THE CATHOLIC CHURCH
AND THE NATION-STATE

The Catholic Church and the Nation-State
Comparative Perspectives

Paul Christopher Manuel
Lawrence C. Reardon
Clyde Wilcox
Editors

As of January 1, 2007, 13-digit ISBN numbers will replace the current 10-digit system.
Paperback: 978-1-58901-115-1
Cloth: 978-1-58901-114-4

Georgetown University Press, Washington, D.C.

Library of Congress Cataloging-in-Publication Data

The Catholic Church and the nation-state : comparative perspectives / [edited by] Paul Christopher Manuel, Lawrence C. Reardon, Clyde Wilcox.
    p. cm. — (Religion and politics series)
  Includes bibliographical references and index.
  ISBN 1-58901-114-7 (Hardcover : alk. paper) — ISBN 1-58901-115-5 (pbk. : alk. paper)
    1. Christianity and politics—Catholic Church. 2. Manuel, Paul Christopher.
II. Reardon, Lawrence C. (Lawrence Christopher) III. Wilcox, Clyde, 1953–
  IV. Series: Religion
and Politics series (Georgetown University)
  BX1793.C355 2006
  261.7088'282—dc22

                                             2006003022

Printed in the United States of America

13 12 11 10 09 08 07 06   9 8 7 6 5 4 3 2
First printing

Contents

Tables

Foreword: Faith and Culture in a Turbulent Age

"IN ALL YOU DO YOU should seek advice," wrote Anselm of Canterbury in 1076, and "let your advisers be one in a thousand." This book takes up Anselm's call, for it offers a dialogue across disciplines that rarely engage one another. The authors come from political science, history, theology, and comparative religion; they include lay scholars and clerics. They all wrestle with one of the crucial issues of our age: the interplay of religion and politics in a turbulent world.

The book analyzes the familiar rubric of church and state—and explores it around the globe, from East Timor to Ireland, Poland to Rwanda, China to Chile. Grounding their studies in the experiences of the world's people, the authors do not shy away from controversy. They squarely face the legacy of colonialism, the tension between faith communities, the prohibitions imposed by anxious governments, and the conflict—sometimes horrifying conflict—within many cultures. However, the reader will also find a more inspiring theme running across these chapters: In every case, in every country, the authors describe a struggle to speak for the poor and empower the dispossessed. Taken together, they testify to the force of faith as it moves across politics, culture, and history.

This volume suggests a fresh approach to studying the relationship between the church and the state. The phrase itself—"church and state"—fails to capture the rich, complex, lived reality. The authors expand our categories to the more embracing notions of "religion and society" and "faith and culture." These are essays that linger in a real world of fear and hope, conflict and community, transgression and forgiveness. It is all a far cry from dusty abstractions regarding jurisprudence, legal precedents, and court cases.

The focus of all these national case studies is squarely on the Roman Catholic Church as it emerged from the Second Vatican Council, held from 1962 to 1965, to reengage the world. The contemporary church mixes its missions—it is social as well as theological, civic as well as religious, political as well as moral. Each case offers another portrait of the church engaging in its own transformation as it confronts challenges—both unique and universal. Around the world we find the church facing class divisions, global (sometimes bare-knuckled) capitalism, hostile regimes, new forms of national identity, and terrible violence. Through it all, the Catholic Church maintains a robust moral and political presence in practically every nation and across virtually all cultures.

Although decidedly "Western" in its origin and outlook, the Catholic Church has played a major role almost everywhere. Its historical legacies, wrapped up with colonialism and "the age of discovery," are still strongly felt today. In its own way, each chapter of this book carefully examines the religious, diplomatic, and political actions that shaped our world—the authors do not flinch as they explore both the admirable and the regrettable. In the process, they reveal themselves to be astute observers of very different regions; each displays a keen eye for the many forces that shape the interaction of church and state—governmental structures, historical legacies, geography, demography, culture, and more.

The authors of this foreword, a theologian who teaches at the Weston Jesuit School of Theology and a political scientist who teaches at Brown University, see this volume as a kind of promise. We hope that the careful, respectful cross-fertilization that the reader encounters in this book will inspire a new interdisciplinary approach. What struck us both as we read these chapters was how rarely we have seen such a convergence of theological and social-scientific perspectives on contemporary life. The intersection of religion and politics is a particularly promising place for academic disciplines to overlap. Each perspective brings to the conversation precisely the material that the other should be eager to engage. Political scientists are fluent in the language of institutional analysis and power relations—considerations that describe and explain the workings of everyday reality. Theologians explore normative concerns about economics, politics, and peoples; they marshal ancient traditions that reflect on the meaning of the good life and offer principled analysis of current states of affairs. Taken together, the two perspectives weave together the empirical and the ethical, reason and revelation, thought and experience. Their joint analytic power describes and explains the world we inhabit, the world we make. What ultimately emerges is a unique picture of how people, as individuals and in groups, make sense of their lives and their aspirations. We gain insight into how they struggle to project a moral order upon the often-booming chaos of real life.

The chapters that follow bear rich witness to the inescapable lesson that people of every culture live with one foot planted in the secular realm and the other in a realm of religious beliefs and values that are not easily swept away by modernity. Our attempts to examine the Roman Catholic Church as a political and strategic actor must be accompanied by a simultaneous effort to portray it as a moral teacher and source of ethical guidance—one revered by hundreds of millions of people across the globe.

We are distinctly aware of the many ways in which this volume invites controversy. Though we are not eager to fan the flames of disagreement and even
rancor, it seems inevitable that most observers will find some aspects of the questions taken up here quite delicate—and even uncomfortable. This is inevitable
in any study of the Roman Catholic Church, an institution that is perhaps unique
in asserting strong moral claims regarding its own mission to advance the cause
of political justice around the world. Witness these words from paragraph 76 of
the influential Vatican II document *Gaudium et Spes*: "The Church has the right
to pass moral judgment even on matters touching the political order, whenever
personal rights or the salvation of souls makes such judgments necessary." Our
subject is no coy organization but rather one aware of its strength. And yet, as
this book makes clear, "passing moral judgments"—even highly informed and
sophisticated moral judgments—is a delicate process, intricately negotiated
between sincere people with genuine differences; the debate always goes on between the orthodox and the progressive, the center and periphery, the clergy and
laity. Across all the honest differences stands an institution ready and eager to
fulfill its mission as an agent of reconciliation for all peoples.

Above all, this volume is about relationships—some robust and well
established, others delicate and in need of nurturing. Most obviously, the reader
will encounter rich, new relationships among intellectual disciplines—theology,
political science, history, and cultural studies. The chapters that follow also push
us to engage a broad spectrum of opinions, from liberal to conservative, from
radical to reactionary. These views defy neat categorization; they are not ad-
equately captured by any simple spectrum from left to right, and they always end
up messier than we first imagined. Finally, and most important, these chapters
challenge us to think about the relations within and between the world's communities. It is impossible to read these dispatches from across the globe without
feeling saddened, moved, hopeful, and inspired—in short, this book forces us to
confront the human prospect in the twenty-first century.

THOMAS MASSARO, S.J.
Weston Jesuit School of Theology

JAMES MORONE
Brown University

Acknowledgments

THIS VOLUME IS A RESULT of papers presented and discussed at two scholarly meetings that examined how the Vatican and the local national churches try to influence politics and public policy. The initial roundtable took place at the annual meeting of the New England Political Science Association (NEPSA) in Providence in May 2003, followed by a two-day interdisciplinary Research Symposium at the New Hampshire Institute of Politics at Saint Anselm College (NHIOP) in Manchester in April 2004. In the end, perhaps the real value of these two meetings, and this corresponding volume, has been the fruitful dialogue between and across disciplines on the political role of the Roman Catholic Church in national politics.

This volume would not have been possible without the diligent work of Lorie Cochran, the administrative assistant of the NHIOP Academic Research Center. Thomas Massaro, S.J., of the Weston Jesuit School of Theology in Cambridge, Massachusetts, greatly assisted in organizing the Research Symposium and subsequently participated in it as a discussant. Clark Cochran of Texas Tech University served admirably as a panel discussant, and he offered many valuable insights. The Center for the Humanities at the University of New Hampshire (UNH) provided partial symposium financing, and the UNH Vice President's Office provided a Faculty Scholars Fellowship to Lawrence Reardon, giving him the time needed to edit the manuscript. The UNH Department of Political Science also partially funded Reardon's trip to China and Hong Kong for research on his chapter.

Anne Botteri, NHIOP executive director, Marie George, executive vice president of Saint Anselm College, the Reverend Augustine Kelly, O.S.B., Saint Anselm College academic dean, and Dan Reagan, chair of the NHIOP Academic Advisory Board, have all been enthusiastic supporters of this project from the very beginning. Brown University professor James Morone, who served as president of the New England Political Science Association in 2003, promoted the project from its earliest conception, and Dan Krislov encouraged the formation of the 2003 NEPSA roundtable in Providence. Saint Anselm College faculty members Montague Brown, Peter Josephson, and Kevin McMahon offered very helpful comments throughout the planning of the research symposium and as panel discussants. Joshua Chamberlain performed admirably as the symposium rapporteur. Saint Anselm College student John D'Arpino, class of 2005, assisted with the symposium and with the religious concentration chart, which appears in an appendix. Georgetown University graduate student Louis Dezseran prepared the timeline of events that appears in an appendix. Lawrence Reardon's mother, Rosemary Reardon, made useful comments and suggestions on editing the manuscript.

We are grateful to the editors of the Religion and Politics Series at Georgetown University Press for their support of this project, especially Ted Jelen. Richard Brown, director of Georgetown University Press, has been patient with us and a champion of the project. Thanks also go to all the people at Georgetown University Press who helped with the production of this volume. We would also like to acknowledge and thank the outside reviewers for their useful critiques of the original manuscript. Their observations and criticisms greatly assisted us in crafting an expanded and improved final product.

Most important, we would like to thank our families for their counsel, assistance, understanding, encouragement, and patience throughout this project. This book is dedicated to them, and especially to five-year-old Maria Teresa Manuel and four-year-old Rosa Caterina Manuel, who, now that this volume is finally completed, can at last have the full attention of their father.

Introduction: Theoretical Considerations on the Relationship between the Catholic Church and the Nation-State

IN 2004, THE ROMAN CATHOLIC Church was intensely involved in an amazing range of international, national, and subnational politics around the world. Internationally, the Church was actively influencing the language of international agreements being negotiated within various United Nations organizations. Pope John Paul II spoke eloquently in opposition to the American invasion and occupation of Iraq, including during his private discussions with the American president, George W. Bush. For his part, since his 2005 election as pope, Benedict XVI has been warning the world about the dangers of a "dictatorship of relativism," which rejects absolute truth and exalts personal desires.

At the national level, the Chilean Church lost a battle to stop the legalization of divorce but convinced legislators to require a longer period of separation before a divorce could be granted. Some American bishops influenced the 2004 presidential elections by announcing that they would deny Holy Communion to Senator John Kerry, the first Catholic presidential candidate in a generation, because he was pro-choice. In Europe, the Spanish Church became the focus for national mourning and consolation as it conducted the March 2004 state funeral mass for the victims of the Madrid train bombing. The Polish Church lobbied a leftist government to maintain strict antiabortion policies. In Africa, Bishop Ernest Kombo openly criticized the conduct of officials from the Congolese government and the Congolese Church. At the subnational level, the Church was actively involved in lobbying state legislators in the United States, Brazil, and Germany on a range of issues from antipoverty policies to sex education to health care programs to laws affecting Church-run schools and hospitals.[1]

Conceiving of the Church in the Political Sphere

Making sense of this range of activity is complicated, and the sheer diversity of cases poses a severe challenge for any inductive understanding of Catholic

politics. Although core Church theology and teachings are consistent across nations, national churches vary considerably in the emphasis of their teachings and
in the scope and nature of their political involvement. These cross-national differences have themselves varied across history. Casanova traces the transformation of the Catholic Church in Brazil from a supporter of oligarchy to an
institution strongly based in popular sectors, from a disestablished church that
sought to protect the country against foreign rule to a national church providing space for resistance to communism in Poland, and from an insecure sect to
an assertive public actor in the United States.[2]

In this volume, experts from the United States and abroad describe how the
Vatican and the national churches influence politics and public policy debates
in a variety of countries across the globe. From these cases, the book seeks to
build a broader understanding of the role of the Church in cross-national politics. The first two chapters provide useful insights into just how we should con-
ceive of the Church in national and international politics. In chapter 1, Kenneth
Himes provides a theological conception of the role of the Church, and he shows
how theological change can lead to a change in the way that the Church engages in politics. He notes that Vatican II consolidated a set of ideas that had
been on the margins of Catholic thought into the "warm center of Catholic
theology, spirituality, and practice." He then lays out five metaphorical images
of the Church—as sacrament, as servant, as communion, as the people of God,
and as ecumenical—each of which captures some important theological aspect
of the role of the Church in society and politics.

The first metaphor, of Church as *sacrament*, focuses on the role of the Church
to make grace incarnate. Here Himes reminds us that the Church must be exemplary in its embodiment of Christ's teachings. There are clear examples in this
book where the Church has fallen short of this most high standard—in the failure to strenuously resist genocide in Rwanda, for example, and in the clergy sex
scandal in the United States. Yet in many countries Catholic leaders have enhanced their prophetic role by the purity of their religious vision as evidenced
in their lives. Church as *servant* focuses on the "responsibility to assist in the
transfiguration of the world." The Church's role as servant is very evident in
India, where the Church has played a key role in providing needed services in a
poor country, and in the United States, where Catholic-run hospitals are important actors in civil society.

Church as *communion* invites us to consider the great diversity of national
Churches that come together under the broad rubric of the Roman Catholic
Church—a diversity that is abundantly evident in the case studies that follow.
Indeed, the diversity of concordats negotiated between the Vatican and national
churches with the state is remarkable. Examples include the Lateran Pact concluded by Mussolini's fascist regime, described by Manuel and Mott in chapter
3; the changing political role of the Church in Poland, described by Byrnes in

chapter 6; and the transformation of the Church from colonial instrument to national institution in a new democratic regime, described in various chapters on Latin America, Africa, and Southeast Asia. Church as communion also reminds us of those areas where the Church remains divided, such as Rwanda (chapter 10), India (chapter 12), and China (chapter 13).

Church as *people of God* reminds us that the Church is in fact made up of hundreds of millions of lay members who are part of an international community of faith that is involved in politics and society. This is evident in many of the cases, where diverse opinions within the Church lead to complex patterns of church–state relations. Finally, Church as *ecumenical* reminds us that the Church works with other religious and secular institutions. The Catholic Church is but one of a large number of religious groups competing for adherents and cooperating for common good in the United States, and there the Church has often supported state policies to help religious minorities. In other countries, however, the Church has more of a monopoly power, and it has sought policies and laws to make it harder for religious minorities to proselytize.[3] In the coming century, the Church will face struggles to consider its relations with non-Christian faiths, where it shares some key values but differs on others. The similarity of the Church's social welfare role and that of many Islamic groups, for example, and the shared opposition to abortion and same-sex marriage contrast with very different values taught by these faiths on other questions.

In chapter 2, Lisa Ferrari argues that the Church occupies an ambiguous position in international politics. On the one hand, the Vatican is a peculiar type of state, with the pope as absolute monarch of slightly fewer than 110 acres inside the state of Italy. Although Ferrari does not focus primarily on the Church as state, it is worth noting that such a perspective invites us to consider the Church as a rational actor seeking to maximize its various resources—money, members, and political power. Although the Vatican is small and has no military except the Swiss Guard, its hierarchical organization makes it easier for it to pursue its policy goals than many other nations.[4]

This conception is obviously highly relevant to the Church's historic role as a European political force, but it has implications for the Church's current involvement in various issues and political disputes around the world. It reminds us that unlike many religious bodies, the Vatican's hierarchical structure allows for separate negotiations with different political regimes, much the way nations seek different types of agreements with different countries. In chapter 11, Linda Heywood describes the arrangements between the Vatican and Portuguese colonial rules that guaranteed the survival of the Church in the face of Protestant missionary activity but that "drew the Angolan Church deeper into the oppressive colonial system, and weakened its prophetic voice." In chapter 13, Lawrence Reardon describes how the Vatican's attempt to reestablish diplomatic relations with the People's Republic of China failed in 2000 when Chinese authorities insisted upon their right to appoint Chinese bishops. Despite a deepening division between those Chinese Catholics who support the official Church and those who support the nonofficial Church, the Vatican considered its greater interest lay in preserving the pope's hierarchical and spiritual authority. In both the Angolan and Chinese cases, the Church learned how to maximize its self-interest by cooperating with or rejecting the authoritarian state.

Nation-states frequently act to maximize their self-interest, including their resources and power. Historically, the Church has sought to expand its resources and power in many countries. It has sought to maximize its wealth and resources, and to enact laws and policies that protect it against competitors such as Protestant Christianity and other faiths.

Yet the Church is more than a self-interested nation. Ferrari also notes that the Church acts in international politics as a transnational moral actor, a large nongovernmental organization with powerful resources. Her chapter shows the Vatican using its resources to pursue public policies consistent with the Church's theology, such as Amnesty International and other similar transnational groups. The Church's policy goals may come from its unique role—in chapter 1, Himes argued that the Church seeks to embody and establish Christ's reign in history—but it pursues those policy goals with many of the typical strategies and tactics of interest groups.

Ferrari's conception invites us to consider the Catholic Church as an interest group, competing with other interests in both international and national politics.[5] In national and international politics, this means that the Catholic Church sometimes forms unusual alliances to pursue public policies; negotiates strategically with political parties and leaders; uses both inside and outside strategies to persuade and pressure policymakers; and generally can be viewed as any other actor with policy goals, resources, and constraints. This was evident when the Church in the United States entered into political negotiations in the early 1990s over national health insurance, and internationally when the Church worked with Muslim groups in UN policymaking.

Interest groups are constrained by their own internal bureaucracies, by disagreements in policy goals among group leaders and between leaders and members, and by a need to maintain a committed membership while pursuing policy goals. Interest group membership is most important as a resource when a majority of members support key policy goals, but surveys show that a majority of Catholics in many nations oppose the Church's position on contraception. In chapter 5, William Lies and Mary Fran Malone show that a majority of practicing Catholics in Chile have come to oppose the Church's position on divorce. Interest groups also use their credibility as a resource. Ted Jelen demonstrates in chapter 4 how the clergy sex abuse scandal has weakened the American Church's credibility, while Elisée Rutagambwa argues in chapter 10 that the Rwandan Church's integrity has been compromised by the complicity of Church elites in genocidal acts. Yet in all these countries, the Church still has important resources. It has many members, a vast infrastructure, great financial resources, a hierarchical structure affording the pope's voice singular authority within it, and moral influence in the larger community.

Taken together, the chapters by Himes and Ferrari provide many useful perspectives from which to view the national case studies that follow. These rich cases differ along many key dimensions. This introduction first discusses four of the most important dimensions on which the cases differ, and it then turns to the book's organizing framework—the challenges faced by the Church.

The Church and National Identity

The first dimension distinguishes between cases where the Church is deeply rooted in national identity and culture, and those where it has been imposed by external forces, generally as a tool of colonial masters. Of course, in most of these countries the Church was at some point an outsider religion. Yet today the Church is so deeply embedded in history and culture that it is a source of national unity and pride, even among those who oppose its policies. In other countries, the Church first worked to suppress nationalism and then embraced it. And in still other countries, it remains a minority faith, outside mainstream cultural traditions.

In chapter 6, Timothy Byrnes provides perhaps the strongest case, where Polish national identity is very deeply rooted in Catholicism. Poland embraced the Catholic Church in 966, and the Church remained the voice of Poland as its borders expanded and contracted wildly over the next thousand years. During communist rule, the Church was the center of resistance, so Lech Walesa signed an accord with the government using an oversized pen with a picture of the pope and sporting a badge of the Black Madonna.[6] Catholicism is also deeply linked to national identity in Latin Europe, as Manuel and Mott point out in chapter 3. William Crotty describes in chapter 7 the 1937 Irish Constitution, which called the Church the "guardian of the faith professed by the great majority of citizens."

In Latin America, the Church arrived with the Spanish and Portuguese armies, and it proceeded to eradicate indigenous religions. Within a relatively short time, however, some Church leaders dissented from the agreements that embedded Church activity in colonial rule. Some Catholic leaders, such as Bartolomeu de las Casas, the Spanish Dominican priest, condemned the treatment of native peoples by the Spanish authorities and secured better imperial policies for them by the Crown, at the same time that others worked with the colonial powers. Today Catholicism is well ensconced in the national identity of most Latin American countries, coexisting with scattered indigenous religious practice and incursions by evangelical Protestant and Mormon churches. In chapter 9, Christine Kearney traces the evolution of the Brazilian Church from imperial instrument to supporter of nondemocratic, nonegalitarian regimes to active participant in democracy.

In other countries, the Catholic Church arrived as a tool of conquest and oppression and remained a key part of imperial rule for an extended period. In Angola (chapter 11) and in East Timor (chapter 8), the Church was an instrument of Portuguese conquerors; in the Congo (chapter 14), it accompanied French colonial troops. Yet in each case, the Church's position gradually shifted. Consider, for example, the story of East Timor, as told by Alynna Lyon. Initially the Church was an instrument of colonial rule, which aided the suppression of the 1930 independence movement; the colonial state also took control of Church operations, much as it did in Angola. When Indonesia annexed East Timor, the Church came under the direct control of the Vatican, which resisted Indonesian efforts to consolidate its rule, and it opposed the family-planning and sterilization programs that Indonesia sought to implement. The Church coexisted with the resistance movement, and the pope eventually declaimed the genocide in East Timor. In the end, the Church that first came as part of a conquering army became a conduit for nationalism, collective action, and liberation. In chapter 14, Yvon Elenga describes a complex history of the Church and colonial and postcolonial governments in the Republic of the Congo.

Finally, in some societies the Catholic Church remains primarily an outsider institution. In chapter 12, Mathew Schmalz describes demonstrations in the streets of India's cities protesting Catholic conversions, and efforts by Hindu leaders to marginalize the Church by denying Scheduled Caste status to converts. Although the Church has attempted to adapt to the Indian culture by adopting symbols such as the lotus, this has met with resistance from Indian Catholics, who are a tiny portion of the nation's population. In chapter 13, Lawrence Reardon describes a splintered Church in China, where traditional Confucianism, Buddhism, and Taoism have been supplanted by a Marxist state. Here the Vatican has tried to engage both an official, state Church and an underground Church, but these divisions remain a liability for the Church in a society where it is clearly not indigenous. In China, the Church has an uphill battle to define cultural values in the face of an established Marxist regime and a surging capitalist ethos.

The Church and Democracy

In some countries, the Church has been a force for democracy, providing open space for civil society and working well with other religious and secular groups. In other countries, the Church has been complicit with authoritarian regimes that engaged in human rights abuses. And in some countries, the Church has opposed and supported democracy in various periods, while in others Church leaders have taken opposite sides in the same conflicts.

The Church was once closely linked with antidemocratic elites in nearly every country of the world. As Casanova notes, the Church "fought capitalism, liberalism, the modern secular state, the democratic revolutions, socialism, and the sexual revolution. In brief, it has been the paradigmatic form of anti-modern public religion."[7] In 1832, Pope Gregory XVI issued an encyclical that placed the Church firmly in opposition to "elected assemblies, freedom of the press, freedom of conscience and the separation of Church and state. . . . (He) described representative government as a 'pernicious opinion.'" Throughout the 1800s in Europe, the Church generally fought against the process of democratization. When Catholic priests became active in political parties, they were generally the parties of the landed aristocracy. There is evidence that in the middle of the twentieth century, the Church collaborated with fascist regimes in Italy, Spain, and elsewhere.[8] In this volume, the most difficult case is Rwanda, where the Church was silent in the face of genocide, and in some cases complicit in the atrocities. Elisée Rutagambwa in chapter 10 quotes a Catholic bishop who defended the genocide in 1995, although Rutagambwa believes that the Church has a role to play in the reconciliation in that country. To a lesser extent, the Congolese Church also fit the antidemocratic label.

Yet in many parts of the world, the Church has also provided important resources, including protected space for civil society to oppose repressive regimes. In Eastern Europe, especially in Poland, the Church was one of the few institutions in which dissent could be expressed during the communist years, and it was critical to the success of the Solidarity movement. It is a key institution providing space for dissent in China today, as Lawrence Reardon notes in chapter 13. In the United States, the Catholic Church was the center of civil society for many immigrant communities from southern and eastern Europe, as Ted Jelen describes in chapter 4. Because Catholics were a persecuted minority, the Church has traditionally both been supportive of civil liberties and worked in alliance with disadvantaged groups.

In many countries, the role of the Church is difficult to categorize, varying over time and among Catholic elites at any given time. Thus the liberation theology of some priests in Latin America was matched by close connections of other priests at the same time with ruling military dictatorships. While embracing democracy and advocating worker's rights, the Church has also maintained an anticommunist and even antisocialist stance. Here the Chilean case in chapter 5 is fascinating. Originally an element of Spanish conquest, the Church after independence sided with wealthy and conservative interests. In the 1930s, many Church leaders focused their attention on the needs of the poor and workers, in part to help thwart a socialist movement but in part also because of a genuine theological change in views of the role of the Church in politics and society. Although Church leaders initially sought to work with the socialist president, Salvador Allende, they later endorsed General Augusto Pinochet's military coup, which proceeded to use torture and murder to stay in power. During the Pinochet era, the Church was an important source of opposition, but since the return to democracy the Church has been allied with rightist parties because it has prioritized its teachings on divorce and abortion, thus returning in a sense full circle to the role of the Church in the first democratic era.

The Church as Moral Actor or Self-Interested Institution

The case studies presented in this volume also show very different views of the essential nature of the Church's involvement in politics. Some cases identify the Church as a strategic moral actor, interested in standing up for its articulated moral causes and purposes. Other cases identify the Church as a strategic institutional actor, concerned with maximizing its resources through ties to political elites, and with protecting itself from human rights abuses, sex scandals, and other problems from within. These are not entirely contradictory notions, for a bankrupt or politically impotent Church cannot affect politics or even societal values.

What is striking is the complexity of the cases. Some tell of a national church that is simultaneously acting as a strategic moral and institutional actor. In the American case, Jelen tells of an institution that has sought to cover up its growing sex abuse scandals but has also maintained unpopular positions on issues such as contraception in the face of considerable dissent from the laity.

Others show an institutional strategic actor that reluctantly appears to stake out a more prophetic voice, with varying levels of authenticity. Manuel and Mott describe the Spanish Church that supported Franco and only reluctantly accepted democratization but that maneuvered adroitly during that process to emerge as an institution positioned quite differently in the new democracy. Heywood describes the reluctance of the Angolan Church to support independence even when most Protestant churches opposed the colonial government; yet by the end the Angolan Church exerted a prophetic voice on behalf of social justice. And some cases show a retreat from the prophetic voice. Kearney shows that the Brazilian Church maneuvered through a period of support for a colonial slaveholding society, through an elite-dominated corporatist society dominated by patron–client relationships, and emerged for a time as an institution committed to liberation theology, before retreating from that position more recently.

Multiple Contexts, Multiple Challenges

The last organizing theme of the book, the primary challenges facing the Church, has been used to divide the case studies into five separate parts. The first part includes the two chapters by Himes and Ferrari depicting the broad political and theological challenges that the Church faces worldwide as it deals with international and national politics.

The second part focuses on the challenge of secularization, as the Church seeks to maintain its moral voice in the face of growing numbers of citizens who reject its authority to define morality. This is especially true in southern European countries such as France, Italy, Spain, and Portugal, but also true to a lesser extent in Chile. In the United States, there is controversy about whether secularization is taking place, but there is little doubt that the Church's ability to define morality for its members has been reduced in recent years. In these countries the Church competes with many secular voices to frame issues such as sexuality, marriage, divorce, and abortion. The recent decision by Spain to legalize same-sex marriages—a move bitterly opposed by the Church—is but one of many examples.

The third part presents cases where the Church's main challenge has been, until recently, providing opposition to a foreign power. In the cases of Poland, Ireland, and East Timor, the Church exerted a powerful nationalist voice in opposition to foreign powers with different values (communist, Protestant, and Muslim). In Poland, the Church is now in transition to a new role, as memories of Soviet occupation fade.

The fourth part focuses on the challenges for the Church in confronting contentious national issues of social justice and ethnic hostilities. In Brazil the Church has struggled with its response to massive economic inequality, first siding with landed elites, then promoting liberation theology, and then retreating to a more purely spiritual role. In Rwanda, the Church was in some ways complicit in a horrific genocide, and it now seeks to help a brutalized society heal. In Angola, the Church confronted a bloody civil war, and it played an important role in bringing peace.

The fifth and final part focuses on countries where the Church faces challenges in dealing with civil authorities. In these countries, the Church has fewer resources and in some cases confronts a hostile government. In India, the long-established Church represents a tiny fraction of the public, and it faces hostility both from those who want a secular India and from those who support Hindu nationalism. In China, an official Church and an unofficial Church must deal with each other while facing an officially atheistic state amid rapid economic transformation. In the Congo, the Church has more members but still faces difficulties in dealing with government.

Taken together, the chapters in this volume provide a rich portrait of the Roman Catholic Church as a complex and paradoxical institution whose political role has varied historically and geographically. It is the authors' hope that the considerations and analyses presented in this volume will engender a deeper understanding of the role of the Church in the world and will lead to future research.

Notes

1. Carin Larson, David Madland, and Clyde Wilcox, "Religious Lobbying in Virginia: How Institutions Can Quiet Prophetic Voices," in *Representing God at the Statehouse: Religion and Politics in the American States*, ed. Edward Cleary and Allen Hertzke (Lanham, Md.: Rowman & Littlefield, 2005).

2. Jose Casanova, *Public Religions in the Modern World* (Chicago: University of Chicago Press, 1994).

3. Anthony Gill, *Rendering unto Caesar: The Catholic Church and the State in Latin America* (Chicago: University of Chicago Press, 1998).

4. Peter J. Katzenstein, "Conclusion," in *Between Power and Plenty: Foreign Economic Policies of Advanced Industrial States*, ed. Peter Katzenstein (Madison: University of Wisconsin Press, 1978), 306–32.

5. Stathis Kalyvas, *The Rise of Christian Democracy in Europe* (Ithaca, N.Y.: Cornell University Press, 1996); Gill, *Rendering unto Caesar*; Carolyn M. Warner, *Confessions of an Interest Group: The Catholic Church and Political Parties in Europe* (Princeton, N.J.: Princeton University Press, 2000).

6. Steve Bruce, *Politics and Religion* (Cambridge: Polity Press, 2003).

7. Casanova, *Public Religions*, 9.

8. Bruce, *Politics*.

Bibliography

Evans, Peter B., Dietrich Rueschemeyer, and Theda Skocpol, eds. *Bringing the State Back In*. New York: Cambridge University Press, 1985.

Gill, Anthony. "Religion and Democracy in South America: Challenges and Opportunities." In *Religion and Politics in Comparative Perspective: The One, the Few, and the Many*, ed. Ted G. Jelen and Clyde Wilcox. New York: Cambridge University Press, 2002.

Hallum, Anne Motley. "Looking for Hope in Central America: The Pentecostal Movement." In *Religion and Politics in Comparative Perspective: The One, the Few, and the Many*, ed. Ted G. Jelen and Clyde Wilcox. New York: Cambridge University Press, 2002.

Jelen, Ted G., and Clyde Wilcox. *Religion and Politics in Comparative Perspective: The One, the Few, and the Many*. New York: Cambridge University Press, 2002.

Manuel, Paul Christopher. "Religion and Politics in Iberia: Clericalism, Anti-Clericalism, and Democratization in Portugal and Spain." In *Religion and Politics in Comparative Perspective: The One, the Few, and the Many*, ed. Ted G. Jelen and Clyde Wilcox. New York: Cambridge University Press, 2002.

Olson, Mancur. *The Rise and Decline of Nations*. New Haven, Conn.: Yale University Press, 1982.

Rueschemeyer, Dietrich, and Peter B. Evans. "The State and Economic Transformation: Toward and Analysis of the Conditions Underlying Effective Intervention." In *Bringing the State Back In*, ed. Peter B. Evans et al. New York: Cambridge University Press, 1985.

Sahu, Snil K. "Religion and Politics in India: The Emergence of Hindu Nationalism and the Bharatiya Janata Party (BJP)." In *Religion and Politics in Comparative Perspective: The One, the Few, and the Many*, ed. Ted G. Jelen and Clyde Wilcox. New York: Cambridge University Press, 2002.

Wilcox, Clyde, and Ted G. Jelen. "Religion and Politics in an Open Market: Religious Mobilization in the United States." In *Religion and Politics in Comparative Perspective: The One, the Few, and the Many*, ed. Ted G. Jelen and Clyde Wilcox. New York: Cambridge University Press, 2002.

Part One

THE THEOLOGICAL AND POLITICAL CHALLENGES OF THE VATICAN

THE VOLUME OPENS WITH TWO contributions on the theological and political challenges faced by the Vatican. To begin, the theologian Kenneth Himes reviews the Vatican's political role throughout history. He argues that the Second Vatican Council represented a moment of choice in the theological and political identity of the Roman Catholic Church, resulting in five new models of the church: church as *sacrament*, church as *servant*, church as *communion*, church as *people of God*, and church as *ecumenical*. As such, Himes describes how a retrieval of metaphors drawn from the Roman Catholic biblical and theological tradition helped form a new self-image of the Catholic Church. Vatican II allowed a public church to emerge, one open to pluralism and to liberal democracy.

Using the language of international relations theory, the political scientist Lisa Ferrari offers an insightful contribution on the global role of the Vatican as an international player in chapter 2. She contends that the influence of the Roman Catholic Church is an enduring fact of international relations, even though it lacks a military—notwithstanding its Swiss Guard. She further contends that the Vatican can be partially understood as both a nongovernmental organization and a sovereign state. Borrowing from Pope Paul VI's terminology, the theme of "a universal church without boundaries or frontiers" is very pronounced in this offering.

Chapter 1

Vatican II and Contemporary Politics

KENNETH R. HIMES, O.F.M.

INVOLVEMENT IN POLITICAL LIFE IS not something new for the Roman Catholic Church. There are abundant illustrations available throughout history that Catholicism has engaged the political order. There also is the record of service evidenced by the multitude of institutions sponsored by the Catholic Church. Add to these the various movements for social reform that have been allied with and supported by the Church and the historical record is clear. The Church in every age has had to consider how it will relate to the political order.

For example, Paul in chapter 13 of his Letter to the Romans encouraged obedience to the state, paying taxes and tolls as required, and respecting magistrates and public officials. Paul wrote at a time when the Roman Empire treated the fledgling faith with benign neglect. He saw civil authority as unwittingly assisting his ministry by its establishment of relative peace, physical safety, ease of transportation, and the rule of law.

The author of Revelation, chapter 13, saw the empire as a beast that blasphemes and, consequently, the author paid no respect to civil authority even as he recognized the coercive power of the state. By this time Rome had become an active agent of persecution, working against the spread of the faith. The judgment found in the book of Revelation about the state was much different than that of Paul.

Another point to note about the different approaches to the state is the role of the Church in society. When the writer of Revelation finished lamenting and decrying the empire, he did not issue a call to social reform. Instead, the passage ended with a warning to his readers that "if anyone is to be taken captive, to captivity he goes" and if anyone takes up the sword with the sword they will be slain. In short, though unjustly accused, Christians will still wind up in prison; and if they seek to rebel, then they will be violently crushed. Following this warning was the statement that the Christian community must patiently endure.[1]

The context for this, of course, was that the Christian community had no political or military clout; it had no hands on the levers of power and no ability to bring about social change. In the face of oppression by a powerful state, resistance was fruitless. What a good Christian could do was patiently endure. And so that was the counsel given.

In the fourth century, Ambrose, as bishop of Milan, wrote a treatise, *De Officiis*, with the intent to explain how Christians can be good civil servants and reconcile their authority with the gospel. At the time, the Church was not only free from persecution but also populated with figures holding civil power. Ambrose saw the state as an instrument whereby God's purposes can be effected, at least to a degree. Christians, as full members of the empire and significant role-players in its governance and operations, must assume different roles and take on new duties. This was no longer Paul's world or that of the author of Revelation, and so the bishop of Milan developed yet another way of relating church and politics.

The examples could be easily multiplied, citing other biblical and patristic texts. The point is that the early Church was always cognizant of the political realm but tended not to develop political theories as much as pastoral strategies. The immense differences in thinking regarding the political order are explained by the various ways in which the Church experienced the state's power and the options available to the Church in a given setting. We do not find in the early Christian literature a political philosophy as much as prudential judgments about how to deal with a particular political order.

Vatican II, then, did not establish the tradition of sociopolitical engagement. But the Second Ecumenical Council did initiate a distinctive era in the story of Catholicism and politics. As one friendly Protestant observer put it, "The Second Vatican Council (1962–1965) expressed a sea change in Catholic thinking about church–state relations, religious liberty, and issues of political participation in the modern world."[2]

This chapter explains the nature of the "sea change" in Catholicism that led to a different way of engaging the realm of politics. It proceeds by first describing significant elements of the conciliar renewal that have shaped Catholic political engagement, and it then turns to an examination of several areas of the post–Vatican II situation that reveal the council's significance for understanding Catholicism and contemporary politics.

Vatican II and the Political Realm

The movement for renewal in the Catholic Church did not begin with the Second Ecumenical Council. Most of the dominant themes during the four autumn sessions of the council that began in 1962 were preceded by work that was initiated in the mid–nineteenth century. During the decades between the First and Second Vatican Councils, an array of "intellectual, organizational and pastoral movements in the Church" laid the groundwork for what transpired during the four sessions of Vatican II.[3] Renewal in the area of biblical studies, the development of a liturgical reform movement, a call to retrieve the social meaning of Catholic doctrine, the beginning of Catholic ecumenical conversation—all these had started before Vatican II.

What the council did was bring these ideas "in from the cold" where they had weak support and marginal impact on ecclesial life, to the warm center of Catholic theology, spirituality, and practice. Due to the council, ideas and themes that small numbers of committed Catholics in a few locales discussed and hoped to someday implement became widely shared commitments backed by papal and episcopal approval.

Among the important aspects of the biblical, liturgical, and theological renewal brought on by Vatican II was that it offered the Church a broader array of images and metaphors for ecclesial self-understanding. That, in turn, led to new thinking about the Church and politics.

An Array of Images for Self-Understanding

From one perspective, the Church underwent an identity crisis during Vatican II. Crisis is not used here in a negative sense, but as a moment of choice and transition; a familiar identity was being reconsidered in favor of a new self-image shaped, in part, by a retrieval of metaphors drawn from the biblical and theological tradition that supports Catholic faith and practice. A brief review of some of these new, yet traditional, images of the Church will suggest how the conciliar renewal affected the Catholic approach to political life.

Church as Sacrament

The opening paragraph of Lumen Gentium states, "the Church is a sign as well as an instrument of salvation."[4] That is, prior to the seven sacraments familiar to Catholics, the Church itself is a sacrament. There are two points to underscore this claim.

First, a sacrament "causes" grace by signifying, that is, incarnating the reality of grace. For example, the performance of lovemaking between a married couple is not simply an indicator of love between them but is the very embodiment of their love. Sexual intercourse is their love given expression, and the very expression also deepens and makes their love for each other real. The grace of married love comes to be incarnated in the symbolic act of conjugal intimacy. Sacraments are not simply pointers to grace "over there" or in another event. The sacrament itself is the "bodying forth" of the graced reality. Sacraments make the graced reality present by giving it material expression.

Therefore, if the Church is a sacrament it, too, must be capable of incarnating or "enfleshing" the reality it seeks to communicate. Like all the other sacraments, the Church does not bring grace to a situation that is wholly profane;

rather, it illuminates the presence of grace in situations that we only imagined profane but that were already graced by God's presence. Put differently, the Church assembly is not "more holy" than other assemblies of people; we only claim that the Church is the assembly of people who are conscious of the gracious presence of God whenever two or three gather in his name. The Church is the place where people make explicit what is always going on implicitly: God's gracious presence is being made available.

To be a sacrament in this framework requires that the Church's internal life be an adequate expression of its message to others. The Christian community must live in such a way—by its devotion to love and forgiveness, justice and compassion, freedom and truth—that when others look at the Church they are reminded of God's grace at work in the world.[5] It is for this reason that the bishops of the United States pointed out in their pastoral letter on economic justice that "all the moral principles that govern the just operation of any economic endeavor apply to the Church and its agencies and institutions; indeed the Church must be exemplary."[6] Therefore, Church reform is important not just for the membership of the Church but also for the sake of the external mission to witness to others. The sacramental witness of the Church is betrayed when its internal life embodies something radically other than the gospel.[7]

Church as Servant

The Church understands itself as having a religious mission that entails a commitment to serve the rest of humankind. Drawing upon the claim about its sacramental character, the Church is portrayed by the bishops at the council as the "universal sacrament" of God's salvation.[8] The Church does not exist only for its own members but for all humanity. Just as Christ came to save all, the Church cannot accept a narrower mission of catering only to those in formal membership.

The Church must be wary of what the Protestant theologian James Gustafson has called "the sectarian temptation" because the Church has the responsibility to assist in the transformation of the world, not simply tell its message to itself.[9] Within Catholic theory and practice, the sectarian impulse has been incorporated through certain theologies and spiritualities that characterized the life of vowed religious. There have been times when religious life was interpreted as a flight from the world, a refusal to sully one's hands with the world's work. Additionally, generations of Catholics have heard misguided homilies on the gospel passage that allegedly rebukes Martha and praises Mary for the latter's contemplative posture and freedom from the "busyness" of material concerns.

Gaudium et Spes situated the Church within the world, as a part of the human community, not set apart from it. In its opening words, *Gaudium et Spes* describes disciples not as separate from the rest of humankind but as devoted to serving others: "The joys and hopes, the griefs and anxieties of the people of this age, especially those who are poor or in any way afflicted, these too are the joys and hopes, the griefs and anxieties of the followers of Christ."[10]

Combined, the gospels of Mark, Matthew, and Luke, also known as the synoptic gospels, make clear that the coming of the reign of God was at the core of Christ's teaching, and accordingly, the challenge to his listeners was to respond appropriately to the good news of the in-breaking of God's reign in history (Mk. 1:15). The bishops at the Second Vatican Council understood that the mission of the Church must be in conformity with the ministry of Jesus.[11]

According to the council, the reason for the Church's existence is to continue "the mission of proclaiming and establishing among all peoples the reign of Christ and of God." Furthermore, and in keeping with the sacramental view of the Church, the council declared that the Church is "the seed and the beginning of that reign." Although remaining incomplete on this side of history, the Church is called to be an anticipatory presence of God's reign in the midst of humankind.[12] Human beings can create communities that effectively point to the goal of history—the fulfillment of creation through the establishment of God's reign over all historical realities, including human hearts and minds.

In accord with the Catholic principle of mediation, the bishops at Vatican II maintain that it is not divine action alone that brings about God's reign but God acting through, with, and in us.[13] Human activity, therefore, has significance and meaning, for we can cooperate in God's plan for creation or seek to frustrate it by pursuing our own designs. The Church, for its part, must always place itself at the service of God's reign, helping to establish it in history, pointing to its fulfillment beyond history, seeking to embody it in its own internal life and external ministry. Yet the fullness of God's reign is in the future, and even the best of human activity falls short of that future. Therefore, the status quo can never be sacralized and placed beyond scrutiny or considered immune from the necessity of ongoing reform.

Church as Communion

The communion of churches implies that the Universal Church is composed of many churches that are united in faith, worship, and mission. The Church Catholic is not only realized universally but also locally and regionally. "The Church of Christ is really present in all legitimately organized local groups of the faithful, which, insofar as they are united to their pastors, are also quite appropriately called Churches in the New Testament."[14] Without question, the Church is transnational, as Lisa Ferrari suggests in chapter 2 of this volume, but it is also national and has deep roots in particular cultures and histories. This accounts for the distinctive experience of Catholics in Poland, France, Spain, Rwanda, Brazil, China, the United States, and the other countries discussed in this volume. Though the Church professes "one Lord, one faith, one baptism" (Eph. 4, 5), a legitimate diversity is found that permits differences in issues and strategy when the Church turns to the political realm. Diocesan, national, and regional expressions of Church will give rise to a variety of goals and methods for Church engagement with politics.

Two examples that can be cited here are the work of the Latin American episcopate (Consejo Episcopal Latinoamericano, CELAM; Latin American Episcopal Conference) and the bishops of the United States (United States Conference of Catholic Bishops, USCCB). The Latin Americans were not a particularly powerful or influential force at Vatican II; compared with the Europeans, they had not found their collective voice. However, the experience of the council led the Latin American bishops to increase communication among themselves and to act on a desire to match their experience with the teaching of Vatican II. I will not belabor a story that has been told very well by others, including Christine Kearney in chapter 9, but it should be emphasized that the Latin American Church leaders returned to their own continent not content simply to apply the teaching of Vatican II to their situation.[15] Instead, they sought to interpret the teaching so that it spoke to a situation they knew was far different from the history and culture of European Catholicism.

In the United States, one notable consequence of the council's vision was the gradual willingness of the episcopacy to assess its own national experience and begin an effort to develop a new pastoral agenda. This agenda moved the Church beyond the strategy that had guided the pastoral care of the tens of millions of immigrant Catholics who came to the United States in the nineteenth and twentieth centuries. No longer was the American Church best understood as urban, ethnic, and working class. By the middle of the twentieth century, substantial segments of the American Catholic population had become suburban and assimilated and were members of the managerial and professional classes.[16] In this new situation the bishops, after some fits and starts, eventually hit upon a process of formulating pastoral letters that became notable contributions to the political life of the United States.

In both these cases, it was the conciliar support for episcopal leadership in the local Church and the initial encouragement given to national and regional bodies of bishops that made possible the Medellín and Puebla documents of CELAM as well as the pastoral letters on war and peace and economic justice by the USCCB. The ability of a local Church to name its own reality and devise a pastoral strategy in response accounts for the development of various initiatives that have had political significance in particular locales.[17]

Church as People of God

Chapter 4 of *Lumen Gentium* and *Apostolicam Actuositatem* clearly and emphatically support what *Gaudium et Spes* called the layperson's "own distinctive role."[18] Further, the bishops acknowledge that secular life and its activities belong "properly" to the laity. This suggests an appropriate degree of autonomy from clerical oversight and direction. As the bishops make clear, laypersons should follow their own well-formed consciences in seeking to live the faith in everyday life. There should not be the presumption that "pastors are always such experts, that to every problem which arises, however complicated, they can readily give" an answer to the layperson. Indeed, to play that role is not the mission of the clergy.[19]

There is a turn in the council documents away from a model of lay activity known as Catholic Action.[20] Identified especially with Pius XI's papacy, this model presumed that lay people participated in the ministry of the Church as infantry serving in the Church's army under the command of clerical officers.

It was the universal call to holiness articulated in *Lumen Gentium* that reasserted a different understanding of the Christian life. According to the council, all persons of "whatever rank or status are called to the fullness of Christian life," and "one and the same holiness is cultivated by all who are moved by the Spirit of God."[21] Laypersons were encouraged to see their baptismal commitment as a true vocation, one that encouraged taking responsibility for the quality of witness to the world that was given by the community of faith.

The image of the Church as the people of God undercut the abuses of clericalism and emphasized the significance of family life, the workplace, and secular culture and its organizations as the locale where laypeople work out their salvation. In accord with *Apostolicam Actuositatem*, no person in the Church can be understood as passive, for each person has a part to play in the work of the Church. In a particular way, laypersons are charged with "penetrating and perfecting the temporal sphere of things through the spirit of the gospel."[22] This is done through a committed effort to witness to the truth of gospel values while functioning in a variety of roles, including spouse, parent, neighbor, worker, manager, employer, consumer, and citizen.

Recapturing the vital importance of laypeople's worldly activities and its connection with Christian witness has forced the Church to see the world of politics as an important sphere of concern. Politics is not prized because the Church can pursue its institutional self-interest but as an important realm for faithful witness and as a way of living the mandate to love the neighbor, especially the distant neighbor who will be touched not through personal contact but by the instrumentality of just institutions.

Church as Ecumenical

Among the signal moments of the Second Vatican Council was the promulgation of *Unitatis Redintegratio*, which reads in part: "All who have been justified by faith in baptism are incorporated into Christ; they therefore have a right to be called Christians, and with good reason are accepted as brothers and sisters by the children of the Catholic Church."[23] This opening to the movement of unity among Christians was widened by *Nostra Aetate* to the point that subsequent documents of Catholic social teaching have followed the lead taken by John XXIII in *Pacem in Terris* and been addressed to all people of goodwill.[24] Encyclicals, originally sent as circular letters by the bishop of Rome to other bishops, now routinely include a wider audience when they are on topics of social teaching.

Church leaders, on any number of occasions, have professed their willingness and desire to work with others on social issues that touch upon the common good of a society, be that local or global. Behind that commitment is the Catholic belief in human dignity as the foundation for moral reasoning on matters of politics. In short, there is no claim that there is a Catholic solution to arms proliferation or drug trafficking, no body of Catholic teaching that constitutes a "third way" between capitalism and socialism when thinking about the role of the state in a free market economy. The goal is not to establish a Catholic political party or Catholic state but a humane set of social institutions that serve the human dignity and well-being of all.

In this way the council disavowed a triumphal approach in favor of a dialogical partnership when engaging social questions. Indeed, the bishops go so far as to state that the Church "has greatly profited and still profits from the antagonism of those who oppose or persecute her."[25] Even more common has been the assistance the Church has received from people of goodwill who have helped the Church learn through "the experience of past ages, the progress of the sciences, and the treasures hidden in the various forms of human culture."[26]

Martin Marty, the respected Church historian, has written of what he calls the emergence of a "public Church" in American society. He means by this an ecumenical alliance of churches that share three commitments. First is the willingness of a church to accept a measure of responsibility for the temporal good of society. This was clearly affirmed in both *Lumen Gentium* and *Gaudium et Spes*. Second is the Church's acknowledgment of the legitimate autonomy of other social institutions to develop and act upon their self-understanding and mission. This is a consequence of secularization and is clearly approved by *Gaudium et Spes* and *Dignitatis Humanae*.[27] Finally, there is a commitment by the Church to work with all others of goodwill to promote the common good of a society. *Unitatis Redintegratio* and *Nostra Aetate*, along with *Gaudium et Spes*, affirm this principle. In sum, Vatican II embraced the framework of what Marty calls the "public church."[28]

A Synthesis of Conciliar Teaching

All the above elements in the shift of ecclesial self-understanding provided grounds for the way the Second Vatican Council discussed the relationship of the Church and the modern world. The effort to describe that relationship resulted in the single longest document ever written by an ecumenical council during the two-thousand-year history of Catholicism. *Gaudium et Spes* is a document in two parts. The first part provides a synthetic statement of the theological foundations for why the Church is engaged with secular questions of politics, economics, culture, and family life. The second part takes up certain questions of "special urgency," among which is the life of the political community. Taken together, the first part (nn. 1–45) and the specific section on politics (nn. 73–76) offer a reflection on how the Church understands its rightful place in the world, the competence it possesses in world affairs, and the manner in which it comports itself in the world.

Engagement with politics falls under the heading of the social mission of the Church. Throughout the modern era, there was always an implicit assumption that the Church could and even should involve itself with political affairs. *Gaudium et Spes* transformed the implicit assumption into a theological conceptualization that integrated the social mission with the rest of ecclesiology. It did this in a series of moves that both repositioned the social mission while preserving the integrity of the Church's religious identity and the secular independence of the political realm.

Gaudium et Spes is clear that there is no proper political mission for the Church; rather, its mission is religious.[29] That religious mission is to proclaim the reign of God, which penetrates human existence and connects with human history in a variety of ways: defending human dignity, protecting human rights, promoting unity within the human family, and assisting people to find meaning in their daily activities.[30]

Part of the good news of the gospel message is the affirmation that humans are creatures of dignity. This belief is rooted in the doctrine of creation (the *imago Dei*) and incarnation (the human is *capax infiniti*). Protecting and promoting human dignity is religiously significant, for the Church serves as a "sign and safeguard" of the transcendent dignity of the person.[31]

Because the person is both sacred and social, a common life must be established that preserves and promotes human well-being. The cause of human rights is to establish those basic conditions whereby persons can live in communion with others while enjoying a basic measure of freedom, truth, justice, and love. The Church's efforts to defend human dignity and human rights, promote human unity, and help people find meaning are part of its religious mission to serve God's reign. In so doing, there will be points of contact with the realms of politics, economics, and culture. The Church, it is claimed, does not engage these realms in the quest for power, wealth, or prestige, or on behalf of any ideology. Rather, the desire to be faithful to the religious mission requires an indirect vocation to transform the realms of social life to serve rather than threaten the human person. The right of the Church to engage the political order is a consequence of its religious mission to be a sacrament of God's reign.

The competence of the Church in matters political is not based on technical knowledge but due to the insights of faith as to the meaning and goal of human life. It is the mission of the Church to anchor what is authentically human against all tides of opinion that may threaten it. The earthly ministry of Jesus as well as his passion, death, and resurrection reveal the true nature of human existence: the values that affirm our humanity and the end for which our lives are destined.[32] On the basis of that revelation, the Church claims a limited competence to teach and act on matters political; it is a competence that extends to the moral dimension of political life. Even that competence, however, is a matter of degree as one moves from matters of basic principle and toward judgments that are based on contingent realities.

Due to its self-understanding, the Church opts for a style of presence that is dialogical. The Church must learn as well as teach, listen as well as speak. *Gaudium et Spes* makes clear that the Church, "by reason of her role and competence," is not to be identified with any political system or movement.[33] The political realm has a legitimate autonomy from the Church. There is no desire to establish a theocracy. The bishops assert that they do not seek political privilege and even are willing to "give up the exercise of certain rights which have been legitimately acquired, if it becomes clear that their use will cast doubt on the sincerity" of the Church's witness.[34]

Acknowledging the many contributions made by other Christians, people of faith, and nonbelievers, the Church admits that it has not always been faithful to the message it preaches and that this is a cause for repentance.[35] There is a modesty of style envisioned by the bishops as they comment on how the Church will teach and act in the political realm.

In sum, what the bishops did in *Gaudium et Spes* was explain why the Church cannot be indifferent to politics, explored what competence it has in the area, and set a tone for the manner in which it will engage the political realm.

As important as the *Gaudium et Spes* was for the topic of Catholicism and politics, it must be coupled with another conciliar document, *Dignitatis Humanae*. It would have been impossible for the bishops to take up the question of Church and world had they not also agreed to deal with a question that had bedeviled Catholicism throughout the modern era and that had still not been satisfactorily addressed before Vatican II.

For centuries, the Catholic Church struggled to adapt to the rise of nation-states and the claims of monarchs, including the emergence of territorial Churches that were a consequence of the "Westphalian synthesis."[36] Part of the dilemma, of course, was the acceptance by both papacy and monarchy of the paternalistic role of the state in society. When the secular state arose in the European situation, often brought in on the tide of anticlerical and even antireligious forces, the ecclesial reaction was defensive and hostile. This reaction was coupled with a longing for an ancien régime that was at least familiar if not always friendly. For a variety of reasons, even in the case of secular states that were not hostile but self-limited in their role in pluralistic societies, Catholic leaders failed to grasp the import of the transition from paternalistic monarchies to limited, constitutional republics.

In the older context, the Church employed what was called the thesis/hypothesis method for assessing church–state relations. The thesis was that the Catholic Church, as the institutional expression of the one, true religion, ought to be given a privileged public role in the life of a nation. The hypothesis was that exceptions to the thesis could be made if implementation of the thesis would lead to civil unrest and severe animosity toward the Church and its members.

Again, in the eyes of a friendly Protestant observer, "The traditional Roman Catholic viewpoint [meant] that the Church should use the state for its own institutional enhancement and to secure cultural victories over competing religious bodies."[37] This traditional approach was discarded by the arguments found in *Dignitatis Humanae* that a right of religious liberty ought to be enshrined in any political community and that states did not have the competence to determine true religion from false. As a result, the state's interest in regulation of religious practice was simply the protection of public order.

The importance of *Dignitatis Humanae* is that it created the condition for a new kind of Catholicism to develop, one that did not employ the state and its coercive or regulatory power to secure its public presence. The possibility of a new model of public Catholicism came as a result of changing the dialogue partner for the Church. Casanova has observed that the role of a church in public life is largely determined by the "structural location any Church accepts between state and society."[38] *Dignitatis Humanae* broke traditional linkages between Catholicism and the state, thus allowing a reconceptualization of how Catholicism and society might be related.

Vatican II was the watershed event when the Church shifted its emphasis from a church–state dialogue to an appreciation of a new partner: civil society. *Dignitatis Humanae* made the switch in partners possible. *Gaudium et Spes* made the dialogue with the new partner far different than it otherwise would have been.

Postconciliar Catholicism and Politics

As already suggested earlier in this chapter, the significance of the Second Vatican Council is that, taken together, the council's documents, along with the event of the council itself, effected an identity transformation for the Catholic Church.[39] And the reconsideration of what it meant to be church led to a revision in how the Church understood its situation in history. For Casanova, "the most important consequence of this collective redefinition of the situation was the transformation of the Catholic Church from a state-centered to a society-centered institution."[40]

The process of reform instigated by the council may take decades to work through all areas of Church life and be truly integrated into the various levels of the institution. We ought not be surprised, therefore, if the pace of renewal varies and the record of implementation appears uneven in the ensuing decades. Three important areas where the Church is still sorting out the implications of the council's teaching in the political realm are *shaping a political culture, the relationship between the local and Universal Church*, and the *relationship between Church leaders and Catholics in public office*. Let us now turn to a brief discussion of each.

Shaping a Political Culture

Gaudium et Spes suggested that the main agenda is the relationship of Church and world. Initially, the council's response to modern culture was positive, perhaps too much so. Certainly the anathema pronounced upon modernity by Pius IX in the *Syllabus of Errors* was removed by *Gaudium et Spes*. Of course, an uncritical embrace is no more satisfactory than an unrelenting opposition; greater discernment is called for in reading the signs of the times. As the philosopher Charles Taylor puts it, neither cultural "boosters" nor "knockers" are helpful. Needed are people who can provide a critical, balanced, and insightful assessment of both the strengths and weaknesses of a culture.[41] The critical task is to influence and renew a culture, not simply oppose or approve it.

How does the Church inform and shape a culture? Within the United States, the Church has been engaged in a conscious effort to transform the public philosophy of the nation.[42] It has tried to inflect the dominant liberalism of the land with a measure of communitarian thought. A sampling of the pastoral letters of the American hierarchy will reveal consistent appeals to the common good, to an understanding of rights as securing conditions for participatory community, reminders of society's obligations that are met by government policies to protect the weak, and the need to express solidarity across boundaries of class, race, gender, ethnicity, and citizenship.[43]

In its efforts to shape public philosophy, the Church works to change the conventional wisdom of a society. One notable effort by the American bishops in this regard has been to link a variety of issues generally kept discrete in public discourse. The consistent ethic of life, or seamless garment ethic, is an attempt to show the analogical connection between issues that tend to be put on opposing sides of the standard political spectrum, for example, opposition to the death penalty and physician-assisted suicide.

If the Church is to be a sacrament of the reign of God, it is important that its witness be to the whole range of values that reflect that reign. Without such a wide perspective, there is the risk of a reductionist understanding of the Church's social mission. To do justice to its sacramental character, the Church must not confine itself to a narrow set of issues. Whatever difficulties single-issue political strategies encounter politically, it is also theologically dangerous to limit the impact of the Church's social mission in a manner that undercuts its character as a sacrament of the reign of God.[44]

Among the challenges facing the Church in its efforts to shape a culture such as that of the United States is the role and importance of modern media. Church-sponsored media outlets are often lack human and financial resources as well as suffer from the image, and often the reality, of limited freedom and creativity in presenting a message. Though individuals and groups in the Church are exceptions to the general rule, the Church has not yet developed an adequate understanding of modern media, nor does one find in most countries an effective pastoral use of the media.[45] It is hard to imagine how the Church will shape modern cultures unless this situation is rectified. The sacramental nature of the Church suffers from this inability.

Local and Universal Church

Modern culture is not monolithic. Shaping the culture in settings as different as Japan, Nigeria, Poland, Brazil, and the United States cannot entail the same approach. So there is no one-size-fits-all strategy.

After Vatican II, the papacy of Paul VI adopted an approach that encouraged national or regional episcopal conferences to express the pastoral agendas of local churches. The "Magna Charta" of the local Church found in the 1971 apostolic letter *Octogesima Adveniens* highlighted this trend.[46] Also during this period, there was a flowering of justice and peace, human rights, and social ministry offices and commissions in direct response to the encouragement of Paul in his 1967 encyclical on development, *Populorum Progressio*.[47]

The papacy of John Paul II placed a strong emphasis on human rights in political life combined with an effort to lessen the influence of episcopal conferences in favor of one-to-one communications between an individual bishop and the Vatican. Such an approach makes for a different dynamic than when bishops meet as a group and understand themselves to have a corporate role in discerning what the gospel imperative is in a given culture. The demise of conference initiatives also changes the political impact that bishops can have, because they no longer speak with the same force as a collective body. Benedict XVI may very well continue John Paul II's policy, but it is too soon to know.

One unfortunate consequence of the declining influence of national episcopal conferences can be seen in the slow corporate response of the U.S. bishops to the emerging scandal of sexual abuse. In January 2002, the *Boston Globe* first published articles on the sexual abuse of minors by clerics. As the revelation of misdeeds became a daily headline and other newspapers began to cover the scandal, the conference of Catholic bishops never met to discuss a response. It was April before a small group of hierarchs, the American cardinals, met with the pope; and it was June before the bishops met as a body to address the topic. When confronted by what was arguably the worst public scandal in the history of the U.S. Catholic Church, the bishops did not take the initiative to hold a special assembly before their normally scheduled meeting. Meanwhile individual bishops were left to respond—sometimes wisely, sometimes not—as local media uncovered one case of sexual abuse after another around the nation. It is hard to imagine that another institution would have allowed so much time to pass before the leadership came together to address a public scandal of historic proportion. At present, it is unclear how long lasting the damage of the scandal will be to the Church's moral leadership.[48]

It is also important to consider the role of a bishop as leader of the local Church. Is a bishop to be viewed as a papal legate to the local Church or as the leader who represents the local Church within the universal college of bishops? Renewed emphasis on centralization during John Paul's twenty-seven-year Pontificate and the lessened role of the local Church in determining episcopal appointments suggests that the former understanding has grown in recent decades at the expense of the latter. The way a bishop understands his role is of crucial significance for both identifying and implementing a pastoral agenda at the diocesan, regional, and national levels. The upshot is that resistance to decentralization and enculturation has marred the image of the Church as communion.[49]

Relations between Church Leaders and Catholics in Public Office

One consequence of the transition from church–state to church–society as the central dialogue is that bishops and other Church leaders have less power for political mobilization and less direct influence over political activity. The American Church sponsors lobbyists, legislative networks, and letter-writing campaigns; it continues to encourage justice and peace committees and social ministry organizations to advance its social mission, but these activities rarely demonstrate substantial political muscle. It is uncommon for Church leaders to deliver a "Catholic vote" in an election or legislative debate.

The Church's engagement with politics loses it attractiveness when it creates the appearance of partisanship, returning to an earlier style of political activity. American Catholics distinguish between the role of religion in public life, which they strongly support, and the role of religion in politics, about which they are dubious. In a sense, one can conclude that American Catholics have accepted the view that the Church ought to engage society but should keep its distance from the state. They want a faith that addresses issues of public life, but they do not want a Catholic political party or even a Catholic political movement. Nor are they much interested in Catholic Action understood as a clerical or Church-directed approach to social engagement.[50]

It will take time for Catholic public officials to work out an adequate under-standing of Vatican II's call to overcome the "false opposition between profes-sional and social activities on the one part, and religious life on the other."[51] Catholic public officials must be able to articulate a more nuanced position than John Kennedy's divorce of his faith from his public role, however reassuring that may have been to non-Catholic Americans in 1960. Indifference to politics is one way of failing to take seriously the conciliar call to engage the world. But relegating moral beliefs to private life and the denial of public significance to Catholic moral teaching is equally a failure.

A recent Vatican statement issued by the Congregation for the Doctrine of the Faith (CDF) illustrates a Church trying to sort out the issues in this post-conciliar situation.[52] The document acknowledges the rightful freedom of conscience and the legitimate autonomy of Catholics and others acting in the political arena. But it laments a cultural relativism that permits one to conclude that any appeal to conscience settles matters. Following one's conscience can beg the question of whether conscience is properly informed or if a good faith effort to be informed has even been attempted. The freedom of conscience must be respected, but freedom includes an obligation regarding conscience formation.

The CDF document is clear in its support for the legitimate autonomy of Catholics in public life. The congregation does not see Catholic officials as rep-resentatives of the Church or as lobbyists for things Catholic. What is a source of concern for the CDF is the state of the culture; the spirit of relativism is iden-tified as the principal enemy of a sound relationship between morality and poli-tics. This latter point is important because the document explicitly states that the topic is morality and politics not religion and politics.

Due to the persistent pluralism on moral matters that we find in modern cul-tures, the task of relating morality and public policy will likely remain contro-versial. The Catholic Church cannot accept a simple divorce of these two realms in light of the teaching of Vatican II, but it has yet to develop a fully convinc-ing strategy for relating them when there is profound moral disagreement within a society. Catholic politicians are caught in this situation, and it has given rise to tensions between civic officials and Church leaders.

Conclusion

The sea change that Vatican II introduced into the life of the Catholic Church has energized a variety of movements that give expression to the disciple's de-sire to serve humankind through social action. Understanding one's efforts at promoting social development as congruent with living one's faith has been an important motivation for many Catholic citizens. Catholics have been taught that to care for the world and its inhabitants is a norm of discipleship. Consci-entious citizenship is one of the roles that believers play in fulfillment of their baptismal vocation.

Still remaining in our present situation is the centuries-old process of discerning what the signs of the times might mean for practical judgments relating faith to the political order. Vatican II provided a new impetus for taking up the question, as well as a new spirituality and set of resources for thinking about it. What it did not provide is a once-and-for-all resolution of the question.

Notes

1. The New American Bible may be found at http://www.usccb.org/nab/bible/.

2. Philip Wogaman, *Christianity and Politics*, rev. and expanded ed. (Louisville: Westminster John Knox Press, 2000), 46.

3. J. Bryan Hehir, "Forum: Public Theology in Contemporary America," *Religion and American Culture* 10, no. 1 (Winter 2000): 23.

4. Vatican II, *Lumen Gentium*, n. 1, in *The Documents of Vatican II*, ed. Walter Abbott (Piscataway, NJ: New Century, 1966). As is customary for citations of Vatican Statements, all references will be to paragraphs rather than to page numbers.

5. As the episcopal synod held in 1971 stated: "Everyone who ventures to speak to people about justice must first be just in their eyes." 1971 Synod, *Justitia in Mundo*, chap. 3, in *Catholic Social Thought: The Documentary Heritage*, ed. David O'Brien and Thomas Shannon (Maryknoll, N.Y.: Orbis Books, 1992).

6. National Conference of Catholic Bishops, *Economic Justice for All* (Washington, D.C.: United States Catholic Conference, 1985), n. 347.

7. This last point indicates an unresolved tension in the life of the Catholic community. Is the Church to be a church of the masses, accepting within its walls many people only partially or hesitantly committed to the gospel message? Or, is the demand upon the Church for faithful witness such that those admitted to membership must constantly and consistently show themselves as a sacramental community that signifies the presence of divine grace in the world? In other words, how distinct from the rest of humankind must disciples be if their witness is to be noticed as more than a pale reflection—and their voice is to be heard as something other than a mere echo—of the wider society?

8. *Lumen Gentium*, n. 48, quoted in *Gaudium et Spes*, n. 45, in *The Documents of Vatican II*, ed. Abbott.

9. James Gustafson, "The Sectarian Temptation," *Proceedings of the Catholic Theological Society of America* 40 (1985): 83–94.

10. *Gaudium et Spes*, n. 1.

11. "The Church seeks but a solitary goal: to carry forward the work of Christ himself," in *Gaudium et Spes*, n. 3.

12. *Lumen Gentium*, n. 5.

13. Richard McBrien's explanation of the principle of mediation is a simple yet standard one: "The theological principle that God is available to us and acts upon us through secondary causes: persons, places, events, things, nature, history." See Richard McBrien, *Catholicism*, vol. 2 (Oak Grove, Minn.: Winston Press, 1980), xxxvi.

14. *Lumen Gentium*, 26. See also *Christus Dominus*, nn. 36–38, in *The Documents of Vatican II*, ed. Abbott.

15. See Edward Cleary, *Crisis and Change* (Maryknoll, N.Y.: Orbis Books, 1985).

16. I do not, of course, wish to deny the importance of the new wave of immigration, composed largely of people of color from continents other than Europe, that is currently transforming the Catholic and general population of the United States. My point is that a major shift in pastoral strategy occurred as the Catholic population in the United States was affected by public policies like the immigration act of 1924 and the G.I. bill after World War II. These measures altered the social characteristics of American Catholicism in several ways.

17. Examples include the Philippine Church and the Marcos Family, the South African Church under Apartheid, and the Nicaraguan Church with Somoza first and the Sandinista regime later.

18. *Apostolicam Actuositatem*, in *The Documents of Vatican II*, ed. Abbott. *Gaudium et Spes*, n. 43.

19. Ibid.

20. Pius XI defined Catholic Action in a letter dated November 18, 1928, as "the participation of the laity in the apostolate of the hierarchy." Note that the laity had no distinctive role to play in the Church's mission. Ministry was the domain of the ordained and/or professed member of a religious order. In fairness to Pius XI, it should be noted that he inherited from the papacy of Pius X an "integralist" tendency in the Church that sought clerical control over all lay Catholic organizations.

21. *Lumen Gentium*, n. 40; ibid., n. 41.

22. *Apostolicam Actuositatem*, n. 2.

23. *Unitatis Redintegratio*, n. 3, in *The Documents of Vatican II*, ed. Abbott.

24. *Nostra Aetate*, in *The Documents of Vatican II*, ed. Abbott; *Pacem in Terris*, in *Catholic Social Thought*, ed. O'Brien and Shannon.

25. *Gaudium et Spes*, n. 44.

26. Ibid.

27. *Dignitatis Humanae*, in *The Documents of Vatican II*, ed. Abbott.

28. Martin Marty, *The Public Church* (New York: Crossroad, 1981).

29. *Gaudium et Spes*, n. 40.

30. Ibid., nn. 41–43.

31. Ibid., n. 76.

32. Ibid., n. 41.

33. Ibid., n. 76.

34. Ibid.

35. Ibid., n. 43.

36. Daniel Philpott, "The Challenge of September 11 to Secularism in International Politics," *World Politics* 55 (October 2002): 71. The three parts of the synthesis are (1) the recognition of state sovereignty, (2) the rule of nonintervention in a state's internal affairs, and (3) the removal of religion from international affairs—the religion of the prince would be the religion of the people.

37. Wogaman, *Christianity and Politics*, 51.

38. Jose Casanova, *Public Religions in the Modern World* (Chicago: University of Chicago Press, 1994), 70.

39. Although the thrust of this section pertains to the general topic of the Church and politics, I will rely upon examples drawn from the experience that I know best,

namely, the way the issue is framed in the United States. I do not mean to imply by my limited range of examples that the American case is the model for others, but only to point out the kinds of issues that can arise when the Church engages pluralistic, open, democratic societies and limited constitutional states.

40. Casanova, *Public Religions*, 71.

41. Charles Taylor, *The Ethics of Authenticity* (Cambridge, Mass.: Harvard University Press, 1991), 22. Here one might ask if the language of a "culture of death" used by some contemporary Church leaders is a useful term of analysis.

42. By public philosophy, I mean the deeply rooted convictions and metaphors that constitute the characteristic way in which public life is discussed and debated in a country. Within the Unites States, for example, this would include certain tenets of liberalism (presumptions about individual liberty, private property, equality of opportunity, and equal standing before the law) and moral idealism (American exceptionalism, the promotion of democracy, and the defense of human rights and freedom). Public opinion, conversely, refers to more transitory and situation-dependent viewpoints that people hold about public affairs. These are judgments susceptible to quick shifts, for they are dependent upon matters prone to change, such as natural disasters, crime waves, business cycles, media attention, and the fear of terrorism.

43. One could interpret the agenda of the Catholic leadership in terms similar to those found in the now famous work of Robert N. Bellah, Richard Madsen, William M. Sullivan, Ann Swidler, and Steven M. Tipton, *Habits of the Heart: Individualism and Commitment in American Life*, rev. ed. (Berkeley: University of California Press, 1985), where there was a call to reintegrate the biblical and republican "languages" with the dominant discourse of individualism in American culture.

44. For my further reflections on this topic, see "Single-Issue Politics and the Church," *America*, May 9, 1987, 377–81.

45. It is surely no coincidence that Vatican II's *Inter Mirifica*, The Decree on Communication, is widely considered one of the least significant documents emanating from the council.

46. Paul VI, *Octogesima Adveniens*, n. 4.

47. Paul VI, *Populorum Progressio*, n. 5.

48. For a fair-minded account of the sexual abuse crisis, see Peter Steinfels, *A People Adrift: The Crisis of the Roman Catholic Church in America* (New York: Simon & Schuster, 2003), chap. 2.

49. Also see Mary Elsbernd, "Whatever Happened to *Octogesima Adveniens*?" *Theological Studies* 56 (1995): 39–60.

50. There is a similar conclusion found in Casanova, *Public Religions*, 205.

51. *Gaudium et Spes*, n. 43.

52. Congregation for the Doctrine of the Faith, "Doctrinal Note on Some Questions Regarding the Participation of Catholics in Political Life," November 24, 2002; http://www.vatican.va/roman_curia/congregations/cfaith/documents/rc_con_cfaith_doc_20021124_politica_en.html.

Chapter 2

The Vatican as a Transnational Actor

LISA L. FERRARI

WHEN THE UNITED NATIONS CALLED its Third International Conference on Population and Development in 1994, the Bill Clinton administration wanted a final document with clear pro-choice language on abortion and that linked population control with development. Because wealthy industrialized states supported the American position, the United States was confident of realizing its policy objectives. In fact, nearly 90 percent of the draft language met the approval of most UN member states.[1] However, the Holy See guaranteed that the remaining 10 percent would prove lethal to U.S. interests. With a small but adamant group of Latin American and Muslim allies, the Holy See focused discussion only on abortion and family planning. Though the great powers complained that the Holy See was derailing negotiations, the conference produced a final document that did not include the pro-choice language of the industrialized West.

An enduring fact of international relations is the considerable influence wielded by the Roman Catholic Church, without a single soldier—notwithstanding the Swiss Guard—or trade agreement of its own. As a member of the American delegation observed, "We didn't know how strong they were."[2] World leaders from George W. Bush to Yasser Arafat have gone out of their way to visit the Vatican. The pope's travels make the front page of the *New York Times*. Many secular leaders in Latin America, Asia, and Africa regard Catholic bishops as politically dangerous.

The Catholic Church has a unique identity in the international system, which allows it to influence international relations in a distinctive way. Like the European Union, the Catholic Church defies easy classification in the simple international relations taxonomy of states, intergovernmental organizations (IGOs), and nongovernmental organizations (NGOs). That is, whereas the European Union falls somewhere between the first two categories, the Church combines elements of the first and third. The fact that the Church can be partially understood either as an NGO or as a state, but fully understood in neither category, reflects differences in ecclesial and secular epistemologies. The Church straddles two categories of political personhood because those categories were formulated by academic analysts looking at secular institutions. As this chapter shows, the Church operates from fundamental beliefs and standards that are largely compatible with secular ways of understanding the world but at times diverge considerably from those understandings.

One way to understand the Vatican is as a sovereign state. The current sovereign borders of the Vatican city-state were drawn in the 1929 Lateran Pacts between Italy and the Holy See. The Lateran Pacts consist of three agreements. The Conciliation Treaty confirms the Church's sovereign status; the Financial Convention sets the terms of Italian reparation to the Holy See for the loss of the Papal States; and the Concordat lays out the terms of Italy's interaction with the Holy See. The pope, who is the head of the Church, is also the absolute monarch in the 108.7 contiguous acres of Vatican City, with extraterritorial jurisdiction over certain buildings in Rome. However, the Church is more than the sum of activities in Vatican City.

Another way to understand the Catholic Church is as a transnational NGO, which is a group of private individuals that operates across sovereign boundaries in pursuit of its aims. A growing body of literature in international relations documents the power of NGOs, and their ontological cousins, the transnational social movements and transnational issue networks.[3] Rather than exerting influence via the traditional instruments of foreign policy, NGOs exert soft power, the ability to bring another actor's desires in line with one's own.

In comparison with other NGOs, the Catholic Church is a massive entity with multiple layers of organization. The Holy See is the ecclesial center of the Church, headed by the pope and staffed by the curia, the administrators and bureaucrats who oversee the Church's work worldwide. The curia includes numerous congregations, tribunals, councils, and commissions charged with overseeing various aspects of canon law, doctrine, and the pastoral care of the faithful.[4] The Holy See, the pinnacle of this organization, oversees the world's bishops, many of whom meet in national or regional episcopal conferences. The bishops, in turn, oversee the various territorial units of the Church, including the dioceses to which local parishes belong. Therefore, an analysis of the Church's political relevance must first determine which of these layers of organization to study, or whether to look at them all simultaneously.

This chapter considers the actions of the Holy See specifically, because the Church elites have the most direct influence on formal channels of ecclesial decision making. In addition, the Holy See is the only portion of the Church that must act transnationally if it is to act at all. Parishes and bishops' conferences may act on matters of local or national concern, but the Holy See has very little business that may be considered purely local.[5] Conversely, a study of the

Holy See cannot ignore the rest of the Church, because the Holy See frequently relies on subsidiary ecclesial structures to carry out its actions.

To summarize, "the Vatican" is actually two separate, if related, entities: the Holy See and the government of Vatican City. The chapters in this volume use the term "Vatican" to refer to the Church's combined roles as sovereign state and ecclesial NGO. In this chapter the terms "Vatican City" and "Holy See" will indicate those individual roles, respectively. The boundaries between the political and ecclesial institutions are not always sharp. For example, the Secretariat of State, an office of the curia, conducts foreign relations for Vatican City. Foreign diplomats are accredited to the Holy See, not to the sovereign government of Vatican City. Therefore, other sovereigns have diplomatic relations not with Vatican City but with the Church per se. The interaction between the Church's roles as sovereign and NGO helps promote its transnational program. In fact, the Vatican's dual identity has important implications for the Church's methods of and purposes for interacting with states.

The Holy See's Interpretation of the International System

The Holy See directs a truly global Church. The Catholic Church's membership reaches around the world, and the Church engages in mission work worldwide. However, an actor may recognize its membership as geographically dispersed without seeking influence in the international system. For example, transnational academic organizations recruit members worldwide without aspiring to influence the global balance of power or distribution of wealth. Such organizations understand the space in which they operate differently than do sovereign states. They regard the world as a patchwork of membership regions and concentrations of intellectual resources. They are at least as concerned with the distribution of universities, libraries, graduate fellowships, and potential research collaborators as they are with the political boundaries that divide sovereigns. Thus, an organization may act in the world of sovereign states without interpreting social or material reality exactly as states do.

States, by their nature, understand themselves as situated in the atomized space of political sovereigns. The Church acknowledges its position among the political units of the international system, yet it does not envision the international system as states do. In the words of Pope Paul VI,

This is how the Lord wanted his Church to be: universal, a great tree whose branches shelter the birds of the air, a net which catches fish of every kind or which Peter drew in filled with one hundred and fifty-three big fish, a flock which a single shepherd pastures. A universal Church without boundaries or frontiers except, alas, those of the heart and mind of sinful men.[6]

Furthermore, the Church interprets the world differently than do secular sovereigns. As Pope Leo XIII wrote, the Church observes the world and "seeks greater things than this. . . . We cannot understand and evaluate mortal things rightly unless the mind reflects upon the other life, the life which is immortal."[7] Thus, the Church calculates its worldly interests by considering divine intention and the universal human impact of pursuing those interests. Few, if any, states claim to use such criteria in policymaking. Certainly the great powers do not.

Most of the Vatican's foreign relations are conducted by the Holy See, which means that an ecclesial organization must interact with other, secular aggregations of humanity that offer different—and often competing—principles for organizing the world. Paul VI comments that

> for the Church it is a question not only of preaching the Gospel in ever wider geographic areas or to ever greater numbers of people, but also of affecting and as it were upsetting, through the power of the Gospel, mankind's criteria of judgment, determining values, points of interest, lines of thought, sources of inspiration and models of life which are in contrast with the Word of God and the plan of salvation.[8]

As a consequence, the Holy See regards phenomena such as urbanization and migration, which political scientists and policy practitioners would likely describe in political or economic terms, primarily in terms of their social and religious implications.[9] John Paul II writes of authentic human development rather than simply economic development, and he offers a "theological reading of modern problems," in which he asks the faithful to reframe political and economic questions in terms of sin and "structures of sin."[10] In his words,

> If certain forms of modern "imperialism" were considered in the light of these moral criteria, we would see that hidden behind certain decisions, apparently inspired only by economics or politics, are real forms of idolatry: of money, ideology, class, technology. I have wished to introduce this type of analysis above all in order to point out the true *nature* of the evil which faces us with respect to the development of peoples: it is a question of *moral evil*, the fruit of *many sins* which lead to "structures of sin."[11]

As John Paul II recognized, sovereign states frame the world in different terms than does the Church.

Nonetheless, historically the Church has made clear its concern with justice in the political order and with international relations specifically. Kenneth Himes provides a useful summary of this perspective in chapter 1 of this volume. In modern times, Pope Leo XIII's 1891 encyclical letter *Rerum Novarum* decried the abuses of the Industrial Revolution that drove the working class toward communism; Manuel and Mott in chapter 3 and Kearney in chapter 9 demonstrate that *Rerum Novarum's* advocation of corporatism was adopted by leaders throughout Latin Europe and Latin America as the key organizing principle to govern society.

Pope John XXIII's landmark encyclical letter *Pacem in Terris* of 1963 offers a wide menu of concerns for the Church. The political, economic, and social realities of the world create the conditions in which the Church must fulfill its pastoral mission. Thus, the Church must recognize temporal realities and be willing to demand change in the course of its ecclesial work. *Pacem in Terris* emphasizes that achieving the common good is the appropriate purpose of authority, and it devotes considerable attention to relations between states, which is one means of achieving the common good. Less explicitly, the encyclical enumerates human rights that mirror those in the United Nations' 1948 Universal Declaration on Human Rights. Even so, the Holy See needed to promulgate its own statement of human rights to reflect the subtle and serious differences between its conception of humanity and the UN's.

The documents of Vatican II provide further evidence that the Church is self-consciously concerned with conditions in the international system, but understands a unique role for itself within that system. *Gaudium et Spes*, promulgated two years after *Pacem in Terris*, revisits themes of John XXIII's encyclical and clearly articulates the global vision and radical egalitarianism that underpin the Church's subsequent commentary on international relations. The introduction to *Gaudium et Spes* famously declares that "the Church has always had the duty of scrutinizing the signs of the times and of interpreting them in the light of the Gospel."[12] Subsequent chapters give substance to the Church's concerns. For example, *Gaudium et Spes* calls for alternatives to war, while eschewing pacifism per se.[13] The Church thus rejects secular political categories for understanding the use of force. *Gaudium et Spes* further calls for new practices of economic development as necessary for a just international community. Even the document's English title evinces the Church's awareness of its position in the international system.

In the years since Vatican II, the Holy See has reiterated the global interests and concerns expressed in *Pacem in Terris* and *Gaudium et Spes*. Through his writings and actions, Pope John Paul II expressed the Church's ongoing concern with global conditions. For example, in his 1991 encyclical *Centesimus Annus*, written on the hundredth anniversary of *Rerum Novarum*, John Paul II argues that:

> the human person receives from God its essential dignity and with it the capacity to move towards truth and goodness. But one is also conditioned by the social structure in which one lives, by the education one has received and by the environment. These elements can either help or hinder a person's living in accordance

with the truth. The decisions which create a human environment can give rise to specific structures of sin which impede the full realization of those who are in any way oppressed by them.[14]

Later in the same document, John Paul II emphasizes the universal destination of material creation.[15] This has widely been read as a critique of unbridled capitalism and consumerism. However, John Paul's general interest in material economic conditions is arguably less important than his specific teaching that everything is intended by God for universal benefit. The latter observation distinguishes the Church's fundamental ethical standards, and their economic and political implications, from those of secular sovereigns.

By the Church's standards, the justice of a political community can be measured by that community's promotion and protection of human dignity, regardless of individuals' social, economic, or political status.[16] According to the Congregation for the Doctrine of the Faith (CDF), proper respect for human dignity compels the faithful to promote religious freedom and the right to life; protect the family as an institution; and attend to the needs of minors, the poor, and the otherwise weak. In sum, human dignity can best be promoted by securing freedom and honoring truth, both publicly and privately.[17]

Two important, and related, preconditions of human dignity are peace and development. Citing the *Catechism of the Catholic Church*, the CDF instructs the faithful that "peace is always the work of justice and the effect of charity. It demands the absolute and radical rejection of violence and terrorism and requires a constant and vigilant commitment on the part of all political leaders."[18] However, the Catholic notion of peace is more expansive than a simple absence of war. Peace is the right ordering of the world according to the divine plan. This definition highlights the tension between the ecclesial and secular ways of interpreting the international system. Thus, John XXIII observes that "peace on earth . . . can be firmly established only if the order laid down by God be dutifully observed."[19] Furthermore, God's universal order includes all facets of human existence, not merely questions of the resort to force. Therefore, nearly three decades later, John Paul II writes:

> It must be remembered that true peace is never simply the result of military victory, but rather implies both the removal of the causes of war and genuine reconciliation between peoples.[20]

The cold war arms race, for example, was not a condition of peace.[21] Furthermore, God's peace does not serve the interest of any particular human institution.

Similarly, the Holy See regards development as a complex condition defined by God and reflecting the nature of humanity, not the balancing of power and interest. In his 1987 encyclical *Sollicitudo Rei Socialis*, John Paul II begins by expressing the complexity of the concept of authentic human development:

> The social concern of the Church, directed towards an authentic development of man and society which would respect and promote all the dimensions of the human person, has always expressed itself in the most varied ways.[22]

The Holy See understands development as broadly as it understands peace. Any matter that impedes authentic human expression and fulfillment is a barrier to development. Indeed, the Church sees a close relationship between development and peace, and not simply in the power-political sense that poverty may breed discontent and violence. In his 1967 encyclical letter *Populorum Progressio*, Paul VI noted that "development is the new name for peace."[23] Discrimination, economic inequality, and other injustices are as central to peacemaking as is refraining from the use of deadly force. Observers of the Holy See might argue that it has three significant areas of political concern—human dignity, peace, and development. In fact, the Church understands these three areas as being a single, if multifaceted, concern.

The Catholic Church as an Atypical Sovereign

The contemporary Church promotes this concern through both its sovereign and ecclesial structures. Of the Church's two structures, the ecclesial is the higher-profile organization, and the most central to the Church's self-understanding, but the sovereign also plays a critical role. However, Vatican City is not a typical state. According to the 1933 Montevideo Convention on the Rights and Duties of States, which provides a frequently cited legal definition of statehood, states must have a permanent population, territory, government, and the capacity to interact with other states.[24] Vatican City has defined territory and government, but it meets the other two criteria rather ambiguously.

In territory, Vatican City is the smallest sovereign entity in the world. At 0.17 square miles, it is less than one-fourth the size of the next largest state, Monaco. However, the borders of Vatican City have been undisputed since 1929; the 1985 revision of the Lateran Pacts did not change the Church's sovereign boundaries.

The government of Vatican City oversees this tiny territory. Although he is the monarch of Vatican City, the pope generally is not involved with the day-to-day governance of the state. Rather, the Pontifical Commission for the Vatican City State, comprising five cardinals, and the president, a sixth cardinal, oversee all state functioning and report periodically to the pope.[25] The government of Vatican City performs many of the functions of other states, including accounting; maintaining civil records and a police department; and providing tourist information, legal, and health services.

Even cursory consideration of Vatican City's population shows its anomalous nature among states. The population of Vatican City is variously estimated at between 500 and 700 persons, but nearly all of these are temporary citizens.[26] If statehood requires a permanent population, Vatican City barely meets the criterion. Furthermore, the miniscule population of Vatican City in no sense comprises the full membership of the Catholic Church. Approximately one-sixth of the world's population is at least nominally Catholic, and many countries have a significant Catholic population.[27] Virtually all Catholics claim native citizenship outside Vatican City, and most are unlikely ever to set foot on the pope's territory; yet the monarch of the sovereign state of Vatican City enjoys a singular authority over a population rivaling that of the People's Republic of China, and he often uses that influence to address issues of political significance.

Even so, the Church's ability to interact with states is not always a function of its statehood. On one hand, Vatican City does interact with some other sovereigns regarding its limited functions. Italy may punish crimes committed in Vatican City, and Italian police may arrest suspected criminals in Saint Peter's Square. International mail from Vatican City is processed by Switzerland. On the other hand, foreign diplomats are accredited directly to the Holy See, not to the government of Vatican City. Vatican diplomacy is an ecclesial matter, and, to date, approximately 175 countries have formal diplomatic ties to the Holy See.[28]

To secular sovereigns this must seem odd. They do not send diplomatic missions to other religious organizations or receive such missions from them. For the Church, however, there is nothing odd about the arrangement. The raison d'être of the Catholic Church is its divinely appointed mission. The Church employs such temporal structures as it needs to fulfill this mission. For much of its history, the Holy See maintained or aspired to greater territory, sometimes as a foothold into greater secular authority. However, in the twentieth century, Pius XII wanted to secure only a small territory on which to headquarter the Church because its apostolic mission would be compromised either without such a temporal base of operations or with greater territorial interests to protect.[29] The Church today regards Vatican City as part of the infrastructure for carrying out its true mission. In the language of international relations, the Church understands itself as an NGO, and it additionally employs the benefits of sovereign status in the service of its advocacy interests.

The Westphalian system of sovereign states emerged from the Thirty Years' War, which was driven by questions of political and ecclesial authority. Philpott notes that "Reformation theology and sovereignty are connected intrinsically and conceptually" in the origins of the Westphalian system.[30] The Reformation removed some powers from the Church, and the secular leaders who took up those powers therefore had an interest in maintaining them. The significance of the Reformation to the rise of sovereignty makes the Church's role in contemporary international relations both ironic and apt. Ironically, the Church nonetheless found a way to make sovereignty work in its favor, maintaining a base for operations that eclipse those of any single Protestant church in their scope. Instead of being a normal sovereign, the Church maintains the trappings of sovereignty while conducting the bulk of its affairs through its incarnation as an NGO. Far from unseating the Catholic Church as a political force, the Reformation-driven Westphalian system ultimately gave the Church a unique position in international relations. Centuries after the Treaties of Münster and Osnabrück, papal nuncios still claim the same privileges as secular diplomats and still have no Protestant counterparts.

Because of its sovereign status, the Church enjoys the privilege of formal roles in various IGOs. Having established a postal service and radio station, Vatican City joined the Universal Postal Union and International Telecommunications Union after World War II. In 1951, the United Nations General Assembly and World Health Organization invited the Vatican to attend sessions on an ad hoc basis. A few years later, the Church indicated that its delegation represented the Holy See per se; in 1964, UN secretary general U Thant extended permanent observer status to that delegation. The Holy See shares permanent observer status at the United Nations with organizations as varied as the Palestinian Authority, League of Arab States, International Committee of the Red Cross, and Commonwealth Secretariat. Today the Holy See has observer status at more than a dozen IGOs, including the International Atomic Energy Agency, Council of Europe, Organization of American States, and Organization for Security and Cooperation in Europe. When the Holy See takes a high-profile controversial position in an IGO, such as its 1994 role in Cairo, critics question whether the Church deserves membership in an organization of states. The failure of these campaigns reflects the Vatican's position of strength in international relations. Without its sovereign identity, the Church could not act as it does in the international system, but that identity is only one aspect of the Church's global profile.

The Catholic Church as an Atypical Advocacy Nongovernmental Organization

The first attribute that distinguishes the Holy See from other NGOs is the sheer size of the Church's membership. This great size can be a great disadvantage. Coordinating the activities of more than a billion people is a huge task. Conversely, most global leaders wish to avoid alienating Catholics, who likely make up a notable portion of their constituency. As a result, political actors are often reluctant to respond as harshly to the Holy See or to domestic Catholic actors as they are to other types of advocates.[31]

Besides this simple structural distinction, there are a number of conceptual ways in which the Church differs from other advocacy NGOs, organizations that exist to promote a set of principles or principled issue positions. These conceptual distinctions may be summarized in terms of moral authority. In his analysis of political influence, Kane uses the term "moral capital" to mean the "respect and approval that is of great political benefit to the receiver" bestowed by people judging the receiver's behavior, and which that receiver can acquire by being "faithful and effective in serving those values and goals" to which the receiver claims to attach importance.[32] Kane further argues that moral capital can be a source of authority, because political actors have need of it, and therefore may be influenced by others with significant stores of it. Though Kane is most interested in exploring the moral capital available to individuals in positions of political leadership, his ideas are equally suitable to states and nonstate actors as units of analysis. Like individual political leaders, aggregate political actors display interests and require others' perceptions of their credibility and legitimacy in order to implement their political programs.

In explaining the importance of moral capital, Kane offers a set of four "sources typically available [to an actor] to build moral capital, to maintain it, and to mobilize it politically."[33] The first of these sources is cause. That is, actors who wish to wield moral capital must consistently promote a coherent goal and rationale for achieving it. The second source is action, the ability to "maneuver and manipulate . . . without seeming to betray core values."[34] Third, actors evince moral capital by being moral exemplars of their cause, living out their values rather than just espousing them. Finally, moral capital depends on an actor's ability to mobilize and sustain support by using rhetoric and symbolism. In each of these four categories, the transnational Catholic Church has assets uncommon to advocacy NGOs. By examining each category in turn, it is possible to understand the Church's distinctive position as a transnational actor and advocate.

Cause

Kane argues that actors accumulate moral capital through firmness and faithfulness in pursuit of their goals. NGOs that remain true to their principles consistently and over time enjoy higher levels of moral capital than do NGOs that do not. By this criterion, the Holy See is likely to succeed. It espouses a coherent and enduring set of values, and it consistently directs its energies toward the service of those values.

However, Clark argues that NGOs succeed in their advocacy when they focus their resources quite specifically.[35] By Clark's criterion, the Holy See is less likely to achieve its advocacy goals, because those goals are broad as compared with those of other advocacy NGOs. For example, Amnesty International seeks just treatment for prisoners of conscience and monitors states' adherence to the Universal Declaration of Human Rights. The Red Cross monitors adherence to the 1949 Geneva Conventions on the Laws of War. Greenpeace, which began as an advocate of nuclear disarmament, has branched out from its original purpose but nonetheless mounts only a limited number of campaigns on selected environmental issues (e.g., against climate change, genetic engineering, and whaling). The Holy See, in contrast, concerns itself with all aspects of human life that may have an impact on peace and human dignity and claims to be "an expert in humanity."[36] Though the Holy See has forbidden certain types of political action, such as holding public office if one is in religious life, and maintains certain understandings of the right ordering of creation, such as the rejection of same-sex marriage, the Church is potentially interested in any area that has a significant impact on the social, economic, or political order. Indeed, the opening lines of *Gaudium et Spes* state:

> The joys and hopes, the griefs and the anxieties of the men of this age, especially those who are poor or in any way afflicted, these are the joys and hopes, the griefs and anxieties of the followers of Christ.[37]

If Clark is correct that advocacy NGOs gain strength from their issue focus, an analysis must conclude that the Church's broad-based concern with human experience is not, in itself, an asset.

In another sense, the breadth of the Holy See's interests indicates that the Church's relationship to the common good is unique among NGOs and may work to the Vatican's political advantage. Most advocacy NGOs unquestionably have well-defined interests. They champion a single issue or closely related set of issues to which they wish states, and perhaps civil society, to attend. Therefore, when these NGOs call upon states, they do so with many competing voices, demanding shares of limited resources for their particular area of concern. The full onus is on states to determine which demands warrant response, and in what ways.

In contrast, the Holy See regards as in its purview any matter that bears on the question of human dignity. The Church's notions of peace and development are so broad as potentially to encompass any aspect of human endeavor that generates injustice or oppression. Because the Holy See nonetheless must operate with finite resources and cannot pursue all its potential goals simultaneously, it must prioritize the causes it cares about and dedicate resources to them accordingly. States know that by the time they receive requests from the Holy See, those requests have been weighed against other demands and prioritized. That, coupled with the Holy See's moral authority as a religious organization, encourages states to take the Holy See's requests more seriously than they take those of other, "special" interests.[38]

Action

The Holy See has a unique array of transnational action channels. The Church is a worldwide network of formal and informal transnational ties, from the administrative structures based in Rome to the grassroots connections be-tween parishes in the developed and developing worlds. Though many of these ties formed during the post–cold war era of NGO proliferation, others are cen-turies old. No other advocacy NGO can claim such historical depth to its ties, or such breadth of membership. These transnational ties can generate inter-national support for a particular cause, even in the face of domestic oppres-sion or unrest. For example, the Chilean Church in the 1970s successfully supported domestic political change by relying on transnational elements of the organization.[39]

Of course, many of these action channels are international rather than transnational, because the Vatican interacts with states as a peer while simulta-neously interacting with them as an interest group. In this sense, it is difficult to distinguish Vatican influence stemming from NGO status from Vatican in-fluence stemming from sovereign status. As an outgrowth of its historic relations with European sovereigns, the Holy See has developed regular diplomatic rela-tions with most of the states in the international system. Many states regard the Vatican as a valuable listening post.

As a result of its diplomatic ties with states, the Holy See has regular ac-cess to heads of state, foreign ministries, and diplomatic delegations. In many countries, the papal nuncio is the dean of the diplomatic delegation, because he represents the longest-standing diplomatic relationship of the sovereign. In addition, the Holy See has long held observer status in several IGOs. Until the end of the cold war, this made the Church nearly unique among NGOs. Today, however, many more NGOs are being afforded such status or are being called upon regularly to offer expert testimony, particularly in the United Nations.[40]

Another important aspect of the Holy See's ability to "maneuver and manipu-late" concerns finances. The Holy See, to a far greater degree than other advo-cacy NGOs, is financially self-sufficient. The Holy See's operating budget depends primarily on income from investments and donations. The recent his-tory of the Vatican bank has been checkered with mismanagement and scan-dal. Nonetheless, in 1994, the Holy See reported 750 billion lire in net assets, including cash, stocks and bonds, gold, and fixed assets.[41] The exact nature of the Holy See's investments is not public information, and in the early 1990s the Holy See clearly operated at a deficit; yet the overall picture is one of financial strength. The pope's financial experts recognize the need for reform, and the absolute levels of wealth in question are large by global standards.[42] In contrast, Sikkink notes that many NGOs struggle with limited or unevenly distributed funding that impedes their ability to advocate their cause. Furthermore, many of these NGOs depend on funding from private foundations, which leaves them vulnerable to funding cycles, fads in charitable giving, or other unexpected losses of revenue.[43]

Moral Exemplars

Kane states that actors with high degrees of moral capital exemplify moral standards in the pursuit of their cause. He proposes Nelson Mandela and Aung San Suu Kyi as two such role models. After his imprisonment on Robben Island, Nelson Mandela embodied the struggle against apartheid in South Africa. As a captive with no public contact, Mandela was relatively easy for the antiapartheid movement to idolize and elevate to the status of martyr.[44] Although Mandela did not seek this position as moral role model, he clearly has honored it. Mandela's conduct toward the apartheid regime after his release was exemplary; therefore, African National Congress supporters could feel confident following in his footsteps.

Another imprisoned dissident, Aung San Suu Kyi of Burma, likewise proved to be a moral exemplar for her cause. However, Kane observes that her credibility was to an extent undermined because of the time she had spent away from Burma and her marriage to a British citizen. As a result, Suu Kyi made deliberate moves to reestablish her credentials as a representative of Burma and a worthy embodiment of her cause.[45] It is clear that both Mandela and Suu Kyi have deliberately held themselves to high standards of conduct at least in part because they understand themselves as under personal moral scrutiny by critics of their political causes.

The Holy See can draw on a number of moral exemplars, including Jesus, Mary, and the saints. All of these provide Catholics with robust role models for lives of faith, and frequently for interacting with the political establishment.[46] More directly in keeping with Kane's model, the pope himself serves as a moral exemplar for the Church. Like his immediate predecessor, Pope Benedict XVI is widely esteemed as a person of great intellect and integrity, even by non-Catholics and observers who disagree with the Church's teaching. For political leaders, association with the pope can send a potent message. For example, in 1987, John Paul II met with President Ronald Reagan during a stopover in Fairbanks, Alaska. Reagan requested that, after the meeting, he and the pope leave in the same car. A Vatican official explained why Reagan's request was flatly denied: "The Pope never rides in the same car with the head of a country. It would look like he was endorsing him. Then Kim in South Korea would want it, Marcos would want it, and Pinochet. We can't do it for the United States but not for other countries."[47] As was the case with John Paul II, Pope Benedict XVI himself is a bearer of moral authority, and that authority arises in no small part because the pope lives in accordance with the dictates of the Church.

Not all the Church's moral examples are unequivocally good, however. Pope Pius XII has been accused of inaction at best and complicity at worst with regard to fascism.[48] Recent sex abuse allegations against a growing number of priests have undermined the ability of Catholic clergy to speak as unquestioned moral role models. These latter cases are especially troubling for Church authority, because weekly or occasional interaction with a priest may be any individual person's most direct contact with the Church's moral exemplars. To the extent that Church political influence is predicated on its ability to influence the Catholic constituents of secular authorities, the Vatican's influence may weaken as the credibility of its grassroots representatives erodes.

Rhetoric and Symbolism

Moral exemplars are not the Vatican's only moral indicators. The Holy See draws upon rhetoric and symbols that have been imbued with meaning over the course of centuries. The *Catechism of the Catholic Church* contains a section detailing the symbols of the Christian faith, including light and darkness, fire, processions, incense, candles, the Lectionary and Gospels, and such actions as circumcising, anointing, and the laying on of hands.[49] In addition, the Church regularly employs additional symbols and iconography, including liturgical colors, the crucifix, Stations of the Cross, the Sacred Heart, bread and wine, and Jesus as the Lamb of God. Many of these symbols are not used exclusively by the Church, but nonetheless have particular resonance with the Catholic faithful. Furthermore, most aspects of Catholic religious observance and worship are highly ritualized.

Ritual and imagery are not the only symbols available to the Holy See for transmitting its messages. Individual persons, or classes of persons, also function in symbolic roles. Schmitt notes that "the Catholic Church is the sole surviving contemporary example of the medieval capacity to create representative figures—the Pope, the emperor, the monk, the knight, the merchant."[50] Thus, the Holy See has an atavistic ability to place its stamp on political interactions, which is not shared with contemporary NGOs. Geertz further explains the transfer of authority from such a symbol to the matters that concern it: "When kings journey around the countryside making appearances, attending fetes, conferring honors, exchanging gifts, or defying rivals, they mark it, like some wolf or tiger spreading his scent through his territory, as almost physically part of them."[51]

Geertz goes on to describe an "inherent sacredness of central authority," which could apply to the Holy See as easily as to secular leaders. Of course, the medieval kings of whom Schmitt writes would have claimed authority as a matter of divine right, thus blurring the distinction between ecclesial and secular authority. In a sense, however, this parallels the condition of the pope today, because he is head of both the Church and the Vatican City State.

Manipulation of symbols is a part of political business as usual. Edelman has discussed at length the use of condensation symbols—encapsulations of deeply resonant associations—in politics.[52] Secular political symbols may include colors, flags, and partisan iconography. Advocacy NGOs have created their own symbols, in the hope of seeing them become condensation symbols. One prominent example is Amnesty International's single candle wrapped in barbed wire. Another is the red cross. However, the Holy See's symbols are loaded with centuries of meaning and enjoy worldwide recognition. No other advocacy NGO can make such a claim. Therefore, the Holy See is drawing on more potent symbols in its attempts to influence international relations than are other advocacy NGOs.

Conclusion

The Vatican is both a sovereign state and an NGO, and analysis of one aspect without the other gives an incomplete picture of the Church in international relations. The Holy See is simultaneously distinct from and similar to the group of transnational nonstate actors known as advocacy NGOs. Like all such NGOs, the Holy See cannot rely on economic or military strength to sway the activities of sovereign states in line with the principles it champions. Therefore, the Holy See relies on its soft power resources to effect change.

One of these sources of soft power is the size and breadth of the Church's worldwide membership. As a result of its large and diffuse body of the faithful, the Church warrants attention, and often careful treatment, from even those states that do not regard the Church as a friend. This means that the Holy See's requests will be heard, even when they are not fully heeded. Given that NGOs' primary means of influencing international relations are through agenda setting, issue framing, and information sharing—all matters of manipulating knowledge—"being heard" is not a minor victory. The first important step to altering discourse is to enter that discourse.

In general, advocacy NGOs are successful because of their clear issue focus, credibility, expertise, and valuation of principle over narrow self-interest. For a variety of theological and epistemological reasons, the Holy See does not understand its role in international relations as defined by a narrow or single issue focus. As a result, it loses some of the benefits that may accrue to NGOs from such a focused stance. However, in terms of credibility and espousal of principle over self-interest, the Holy See is at no disadvantage compared with other advocacy NGOs.

Furthermore, there are several areas in which the Holy See is better situated to affect international relations than are most NGOs, because the Church transcends simple categorization as an NGO. The Holy See is linked directly to a sovereign actor, Vatican City, and relates to sovereign states as their diplomatic and legal peer. This means that the Holy See has action channels available that are critical in international relations and are characteristic of states but not of NGOs. Without any effort to establish new lines of communication with states or IGOs, the Holy See has direct access to heads of state, foreign ministries, major

IGOs, and the diplomatic corps. In addition to these important action channels, the Holy See enjoys another distinction from other advocacy NGOs in that it is self-financed at a very high level. Members' donations are critical to the financial health of the Church, but neither the Holy See nor most levels of Church organization are reliant on funding through foundations or grants-in-aid. Furthermore, the size and geographic distribution of the world's Catholic population affords the Holy See leverage in interacting with states, as does its ability to command a vast array of unusually powerful condensation symbols in global political discourse.

The Church carries out its secular activities in the service of its ecclesial mission. Therefore, analysis must conclude that the Church understands itself primarily as an NGO. Because it has an apostolic mission, the Church regards Vatican City as existing to serve the Holy See, and not vice versa. To the extent that the Church's identities as sovereign state and NGO can be teased apart, however, observation shows that the Holy See's ability to act in the international system is greatly enhanced by its attachment to a sovereign state.

Notes

1. Christine Gorman, "Clash of Wills in Cairo," *Time*, September 12, 1994, 56.

2. M. Faith Mitchell, former director, Bureau of Population, U.S. Department of State, and member of the U.S. Delegation to the 1994 United National International Conference on Population and Development, Cairo, interview by author, July 13, 1995, Washington.

3. For an excellent literature review, see Richard Price, "Transnational Civil Society and Advocacy in World Politics," *World Politics* 55, no. 4 (July 2003): 579–606.

4. For concise information on the offices and functions of the curia, consult any issue of the annual *Catholic Almanac* (Huntington, Ind: Our Sunday Visitor Publications). A more detailed presentation can be found in Eric Hanson, *The Catholic Church in World Politics* (Princeton, N.J.: Princeton University Press, 1987), 59–94.

5. Of course, the pope is the bishop of Rome and thereby has some "purely" local responsibilities. However, any act of the pope, even in his capacity as a bishop, is likely to be scrutinized for its significance to the larger Church.

6. Paul VI, Encyclical *Evangelii Nuntiandi*, 1975, n. 61

7. Leo XIII, Encyclican *Rerum Novarum*, 1891, n. 33.

8. *Evangelii Nuntiandi*, n. 19.

9. See, e.g., John Paul II, Encyclical *Redemptoris Missio*, 1990, nn. 32, 37, 38, 58.

10. John Paul II, Encyclical *Sollicitudo Rei Socialis*, 1987, esp. nn. 36–37.

11. Ibid., n. 37. Emphasis in the original.

12. John XXIII, Encyclical *Pacem in Terris*, n. 84; Vatican II, *Gaudium et Spes*, n. 4.

13. *Gaudium et Spes*, nn. 77–82.

14. John Paul II, *Centesimus Annus*, n. 38.

15. Similar language and argumentation can be found in *Sollicitudo Rei Socialis*, n. 42; *Redemptoris Missio*, nn. 1, 23.

16. *Gaudium et Spes*, nn. 73–93.

17. Congregation for the Doctrine of the Faith, "The Participation of Catholics in Political Life," November 21, 2002, nn. 4, 7.

18. Ibid., n. 4.

19. *Pacem in Terris*, n. 1.

20. *Centesimus Annus*, n. 18.

21. Ibid., n. 18.

22. *Sollicitudo Rei Socialis*, n. 1.

23. Paul VI, Encyclical *Populorum Progressio*, 1967, n. 87.

24. League of Nations Treaty Series 19. The Montevideo Convention was originally an inter-American agreement, signed at the Seventh International Conference of American States. Subsequently, it has been more widely regarded as a set of legal guidelines for determining statehood.

25. Thomas J. Reese, S.J., *Inside the Vatican: The Politics and Organization of the Catholic Church* (Cambridge, Mass.: Harvard University Press, 1996), 18, 20–21; Peter Nichols, *The Pope's Divisions: The Roman Catholic Church Today* (New York: Holt, Rinehart & Winston, 1981), 113–14.

26. Reese, *Inside the Vatican*, 23; Matthew Bunson, ed., *2004 Catholic Almanac* (Huntington, Ind.: Our Sunday Visitor Publications, 2003), 256.

27. Bunson, *2004 Catholic Almanac*, 328. The global Catholic population in 2003 was approximately 1,060,840,000.

28. Ibid., 262–64.

29. Reese, *Inside the Vatican*, 18.

30. Daniel Philpott, "The Religious Roots of Modern International Relations," *World Politics* 52 (January 2000): 224.

31. Barry Rubin, "Religion and International Affairs," in *Religion, the Missing Dimension of Statecraft*, ed. Douglas M. Johnston and Cynthia Sampson (New York: Oxford University Press, 1994), 31.

32. John Kane, *The Politics of Moral Capital* (New York: Cambridge University Press, 2001), 10.

33. Ibid., 38–39.

34. Ibid., 38.

35. Anne Marie Clark, "Non-Governmental Organizations and Their Influence on International Society," *Journal of International Affairs* 48, no. 2 (Winter 1995): 512–13.

36. *Sollicitudo Rei Socialis*, n. 81.

37. *Gaudium et Spes*, n. 1.

38. On the moral authority of religious organizations, and the power of their appeals, see Niall Ferguson, "Think Again: Power," *Foreign Policy* 134 (January/February 2003): 22–23.

39. Darren Hawkins, "Human Rights Norms and Networks in Authoritarian Chile," in *Restructuring World Politics: Transnational Social Movements, Networks, and Norms*, ed. Sanjeev Khagram, James V. Riker, and Kathryn Sikkink (Minneapolis: University of Minnesota Press, 2002), 55.

40. Jessica T. Mathews, "Power Shift," *Foreign Affairs* 76 (January/February 1997): 58-60.

41. Reese, *Inside the Vatican*, 205, 217.

42. Ibid., 226, 229. Reese's figures suggest that the net assets of the Vatican bank are comparable to the endowments of many U.S. colleges and universities.

43. Kathryn Sikkink, "Restructuring World Politics: The Limits and Asymmetries of Soft Power," in *Restructuring World Politics*, ed. Khagram, Riker, and Sikkink, 306–8.

44. See Kane, *Politics*, chap. 5, esp. 126–32.

45. Ibid., 161–62.

46. For a concise discussion, see James A. Bill and John Alden Williams, *Roman Catholics and Shi'ia Muslims: Prayer, Passion, and Politics* (Chapel Hill: University of North Carolina Press, 2002), chap. 3.

47. Thomas J. Reese, S.J., "Three Years Later: U.S. Relations with the Holy See," *America*, January 17, 1987, 33–34.

48. Pius XII's role in wartime Europe has received extensive treatment recently. See Michael Phayer, *The Catholic Church and the Holocaust, 1930–1965* (Bloomington: Indiana University Press, 2001); John Cornwell, *Hitler's Pope: The Secret History of Pius XII* (New York: Penguin, 2000); and Pierre Blet and Lawrence J. Johnson, *Pius XII and the Second World War: According to the Archives of the Vatican* (New York: Paulist Press, 1999).

49. *Catechism of the Catholic Church* (Vatican City: Libreria Editrice, 1994), nos. 1145–62.

50. Carl Schmitt, *Roman Catholicism and Political Form*, trans. G. L. Ulmen (Westport, Conn.: Greenwood Press, 1996), 19.

51. Clifford Geertz, "Centers, Kings, and Charisma: Reflections on the Symbolics of Power," in *Culture and Its Creators: Essays in Honor of Edward Shils*, ed. Joseph Ben-David and Terry Nichols Clark (Chicago: University of Chicago Press, 1997), 153.

52. Murray Edelman, *The Symbolic Uses of Politics* (Urbana: University of Illinois Press, 1964).

Part Two

THE CHALLENGE OF
SECULARIZATION

IN HIS CHRISTMAS 2000 MESSAGE, Pope John Paul II warned of a "culture of death" in those societies that condoned abortion, euthanasia, and the death penalty. He was also disturbed by the increasing commoditization of the human body by pornography, which places pleasure and profit over sacrifice and charity as ultimate values in society. Pope Benedict XVI has continued to voice similar concerns about these issues. The following chapters examine a Catholic Church offering its traditional teaching on life, sexuality, marriage, divorce, and abortion as an antidote to this perceived culture of death. In this, and following *Gaudium et Spes*, we see a Church scrutinizing the signs of the times and interpreting them in the light of the Gospel, in order to influence policymaking in the public square—even as it faces declining mass attendance, financial pressures, a crisis in new vocations, and scandal.

In chapter 3, Paul Christopher Manuel and Margaret Mott capture the complex blend of institutional, cultural, and religious forces in the nation-states of "Latin Europe," which includes France, Italy, Spain, and Portugal. The authors argue that religion and politics in Latin Europe function on both epistemological and ontological levels. Epistemologically, the person living in Latin Europe must choose a religious or secular worldview; ontologically, the people of Latin Europe embrace some sense of the Catholic faith during critical moments of human reality. Secular views tend to define the Latin European during ordinary periods of life, whereas religious beliefs surge during the extraordinary times of life. The authors contend that this epistemological/ontological divide characterizes the contemporary Catholic approach to religion in Latin Europe.

Ted Jelen examines the Catholic Church in the United States in chapter 4. Originally an immigrant church, Jelen shows how the American Church learned to adopt the concept of religious freedom for its own protection. Although anti-Catholic feelings are still pronounced in some sectors of American society, Jelen contends that American Catholics have gradually become part of mainstream individualistic culture in the United States. Vatican II's emphasis on the role of the laity as the "people of God," as discussed by Kenneth Himes in chapter 1, has empowered some American liberal Catholic thinkers to press the Vatican to adopt reforms on birth control, homosexuality, abortion, and female ordination. This has created a *problematique* for the American Church, pitting its morally conservative hierarchy against its very liberal activist base, with a majority of American Catholics caught somewhere in between. Jelen concludes by suggesting that contemporary Roman Catholicism in the United States is a mass of contradictions, not easily resolved.

Chapter 5 focuses on the Church's response to one aspect of secularization by analyzing the debate over legalizing divorce in Chile. Authors William Lies and Mary Fran T. Malone describe the measures adopted by the Church to delay the legalization of divorce in Chile, and they argue that despite the steady erosion of its traditional power base, the Chilean Catholic Church has tried to learn the democratic game of political alliance making to maintain its place and continue to influence public policy debates.

Chapter 3

THE LATIN EUROPEAN CHURCH: "UNE MESSE EST POSSIBLE"

PAUL CHRISTOPHER MANUEL
AND MARGARET MACLEISH MOTT

FOR MORE THAN A THOUSAND YEARS, Latin Europe, which includes the nation-states of France, Italy, Spain, and Portugal, has shared a common Christian and Roman Catholic faith. Yet during the last two hundred years, the modernization process, initiated by the democratic and industrial revolutions, has also introduced far-ranging secularization. In the twentieth century, each state experienced democracy and fascism, and they have recently come together as partners in the European Union. Throughout these periods, the church–state relationship in these historically Roman Catholic nation-states has been a feisty source of political conflict and societal cleavage.

Deep and complex contradictions characterize religion and politics in Latin Europe. Grace Davie usefully cites the funeral mass of former French president François Mitterrand to illuminate this paradoxical relationship. Mitterrand, a proud heir of the anticlerical socialist and republican tradition in France, noted in his last will and testament that *"une messe est possible"* (a mass could be celebrated at my funeral).[1] In fact, two funeral masses were celebrated for Mitterrand: the archbishop of Paris, Cardinal Jean-Marie Lustiger, celebrated the state funeral mass at Notre Dame Cathedral in Paris, and a small family mass was celebrated in his hometown church of Saint-Pierre de Jarnac. Mitterrand's wife, Danielle, attended each mass with their two sons. Also seated with the family was Mitterrand's mistress, Anne Pingeot, and their illegitimate twenty-one-year-old daughter, Mazarine.

Neither supporters nor opponents of Mitterrand were pleased. Feeling that Mitterrand had sold them out in death, the anticlerical left was sickened to have their fallen leader in the hands of the clergy. The clerical right was dismayed that the French Church would grant such privileges to a man who, although baptized a Catholic, lived a non-Christian, perhaps even anti-Christian, life. In their view, even in death, Mitterrand managed to mock their faith when his mistress and illegitimate daughter appeared at mass alongside his wife and legitimate children.

This story about a Catholic funeral mass for an agnostic president may just reveal something fundamental about French culture. In death, Mitterrand seems to have admitted something about himself and about France that he denied in his political life: that his baptism continued to carry some significance for him, and, perhaps more broadly, that the Catholic Church has a singular role to play in French society. This is reminiscent of the fictional character Jean Monneron, created by the French Catholic author Paul Bourget in his 1902 novel *L'Etape*. In this novel, Monneron converted to Roman Catholicism after a secular upbringing by republican, anticlerical parents, explaining, "I've decided to become what my family was for centuries. I want to get back, back to the depths of France. I can't live without my dead."[2]

Together, these anecdotes suggest that Catholicism continues to play an important role in maintaining personal and cultural memory in Latin Europe. Both Mitterrand and Monneron understood that religion, specifically the Roman Catholic religion with its enduring ties to southern Europe, provided more compelling answers to the existential problem of death than anything offered by secularism.

In this regard, religion and politics in Latin Europe may be understood to function on both epistemological and ontological levels: *epistemologically*, in that the person living in Latin Europe has to decide whether his or her worldview will be religious or secular; and *ontologically*, in that his mortality has kept some sense of the Catholic religion close to his heart and soul at the critical moments of human reality. Secular views tend to define the Latin European during ordinary periods of life of *métro*, *boulot*, and *dodo* (metro, work, and bedtime); religious beliefs surge during the extraordinary times of life (birth, marriage, death), as well as during the traditional ceremonial times (Christmas, Easter).

This epistemological/ontological divide may well summarize the contemporary Catholic approach to religion in Latin Europe, and it appears to be what recent Eurobarometer surveys of Catholics indicate.[3] Latin European Catholics continue to participate in the same sacraments, flock to the same pilgrimage sites, venerate the same saints, and look to the Holy See for spiritual guidance. Yet there are also some significant differences from the past. Today, Catholics fulfill their religious obligations less frequently, resulting in empty churches. Their children have not chosen a religious life, which has resulted in a major crisis of vocations. Latin European Catholics also have failed to support the Church financially, which has created financial problems for certain dioceses.

This chapter approaches the question of religion and politics in Latin Europe by proposing three models of church–state relations, followed by a brief examination of the development of church–state relations in the twentieth century, and finishing with a discussion of the contemporary Latin European Catholic

Church as a strategic moral actor. Throughout, it poses two interrelated questions: how popular expressions of religion influence national politics; and to what degree the Catholic Church can sway contemporary public policy choices in the democratic nation-states of France, Italy, Spain, and Portugal.

Competing Models of Church–State Relations

Historically, the church–state relationship in Latin Europe has been rather fluid. Generally speaking, there have been at least three overlapping models of church–state relations in these countries: the *authoritarian* model, the *secular anticlerical* model, and the *strategic actor* model. Though the genealogy of each model can be traced to a particular historical period, the intellectual space they occupy is not bound by time. Further, there is a time lag in each country. That is, whereas each country has experienced these various models, they have rarely experienced them at the same historical moment. The fact that all four countries currently operate under similar economic and political arrangements is a historical oddity, not the norm. In many ways these three distinct models are at once overlapping, contradictory, and divisive. They also neatly sum up the historical evolution of the church–state relationship in Latin Europe.

The Authoritarian Model

The archetypical Catholic authoritarian model of political authority and legitimacy, also known as the divine right of kings, held sway in Latin Europe until the democratic revolutions of the modern era. Monarchs such as the French sun-king Louis XIV successfully used the authoritarian doctrine to centralize power and authority in Paris. In Spain, King Philip implemented the authoritarian, hierarchical, intolerant form of political Catholicism.[4] The Catholic Church legitimized the monarch's claim to divine authority, for which the Church was granted special privileges. The relationship between them was generally stable and jointly advantageous. However, because the Church was closely aligned with the state, it often lost its moral authority.

The Secular Anticlerical Model

In contrast to the authoritarian model, the secular model emerged after the French Revolution of 1789. This model limited, or even removed, ecclesiastical authorities from the political equation. The unification of Italy and the loss of papal territories in 1860 became a great source of political intrigue and turmoil for the Vatican and the new secular democratic regime in Italy. Pope Pius IX argued that the liberal democratic revolutions, which promised free elections and free markets throughout Europe, represented a danger to society and the

Church. In response, he penned *Quantra Cura* (Syllabus of Errors) in 1864, which strongly denounced the materialism and individualism of both liberalism and republicanism. *Quantra Cura* suggests that these modern philosophies are inimical to biblical truth.[5]

Pius IX subsequently convened the First Vatican Council in 1870 to address the challenges of modernity. The council developed a new doctrine of papal infallibility, placing the papacy at the center of Catholic opposition to modernity. Bokenkotter has noted that the results of the First Vatican Council led to the creation of a distinct antisecular Catholic culture.[6] Indeed, the Vatican fought against the democratic and liberal revolutions of the modern era, and it defended traditional authority relations in Latin Europe.[7] Putnam observes that "for more than thirty years the Papal *non expedit* forbade all Catholics from taking part in national political life [in Italy]."[8]

Secular republicans believed that total victory could only be achieved in their democratic and liberal revolutions by eliminating the influence of the Catholic Church from politics, society, and education.[9] Education thus became a major policy battleground precisely because it represented a chance for the state, or the Church, to influence the beliefs and political activities of the next generation.[10] While lacking political authority under the secular model, the Church often increased its moral authority by standing up against a repressive and intolerant secular state and, in turn, in suffering the consequences for its political engagement.

The Strategic Actor Model

The strategic actor model emerged after World War II in France and Italy, and following the democratic transitions of the 1970s in Spain and Portugal. Whereas the First Vatican Council of the nineteenth century led to a growth of anticlerical attitudes among many elite secular groups in Latin Europe, especially in France, this new strategic actor model provided a means for both the institutional Catholic Church and practicing Catholics to participate in democratic society.

During the Fourth French Republic of the late 1940s, the Mouvement Républicain Populaire (Popular Republican Movement) combined Catholic social teachings with the secular welfare state.[11] In Italy, the Christian Democratic Party promoted the Catholic agenda from the late 1940s until the party's demise in the early 1990s.[12] Warner suggests that the post-1945 Church in France and Italy behaved as a strategic actor in the public square.[13] Such a close affiliation with political parties did not exist in Portugal or Spain in the contemporary period, although the Church was supported by right-wing, traditional, and conservative parties in both countries.

Throughout the second half of the twentieth century, the Church's leadership sought to influence public policies in Latin Europe by leveraging its moral authority and its large voting bloc of followers to secure health and welfare benefits; to stop the liberalization of laws on divorce and abortion; to oppose the death penalty; and more recently, to block homosexual marriage. The declarations and documents of the Second Vatican Council, most notably *Gaudium et Spes*, were important catalysts to this new political approach.[14] The values and worldview of Catholicism continue to influence the imagination, identity, and behavior of this population. However, a spiritual allegiance to the Church no longer translates into a reliable, faithful, traditional voting bloc.

Latin European Church–State Relations in the Twentieth Century

These three models—authoritarian, secular, and strategic actor—point to the varying degrees of influence the Church has had on Latin Europe's governments: from the close ties of the Holy Roman Empire, when monarchs such as Philip II depended on the Church for legitimacy; to the hostilities of the eighteenth-century republics, when governments found legitimacy at the expense of the Church; to the strategic maneuvers required when the Church was one of several competing interest groups in the post–1945 period. Let us now turn to a more detailed discussion of the historical development of the church–state relationship in twentieth-century Latin Europe.

The Dictators and the Church

One frequently associates the authoritarian Catholic model of authority relations in the twentieth century with the Iberian dictators. This is a reasonable association, given the longevity of these regimes. However, this model also had resonance in Italy and in France during that period. Binchy demonstrates how some supporters of Benito Mussolini were convinced "that a synthesis between Fascist and Christian doctrine can be achieved."[15] These Catholics were clearly reacting, at least in part, to the secular and anticlerical regime that was the First Italian Republic. For his part, Mussolini negotiated an important concordat with Pope Pius XI in 1929, the so-called Lateran Pact, which undid the anticlerical legislation of the First Italian republic, established Catholicism as Italy's state religion, and arrived at a financial settlement over the Papal States taken during Italian reunification.[16] Despite certain tensions, "Il Duce" was more able to coexist with the Church than the leadership of the First Republic managed to be. One can only wonder how long this absolutist model would have continued in Italy had Mussolini survived World War II.

As for France, a number of conservatives believed that the Catholic Church received a better deal from Henri-Philippe Pétain's government than from the anticlerical and secular Third Republic, especially after the Popular Front swept to power in the 1936 elections. This was an extreme situation, to say the least. Inspired by a perverse sense of nationalism, Marshal Pétain, the eighty-three-year-old French hero from World War I, accepted the German invitation to lead the Vichy government. Of course, the Vichy government was an administrative convenience for the occupying Germans. Yet some conservatives found reason for hope with this new government. Paxton observes:

> Most Catholics longed for official support for religious values and for undoing old wrongs that still smarted: the "expulsion of God" from public schools in the 1880's, the quarrel over church property at the time of the separation of church and state in 1905, laws that discriminated against religious orders. The new Catholic left, while it horrified traditional Catholics by its denunciations of capitalism and the laissez-faire state, was if anything more hostile to the secular republic than the others. And so Monseigneur Delay was speaking for most Catholics when he told Pétain at the end of 1940 during one of the marshal's triumphal tours, "God is at work through you, Monsieur le maréchal, to save France."[17]

Under Pétain, the traditional republican slogan of the French revolution of *liberté, égalité,* and *fraternité* (liberty, equality, and fraternity) was rephrased to *travail, famille,* and *patrie* (work, family, and fatherland). This revised fascist slogan was considered to be more in keeping with traditional French and Catholic values. Even with its long democratic history, significant elements of French civil and political society longed for an authoritarian model well into the twentieth century. The eventual defeat of fascism in World War II returned France to its democratic trajectory, but this absolutist interlude remains noteworthy, and it connects French political development with similar processes throughout Latin Europe at that time.

Of course, the authoritarian model was most rooted in Iberia during the twentieth century. Both Antonio de Oliveira Salazar and Francisco Franco agreed that *Rerum Novarum,* the papal encyclical on the condition of the working class, was a useful tool to justify the banning of interest groups or associations they felt were contrary to the good of the whole. Labor and management were grouped together by type of industry, not by class allegiance. Private property was protected and traditional family values were promoted. Elites orchestrated all changes, which were imposed in a top-down fashion. Particularly in the early years of the dictatorships, those who disagreed were persecuted, exiled, or executed. Of the two, Salazar was closer to the principles of Catholic teaching. Wiarda and Macleish describe Salazar as "a seminarian, trained for the priesthood, and active in Catholic social movements; he was thoroughly imbued with the Catholic-corporatist conception."[18]

Franco, conversely, was a career military man and a pragmatist. Rather than consult Church doctrine to resolve political problems, Franco kept control over powerful interests, such as the Spanish Church. He was also interested in the Falange, whose members were more interested in repressing Marxist or liberal elements than in promoting Christian social justice. Similar to the Falange, the

Catholic religious group called Opus Dei (God's Work) strongly supported Franco. Opus Dei, which was founded in 1928 by Josemaría Esquivá de Balaguer during the civil strife preceding the Spanish Civil War, is an ultraconservative Catholic organization.[19]

Even though the Catholic Church was a competing interest, it occupied a unique space in Spanish civil and political society. The 1953 Concordat signed with the Vatican began with the following decree: "The Catholic, Apostolic and Roman religion, being the only religion of the Spanish nation, enjoys rights and prerogatives which are its due conforming to Divine and Canon Law."[20] The Concordat granted the state the right to intervene in the alteration of ecclesiastical jurisdictions, including the appointment of bishops; this privilege became increasingly problematic as Rome sided more with the concerns of laborers and against the repressive policies of the regime.[21]

Recognized as a "perfect society" and a juridical personality, the Spanish Church received tax exemptions and government subsidies for salaries and the maintenance of cathedrals, parishes, religious orders, and other ecclesiastical institutions. Besides the financial benefits, the Church controlled family matters: Only a Catholic priest could consecrate a marriage; divorce, contraception, and abortion were prohibited; and Catholic religious education was obligatory. The Spanish Church held the right to censure all educational material, while its own publications were free from state censorship.[22]

By contrast, the Portuguese 1940 Concordat used far less insistent language. The appointment of bishops was subject to "objections of a general political nature," and priests were subject to military service, admittedly as chaplains. The state subsidized parochial schools "if they were located in missionary areas," and Catholic religious education was required of all students, unless parents requested an exemption. Public education followed Christian principles, which were understood as "traditional principles." Divorce was banned, unless the parties were not Catholic, a condition that created a two-tiered society where those who stayed wedded remained Catholic and those who divorced became non-Catholic.[23] The moderate and flexible terms of this Concordat may explain why it is the only one still in existence in Europe.[24]

The 1933 Constitution proclaimed Portugal to be both a republican and corporative state. Of the two houses of parliament, one was based on geographical representation and the other on functional representation. Corporatist interests, including the Catholic Church, the military, and the wine industry, were guaranteed a certain number of seats.[25] Yet under the terms of the Constitution, the Church was not formally recognized. Even though Salazar used *Quadragesimo Anno* as a blueprint for his government, the official status of the Church was less visible than in Spain. In article 45 of the Estado Novo Constitution, Portuguese confessionality is represented as follows:

The State, recognizing its responsibilities before God and man, assures freedom of worship and organization to those religious bodies whose doctrines are not contrary to the fundamental principles of the existing constitutional order, nor offend the social order or good morals, and whose worship respects the life, physical integrity and dignity of the person.

Thus, the only religious body "whose doctrines are not contrary to the fundamental principles of the existing constitutional order" is the Portuguese Roman Catholic Church.

Perhaps recognizing that republican virtues were tied to American foreign aid and cognizant of the persistent anticlerical feelings in Portugal's southern region, Salazar did not grant the Church official status. Rather, article 46 recognizes the Church for its role in Portuguese culture: "The Roman Catholic Apostolic Religion is considered to be the traditional religion of the Portuguese nation. The Catholic Church possesses existence as a legal body. The principle regulating relations between the state and religious bodies is that of separation, without prejudice to the existence of concordats or agreements with the Holy See."[26] Through careful rhetoric, Salazar promoted freedom of religion *and* constitutional recognition for the Church, to be both republican and corporatist.

The Democratic Constitutions and the Church

Following the various documents issued by the Second Vatican Council, which redefined the political role of the Catholic Church in the modern world—notably *Gaudium et Spes*, discussed by Himes in chapter 1 of this volume—Rome began to move away from its support of the authoritarian model of political organization in the 1960s.[27] Indeed, after Vatican II, the Spanish Church became more alienated from the regime. Younger priests, who were more familiar with the poverty of the working class than with civil war–era religious persecutions by anticlerical Republican forces, took up the demands of urban pastors. Ecclesiastical base communities appeared in poor and working-class neighborhoods in Madrid and other large cities. As early as 1960, younger clergy, particularly in the Basque region, protested the close ties between the hierarchy and the Franco regime. Much to Franco's dismay, the younger generation found sympathy with Cardinal Vicente Enrique y Tarancón, known as "Paul VI's man," who became the archbishop of Madrid-Alcalá in 1971. Tarancón was eager to bring Spain more in line with Vatican II's teachings and to prepare his flock for life after Franco. He was, in Payne's words, the "optimal" leader during the transition to democracy.[28]

The democratic transitions in Iberia in the 1970s brought an abrupt end to the authoritarian model in Spain and Portugal, and they ushered in a new democratic model of church–state relations. Secular authorities granted all religious organizations equal rights, although the Spanish and Portuguese churches managed to negotiate some special privileges. To keep up with these rapid changes, the Church adopted a strategic actor model by working within established democratic processes to influence public policy. In other cases, the Church has represented the spirit of the nation, as witnessed in the official funeral mass following the Madrid train bombings by the al-Qaeda international terrorist organization in 2004.

Davie suggests that whereas contemporary Italy, Spain, and Portugal remain solidly Catholic—at least in their culture—France displays some unusual characteristics. In her words, "France is a hybrid case. . . . It is culturally part of Catholic Europe but far more like the Protestant North in terms of its religious practice or patterns of belief. It is, moreover, the country of Western Europe which embodies the strictest form of separation of church and state."[29]

Indeed, the secular and anticlerical model has been institutionalized in France to such a degree that it cannot tolerate the idea of any religion in public places. The so-called *affaire du foulard* (headscarf affair) is a case in point. In this situation, the French government had to deal with the question of whether the wearing of Muslim headscarves and other religious symbols at state-run schools by Muslim women—in accordance with their religious beliefs—violated the secular nature of state education. After a long and contentious debate, parliamentary leaders passed a measure banning the practice in 2004: Secular views prevailed over religious convictions. The French Constitution of 1958 incorporates the 1905 French law on the separation of religion and state, and it prohibits discrimination on the basis of faith. The 2001 Picard law on the "Prevention and Repression of Sect Movements" grants the French government the requisite authority to dissolve certain sects it considers illegal.[30]

The so-called crucifix affair in Italy reveals some significant differences with France on church–state issues. In this case, a Muslim immigrant sued the Italian government arguing that Catholic symbols, such as crucifixes, had no place in officially secular state buildings, including schools and courthouses. An Italian high court ruled that since the crucifix is a "symbol of the country's identity," it may remain in public buildings. So, as France distances itself from its religious heritage, Italy appears to be trying to blend its Roman Catholic identity with its secular government.[31] The Italian Constitution recognizes Vatican City as an independent, sovereign entity; the 1984 revision of the 1929 Concordat granted the Catholic Church some rights. The pope and the Italian Bishops' Conference both play important roles in articulating the Catholic vision in the public square, in particular after the collapse of the Christian Democratic Party in 1992.

On its face, the Spanish Constitution of 1978 has also severed all ties between the state and the Church. Section 16, paragraph 3, declares, "No religion shall have a state character." Still, the Roman Catholic Church is the only religion to achieve some amount of formal constitutional recognition, as stated in the very next sentence: "The public authorities shall take into account the religious beliefs of Spanish society and shall consequently maintain appropriate cooperation with the Catholic Church and other confessions."[32] One of the places where that "appropriate cooperation" is most visible is in the matter of education. Paragraph 3 of section 27 guarantees the "right of parents to ensure that their children receive religious and moral instruction in accordance with their own convictions," a guarantee posted on the walls of many a parish. Given the Church's de facto responsibility with respect to the moral and religious education of Spanish students, a service that the state continues to finance, the collective memory of Christian symbols and rites is unlikely to disappear very soon. Unlike neighboring France, where a basic understanding of Christian teaching is precarious, students in Spain continue to recognize Christian references in art and music. Despite constitutional claims to the contrary, democratic Spain continues to provide a de facto church tax system. In Spain and Portugal, private funding for the Church remains generous.[33]

The Portuguese Constitution of 1976 provides for freedom of religion. The two most important documents related to religious freedom are the 2001 Religious Freedom Act and the 1940 Concordat. The former provides non-Catholic religions with the same benefits previously reserved for the Catholic Church; ongoing negotiations seek to revise the latter. Unlike the anticlerical and secular Lei de Separação (Church/State Separation Law) of 1911, which essentially placed the Church under the control of the state, the civil authorities now seek to find a settlement with the Church authorities providing for both secular and clerical space in Portuguese society.

In their totality, these constitutions indicate that the nations of Latin Europe do indeed invite the Catholic Church to participate in the public policy process, not as an official state member but as an important religious organization in civil society.

Has Contemporary Latin Europe Been De-Christianized?

Under the dictators, the Roman Catholic Church enjoyed enormous legal, political, and moral privileges. Yet the Church's effectiveness in creating a truly confessional society, even with these privileges, was marginal. In 1973, the Catholic journal *Vida Nueva* reported that the majority of Spaniards lived their religion as something peripheral, conventional, and formal and with no great depth of conviction and corresponding commitment. By 1975, sociologists were claiming that Spain was experiencing a "phase of de-Christianization." Later, Pope John Paul II would refer to this phenomenon as "Spanish neopaganism."

Terms such as "de-Christianization" and "neopaganism" are a bit misleading in that they suggest an evolutionary process. In all fairness, Catholicism in Latin

Europe was never particularly deep, at least not in a formal sense. Over the years, the faithful of Portugal, most of whom live in central and northern rural areas, may very well have been more interested in making a pilgrimage to the Virgin of Fátima, or in worshiping a local saint, than in following the pronouncements issued in Rome or by the Lisbon archdiocese. One can identify similar patterns in Lourdes. Ruth Harris argues that the devotion to the Blessed Mother had more to do with the religiosity of a small rural community within a secularizing France at the midpoint in the nineteenth century than with the institutional Church.[34] In Spain and in Italy, where local saints still get far more attention than formal doctrine, Spaniards and Italians have historically used the Church for baptisms and weddings, but their experience of the faith has been more local than doctrinal. In the light of this, can we really claim that Latin Europe is truly becoming de-Christianized?

In our view, a better case could be made that Latin Europeans are privatizing their religious life by "cherry-picking" through the Church's social teachings. For instance, a 1994 survey conducted by the International Social Survey Program on "The Family and Changing Gender Roles II" reports that almost half of all Spaniards interviewed believed that abortion was not a bad thing.[35] In Portugal, allowing non-Catholics to divorce created a two-tiered society, where people left the faith, particularly in Lisbon and other large cities, to pursue personal goals.[36]

There is simply not enough evidence to accept the proposition that Latin Europe is being de-Christianized. To the contrary, there is ample evidence of the vibrancy of Catholicism in the region. France, for instance, long known as the eldest daughter of the Church on the one hand, and having gained a twentieth-century reputation as one of the most secular and hostile nations to religion on the other, is actually showing some signs that it could become the Church's prodigal son in the twenty-first century. In this regard, Sahakian-Marcellin and Fregosi have argued that Catholicism in France is not disappearing but rather is presently evolving into a new form.[37] Similarly, Safran notes that

> In many respects, France . . . manages to be a thoroughly Catholic country. The town cathedral remains in subtle ways a focal point for French culture. Most public holidays are Catholic holidays, and public institutions are shut down. There is still little commerce on Sundays, and the major newspapers do not appear on that day. . . . Catholic celebrations tend to be more cultural-familial than theological, and religion in general more personal than institutional.[38]

These words apply throughout the region, and they underline the potential strength of the Roman Catholic Church in Latin Europe. Of course, Pope Benedict XVI is presently seeking to reevangelize the countries of Europe, and it is an open question as to how successful he will be in reintegrating Catholic theology into European cultural and familial life.

Secularization has certainly altered the face of Catholicism in Latin Europe, and scholars such as Davie debate the extent to which religion remains at the center of the European value system. The recent battle over the language in the preamble of the European Constitution suggests that secular humanism is encroaching on what had been the terrain of the Roman Catholic Church. Spain and Italy, along with Ireland and Poland, demanded that the Church receive official recognition of Europe's religious roots. "Either Europe is Christian or it is not Europe," is how the Vatican phrased the issue.[39] "Either Europe is pluralist or it is not Europe," is how Germany and Belgium might have characterized their position. In the end, the published final draft ignored any specific reference to Christianity, recognizing instead "the cultural religious and humanist inheritance of Europe, from which have developed the universal values of the inviolable and inalienable rights of the human person, democracy, equality, freedom and the rule of law."[40]

Conclusion: The Church as a Strategic Moral Actor

On the question of the three models (authoritarian, secular anticlerical, and strategic actor), each provides some insight into the church–state relationship. Though the authoritarian model has lost salience in the contemporary period, Warner insightfully argues that the strategic actor model may now enjoy the most explanatory power, in that all four countries are currently liberal, democratic regimes. Since the end of World War II, the institutional Catholic Church has often acted like an interest group, rallying support and negotiating deals over a variety of public policy issues. Whereas the Church has been on the losing side on abortion decisions, the opposite is true regarding capital punishment. The decision in 2005 by the Socialist-controlled Spanish parliament to legalize same-sex marriage over the Church's staunch opposition casts doubt over its actual strength in policy formation. Of course, the possibility exists that the right-wing Popular Party may undo that legislation when it returns to power. At the very least, the marriage issue in Spain clearly demonstrates that the Catholic Church does not enjoy unqualified influence in public policy formation in even that most Catholic of nations. Warner's argument thus is very useful for interpreting the Vatican II documents as well as Church's attempts to influence public policy in the region.[41]

However, if the strategic actor model were applied to the Church purely in terms of interest group behavior, the analysis would be incomplete. Such a model would be unable to explain why a Socialist French president, who had built his career within an anticlerical tradition, allowed his funeral to be celebrated with a mass; why a Europeanized Spain responded to the railroad bombings in Madrid by celebrating mass—the first state funeral held since Franco's death; or why, in some cases, the institutional Church has fought for policies against the wishes of a majority of its own membership, causing a serious lay/clerical cleavage within the Church itself. To understand these phenomena, the discussion must include the Church's ontological capacity to give meaning to life and death.

In the years since the Second Vatican Council, the Church has behaved more exactly as a "strategic moral actor," in that it has sought political influence and offered important moral criticism of existing systems, not to mention its capacity to make sense of extraordinary events in one's life: its ontological character. Contemporary Eurobarometer polling data point to people's preferences on public policy—their epistemological choices. Ontological aspects, however, are generally not measured by using opinion polls, but speak to how the Church gives meaning to time and space.[42]

In that regard, the Vatican certainly did not push for Mitterrand's funeral mass; this private decision indicates that the Catholic religion can become paramount at critical moments of human reality. The recent state funeral in Madrid after the March 2004 terrorist attack suggests that the Church continues to play an important role in embodying the spirit of the nation. In extraordinary times, the rituals and symbols of the Church still have the power to unite a society at risk of dismemberment.

The new democracies and the ongoing effects of secularization have posed a variety of challenges for the Roman Catholic Church in Latin Europe. The faithful are less likely to obey the Vatican automatically, and there are fewer and fewer priests. At the same time, Chadwick argues that the nature of human fragility and mortality leaves a space for religion and the Catholic Church for many people.[43] The political triumph of secularization notwithstanding, religion serves to comfort and provide answers to the unknown. Even François Mitterrand turned to Rome at the end of his life.

Sociologists of religion suggest that we take a broader look at how religion functions in society, not just as a promoter of Christian values or social corporatism but also as a collective memory. According to Hervieu-Léger, modern societies suffer from "amnesia," whereby traditional practices, including religion, are corroded; they also require solutions to existing problems that often only religion can solve—what she refers to as a need for utopia.[44] Davie describes Hervieu-Léger's conclusions as "the paradox of Modernity, which in its historical forms removes the need for and sense of religion (the amnesia), but in its utopian forms cannot but stay in touch with the religious (the need for a religious future)."[45] Thus, Roman Catholicism is not just the hierarchy or the formal liturgy; it is also Latin Europe's collective memory, a place to go when looking for answers to life's problems.

Secular practices control the quotidian epistemological experience of the average Latin European; religious practices dominate their periodic, ontological moments. As such, this chapter concludes that the 155 million Roman Catholics living in Latin Europe share a "collective memory" of their Church and their faith. The fictional character of Jean Monneron may very well encapsulate this collective memory. His cry "I can't live without my dead" brings us to the onto-logical notion that the shared memories of Catholics in Latin Europe will con-tinue to influence their societal behavior, political activities, and their beliefs in God. The Roman Catholic Church in Latin Europe should not be regarded as one of many political actors hoping to influence public policy formation but more accurately as a strategic moral actor seeking to change the terms of the political debate by opening it up to the larger question of being.

Notes

1. See Grace Davie, *Religion in Modern Europe: A Memory Mutates* (Oxford: Oxford University Press, 2000). Davie reports that on the eve of his death on January 7, 1996, Mitterrand passed this written request to his doctor, Jean-Pierre Tarot.

2. Paul Bourget, *L'Etape* (Paris: Librairie Hachette, 1902), quoted in Owen Chadwick, *The Secularization of the European Mind in the 19th Century* (Cambridge: Cambridge University Press, 1975), 114.

3. A draft version of this chapter contains some relevant Eurobarometer data. See Paul Christopher Manuel and Margaret MacLeish Mott, *"Une Messe est Possible": The Imbroglio of the Catholic Church in Contemporary Latin Europe*, Working Paper 113 (Cambridge, Mass.: Minda de Gunzburg Center for European Studies, Harvard University, 2003). The paper is available at http://www.ces.fas.harvard.edu/publications/ManuelMott.pdf.

4. Renaissance Iberia was home to many centers of humanistic learning for members of the Church hierarchy. See Stanley G. Payne, *Spanish Catholicism* (Madison: University of Wisconsin Press, 1984), 39; and Lu Ann Homza, *Religious Authority in the Spanish Renaissance* (Baltimore: Johns Hopkins University Press, 2000).

5. See Chadwick, *Secularization*.

6. Thomas Bokenkotter, *A Concise History of the Catholic Church* (New York: Image Books, Doubleday 1990).

7. Martin Conway, *Catholic Politics in Europe, 1918–1945* (New York: Routledge, 1997).

8. Robert Putnam, *Making Democracy Work: Civic Traditions in Italy* (Princeton, N.J.: Princeton University Press, 1994), 107. *Non expedit* means "It is not expedient" in Latin, and were the words used by the pope ordering Italian Catholics not to vote in the par-liamentary elections during the First Republic.

9. Robert Gildea, *The Past in French History* (New Haven, Conn.: Yale University Press, 1994).

10. Ralph Gipson, *A Social History of French Catholicism, 1789–1914* (London: Routledge, 1989).

11. William Safran, *The French Polity*, 6th ed. (Boston: Longman, 2003), 84.

12. Frederic Spotts and Theodor Wieser, *Italy: A Difficult Democracy* (Cambridge: Cambridge University Press, 1991), 9.

13. Carolyn M. Warner, *Confessions of an Interest Group: The Catholic Church and Political Parties in Europe* (Princeton, N.J.: Princeton University Press, 2001).

14. Austin Flannery, ed., *Vatican Council II: Constitutions, Decrees, Declarations* (Northport, N.Y.: Costello Publishing, 1996), 163–282.

15. D. A. Binchy, *Italian Fascism and the Church* (London: Oxford University Press, 1941), viii.

16. Spotts and Wieser, *Italy*, 242.

17. Robert O. Paxton, *Vichy France: Old Guard and New Order, 1940–1944* (New York: Columbia University Press, 2001), 149.

18. Howard Wiarda and Margaret Macleish Mott, *Catholic Roots and Democratic Flowers: Political Systems in Spain and Portugal* (Westport, Conn.: Praeger, 1991), 44. Also see Stanley G. Payne, *The Franco Regime, 1936–1975* (Madison: University of Wisconsin Press, 1987).

19. Opus Dei is credited with being the engine behind the Spanish economic miracle of the 1960s and 1970s, when economic growth rates were around 8 percent of the gross national product. It is currently an international organization with "chapters" in at least eighty-seven countries. With its authoritarian hierarchy, Opus Dei puts a contemporary face on statist corporatism. See Robert Hutchinson, *Their Kingdom Come: Inside the Secret World of Opus Dei* (New York: St. Martin's Press, 1999).

20. *World Christian Encyclopedia*, 2d ed., s.v. 690.

21. Audrey Brassloff, *Religion and Politics in Spain: The Spanish Church in Transition, 1962–96* (New York: St. Martin's Press, 1998).

22. *World Christian Encyclopedia*, 690.

23. Ibid., 609.

24. Davie, *Religion*, 19.

25. Wiarda and Mott, *Catholic Roots*, 44.

26. *World Christian Encyclopedia*, 609.

27. Donal Dorr, *Option for the Poor: A Hundred Years of Catholic Social Teaching* (Maryknoll, N.Y.: Orbis Books, 1992).

28. Payne, *Spanish Catholicism*, 213.

29. Davie, *Religion*, 19.

30. See http://www.state.gov/g/drl/rls/irf/2003/24357.htm.

31. Agence France-Presse, "Church and Pope Defend Crucifix in Italian Schools," December 11, 2003.

32. The Spanish Constitution may be found at http://www.igsap.map.es/cia/dispo/ ce_ingles_art.htm.

33. Davie, *Religion*, 41.

34. Ruth Harris, *Lourdes: Body and Spirit in the Secular Age*, 2nd ed. (New York: Penguin Books 2001), introduction.

35. See http://religionstatistics.bravehost.com/gendaten.htm.

36. "A Flock That Strayed," *The Economist*, January 6, 1996.

37. Sophie Sahakian-Marcellin and Franck Fregosi, *Etre Catholique en France Aujourd'hui* [To Be Catholic in Today's France] (Paris: Hachette, 1997), 235–49.

38. Safran, *French Polity*, 33.

39. *New York Times*, November 12, 2003.

40. See http://www.euabc.com/upload/rfConstitution_en.pdf.

41. Warner, *Confessions of an Interest Group*.

42. See http://www.ces.fas.harvard.edu/publications/ManuelMott.pdf.

43. Chadwick, *Secularization*.

44. Danièl Hervieu-Léger, *Vers un Nouveau Christianisme* [Toward a New Christianity] (Paris: Le Cerf, 1986).

45. Davie, *Religion*, 31. Also see Ronald Inglehart, *Modernization and Postmodernization* (Princeton, N.J.: Princeton University Press, 1997).

Chapter 4

The American Church: Of Being Catholic and American

Ted G. Jelen

IN 1960, JOHN F. KENNEDY became the second Roman Catholic to run for president of the United States. As a Catholic, he was repeatedly called upon to clarify his positions on church–state relations and on his possible relationship with the Vatican if he were elected. Speaking to the Greater Houston Ministerial Association on September 12, he strongly reiterated his position on church–state separation, and he asserted that if ever his duties as president should conflict with his religious obligations as a Catholic, he would resign the presidency.[1] Thus, Kennedy was forced, by virtue of his religious affiliation, to defend his candidacy against a charge of divided loyalty. Yet despite his repeated and eloquent statements in this regard, the religious issue was an important determinant of the vote in the presidential election of 1960.[2]

In 2004, another senator from Massachusetts with the initials JFK was the Democratic nominee for president. Like Kennedy, John Kerry was, and remains, a Catholic. Forty-four years after Kennedy's decision to run for the presidency, few Americans would pose the question of divided loyalty to a Catholic candidate for president. However, Kerry's Catholicism posed a political dilemma for the Catholic hierarchy in the United States and the Vatican. As a U.S. senator, Kerry supported both legal abortion and stem cell medical research, both of which were condemned by the Vatican.[3] In November 2003, the United States Conference of Catholic Bishops (USCCB) organized a task force to consider how the American Church should treat Catholic political leaders who seek to make a distinction between their personal convictions and their responsibilities as public officials. Although the task force, headed by Cardinal Theodore McCarrick of Washington, did not make specific recommendations, it did consider penalties that included withholding Holy Communion as well as the extreme penalty of excommunication. Moreover, several American bishops announced that they would withhold the Eucharist from Senator Kerry. Others suggested that Kerry refrain from taking Communion, because his public acts were in violation of the Vatican's teaching.[4]

Such changes in Catholic politics provide an intriguing illustration of the role of the Catholic Church in American politics. The American Church represents a fascinating example of religious politics on a national and global scale. As the representative of the Vatican hierarchy in a nation in which individual liberty is a core value, and in which religious freedom is particularly prized, the American Church is a paradigm case study of the manner in which the obligations of citizenship and discipleship may interact and conflict.

American Catholics represent a minority presence in two senses. Roman Catholics are a large and growing minority of the U.S. population. Thus, they have never been in a position of cultural or political dominance. Moreover, American Catholics are a small minority within the worldwide Roman Catholic Church, and they hold correspondingly limited power within the Vatican's hierarchy. Nevertheless, American Catholics may illustrate in stark terms the manner in which Catholics can retain authentic Christianity in a modern, secular, and pluralistic society. Alternatively, American Catholics have tested the boundaries of Catholic orthodoxy, and they may have set part of the agenda for the Vatican for the past quarter century.

As a force in American politics, the Catholic Church has had an ambiguous legacy. The religious pluralism and liberal individualism that characterize the United States pose unique challenges for the American Church.[5]

Overview

Although not the majority religion, Catholicism is the largest single religious denomination in the United States. The proportion of Roman Catholics among the U.S. population grew steadily throughout the twentieth century; it currently comprises about 25 percent of the population. Most American Catholics are the descendants of immigrants from southern and eastern Europe, although, at the end of the twentieth century, Hispanics were the largest single ethnic group. Indeed, Hispanics have accounted for much of the growth of the Catholic population since 1970.[6]

Geographically, American Catholics are concentrated in the Northeast, with additional concentrations in the urban areas of the Great Lakes region (Chicago, Milwaukee, Cleveland, and Buffalo) and in the areas of the southwest adjacent to Mexico. In absolute terms, Roman Catholics are least numerous in the Southeast and Mountain West, although the Catholic population is growing most rapidly in these areas.

Although the American Catholic population is largely comprised of relatively recent immigrants and their descendants, their socioeconomic status has improved rapidly since World War II.[7] As American Catholics have assimilated into the broader culture, they have become less distinctive in a number of ways. Large majorities of Catholics regard the Eucharist as the core Roman Catholic sacrament, which is very important to their Catholic identity.[8] Yet, overall participation in the sacraments and church attendance has been declining for a generation.[9] Rates of intermarriage between Catholics and adherents of other faiths have increased during the same period.[10] Further, religious vocations have declined precipitously.[11] The decline in vocations, along with the mortality of an aging clergy, poses a serious problem for the American ministry, as well as a persistent source of tension between the American Catholic laity and the Vatican.[12]

Catholics in America: Historical Background

Although one of the earliest churches to be established in North America, the American Church is considered an immigrant church. Three waves of Roman Catholic immigration made the Catholic presence in the United States politically consequential. The first wave occurred during the 1840s and 1850s, and was comprised primarily of Catholic immigrants from Ireland and Germany. In particular, the Irish potato famine of the 1840s provided the motivation for large numbers of Irish Catholics to relocate in the New World. The second wave occurred during the years surrounding World War I, and generally consisted of immigrants from Poland, Czechoslovakia, and Italy. Finally, in the years after World War II, a large number of non-European Catholic immigrants arrived from Latin America and Asian nations with large Catholic populations, such as Vietnam, the Philippines, and South Korea.[13] This description does not account for the rapid increase of people emigrating from particular countries. There was a relatively large influx of Catholic Polish immigrants in the immediate aftermath of World War II, and during the Solidarity period of the early 1980s—discussed by Byrnes in chapter 6 of this volume. Likewise, following the Castro revolution of 1959, large numbers of Catholic Cuban émigrés arrived in southern Florida.

Thus, between the Civil War and World War II, Americans inextricably connected this "immigrant" Church with questions of "authentic" citizenship and nativism. Issues such as public education, language instruction, and temperance created conflict between American Catholics and Protestants.[14] In 1875, Representative James Blaine of Maine introduced the Blaine Amendment, which prohibited the use of public funds for sectarian purposes. Widely understood as an anti-Catholic measure, the Blaine Amendment passed the House of Representatives overwhelmingly, but it was narrowly defeated in the U.S. Senate. However, versions of the Blaine Amendment were adopted in various state constitutions, mostly in the Western states.[15] Reichley has suggested that white American Protestants supported Prohibition following World War I because of anti-Catholic and anti-immigrant feelings.[16] Moreover, the battles over school prayer that occurred in the late nineteenth and early twentieth centuries were largely inspired by conflicts between groups of nativist Protestants and immigrant Roman Catholics.[17]

The immigrant nature of American Catholicism had at least two important consequences. First, many Catholic immigrants migrated to ethnic enclaves in large cities in the Eastern and Great Lakes regions of the United States. For many such immigrants and their descendants, religious and ethnic identities were difficult to distinguish.[18] Second, first- or second-generation Catholics felt pressured to assimilate American values of religious freedom and church/state separation to demonstrate that their primary allegiance was to the United States and not to a foreign state. Indeed, Zoller reports that the ethnic identification of many German parishes in the United States was quietly deemphasized during both world wars.[19]

Overt anti-Catholicism ended after World War II, as anticommunism emerged as the main rationale underlying American foreign policy.[20] Prominent American Catholics such as Bishop Fulton Sheen and the journalist William F. Buckley had allied the goals of U.S. foreign policy with the Vatican's anticommunist stance. Further, the economic, educational, and social mobility of American Catholics freed Catholic and Protestant alike from the "ghetto mentality" with which earlier generations of American Catholics had been identified.

However, the postwar transformation of American attitudes toward Catholics was incomplete. Paul Blanshard's 1949 book *American Freedom and Catholic Power* was one of many works to question the commitment of Catholic citizens to core American political values. Similarly, though the election of John F. Kennedy symbolized the demise of American anti-Catholicism, both journalistic and scholarly accounts of the election suggest that Kennedy's religious identification was a potent issue, which likely cost him substantial votes in both the primary and general elections.[21] Nevertheless, the association of Roman Catholicism with "alien" cultures had largely ended by the middle of the twentieth century.

The Constitutional Context

The conduct of church–state relations largely occurs within the context of the religion clauses of the First Amendment to the U.S. Constitution, specifically: "Congress shall make no law respecting an establishment of religion, or prohibiting the free exercise thereof." Yet the two constitutional clauses related to religious freedom have been an enduring source of political and legal conflict in the United States. Essentially, the Constitution's establishment clause creates a constitutionally based freedom *from* religion, while its free exercise clause protects the right to freedom *of* religion.[22]

In essence, the source of tension between the establishment and free exercise clauses centers on the public nature of the free exercise of religion. People may influence government to enact policies based on their values; the free exercise clause provides special constitutional protection for the expression of religiously based values. However, the establishment clause guarantees that government will not endorse specifically religious values.[23]

In 2003, the federal court enjoined Alabama Judge Roy Moore to remove a large replica of the Ten Commandments from the courthouse in which he worked. Opponents of the statue argued that the public display of religious symbols on government property amounted to an impermissible endorsement of religion, which violated the establishment clause. Conversely, Moore and his supporters argued that the community supported the public display of the Ten Commandments, whose removal represented an unconstitutional violation of the free exercise rights of Judge Moore and a majority of Alabamians.[24] Thus, because church–state jurisprudence in the United States is often framed as either one of religious establishment or free exercise, rulings are inconsistent.[25]

The American system of divided government also exacerbates the church–state conflict. Elected officials have overlapping but distinct constituencies, which enables them to benefit politically by raising issues of church–state relations, even if the proposals are of dubious constitutionality or have little chance of being enacted. Thus, since the 1962 case of *Engel v. Vitale*, in which the U.S. Supreme Court declared mandatory prayer in public schools unconstitutional, more than a hundred measures restoring prayer to public schools have been introduced in the House of Representatives.[26] Some members of the House represent religiously homogeneous constituencies, in which such proposals are quite popular.

The 1940 case of *Cantwell v. Connecticut*, in which the Supreme Court "incorporated" the Bill of Rights of the Constitution into the acts of state and local governments, placed church–state relations in the forefront of political debate. Since *Cantwell*, there has been a virtual explosion of church–state litigation in the United States.[27] Though mostly involving the Amish, Seventh-Day Adventists, or Jehovah's Witnesses, church–state litigation has sometimes involved the American Church.[28]

In the pre–*Cantwell* era case of *Pierce v. Society of Sisters* (1925), the Supreme Court held that the Constitution required state governments to recognize sectarian education as a valid alternative to compulsory public education. In 1952, the Court held in *Zorach v. Clauson* that states could provide released time from public school for the purpose of allowing students time for religious instruction without violating the establishment clause. The Diocese of San Antonio was a party to the 1997 case of *City of Boerne v. Flores*, which reaffirmed substantial limits to the scope of the free exercise clause. The American Church was an interested observer in the 2003 case of *Zelman v. Simmons-Harris*, in which the

Court upheld the constitutionality of an Ohio law providing tuition vouchers for the parents of children who attend private schools. As the operator of the nation's largest private school system, the American Church had a clear interest in the outcome of this case. Indeed, the Catholic League submitted an amicus curiae brief to the Supreme Court.

The American Church has been a party to a major religious free exercise controversy at the state level. The California Supreme Court ruled that Catholic Charities of Sacramento was required to provide employees with contraceptive coverage as part of its health care plan. Catholic Charities had argued that contraception is contrary to the Vatican's teaching. Thus the organization should be exempt from providing such coverage under the free exercise clause of the Constitution. The California Supreme Court ruled that, although the legislation in question (termed the "Women's Contraception Equity Act") included a "conscience clause," which created an exception for certain religious employers, Catholic Charities did not meet the criteria posed by the legislature.[29] Although the ruling in *Catholic Charities of Sacramento, Inc., v. Superior Court of Sacramento* appears consistent with the Supreme Court's definition of the scope of the free exercise clause in *Employment Division v. Smith*, the ruling does make clear that the American Church is an active participant in contemporary church–state jurisprudence.

The American Church and the Vatican: Cultural Congruence and Incongruence

As Ferrari argues in chapter 2, the discussion of relations between the Vatican and the United States must be one of relations between the Holy See in Rome and the American Church. Because Americans value the separation of church and state, formal diplomatic relations between the United States and Vatican City did not begin until the Ronald Reagan administration of the early 1980s.

The status of the American Church as a minority church, comprised primarily of recent immigrants, has had a profound effect on the development of Catholic doctrine and practice in the United States. Despite the persistent claims to being the "one true Church," the American Church has never enjoyed political or religious hegemony. By necessity, the American Church has been forced to accept its role as one of several Christian sects and to adopt the value of religious freedom for its own protection.[30]

The Holy See has never easily accepted the views of the American Church. Although the precise authority of the pope has evolved unevenly throughout the Church's history, the Holy See has aggressively exerted its central authority since the late nineteenth century.[31] Pope Pius IX's *Quantra Cura* listed religious freedom and tolerance among the fallacies to be avoided by authentic Catholics. As the source of the one true faith, the Catholic Church had a unique epistemological status among belief systems, and it was not obligated to grant rights to other, erroneous creeds. It seems quite clear that the *Quantra Cura* was largely directed at emerging secular democracies in Europe and especially the United States.

The First Vatican Council, also held during the papacy of Pius IX, occurred shortly after the American Civil War (1869–70), and it represented a formal assertion of the doctrine of papal infallibility.[32] Limiting the scope of papal infallibility to the realm of "faith and morals" constituted a strategic retreat on the part of the Church.[33] By delimiting the boundaries of papal authority, the Vatican ceded some of its prior claims to temporal authority. Nevertheless, the reaffirmation of the Vatican's authority, occurring as it did during the first wave of Catholic immigration to the United States, was a stark reminder of the potential conflict between discipleship and citizenship for newly Americanized Catholics.

The papal successors to Pius IX were even more explicit in their rejection of pluralism and religious freedom. In 1899, Leo XIII specifically rejected "Americanism" as a false ideal. By "Americanism," Leo appears to have meant religious toleration and a more liberal view of the role of the Catholic Church in a democratic society. Leo's successor, Pius X, was even more explicit in his condemnation of "modernism" and his determination to silence dissent within the Church.[34]

Although much of the antimodern, antidemocratic teaching of the Holy See in the late nineteenth century was clearly inspired by political developments in the United States, the extent of the relationship between Vatican pronouncements and the practice of American Catholicism is unclear. Wills suggests that Church doctrine and teaching had little in common with the daily experiences of lay American Catholics and clergy at the parish level.[35] It seems equally clear that *Quantra Cura*, as well as the pronouncements of Vatican I and by Popes Pius IX, Leo XIII, and Pius X, provided grist for the mill of anti-Catholic propaganda in the Western Hemisphere. Thus, during a period in which the allegiance of Catholic immigrants to the United States was being questioned, the Vatican was doing its best to realize the stereotypes promulgated by the Church's critics in the United States. Though Catholics of European descent were demonstrating their commitments to central aspects of the American political culture, the Vatican was explicitly defining Catholic discipleship as opposition to those very values.

Even though the political role of the Vatican in the mid–twentieth century was quite controversial, the Vatican did not explicitly use antidemocratic rhetoric during and immediately following World War II. Perhaps the cooling of papal opposition to religious freedom and modernity represented a strategic retreat in the face of growing liberalism throughout the West.[36] Conversely, it may be that the emergence of communism as a perceived threat to democracy *and* religion occasioned tacit papal cooperation with the more independent American Church. What is clear is that the emergence of anticommunism as a rationale for postwar American foreign policy, and the explicit anticommunism of the Vatican, ameliorated the questioning of American Catholic loyalty.

The effects of the Second Vatican Council (1962–65) on the practice of American Catholicism were extremely profound. The shift of the mass from Latin to the vernacular, changes in the liturgy and style of the mass, and the relaxation of Lenten and other dietary restrictions (e.g., abstinence from meat on Fridays) were all highly visible changes in Catholic worship styles and lifestyles. Moreover, Vatican II included a specific endorsement of religious freedom.[37] Thus, the writings of John Courtney Murray, which had been informally suppressed before the council, influenced many council documents.[38]

Second, the Vatican Council was a fundamental reconceptualization of the nature of the Church, or at least a shift in emphasis on the Church's components. As discussed by Himes in chapter 1, Vatican II emphasized the Church as the "people of God" and deemphasized the role of the hierarchy.[39] The laity was to assume more active roles in the Church and to eschew the traditional pattern of "pray, pay, and obey." While acknowledging the existence of essential differences between clergy and laity, Vatican II ushered in a more horizontal, egalitarian, and pluralistic Church.[40]

Third, the council provided a theological resource for recognizing the important contributions made by the laity to the Church's religious life. Diverse religious structures such as fraternal organizations, universities, elementary and secondary schools, and charities have long enriched the life of the American Church. The laity's role has increased in importance during the decline in religious vocations in the United States.[41]

Fourth and finally, Vatican II represented a shift in Catholic epistemology. Though the hierarchy retained much of its formal authority, "the rhetorical style of the Council documents themselves provided a template for the Church's institutional shift from hierarchical decree toward an engaged deliberative community."[42] Truth was to be discerned by a *process* of prayerful deliberation, in which all members of the "people of God" should participate. Both the content of the documents of Vatican II and the process whereby the council was conducted legitimized the validity of interpretive diversity within the Church. Vatican II did not represent the Church's adoption of secular liberalism as either ideology or epistemology, nor did it question the existence of objective doctrinal and moral truths. Unlike classical liberalism, the Church is not agnostic as to the nature of Christian ontology.[43] Rather, Vatican II simply represented openness to alternative methods of discerning the Truth. Nevertheless, the changes in doctrine and process initiated by the council were easily compatible with the dominant political culture of the United States, and they struck a receptive chord with many American Catholics.

Assessing the effects of Vatican II on the practice of American Catholicism without reference to religious ideology is rather difficult. To supporters of the council, Vatican II saved the American Church by bringing contemporary Catholicism into closer congruence with American political culture.⁴⁴ Indeed, the fact that the American Church has continued to grow may be interpreted as evidence.⁴⁵ Opponents have suggested that the liberalization associated with Vatican II has resulted in a disturbing, if not fatal, decline in the orthodoxy of American Catholics.⁴⁶ Conservative critics can point to the decline in religious vocations and lay participation in the sacraments, as well as increased acceptance of sex outside of marriage, birth control, and homosexuality as evidence of the secularization of American Catholics.

Whatever the case, Americans have pressed for changes in the moral teachings of the Church, and they have made extensive use of the rhetorical and intellectual resources provided by Vatican II. Groups such as Dignity (a Catholic group favoring gay rights), Catholics for a Free Choice, and the Women's Ordination Conference have demanded changes in traditional Church teachings in the areas of homosexuality, abortion, and female ordination. Such movements have not adopted the language of secular liberalism, with its emphasis on personal choices and individual rights. Rather, these agents of reform within the American Church have attempted to recover what is regarded as an older, more authentic, conception of Catholicism, which predates and supersedes the authoritarian structure and method of the Church following Vatican I.⁴⁷ The interaction between the theological insights of the Second Vatican Council and American liberal individualism has placed the American Church at the cutting edge of religious and moral innovation within global Catholicism.

Of course, the *aggiornamento*, or updating, of Catholic doctrine and practice has induced a good deal of conservative or, perhaps more accurately, traditionalist reaction both in and outside the United States. Groups such as the Society of Saint Pius X or the Catholic Traditionalist Movement have found a following among American traditionalist or separationist Catholics who are disgruntled with the post–Vatican II Church. To some dissident Catholics, John Paul II restored the teaching authority that the Church enjoyed after Vatican I; for others, he represented nothing more than a diluted continuation of the problems associated with John XXIII and Paul VI.

With respect to American Catholicism, there are two clear features of John Paul II's pontificate. First, John Paul did not reverse any of the explicit innovations of Vatican II. Changes in the liturgy, dietary regulations, support for religious freedom, and other post–Vatican II changes remained intact. However, the pope also prevented the American Church from further implementing more post–Vatican II innovations. What is not clear is whether such resistance was a reactionary attempt to reverse the legacy of Vatican II or was consistent with a period of consolidation, which is arguably necessary after such

major changes. Nevertheless, John Paul II clearly reaffirmed Catholic orthodoxy in a period of substantial change in the practice and theology of contemporary Catholicism.

In his encyclical letter *Veritatis Splendor* of 1993, John Paul reminded the faithful that there *are* objective truths that are to be discovered rather than to be created. Truth is an ontological, rather than an epistemological state, which
well-guided consciences are instructed to seek. Though *Veritatis Splendor* in no
way represented a reversal of any aspect of Vatican II, it refocused attention on
the nature of truth to be discovered rather than on the process whereby truth is
to be discerned. Moreover, the encyclical reminded the faithful of the objective
limits that the well-formed conscience should not exceed. With respect to the
American Church, John Paul II defined both the process and content of that
objective truth. He aggressively limited the authority of the bishops' conferences.[48] This trend began with Paul VI's response to the varying reactions of
bishops' conferences to *Humanae Vitae*, when Paul VI deemphasized the "colle-
gial" aspects of the post–Vatican II institutional Church.[49] John Paul also reasserted papal authority over individual clergy and theologians. Thus, Father
Robert F. Drinan, the Jesuit priest and Democratic representative from the Fourth
Congressional District in Massachusetts, was ordered to leave his seat in the
House of Representatives; Charles Curran, a Catholic theologian who expressed
heterodox views on matters dealing with sexual ethics, including contraception,
was dismissed from Catholic University; and Bishops Walter Sullivan and
Raymond Hunthausen were investigated for their alleged permissiveness toward
unorthodox beliefs.[50]

On the level of doctrine, John Paul II reaffirmed the exclusively masculine
nature of the priesthood by dismissing the subject of female ordination as inap-
propriate.[51] Taken with Paul VI's reaffirmation of requirement of celibacy for
Catholic priests, the unwillingness of the pope to consider the ordination of
women was very controversial among some American Catholics.[52] Given the
rapid decline in religious vocations during the past generation, some American
Catholics have protested the unwillingness of the Vatican to open the priesthood to women and married people of both genders.[53] In matters of education,
Pope John Paul II issued the Apostolic Constitution *Ex Corde Ecclesiae*, which
imposed stringent requirements on Catholic colleges and universities. Most important among these is a mandate that a majority of faculty at such institutions
must be Catholic.[54]

These brief examples illustrate that John Paul II reasserted the authority of
the Vatican, as well as doctrinal orthodoxy, to the faithful in the United States.
Indeed, Wills has suggested that John Paul II's pronouncements on moral issues
had the tenor of quasi-infallibility.[55]

The American Church as a Domestic Political Actor

True to its American setting, the Church has used its teaching capacity to influence public policy. Of course, the hardy perennial of Catholic politics in America is the issue of abortion. The American Church has been consistently "pro-life" in its approach to the abortion issue. Following the landmark *Roe v. Wade* decision of 1973, the National Conference of Catholic Bishops issued a document titled *The Pastoral Plan for Pro-Life Activities*, which was a detailed blueprint for organized pro-life political activity in the election of 1976.[56] Subsequently, Bishop James Rausch deemphasized the strong focus on abortion by issuing *Political Responsibility: Reflections on an Election Year*. In this document, Rausch discouraged clergy from endorsing candidates for office, and he provided a long list of issues—including abortion—that Catholics should consider when making electoral choices.[57]

The fact that the bishops' conferences are not intermediate sources of authority between the Vatican and diocesan bishops, and that the pope has direct authority over individual dioceses, has ironically meant that individual bishops have a good deal of discretion in dealing with the abortion issue.[58] The late Cardinal John O'Connor of New York and others have aggressively confronted abortion by arguing that the sacraments should be withheld from elected Catholic officials who violate Church teachings on this matter. Others, such as the late Cardinal Joseph Bernardin of Chicago, have integrated the abortion issue into a broader context of social and moral concerns. Bernardin's concept of a "seamless garment" locates abortion in a complex web of pro-life issues, including opposition to nuclear weapons and the death penalty, as well as support for public policies that assist the poor. Bernardin's "consistent ethic of life" is neither liberal nor conservative but attempts to present a consistent pro-life approach cutting across ideological and partisan lines.

American Catholic bishops have taken public positions on other issues, including their 1983 pastoral letter, *The Challenge of Peace*. Partly in response to the aggressive international stance taken by the Reagan administration, the bishops expressed their concern about the morality of nuclear war; their 1986 pastoral, *Economic Justice for All*, criticized American capitalism. The bishops made clear the distinction between "the faithful" (Roman Catholics, who accept the Church's teaching authority in some fashion), and "people of good will" (non-Catholics, who have no obligations to accept Catholic teachings, but who welcome arguments made by the Church's representatives). Thus, the bishops respect the American concept of church/state separation, even as they have participated in the political process.

Recently, the American Church has renewed its opposition to abortion, and has opposed embryonic medical research as well. The USCCB has supported the Vatican's opposition to same-sex marriages.[59] Indeed, the Vatican document requires Catholic lawmakers to oppose gay marriage in any form. However, domestic partnership laws have been considered in heavily Catholic states such as New Jersey and Massachusetts.[60]

Of course, no discussion of Catholic politics in the United States would be complete without mention of the child sex abuse scandal among priests. While a worldwide problem, the issue has received special notoriety in the United States. Because of the extent of the scandal and the size of the legal settlements, the scandal is perhaps the most serious crisis in the history of the American Church. The sex abuse scandal has not only cost the American Church a great deal of money but also, more important, a great deal of credibility across most or all of the issues in which the Church has an interest.[61]

Belatedly, the USCCB has drafted a zero tolerance policy toward sex abuse, titled the *Charter for the Protection of Children and Young People*; it has also created a national review board to oversee diocesan compliance. However, the USCCB's policymaking powers are complicated by the relationship of American bishops to the Vatican. The Vatican has commissioned its own study of the USCCB's proposed policy, which has been quite critical of the zero tolerance policy.[62] The possibility that the Vatican may intervene has caused some Catholic and non-Catholic Americans alike to question the Vatican's authority. Indeed, several state legislatures have considered measures that would erode or eliminate legal protections, such as the confidentiality of the confessional, which the Church has traditionally enjoyed in the United States.[63]

The long-term effect of the sex abuse scandal on the American Church is difficult to predict. Vatican II's reconceptualization of the Church may help its long-term survival. If American Catholics indeed regard the Church as the "people of God," and consider the pedophile priests and protective bishops as flawed stewards, the laity may well regard the Church as capable of reform. After all, the history of the organized Catholic Church contains several unsavory chapters.[64] The current scandal is certainly neither the first nor the worst instance of pervasive sin in church history.

Conversely, a close identification between the interests of the Church and those of the Church leaders who bear responsibility for the scandal could have devastating consequences. The scandal may have constitutional implications as well. In recent years, the Supreme Court has taken an increasingly restrictive view of the free exercise clause.[65] The American Church's resistance to the investigation and prosecution of alleged sex offenders could result in the curtailment of prerogatives that the American Church has traditionally enjoyed.

The Changing Theology and Politics of the Catholic Laity

Observers suggest that the American Catholic laity has undergone a process of "Protestantization." American individualism in conjunction with the theological spirit of Vatican II have produced a distinctive Catholic laity who are less observant and less committed to the institutional authority of the Church, despite the high levels of subjective commitment and religiosity observed among many of them.[66]

Of particular interest, the lack of orthodoxy among American Catholics exists in the areas of ethics and morality rather than doctrine. The vast majority of American Catholics reject the possibility that one can be a "good Catholic" without believing in the bodily resurrection of Christ, or without believing in transubstantiation during the Eucharist. However, they also believe that one can be a "good Catholic" without attending weekly mass or obeying the Church's teachings regarding birth control, divorce, and remarriage. A smaller yet substantial majority believe one can be a good Catholic without obeying the Church's teachings on abortion or without devoting time or money to helping the parish or the poor.[67] Far from having become secular or relativists, American Catholics have largely made a distinction between core Catholic beliefs and the ethical teachings of the Church. For many Catholics in the United States, the latter are regarded as advisory.

Not surprisingly, there exist significant generational differences in Catholic attitudes about Church teaching on questions of morality.[68] American Catholics raised in the post–Vatican II era are considerably less likely to embrace Catholic social teaching on homosexuality, abortion, marriage, and birth control than their elders. However, the continued importance of the Eucharist, and of other core beliefs, suggests that Catholicism as a faith community retains its salience across generations.

These patterns appear to correspond to the attitudes of the American priesthood. A recent survey of Catholic pastors reveals consensus and controversy across a number of issues.[69] Though American priests are unanimous in their acceptance of the virgin birth of Christ, a literal devil, and the return of Jesus Christ, only 57 percent regard the sacraments as essential for salvation. A small but consequential minority agree that "all great religions are equally good and true." Similarly, although 96 percent of all Catholic priests surveyed reject the death penalty, only 38 percent endorse a constitutional amendment banning abortion. Though this does not suggest that pro-choice attitudes are widespread among Catholic clergy, it does represent a rejection of the position taken by the National Council of Catholic Bishops in the wake of the Roe v. Wade decision.[70]

The long-term trends of such nonorthodoxy are not easy to discern. A few studies suggest a marked increase in the doctrinal orthodoxy of much younger Catholic priests.[71] It is not clear whether such clerical attitudes will persist as these younger priests mature and replace their elders in leadership positions. It is also unclear how an increasingly traditionalist clergy will be received among the laity.

Politically, there has historically been a strong link between American Catholics and the Democratic Party. During the late nineteenth century, the Democratic Party was considered the party of "rum, Romanism, and rebellion." The alliance between Catholics and the Democratic Party was renewed by the presidential candidacy of New York State governor Al Smith in 1928—the first Roman Catholic to be nominated for the presidency by a major party—and solidified through the New Deal.[72] The candidacy of John Kennedy in 1960 represented a high point in Catholic support for the Democratic Party.[73] The social and economic mobility of American Catholics has led observers to predict a movement of Catholic voters toward the Republican Party.[74] Although not nearly as supportive of the Democratic Party as they have been in the past, American Catholics have consistently been more Democratic than their Protestant counterparts.[75] Though some Republican presidential candidates have attracted substantial numbers of Catholic voters in specific elections, the cultural conservatism of some religiously observant Catholics has not resulted in major shifts to the Republican Party; instead, Catholics have become an important "swing vote" in U.S. elections, such as the 2004 presidential contest.[76]

The survey of Catholic pastors reveals similar attitudes among Catholic priests. A substantial plurality of priests identified with the Democratic Party, and a small plurality supported Bill Clinton over Bob Dole in 1996. In 2000, George W. Bush won a substantial majority over Al Gore among the priests in the survey. In general, the Democratic partisanship of Catholic priests seemed related primarily to attitudes on economic issues.[77]

It is not clear why a plurality of American Catholics have remained affiliated with the Democratic Party, despite their relatively high levels of social conservatism, economic prosperity, and education. Though partisan attitudes may represent nothing more than attitudinal inertia, some observers suggest the existence of a "Catholic ethic," which promotes economic liberalism and tolerance of differences among people.[78] The identification of the Church under Vatican II as the "people of God" may have engendered a communal ethic among the Catholic laity, which acts as a counterweight to American individualism. Although the evidence is far from conclusive, American Catholic political attitudes have an irreducible religious basis, which cannot be explained by differences in economic prosperity or social location. However, generational change has weakened Catholic distinctiveness.[79]

Conclusion

Contemporary Roman Catholicism in the United States remains a mass of contradictions. The hierarchical structure of the Church has rooted and flowered in the apparently inhospitable soil of American liberal democracy, albeit while undergoing substantial adaptation to the local political and intellectual climate.

One relatively constant feature of American Catholicism has been the tension between Christian discipleship and democratic citizenship. Due to their historical and political circumstances, American Catholics were forced to accept the values of religious freedom, pluralism, and church/state separation long before they were accepted by the hierarchy in Vatican II. Though the Second Vatican Council did not represent the acceptance of secular liberalism, its openness and communal spirit were more compatible with American political culture than was the authoritarian stance taken by successive popes in the late nineteenth and early twentieth centuries.

Furthermore, the relationship between American Catholics and Pope John Paul II was largely influenced by the American response to Vatican II. It is not clear whether John Paul sought to reverse the communal, participatory trend that Vatican II has inspired, or whether papal policies were intended simply to correct excesses and errors in the implementation of the council's principles. However, Vatican II provided American Catholics with religiously accredited alternatives, within which American Catholics can reaffirm their Catholic identity. In light of the recent failings of the hierarchy, Vatican II's reemphasis on the Church as the "people of God," as Himes discusses in chapter 1, may provide the intellectual and theological resources necessary to weather hard times.

The recent troubles of the American Church are the most recent installment of a story as old as the European presence in the New World. Several chapters in this volume detail the Church's resistance against overt repression by the state and the Church's strength in maintaining its autonomy and identity in the face of such opposition. For example, I am aware of no credible account of the fall of communism in Eastern Europe that does not credit John Paul II's important contribution.

However, democracy and toleration also challenge American Catholicism and the West. Authentic Catholicism cannot be authoritative and plausible to a lay population that places such a high value on individual autonomy. To maintain its plausibility, the American Church must evince some compatibility with the national culture. Conversely, to serve as a genuinely prophetic voice in political and social life, the American Church must maintain its distance from the popular culture and retain some vestige of its moral teaching authority. Despite inhabiting an increasingly hospitable environment, the challenge of being both Catholic *and* American is formidable for hierarchy and laity alike.

Notes

The author thanks Clarke Cochran, Paul Manuel, and Clyde Wilcox for helpful comments on an earlier version of this chapter.

1. Theodore H. White, *The Making of the President, 1960* (New York: Anthenem, 1961), 393.

2. "I refuse to believe I was denied the right to be president on the day I was baptized." See White, *Making of the President*, 107. Phillip E. Converse, "Religion and Politics: The 1960 Election," in *Elections and the Political Order*, ed. Angus Campbell, Phillip E. Converse, Warren E. Miller, and Donald Stokes (New York: Wiley, 1966), 97–99.

3. The Vatican has specifically objected to embryonic stem cell research.

4. Katherine Q. Seelye, "Kerry Attends Easter Services and Receives Holy Communion," *New York Times*, April 12, 2004.

5. See, generally, John T. McGreevy, *Catholicism and American Freedom: A History* (Notre Dame, Ind.: University of Notre Dame Press, 2003); Michael Zoller, *Washington and Rome: Catholicism in American Culture*, trans. Steven Rendall and Albert Wimmer, (Notre Dame, Ind.: University of Notre Dame Press, 1999), 186–89.

6. Bryan T. Froehle and Mary L. Gautier, *Catholicism USA: A Portrait of the Catholic Church in the United States* (Maryknoll, N.Y.: Orbis Books, 2000), 17.

7. Froehle and Gautier, *Catholicism USA*, 16.

8. Dean R. Hoge, William D. Dinges, Mary Johnson, and Juan L. Gonzales Jr., *Young Adult Catholics: Religion in the Culture of Choice* (Notre Dame, Ind.: University of Notre Dame Press, 2001), 53–54.

9. Mark Chaves and James C. Cavendish, "More Evidence on U.S. Catholic Church Attendance," *Journal for the Scientific Study of Religion* 33 (1994): 376–81.

10. James D. Davidson, "Outside the Church: Whom Catholics Marry and Where," *Commonweal*, September 10, 1999, 14–16.

11. Froehle and Gautier, *Catholicism USA*, 128–35.

12. Zoller, *Washington and Rome*, 225–26.

13. Ted G. Jelen, "Catholicism," in *Encyclopedia of American Immigration*, ed. James Climent (Armonk, N.Y.: M. E. Sharpe, 2001), 261–73.

14. Climent, *Encyclopedia*, 868–73.

15. Laurie Goodstein, "In States, Hurdles Loom," *New York Times*, June 30, 2002.

16. James A. Reichley, *Religion in American Public Life* (Washington, D.C.: Brookings Institution Press, 1985), 216.

17. Joan Delfattore, *The Fourth R* (New Haven, Conn.: Yale University Press, 2004), 32–51.

18. Garry Wills, *Why I Am a Catholic* (Boston: Houghton-Mifflin, 2002), 12–15.

19. Zoller, *Washington and Rome*, 146.

20. Hoge et al., *Young Adult Catholics*, 8–9.

21. White, *Making of the President*, 97–108; 356; Converse, "Religion and Politics," 120–21.

22. Derek Davis, "Resolving Not to Resolve the Tension between the Establishment and Free Exercise Clauses," *Journal of Church and State* 39 (1996): 455–56.

23. Davis, "Resolving Not to Resolve"; Ted G. Jelen, *To Serve God and Mammon: Church–State Relations in American Politics* (Boulder, Colo.: Westview Press, 2000), 3–4.

24. I have argued elsewhere that most attempts to resolve the tension between the religion clauses of the First Amendment amount to declaring that one of the clauses supersedes another. See Jelen, *To Serve God and Mammon*, 16.

25. John Witte, *Religion and the American Constitutional Experiment* (Boulder, Colo.: Westview, 1999), 217–21.

26. Jelen, *To Serve God and Mammon*, 69.

27. For an overview, see Ted G. Jelen and Clyde Wilcox, *Public Attitudes toward Church and State* (Armonk, N.Y.: M. E. Sharpe, 1995), 21–24.

28. F. Way and B. Burt, "Religious Marginality and the Free Exercise Clause," *American Political Science Review* 77 (1983): 654–65.

29. Bob Egelko, "High Court Declines Religious Dispute over Contraceptives," *San Francisco Chronicle*, October 5, 2004.

30. Zoller, *Washington and Rome*, 243–46.

31. Wills, *Why I Am a Catholic*, 127–54; Hans Küng, *The Catholic Church: A Short History*, trans. John Bowden (New York: Modern Library, 2003), 55–76.

32. Wills, *Why I Am a Catholic*, 258.

33. Gene Burns, *The Frontiers of Catholicism: The Politics of Ideology in a Liberal World* (Berkeley: University of California Press, 1992), 30, 57.

34. Burns, *Frontiers of Catholicism*, 33–34; Küng, *Catholic Church*, 172–73.

35. Wills, *Why I Am a Catholic*, 5.

36. Burns, *Frontiers of Catholicism*, 22–46.

37. *Dignitatis Humanae*, 1965, in *Vatican Council II: The Conciliar and Post-Conciliar Documents*, ed. Austin Flannery (Northport, N.Y.: Costello Publishing, 1980). See Walter Abbott, ed., *The Documents of Vatican II* (New York: Herder and Herder, 1966).

38. Wills, *Why I Am a Catholic*, 233, 237.

39. Burns, *Frontiers of Catholicism*, 63, 70; John O'Malley, *Tradition and Transition: Historical Perspectives on Vatican II* (Wilmington, Del.: Michael Glazier, 1989), 15–24.

40. Abbott, *Documents of Vatican II*, 27, 39. Michele Dillon, *Catholic Identity: Balancing Reason, Faith, and Power* (New York: Cambridge University Press, 1999), 48–53.

41. Peter Steinfels, *A People Adrift: The Crisis of the Roman Catholic Church in America* (New York: Simon & Schuster, 2002), 103–61.

42. Dillon, *Catholic Identity*, 48.

43. Ted G. Jelen, "Catholicism, Conscience, and Censorship," in *Judeo-Christian Traditions and the Mass Media*, ed. Daniel Stout and Judith M. Buddenbaum (Newbury Park, Calif.: Sage, 2004), 43–48.

44. Burns, *Frontiers of Catholicism*, 97–129.

45. Froehle and Gautier, *Catholicism USA*, 3–5.

46. For further analyses, see Patrick Allitt, *Catholic Intellectuals and Conservative Politics in American, 1950–1985* (Ithaca, N.Y.: Cornell University Press, 1993); and Michael W. Cueno, *The Smoke of Satan: Conservative and Traditionalist Dissent in Contemporary American Catholicism* (New York: Oxford University Press, 1997).

47. For a superlative account of such arguments, see Dillon, *Catholic Identity*, 164–94.

48. Wills, *Why I Am a Catholic*, 255–70; David Gibson, *The Coming Catholic Church: How the Faithful Are Shaping a New American Catholicism* (San Francisco: HarperSan Francisco, 2003), 282–86. John Paul II, *The Splendor of Truth: Encyclical Letter of John Paul II* (Boston: Daughters of St. Paul, 1993).

49. Steinfels, *People Adrift*, 352–53. Timothy Byrnes, *Catholic Bishops in American Politics* (Princeton, N.J.: Princeton University Press, 1991), 137–38.

50. Wills, *Why I Am a Catholic*, 274; Burns, *Frontiers of Catholicism*, 102–3.

51. John Paul II, *Ordinatio Sacerdotalis* [On Reserving Priestly Ordination to Men Alone], http://www.vatican.va/holy_father/john_paul_ii/apost_letters/documents/hf_jp-ii_apl_22051994_ordinatio-sacerdotalis_en.html; Wills, *Why I Am a Catholic*, 252.

52. More recently, a Vatican spokesperson issued a statement condemning the "lethal effects" of feminism. See Daniel Williams and Alan Cooperman, "Letter Denounces 'Lethal Effects' of Feminism," *Washington Post*, July 31, 2004.

53. Dillon, *Catholic Identity*, 77–115.

54. D. Paul Sullins, "The Difference Catholic Makes: Catholic Faculty and Catholic Identity," *Journal for the Scientific Study of Religion* 43 (2004): 82–85.

55. Wills, *Why I Am a Catholic*, 252–54.

56. The National Conference of Catholic Bishops was reconstituted as the United States Conference of Catholic Bishops in 2000.

57. Byrnes, *Catholic Bishops*, 69.

58. Mary C. Segers and Timothy A. Byrnes, *Abortion Politics in American States* (Armonk, N.Y.: M. E. Sharpe, 1994).

59. Vatican Congregation for the Doctrine of the Faith, "Considerations Regarding Proposals to Give Legal Recognition to Unions between Homosexual Persons," *Origins* 33, no. 11 (August 14, 2003): 179.

60. Mary C. Segers, "The Sex-Abuse Scandal and the Public Agenda of the American Catholic Bishops," paper presented at the annual meeting of the Midwest Political Science Association, Chicago, April 2004.

61. See especially ibid.

62. Daniel Williams and Alan Cooperman, "Report Criticizes U.S. Catholic Church's Policy on Child Abuse by Priests," *Washington Post*, February 24, 2004.

63. Associated Press, "Nevada Bill Requires Priests to Report Confessed Abuse," *Las Vegas Sun*, March 4, 2003; http://www.lasvegassun.com/sunbin/stories/sun/2003/March/04/030410275.html.

64. Küng, *Catholic Church*; Wills, *Why I Am a Catholic*.

65. Jelen, *To Serve God and Mammon*, 66–68.

66. Patrick H. McNamara, *Conscience First, Tradition Second* (Albany: State University of New York Press, 1992); William V. D'Antonio et al., *Laity*; *American and Catholic: Transforming the Church* (Kansas City: Sheed and Ward, 1996), 43–64; James D. Davidson et al., *The Search for Common Ground: What Unites and Divides Catholic Americans* (Huntington, Ind.: Our Sunday Visitor, 1997), 126–31.

67. Hoge et al., *Young Adult Catholics*, 34–35.

68. Ibid., 33–35.

69. Mary E. Bendyna and Ted G. Jelen, "Roman Catholic Priests: Theology and Politics in the American Context," in *Pulpits and Politics: Clergy and the 2000 Presidential Election*, ed. Corwin Smidt and James Penning (Waco, Tex.: Baylor University Press, 2005); Jelen, "Catholicism, Conscience, and Censorship," 243.

70. Byrnes, *Catholic Bishops*, 57–58.

71. Steinfels, *People Adrift*, 318–20; Ted G. Jelen, "Catholic Priests and the Political Order: The Political Behavior of Catholic Pastors," *Journal for the Scientific Study of Religion* 42 (2003): 595.

72. Froehle and Gautier, *Catholicism USA*, 29.

73. Converse, "Religion and Politics," 96–124.

74. William B. Prendergrast, *The Catholic Voter in American Politics: The Passing of the Democratic Monolith* (Washington, D.C.: Georgetown University Press, 1999).

75. Mary E. Bendyna, "The Catholic Ethic in American Politics: Evidence from Survey Research," Ph.D. diss., Georgetown University, 2000; Mark D. Brewer, *Relevant No More? The Catholic/Protestant Divide in American Electoral Politics* (Lanham, Md.: Rowman & Littlefield, 2003).

76. Ted G. Jelen, "Culture Wars and the Party System: Religion and Realignment, 1972–1992," in *Culture Wars in American Politics: Critical Reviews of a Popular Thesis*, ed. Rhys H. Williams (New York: Aldine de Gruyter, 1997), 145–58. Mary E. Bendyna and Paul M. Perl, "Political Preferences of American Catholics at the Time of Election, 2000," CARA Working Paper 2 (Washington, D.C.: Center for Applied Research in the Apostolate, Georgetown University, 2000). Garry Wills, *Reagan's America* (New York: Penguin, 1988). Catholic News Service, "Catholics Key Swing Vote This Election," *Catholic Standard*, November 1, 2000.

77. Jelen, "Catholic Priests and the Political Order," 595.

78. Bendyna, "Catholic Ethic in American Politics"; John E. Tropman, *The Catholic Ethic in American Society: An Exploration of Values* (San Francisco: Jossey-Bass, 1995). See also Hoge et al., *Young Adult Catholics*, 55–58; Froehle and Gautier, *Catholicism USA*, 32–35.

79. Stephen T. Mockabee, "The Changing Catholic Voter," paper presented at the annual meeting of the Midwest Political Science Association, Chicago, April 2004.

Chapter 5

The Chilean Church: Declining Hegemony?

WILLIAM LIES, C.S.C., AND MARY FRAN T. MALONE

IN THE YEARS SINCE THE 1990 Chilean transition to democracy, the Catholic Church has faced several challenges to its political power. Traditionally, the Church has adopted the corporatist approach promoted by Pope Leo XIII's *Rerum Novarum* by aligning itself with Chilean political and economic elites, just as the Church has done throughout the world—also discussed in this volume by Ferrari in chapter 2, Manuel and Mott in chapter 3, and Kearney in chapter 9. These alliances, coupled with a considerable popular base of adherents, have rendered the Church a key player in politics far beyond its separate legal status. However, under the current wave of democratization, the Church has faced a steady erosion of its traditional power base.

Religious freedom laws and increasing religious pluralism have challenged Catholic hegemony in Chile, as well as throughout Latin America. And yet the Chilean Church has demonstrated remarkable resilience in pressing its political agenda, particularly in the realm of public policy. Most notable is the Church's success at delaying the legalization of civil divorce. Although a sizable majority of Chileans and their political leaders have supported the legalization of divorce for some time, the Church led a successful conservative coalition that delayed the initiative, finally losing the battle when a new divorce law was adopted in May 2004.[1] Even at the end, however, the Church could claim a modicum of success as it managed to temper the final legislation by adding marriage counseling provisions before a divorce could become final.

What accounts for the Church's relative success in this case, given its declining hegemony? To answer this question, this chapter examines the historical role of the Chilean Church, with particular emphasis on the challenges democratization has posed for the Church's power. It will examine the Church's responses to these challenges, focusing on the mechanisms it has employed to promote its public policy goals.

Historical Overview of Church–State Relations in Chile

The proper role of the Roman Catholic Church in Chilean society has been intensely debated since the very birth of the nation in 1818, when it won its independence from Spain. Indeed, the debate over church–state relations differentiated the platforms of the original political parties.[2] The Conservative Party championed the Chilean Church's central role in defending the social order of the previous colonial era, striving to preserve the Church's control over the educational system, as well as the confirmation and recording of births, marriages, and deaths.

The Liberal and Radical parties, conversely, sought a more secular order. They called for the separation of church and state, demanding that the newly independent government assume primary responsibility for education and guard its jurisdiction over civil matters. The Liberals and Radicals drew on the ideals of the Enlightenment and promoted the liberal doctrine of political rights and citizenship. Gaining in power and popularity in the second half of the nineteenth century, the Liberals succeeded in expanding the authority of the state over that of the church. The official separation of church and state, however, was not achieved until the adoption of the 1925 Constitution. Despite this official separation, the Chilean Church involved itself in politics in a variety of ways and with varied intensity throughout the last century.

Through the first half of the twentieth century, Vatican directives increasingly put pressure on the Church's traditional alliance with more conservative parties. Papal encyclicals such as *Rerum Novarum* (1891) and *Quadragesimo Anno* (1931) encouraged bishops, priests, and Catholic laity to adopt more progressive social teachings. Church leaders devoted more attention to the rights of workers and the plight of the poor. Such a focus was both biblically derived and politically useful, as the Chilean Church sought to mollify a growing atheistic Marxist political movement by articulating a Catholic vision of social justice and human rights.

As social justice and reform issues dominated their political agenda, the Chilean Church shifted its allegiance to the Christian Democratic Party of Chile (Partido Demócrata Cristiano de Chile, or PDC). Inspired and guided by Catholic social teaching, this party emerged in 1957 to occupy the center of the political spectrum and became a major political force. The political power of the Christian Democrats grew rapidly with the Church's support, especially among women and rural voters. By 1964, the PDC won the presidency with their candidate Eduardo Frei Montalva.

In the 1960s, the Church's political agenda continued to center on reform. Inspired by the spirit of the Second Vatican Council, the Holy See appointed progressive bishops to leadership positions in Chile and throughout the Latin American Church.[3] Focusing their attention on the dignity and rights of the poor, the bishops criticized the widespread social and economic inequalities that have long plagued Latin America. The Second Vatican Council, reaffirmed at the 1968 Latin American bishops' meetings in Medellín, Colombia, further legitimized President Frei's policy agenda on social issues. Ultimately, however, Frei's reforms were ineffectual, which became a factor in Salvador Allende's 1970 electoral victory.[4]

Allende's tenure was a tumultuous time in Chilean politics. Having been elected by a plurality, with only 36.2 percent of the popular vote in a multi-candidate election, Allende became the first Marxist candidate in the world to be elected to the presidency of a nation. Utilizing his Popular Unity coalition to advocate a social revolution through democratic means, Allende hoped to redistribute wealth and nationalize the industries that were vital for Chile's economic growth. Several of his political goals were similar to those of the PDC: agrarian reform, increased benefits for workers, clean government, and free milk and education for all children.

Although Allende and the PDC shared some political goals, the implementation of Allende's policies did not meet with PDC approval. By late 1971, Allende's radical economic reforms alarmed the middle and upper classes, who felt threatened by the rapid pace of reforms and angered that a minority-elected president would press for such comprehensive changes. The United States reacted by imposing an economic boycott, which greatly diminished foreign investment in the Chilean economy. The resulting economic crisis created even more political instability. Strikes and demonstrations became common as Allende's supporters and opponents clashed in the streets. The Chilean electorate grew sharply polarized, and the political parties were locked in a stalemate. Though Chile had been famous for its long and stable democratic history, by 1973 democracy was in jeopardy.

The Catholic hierarchy attempted to facilitate a peaceful resolution to the impending breakdown of the Allende government.[5] The Church urged political leaders and the public to reach a compromise that would preserve peace and Chilean democracy. The Church sponsored a series of candlelight vigils, appealing to Chileans' Catholic identity as a means to find common ground and bridge the growing political divide.

The polarization of Chilean civil society also caused some divisions within the Church itself. Notably, the group called the Cristianos por el Socialismo (Christians for Socialism), which was formed in April 1971 and led by a Jesuit priest, Gonzalo Arroyo, supported Allende's economic plans and publicly criticized the Church hierarchy for its conservative stands. Several of its founding members met with Fidel Castro during his visit to Chile in November 1971. A few of them even went to Cuba to join in the sugarcane harvest and to have a first-hand look at socialism. Despite Chilean Cardinal Raul Silva's best efforts at communication with them, the group was becoming increasingly radicalized and unwilling to compromise. As a result, the bishops eventually dismissed the

Christians for Socialism as "a new sect, only marginally associated with the hierarchical ties of the ecclesial community," and they finally banned its clergy from political participation altogether in April of 1973.[6]

As the political crisis reached the breaking point, Cardinal Silva hosted meetings between Allende and the leaders of the PDC, the most important of the opposition parties. Allende met with Patricio Aylwin in the cardinal's home less than a month before his overthrow. Unfortunately, the meetings produced little in the way of resolving the political chaos. On September 11, 1973, General Augusto Pinochet led a coup d'état against the seat of government, the Moneda. Allende died during the military action that day.

The coup dramatically altered the traditional role of the Church in Chilean politics. At first the bishops endorsed the military coup by publicly blessing the new junta leaders during Independence Day ceremonies.[7] Like many Chileans, the Church viewed the military occupation as a temporary affair, and it assumed that the armed forces would return to the barracks once they had reestablished order. The Church was initially reluctant to criticize the military government in the hope that it was possible to influence the new government through private negotiations. However, when the military started to routinely use torture and murder to remain in power, the Church assumed a more antagonistic role.[8] By mid-1976, in the face of direct attacks against the Church, its personnel, and its programs, the bishops solidified their critique of the Pinochet regime.

Led by Cardinal Silva, the Chilean hierarchy placed itself in opposition to the Pinochet government. The Chilean Church, particularly the archdiocese of Santiago, sheltered intellectual, party, and union leaders. The Church thus became the natural ally of many progressive groups of the political center-left, which could freely organize their opposition activities under Church protection.[9] The most important institutional response was the Vicaría de la Solidaridad (the Vicariate of Solidarity), which provided legal defense and support to victims of the dictatorship.[10]

In 1983, Cardinal Juan Francisco Fresno succeeded Cardinal Silva as Santiago's archbishop. Though more conservative, Cardinal Fresno supported the Church's work in protecting human rights and encouraging a return to democracy. During the waning days of the dictatorship, Fresno brokered the Acuerdo Nacional para la Transición a la Plena Democracia (National Accord for Transition to Full Democracy), a statement drafted by representatives of nearly all Chilean political parties save those furthest left and furthest right. This document articulated the fundamental legal and economic guidelines for the return to democracy. As a 1988 plebiscite on the Pinochet government approached, the Chilean bishops criticized the junta's plan as antidemocratic and urged Pinochet to step down. Following his defeat in the plebiscite, Pinochet allowed the nation to return to democracy, although he retained some political power and warned that he would lead another coup against the government if necessary.

Seventeen years of the Chilean dictatorship had exacted a heavy toll. The military junta murdered at least 3,000 Chilean civilians, while many more were tortured in soccer stadiums converted to concentration camps. During the initial period of democratic restoration, the Chilean Church was one of the strongest political players. Though political parties had been forced underground during the dictatorship, the Church's institutional structure remained intact. Furthermore, the Church enjoyed high levels of popular legitimacy. Many Chileans held the Church in very high regard, because it had successfully challenged the dictatorship, protested against human rights abuses, and provided sanctuary to those fleeing from the military regime.

The Return to Democracy

Democratization confronted the Chilean Church once again with the nagging question of its appropriate involvement in the political arena. The Vatican's wishes were clear. Desiring to disentangle the Chilean Church from its intense political involvement, the Vatican encouraged the Chilean Church to return to matters of spiritual and moral concern. Shifting from an earlier concern about a "preferential option for the poor," the Church hierarchy placed a renewed emphasis on an "evangelization of culture." The bishops worried that the newly opened culture and society was turning away from its religious values and tradition. According to Kearney in chapter 9, a similar change of emphasis occurred in Brazil, where John Paul II desired to move the Brazilian Church from emphasizing liberation theology to more traditional religious concerns.

The Chilean bishops initially articulated this conservative agenda on the very eve of the democratic transition. In an open letter issued in November 1989, the bishops clarified the Church's stance on various issues with regard to the transition.[11] The document touched on the progressive themes that had concerned the Church during the dictatorship, such as economic justice, the dignity of the worker, and a concern for human rights, justice, and reconciliation. Furthermore, the bishops voiced their concern for the culture and its moral values: the crisis of modernity, the crisis of the family and youth, consumerism, permissiveness, and secular positivism. Referring to secular society as "atheistic," the bishops took an aggressive stance, pitting modern values against the values of the Church.[12]

The 1989 bishops' letter also emphasized the importance of political participation, calling on all Chileans to participate in the electoral process and in political life. In this context, the bishops stressed the essential nature of the unity of belief among Catholics. Acknowledging the need for "a legitimate diversity of opinions on debatable topics," the bishops warned against divisions that impede dialogue and break down effective communication.[13] The bishops also

94   THE CHALLENGE OF SECULARIZATION

encouraged Catholic lawmakers to prevent the adoption of laws that opposed
Church teachings. They argued that the objective moral norms espoused by the
Church were appropriate for all Chilean people and society.

As democratization continued, the Church faced increased competition in
both the political and spiritual arenas in pursuing this conservative social agenda.
As political parties and interest groups reestablished themselves, the Church
faced more competitors than it had under dictatorship, when it was one of the
few organizations permitted to operate relatively freely. Parallel to the case of
Brazil described by Kearney in chapter 9, the Church also faced growing religious competition from Pentecostalism.[14] Increasingly, Chileans drifted from
Catholicism to other Protestant religions, although as of 2004, some 89 percent
still identified themselves as Catholic.

Despite this potential loss of political and spiritual hegemony, the Chilean
Church achieved many of its political goals. The Church has proven to be a savvy
political actor, capable of building alliances with both liberals and conservatives
to meet its varied goals, such as impeding divorce legislation. Until May 2004,
Chile did not recognize divorce, despite the fact that the vast majority of Chileans approved of legislation to legalize divorce.[15] To understand the Chilean
Church's political influence, this chapter turns now to discuss the case of divorce
in Chile.

The Church's Opposition to Divorce

The Chilean hierarchy openly pressured the Catholic laity and politicians to
prevent the adoption of divorce legislation. Despite this pressure, the World
Values Surveys conducted in Chile throughout the 1990s indicated that at least
half of the Chilean public supported some type of divorce legalization; these findings are presented in table 5.1. At the beginning of the democratic transition,
slightly less than half regarded divorce as unjustifiable on any grounds. By 2000,

TABLE 5.1.   CHILEAN ATTITUDES TOWARD
DIVORCE: PERCENTAGE RESPONDING THAT
DIVORCE CAN NEVER BE JUSTIFIED,
SELECTED YEARS, 1990–2000

1990	1995–97	1999–2000
46.1	34.0	26.8

Source: World Values Surveys, available through
the Inter-University Consortium for Political
and Social Research, http://www.icpsr.umich.edu.

however, that number had dwindled to only 26.8 percent. Likewise, support for divorce among Catholics has increased steadily. As table 5.2 demonstrates, surveys conducted by the Centro de Estúdios Públicos (Center of Public Studies) reveal a substantial increase in support for divorce from the inception of democracy to the present.

Despite widespread popular support for legalized divorce and heated debate, the Chilean Congress between the late 1990s and early 2000s failed to gain enough support for passage, largely due to persistent lobbying by the Chilean Church and its conservative allies. And yet Chileans were actually divorcing at a rate comparable to their South American counterparts—enterprising Chileans were not thwarted by the failure to enact divorce legislation, and they exploited a series of loopholes to dissolve their marriages. Popularly referred to as *divórcio a la Chilena* (divorce Chilean-style), many couples argued that due to procedural errors at the time of their wedding, their marriage never truly existed in the first place. Most couples presented the required number of witnesses to testify that the address given on their marriage certificate was false, invalidating the original proceedings and rendering their marriage null and void. Though this loophole allowed couples to dissolve their marriages, it failed to provide a legal framework for the division of assets and child support. In practice, *divórcio a la Chilena* had enormous adverse effects on women. In most cases, women assumed custody of their children following the dissolution of the marriage. They found themselves in a weak legal position for demanding child support payments.

Figures published by the Instituto Nacional de Estadísticas (National Institute of Statistics) indicate that the number of annulments rose from 3,072 in 1980 to 6,269 in 1998, as presented in table 5.3. The actual number of separations of married couples is much higher, especially among those who lack the means to hire the necessary annulment lawyers.

Although popular pressure for divorce was strong, political pressure for change was tepid. Many center and center-right politicians did not wish to antagonize the Church's powerful conservative lobby by supporting divorce legislation. Still,

TABLE 5.2.   CHILEAN SUPPORT FOR DIVORCE:
PERCENTAGE SUPPORTING THE LEGALIZATION OF DIVORCE,
1991 AND 1999

Group	1991	1999
Practicing Catholics	39.5	66.0
All Chileans	56.0	79.0

Source: Centro de Estúdios Públicos (Center for Public Studies) Surveys.

TABLE 5.3.   MARRIAGES, ANNULMENTS, AND THE RATE OF ANNULMENTS,
CHILE, 1980–2002

Year	Marriages	Annulments	Rate of Annulments (%)
1980	86,001	3,072	3.6
1990	98,702	6,048	6.1
1998	73,456	6,269	8.5
2002	60,971	7,080	11.6

Source: Instituto Nacional de Estadísticas, *Anuarios de Demografía y Justicia*, 1980–98. Also see Merike H. Blofield, *The Politics of "Moral Sin": A Study of Abortion and Divorce in Catholic Chile since 1990*, Nueva Serie (Santiago: Facultad Latinoamericana de Ciencias Sociales, 2001). Loreto Ditzel Lacoa, *The Support of Family's Primary Function*, 2004. See www.iin.oea.org.

support for legalization in 1997 was strong enough to pass in the Chamber of Deputies, the lower house of the Chilean Congress.[16] However, Senate debate on the measure was blocked and delayed. Finally, in January 2002, the Commission of the Senate Constitution initiated a debate in the upper house on a marriage law that would include the legalization of civil divorce. Proposals during the commission's debate reflected the diverse political sectors invested in the discussion.[17] In passing by a narrow margin, the approval of this discussion marked a significant victory for those who aimed to legalize divorce in Chile.

Responding to such legislative challenges, the Church renewed its efforts to unite Catholics and Catholic legislators behind its agenda. In a statement released after the November 2001 Episcopal Conference, the bishops argued that cultural chaos and societal collapse would result from the loosening of fundamental social morality. They noted that "central to Church opposition to specific politics is the belief that allowing even a minor relaxation of existing norms risks opening the door to eventual moral chaos. . . . Abortion is seen as a probable eventual consequence both of sex education and the legalization of divorce."[18] This declaration both reiterated and advanced bishops' objections to divorce, which weakened the family union and the resolve to remain faithful to one's spouse. Divorce would cause the disintegration of the family, leading ultimately to delinquency and drug addiction. Haas makes a compelling argument that such threatening discourse, especially in light of the social chaos of the Allende years and the resulting military coup, put the Chilean Catholic hierarchy in a precarious position with regard to its support for democracy.[19]

Given the widespread support for divorce legislation, it is notable that the Church stymied legalization efforts for fourteen years. By May 2004, President Ricardo Lagos signed the bill after it had passed in the Chamber of Deputies and the Senate. Heralding the legislation as important for Chile and its families, Lagos acknowledged the Church's opposition by stating, "We cannot impose the

positions of one sector of our society on all Chileans." Yet the Church did dilute the final legislation by successfully lobbying lawmakers to have provisions
included that required couples to undergo counseling for at least sixty days and
to be separated for one to three years before divorcing.

The Church's Political Alliances

Each of the three democratic administrations of Aylwin, Frei Ruiz-Tagle, and
Lagos has increasingly moved in a secular direction on social issues. In particular, the Chilean bishops' conference has voiced strong reservations about the
Lagos administration, and it even created a special committee to prepare coun-
termeasures to initiatives Lagos had articulated during the presidential campaign.

Furthermore, the Church's conservative stance on social issues has prompted
a strong response from Chilean citizens, legislators, and above all other churches.
The Order of Masons deemed the Church's position on divorce as a "renewed
fundamentalism that echoes the intolerance" that in another age had people
being "burned at the stake."[20] Evangelical Protestants entered the fray as well.
The president of the Council of the Evangelical Pastors, Bishop Emiliano Soto,
accused the Catholic bishops of using "fundamentalist" criteria in their efforts
against divorce. He denounced the Chilean Catholic Church for imposing its
vision on the entire society and for pressuring deputies and senators not to pass
the divorce law.

During the dictatorship, the Church had been an ally of the left as it protested against the Pinochet government. Under democracy, the Church has found
a special ally in the political right. Largely because of their shared traditional
perspectives on the family, women, and sexuality, the bishops and politicians of
the right have found it advantageous to work together in advancing their political goals. The bishops' current alliance with the political right stands in stark
contrast to the largely antagonistic relationship that existed between the two
during the Pinochet dictatorship, when a number of right-wing politicians were
critical of the Church's intervention on behalf of human rights. The support from
parties to the center and left of the political spectrum has been tepid, with only
their most conservative members supporting the Church's moral agenda. Bishops have "called in the debt" by arguing that left-wing factions should follow
their lead in return for the Church's protection of them during the dictatorship.

This realignment has important implications not just for the Chilean Church's
policy interests but also for political parties. As the Catholic bishops increasingly disagree with the PDC on an important array of social issues, they have
sought alliances with parties to the right, such as the National Renewal Party
(Renovación Nacional) and the Independent Democratic Union (Unión
Demócrata Independiente). As these alliances deepen, these parties take on an
increasingly Catholic character, particularly through their stronger ties with

Catholic organizations like Opus Dei and the Legion of Christ. The near-election to the Chilean presidency in December 1999 and continued popularity of Joaquin Lavin, a member of Opus Dei, has given particular vigor to the efforts of these Catholic movements.

The Church's moral stance has also created divisions within political parties. The PDC has been polarized by the debate on a number of social issues, such as divorce. Within this centrist party, the more conservative members are generally prone to follow the Church on moral issues, while a growing number of members are beginning to uphold a position independent of Church teachings. As social liberalization grows among the Chilean public, the PDC legislators must increasingly maintain a delicate balancing act to remain in the political middle. The Church's alliance with the right may jeopardize the PDC's role as the mediating party of the center.

In addition to alliances with political parties of the right, the Church has pursued alliances with interest groups as well.[21] The most important organized support for the Church's moral agenda has come from key groups within the Church, namely, Opus Dei and the Legion of Christ. These groups are dedicated to promoting adherence to Catholic morality both within society and in the political realm. Other well-organized interest groups have effectively promoted the Church's conservative social policies because they also wish to preserve traditional family structure within Chilean law. These groups include Investigación, Formación y Estudios sobre la Mujer (the Investigation, Formation, and Studies about Women); Porvenir de Chile (the Future of Chile), Hacer Familia (Building the Family); and Fundación Chile Unido I (United Chilean Foundation I). The last organization, formed in 1998, is among the strongest of these groups.

A symbiotic relationship has thus developed between these interest groups and parties on the right, particularly the Independent Democratic Union. Morality issues of the Chilean Church are now the political priorities for the right. These groups have also played an important role in enabling the Church to appear less isolated from society. As calls for socially conservative legislation emanate from more lay groups and organizations, the Church enables the right to offer a clearer, uniform message.[22] With the support of the conservative political parties, the Church's hierarchy has placed moral issues on the legislative and societal agendas, but it has also postponed problems that would otherwise have been debated.

Conclusion

Democratization has brought many changes to the church–state relationship in Chile. In the end, Chilean democracy will benefit as all religious groupings, and particularly Catholicism, start to occupy roles equal to other interest groups within Chilean civil society. And as the issue of legalizing civil divorce shows, the Chilean Church has demonstrated remarkable resilience in pressing its political agenda in the realm of public policy, and it will remain an important moral force in Chilean civil society.

Notes

1. See http://news.bbc.co.uk/1/hi/world/americas/3693627.stm.
2. Timothy Scully, *Rethinking the Center: Party Politics in Nineteenth and Twentieth Century Chile* (Stanford, Calif.: Stanford University Press, 1992); Scott Mainwaring and Timothy Scully, *Building Democratic Institutions: Party Systems in Latin America* (Stanford, Calif.: Stanford University Press, 1995).
3. See Jeffrey Klaiber, *The Church, Dictatorships, and Democracy in Latin America* (Maryknoll, N.Y.: Orbis Books, 1998).
4. Allende prevailed in the 1970 Chilean presidential election as the nominee of a Marxist-leaning coalition called Unidad Popular (Popular Unity) by a razor-slim plurality of 36.2 to 34.9 percent over Conservative Jorge Alessandri. The Christian Democratic Party (PDC) but offered an electoral platform similar in many ways to the Unidad Popular only managed 27.8 percent of the vote. They were led by Radomiro Tomic. See http://www.reference.com/browse/wiki/History_of_Chile.
5. See Klaiber, *Church, Dictatorships, and Democracy.*
6. See Brian H. Smith, *The Church and Politics in Chile: Challenges to Modern Catholicism* (Princeton, N.J.: Princeton University Press, 1982), 256.
7. Smith shows that over 70 percent of all respondents said that "military intervention was necessary at the time;" that is, 90 percent of bishops, 76 percent of the priests, over half of the nuns and almost two-thirds of the laity who were interviewed indicated that "there was no other viable alternative." See Smith, *Church and Politics in Chile,* 209; 313.
8. See Paul Drake and Ivan Jaksic, "Introduction: Transformation and Transition in Chile: 1982–1990," in *The Struggle for Democracy in Chile,* ed. Paul Drake and Ivan Jaksic (Lincoln: University of Nebraska Press, 1995); Klaiber, *Church, Dictatorships, and Democracy*; and Brian Loveman, "The Transition to Civilian Government in Chile: 1990–1994," in *Struggle for Democracy in Chile,* ed. Drake and Jaksic.
9. Penny Lernoux, *Cry of the People: United States Involvement in the Rise of Fascism, Torture, and Murder and the Persecution of the Chilean Church in Latin America* (Garden City, N.Y.: Doubleday, 1980).
10. Cynthia Brown, *The Vicaría de la Solidaridad in Chile* (New York: America's Watch Committee, 1987); Cristían Precht, *A Sign of Hope: The Past and Present of the Vicaria de la Solidaridad* (Notre Dame, Ind.: Center for Civil and Human Rights, Notre Dame Law School, 1993); Pamela Lowden, *Moral Opposition to Authoritarian Rule in Chile: 1973–1990* (New York: St. Martin's Press, 1996).
11. Conferencia Episcopal de Chile, "Certeza, coherencia y confianza: Mensaje a los católicos chilenos en una hora de transición" [Certainty, Coherence, and Trust: Message to the Catholic Chileans in the Hour of Transition], November 1989.
12. See Liesl Haas, "The Catholic Church in Chile: New Political Alliances," in *Latin*

American Religion in Motion, ed. Christian Smith and Joshua Prokopy (New York: Routledge Press, 1999); Justino Gomez de Benito, *Proyectos de iglesia y proyectos de sociedad en Chile:1961–1990* [Projects of the church and projects of society in Chile] (Santiago: Ediciones San Pablo, 1995); Cristián Parker, "Religión y cultura" [Religion and Culture], in *Chile en los noventa* [Chile in the nineties], ed. Cristián Toloza and Eugenio Lahera (Santiago: Dolmen Ediciones, 1998); and Jean Daudelin and W. E. Hewitt, "Churches and Politics in Latin America: Catholicism Confronts Contemporary Challenges," in *Religion, Globalization, and Political Culture in the Third World*, ed. Jeff Haynes (London: Macmillan, 1999).

13. Conferencia Episcopal de Chile, "Certeza, coherencia y confianza."

14. Michael Fleet and Brian Smith, *The Chilean Church and Democracy in Chile and Peru* (Notre Dame, Ind.: University of Notre Dame Press, 1997).

15. Malta and the Philippines have not legalized divorce. Ireland legalized divorce in 1996.

16. See Merike Blofield and Liesl Haas, "Legislative Dynamics in Chile: Exploring Left Influence on Policy, 1990–1998," paper presented at the Latin American Studies Association Meeting, Miami, March 16–18, 2000.

17. Congressional Records; see *La Tercera*, January 17, 2002.

18. Conferencia Episcopal de Chile, "Busquemos el bien de la vida familiar y de sus hijos" [We seek the good of family life and the children], 2001; Conferencia Episcopal de Chile, "Responisbilidad moral y elecciones próximas" [Moral responsibility and the next elections], 2001.

19. Haas, "Catholic Church in Chile," 49.

20. *El Mercurio*, November 13, 2001.

21. See Merike Blofield, *The Politics of 'Moral Sin': A Study of Abortion and Divorce in Catholic Chile since 1990*. Nueva Serie (Santiago: Facultad Latinoamericana de ciências sociales, 2001).

22. Ibid.

Part Three

THE CHALLENGE OF OPPOSITION

POLAND, EAST TIMOR, IRELAND, AND Northern Ireland each provide examples of the Roman Catholic Church acting as an indigenous institutional and cultural expression against an outside occupying force. These case studies speak strongly to three interwoven themes: first, the church as a strategic moral actor battling foreign occupiers; second, the church as distinctive cultural space, which insulates and protects indigenous peoples from a foreign belief structure—be it communism, Islam, or, Protestantism; and finally, to a lesser extent, the church in opposition to modernism and secularization in various forms. These chapters echo Kenneth Himes's concept of the church as servant, in that the church strengthened the peoples' inner resolve to resist the dominant paradigm of the occupier.

We find these themes clearly in Timothy Byrnes's case study of the Church in Poland in chapter 6. He first looks at the role played by the Church during the decades of national crisis during Soviet domination up to the revolutionary period of the 1980s. He next examines the consolidation period of the 1990s, when the Polish Church scrambled to maintain the Catholic character of the Polish nation during the early days of independence (with special emphasis on the important role of Polish-born Pope John Paul II). Finally, he brings us to the present day, when the struggles of the Polish Church resemble the challenges faced in Latin Europe and elsewhere in the democratic, secular world—namely, how to maintain the country's Catholic identity in the face of secularizing pressures from a democratic parliament and the European Union.

In chapter 7, William Crotty accentuates the theme of the church's indispensable role in resisting outside forces in his treatment of the Irish and Northern Irish Church. In the case of the Republic of Ireland, he shows how the church fortified cultural and religious resolve against the English occupier. In recent years the Irish Church has argued its case in the public square in the face of secularizing pressures from the Irish parliament and the European Union. For its part, the Northern Irish Church has sought to protect and support its minority population from sectarian violence and other violations of their civil rights by the Protestant majority. Crotty leaves us with the hope that the "Good Friday" agreements of 1998 will lead to a lasting peace in Northern Ireland.

In chapter 8, Alynna Lyon explains how the Roman Catholic Church shifted from the role of "oppressor" to "liberator" in the story of East Timor. She traces the early days of Portuguese colonialism to the mid-1970s, and she highlights the watershed date of December 7, 1975, when Indonesia invaded East Timor. The Indonesian occupation was characterized by unusual cruelty, with an estimated 40 percent of the total population dying from 1975 to 1980. Unlike World War II, when the Roman Catholic clergy fled the island to avoid Japanese occupation, the clergy—both native and foreign-born—stayed this time, and they suffered and died with the local population. As such, a bond was established between the Timorese nationalist revolutionaries and the Catholic priests against the Islamic Indonesian invading force, which transformed the Catholic Church into an indispensable element of East Timor society. The Catholic Church's essential role as a strategic moral actor provided the independence struggle with a dimension of respect for human dignity.

Chapter 6

The Polish Church: Catholic Hierarchy and Polish Politics

Timothy A. Byrnes

THERE ARE TWO KEYS TO understanding the important role that the Roman Catholic Church plays in contemporary Polish politics. First, there has been a long-standing, intimate relationship between Catholicism and Polish national identity. From the creation of the Polish state in A.D. 966, during the national crises of partition and occupation between 1795 and 1948, to the communist era when the Church was the alternative locus of legitimate public authority, the Polish Church has continuously played an important political role. Therefore, it should come as no surprise that the Church continues to play a similar political role today.[1]

The second important key to understanding the Polish Church's involvement in politics is a more recent phenomenon. Pope John Paul II, the supreme pontiff of the Universal Church from 1978 to 2005, was Polish.[2] Karol Wojtyla used the enormous resources of his office to focus world attention on his homeland. He targeted his considerable personal energy on radically reformulating Polish politics and government, as well as using the Polish model to effect systemic change in the social and political life of the European continent.

This chapter focuses on these two key factors and argues that they are the foundation of the important role that the Church continues to play in Poland, even following the death of Karol Wojtyla in 2005. Moreover, the chapter analyzes the close relationship *between* these two factors to argue that Catholicism's traditional role in Polish society is itself the key to understanding Pope John Paul II's approach to political questions. Though the pope certainly deepened the political role of the Polish Church, it is equally true that the role played by the Polish Church formed the core of the pope's grander vision for a reunified, reevangelized Christian Europe.

The chapter is divided into three sections corresponding to three recent aspects of the Polish Church's role in politics. The first, "Revolution," refers to the well-chronicled role of the church in preserving Polish autonomy through decades of national crisis, as well as to the role Catholic leaders played in the epoch-shaping events of the 1980s. The second section, "Consolidation," analyzes the 1990s, when the Polish Church, under the aggressive and unambiguous leadership of its pope in Rome, worked with remarkable energy to consolidate its victory by preserving the faithfulness and the so-called Catholic character of the Polish nation. The final section, "Return to Europe," analyzes the contentious debate within Polish Catholicism over the questions of Poland's membership in the European Union and Poland's role in defining the European continent as a political and cultural idea, rather than as merely a geographic designation.

Revolution

In helping to realize the revolution of the 1980s, the Polish Church primarily provided free space, uncontrolled by the communist government, where Poles could develop modes of thought and patterns of social interaction in which democratic values and processes could develop. The Polish dissident Adam Michnik, who is certainly no friend of the Church on either religious or social grounds, credits Polish Catholicism with preserving a redoubt of civil society within communism where Poles could pretend, even for just an hour per week, that the government did not exist.[3] Unlike the Church in Communist China, examined by Reardon in chapter 13 of this volume, the Polish Church served as a place where Poles freely gathered in what they considered an authentically Polish setting.

Authenticity is a particularly important issue in Poland because of the country's long history of partitions and foreign occupations.[4] By 1795, the Polish state was erased from all European maps. Although reestablished after the 1919 Treaty of Versailles, Poland suffered brutal occupation during World War II and was dominated by the Soviet Union over the long decades of communist rule. Because of this brutal history, the question of national identity and its relationship to state sovereignty is perhaps more contested in Poland than any other European state. Within this particular historical context, the uncontested cultural centrality of Polish Catholicism became a major political factor. The Polish Church is a political institution because history has identified it as an authentically Polish alternative to an alien governing power. Specifically, the Church under communism was transformed into an indispensable substitute for the civil society that Michnik and other dissidents so desired but that the Soviet system so explicitly disallowed.

Therefore, when Polish political autonomy exploded in Poland in the form of the Solidarity trade union, it did so in a distinctively Catholic idiom. From the Black Madonna pin in Lech Walesa's lapel and the striking miners lining up to receive Holy Communion to the revolutionary rallies held in Father Jerzy Popieluszko's Warsaw parish, the articulation of free-thinking opposition to the

Polish communist government was deeply imbedded in the only viable noncommunist institution to which Poles could turn, the Polish Church. Beginning with the Church's millennial celebrations in 1966, gaining steam with the welcome afforded the Polish Pope in 1979, and culminating with the Church's institutionalized participation in the epoch-shaping roundtable talks of 1989, the Polish Church was at the very heart of the complex protest cycles that toppled communism in Poland.[5]

Nevertheless, the hierarchical leadership of the Polish Church was more cautious than capricious, more responsible than revolutionary. In chapter 1, Himes argues that the early church focused on pastoral strategies and less on the political situation or philosophy. In Poland, Cardinal Stefan Wyszynski and his successor, Cardinal Josef Glemp, did not see themselves as leading a revolutionary social movement; they never fully imagined an end of Polish communism. Instead, they believed themselves to be the only Poles with the legitimacy to mediate between Solidarity and a presumably permanent governing system. History already views Wyszynski as the man who was primarily responsible for preserving and defending the autonomous Catholic space out of which the revolution grew. However, neither he nor Glemp were themselves revolutionaries but were simply patriotic Poles preventing a conflagration between a romantic Polish people and an implacably repressive state.

Wyszynski and Glemp, and the Polish pope, were all concerned that the Polish state of the 1980s would be consumed with hatred, tragedy, and bloodshed. But unlike the Polish cardinals, the pope was committed to the establishment of true, absolute Polish autonomy in both political and cultural terms. This was the necessary first step to reinvigorating an authentic Christian heritage in a united Europe.

The post–cold war generation has difficulty appreciating the radical worldview that Karol Wojtyla brought with him to the papacy in October 1978. The new pope was not a follower of Pope Paul VI's Vatican *Ostpolitik*. The role of the Church was not to preserve small spaces of freedom within otherwise oppressive circumstances. Instead, Pope John Paul II completely rejected the legitimacy of communist government in Poland and throughout Eastern Europe. He rejected the very idea of an *eastern* Europe, and spoke in unprecedented terms of a single continental identity, from the Atlantic to the Urals, that had been torn apart by Yalta, Soviet imperialism, and the so-called realities of the cold war.[6]

Moreover, he believed that he was predestined to play a special role in human history. The pope carried the spirit of Polish messianism to Rome, and he did his utmost to redress the wrongs done to his people and to their neighbors. In a typically sweeping statement in 1979, the pope stated, "Is it not Christ's will, is it not what the Holy Spirit dispenses, that this Polish Pope, this Slav Pope, should at this precise moment manifest the spiritual unity of Christian Europe?"[7]

In time, the pope and the Vatican provided substantial concrete support to the anticommunist movements in Poland and elsewhere. The key to John Paul II's political role at that time was the symbolic spiritual one, to which he was referring in the speech quoted above. His existence as a Polish pope and the ecstasy with which his accession was greeted on the streets of Warsaw, Krakow, and Gdansk demonstrated in Stalin's descriptive phrasing that communism fit Poland about as well as a saddle fit a cow. In the ensuing years, the world grew used to the idea of a Polish pope. When John Paul II entered Warsaw in triumphant glory in 1979, and when he defiantly and repeatedly uttered the loaded word "solidarity" before Polish audiences suffering under martial law in 1983—these were the crucial, purposefully symbolic acts of a very resourceful subversive.

Even more surprising than the pope's belief in the unity of a single Europe is the actual realization of such a complex creation. Leaving aside the debate over the pope's influence on these events, John Paul II was right about the fundamental weakness of the communist system and about the profound effect of a Polish revolution. From the perspective of a Polish pope sitting in the Vatican, it must have seemed as though God, or at least the Holy Spirit's chosen agent, was at work shaping the trajectory of European history.

Undoubtedly, the Polish pope recognized that the movements toward political freedom and national autonomy in Poland and elsewhere were the first steps in a very long and complex struggle. As Lech Walesa moved into the presidential office, and as McDonald's and Marriott opened for business in Warsaw, the struggle for the soul of Europe had begun. In the heady days of 1990 and 1991, the pope was one of the few leaders to realize that capitalism and consumerism, pluralism, and democracy might prove to be more insidious obstacles to the creation of a unified Europe than communism and Soviet troops. Once the Poles had tasted freedom, license, and Western consumerism, the Vatican could have difficulty in using Poland as the vanguard for the reevangelization of Europe.

Consolidation

For the Polish Church, consolidation of the victory over communism involved two closely related projects: the deepening of the Church's institutional viability and independence, and its ability to shape public policy. The first project required two concrete outcomes: first, a new democratic constitution that reflected the role that Catholicism had played in Polish history; and second, a concordat or formal agreement of relations between the Vatican and the Polish government that guaranteed Church autonomy in construction, episcopal appointments, parochial education, and the like. The second project required that public discussions of questions like abortion must reflect the social teachings of the religious community to which more than 90 percent of the population belonged.

The Polish Church focused on a number of fundamental constitutional issues. The bishops wanted their new national constitution to recognize Roman Catholicism as an organic element of national identity. The preamble was to include a reference to God; the constitution also would describe the degree to which the Church had been integrated into the Polish nation over the centuries. They also wanted the constitution to codify religious foundations for state law on a number of moral issues. According to Bishop Tadeusz Pieronek, the secretary general of the Polish Bishops' Conference, "The constitution should also explicitly prohibit everything that is an obstacle to or destroys man's links to God, as well as man's links to other men, particularly in the natural forms of interaction."[8] Pieronek probably was calling for a constitutional ban on abortion from the point of conception and for limiting marriage to relationships between men and women.

The bishops viewed the national debate over the constitutional text as a crucial political process that would shape Polish public life for decades. They were absolutely determined that the Polish Church should play a prominent place in that debate. Thus, the bishops' conference focused all its energy on influencing the exact wording of the text.

However, the bishops were disappointed in the final constitutional text submitted to a popular referendum. The constitution's reference to God was settled by a compromise that referred with equal emphasis to "those who believe in God" and to "those not sharing such faith but respecting those universal values as arising from other sources."[9] The text limited marriage to "a union of a man and a woman" and stated that "the Republic of Poland shall ensure the legal protection of the life of every human being."[10] Though this oblique reference to abortion would in practice restrict access to abortion, the bishops were unable to effect a constitutional declaration that all human life was sacred and inviolable from the point of conception.

From the Church's perspective, the most important constitutional clause stated explicitly that "relations between the Republic of Poland and the Roman Catholic Church shall be determined by international treaty concluded with the Holy See."[11] This treaty, or concordat, guarantees the Church's institutional autonomy and sets the basic parameters of the Church's public role in the new, postcommunist Poland. The Church's leadership thus establishes all diocesan boundaries and controls all appointments of Catholic bishops. The concordat also guarantees Catholic wedding ceremonies equal status to civil ceremonies and the right to manage parochial schools, and it commits the state to religious instruction (i.e., Catholic catechism) in public nursery schools and kindergartens. Finally, it ambiguously states that "activities serving humanitarian, charitable, health care, research, and educational purposes, pursued by legal persons of the Church, shall under law be equal with activities serving similar purposes and carried out by state institutions."[12]

Not surprisingly, the concordat was the source of considerable political controversy. Opponents argued that the Church was allowed to control religious instruction for Poland's youngest and most impressionable children, and to determine all marriage ceremonies and rituals. As for issues related to property taxation and the regulation of Church activities, opponents argued that the state would now be required to enter into diplomatic negotiations with Vatican officials. Despite such opposing views, the Polish Church enjoyed a significant victory when the nation's supreme constitutional law eventually recognized the concordat's legitimacy.

Interestingly, the Polish bishops viewed their efforts to influence the shape of the constitution as having failed because many of the key constitutional issues were resolved through unsatisfactory compromises. In the days leading up to the constitutional referendum, prominent bishops spoke about their moral doubts concerning constitutional provisions, which created a text "lack[ing] of understanding for the believing majority" of the Polish population.[13]

Despite the bishops' reservations, 53 percent of the Polish voting-age population ratified the constitution. It is arguable that the Polish Church had a significant, albeit less than absolute, effect on the constitutional text. The so-called disappointments were mostly symbolic and rhetorical in nature, such as the failure to secure an explicit reference in the preamble to God and to the Church's central role in Polish national history. However, the Church's positions and interests were manifested in key sections, such as the inclusion of a concordat, specific textual references to the nature of marriage, the scope of religious education, and access to abortion.

The contentious constitutional debate clearly showed that, by the mid-1990s, the Catholic Church was no longer the unrivaled embodiment of authentic Polish identity. Though remaining an important political actor, the Church could no longer define what was acceptable, legitimate, or authentically Polish. Instead, the bishops were forced to learn how to participate in pluralist democratic politics. Consolidation of the Church's role in Polish society was not the inevitable outcome of the Soviet defeat. The Church was forced to navigate complex new political waters and to reassert faithfulness to an authentically free Polish people.[14]

Pope John Paul II strongly supported his Polish colleagues' political agenda throughout the 1990s. He was passionately committed to the recognition of God and the Polish Church as the bases of Polish history and identity. He was a signatory to the crucial concordat and spoke out clearly—even angrily—about the outlawing of abortion in a free, Catholic, and authentically Polish Poland. At the same time, however, the Polish pope placed these political issues within a broader program of social and cultural reform, specifically the human response to commercial temptation.

The pope feared that the Polish people would drift away from their heritage and devotion to Catholicism through their embrace of capitalist structures and commercial culture. As capitalism arrived in Poland literally overnight in 1990, the pope watched anxiously as Poles sought to balance tradition with opportunity, Catholicism with commercialism. The tone of the pope's first visit to democratic Poland in 1991 was markedly different from that characterizing his triumphant pilgrimage in 1979 or his inspiring challenges to martial law in 1983. Instead of playing the role of courageous protector and national spokesman, John Paul arrived as a disappointed pastor who advised, implored, and scolded his Polish congregation that was reeling from the aftershocks of revolution. "Don't let yourself get caught up," he said in Wlocawek in 1991, "by the civilization of desire and consumption . . . which has infiltrated our circles. . . . [Do not be] trapped by all of these forces of desire which slumber in you as a source of sin."[15]

These entreaties were not just directed to a tempted people but were also statements of the pope's political principles and geopolitical vision. They indicated the depth of his desire for the Polish nation to retain its faithfulness and its Catholic distinctiveness. As his homeland reclaimed its rightful place among the European community of nations, he envisioned Poland as an instrument of the new European evangelization. During the same trip in 1991, he said that "we [Poles] do not have to enter Europe because we helped to create it, and we did so with greater effort than those who claim a monopoly on Europeanness."[16]

These statements clearly echoed the pope's earlier discussions of a unified Europe. They practically applied his interpretation of history and contemporary circumstances that had led to his designation of Saints Cyril and Methodius— the brothers who had evangelized parts of Germany and Poland in the 870s, and were thus known as "Apostles to the Slavs"—as "patrons of Europe" in the 1980s.[17] For the pope, the consolidation of the Church's role within a newly liberated Poland and other Eastern European communist states would bring about the reevangelization of a European continent that had drifted away from its heritage. The pope was perfectly happy to have Poland rejoin Europe, so long as that meant that Europe would in time become more like Poland, rather than the other way around.

Return to Europe

Eastern European accession to the European Union is very controversial both among the member states as well as within eastern Europe itself. In addition to questioning the accession's economic benefits, the controversy often focuses on the cultural symbolism and its connection to national and continental identity. The European Union enjoys great symbolic value as the institutional home of what is often called the West. This symbolism is overwhelmingly attractive to political elites of the former Soviet bloc states, who perceive E.U. accession as essential to joining the West. Membership thus would consolidate the institutional and economic ties that lie at the heart of internationalist liberal capitalism. Yet opponents in east central European countries like Poland question the desirability of such ties and consolidation.

As with so many issues over the quarter century of his pontificate, Pope John Paul II's views on European integration did not fall easily into either one of these broadly defined camps. John Paul II was in favor of enlarging the European Union to include Poland and the other former communist states. But he did not want those states simply to join the West and adopt Western values. To the contrary, he wanted Poland and the others to *join the West in order to transform the West.* This newly reunified Europe would witness a new evangelization that could only occur if the East retained its authentically Christian heritage and challenged the secular West to return to the shared European tradition of Christian civilization.

John Paul II was not a man of timid vision. Indeed, the man who envisioned the crumbling of communism and called for Polish freedom in the early days of his pontificate was the same man who called for a recommitment to Catholicism and a reevangelization of Europe in his waning days. Two events clearly defined John Paul II's broadly conceived view of Europe's future and the role of Poland. The first was his visit to his homeland in 1997 as the issues of European Union expansion and Poland's role in the post–cold war European political order were heating up. The second event was the convening of the European synod of bishops, which culminated with the pope's comprehensive statement, *Ecclesia in Europa.*

During his 1979 visit to the Polish city of Gniezno, the pope delineated his vision for Europe's future and his role in realizing that future: "We know that the Christian unity of Europe is made up of the two great traditions of the West and of the East. . . . Yes, it is Christ's will, it is what the Holy Spirit disposes, that what I am saying should be said in this very place and at this moment in Gniezno."[18] Speaking in the same city in 1997 but under very different political circumstances, the pope repeated those historic words. This time, he further laid out his concept of European Union: "There will be no European unity until unity is based on unity of the spirit. . . . The foundations of the identity of Europe are built on Christianity. And its present lack of spiritual unity arises principally from the crisis of this Christian self-awareness."[19] Warming to the theme, he asked: "How can a 'common house' for all Europe be built if it is not built with the brick of men's consciences, baked in the fire of the Gospel, united by the bond of fraternal social love, the fruit of the love of God?"[20]

The pope was always clear about the place his native Poland should play in this unified Europe. By 1997, he was speaking of Poland's "*right* to take part, on a par with other nations in the formation of a new face of Europe," and of his conviction that "the Church in Poland can offer Europe, as it grows in unity, her attachment to the faith, her tradition inspired by religious devotion, the pastoral efforts of her bishops and priests, and certainly many other values on the basis of which Europe can become a reality endowed *not only with high economic standards but also with a profound spiritual life*" (italics added).[21] To emphasize this point, the pope argued that "the West so much needs our deep and living faith at the historic stage of the building of a new system with many different points of reference."[22] In 2002, a visibly frail and failing pope making his last trip home returned to the same theme of the 1997 Polish trip: "I hope that Poland, which has belonged to Europe for centuries, will find its proper place in the structures of the European community. Not only will it not lose its identity, but it will enrich the continent and the world with its tradition."[23]

These notions of identity and its relationship to the community were the center of discussion of a 1999 European synod of bishops, whose findings are reflected in the "post-synodal apostolic exhortation" of Pope John Paul's *Ecclesia in Europa* of 2003.[24] It was his most extensive communication on what he saw as the proper role for the European Church, and as such deserves to be quoted at some length. The pope again called for a new evangelization of his native continent, the purpose of which would be to bring "the liberating message of the Gospel to the men and women of Europe."[25] Turning to the historic role of Catholicism in European society, the pope reminded his readers that "Europe has been widely and profoundly permeated by Christianity." "There can be no doubt," he said, "that the Christian faith belongs, in a radical and decisive way, to the foundations of European culture. Christianity in fact has shaped Europe," he argued, "impressing upon it certain basic values."[26]

Yet, as "today's Europe . . . is in the process of strengthening and enlarging its economic and political union, [it at the same time] seems to suffer from a profound crisis of values." "Europe needs a *religious dimension*," he wrote, adding italics in the original. Europe needs to "open itself to the workings of God," as it "call[s] upon authentic values grounded in the universal moral law written on the heart of every man and woman." In practical terms, this translates into a European Constitution that should "include a reference to the religious and in particular the Christian heritage of Europe."[27] The European Union, as it both enlarges and deepens, should regard the Catholic Church as a "model of essential unity in diversity of cultural expressions, a consciousness of membership in a universal community which is rooted in but not confined to local communities, and a sense of what unites beyond all that divides."[28]

Above all, Pope John Paul II was exhorting the readers of *Ecclesia in Europa* to ensure that as "the European Union continues to expand," it should not be "reduced to its merely geographic and economic dimensions."[29] Indeed, the heart of the Polish pope's European policy was that the European Union must "consist above all in an agreement about the values which must find expression in its law and in its life."[30]

For the pope, this vision of a Christian Europe was perfectly consistent with Polish membership in the European Union. Indeed, he saw the latter as an important step on the path to the former. His views were obviously influential inside Poland, particularly within the ranks of the Polish Catholic hierarchy. However, leading Polish bishops did not enthusiastically accept many of the specific policy preferences drawn by the pope in favor of Polish accession to the E.U. During the early postcommunist years, Polish Church leaders expressed serious reservations about Poland's rejoining Europe through accession. Like their celebrated colleague in Rome, the Polish bishops were vaguely insulted by any formulation that required the home of Chopin and Mickiewicz to apply for admission to Europe, or to submit to a process of Europeanization. More fundamentally, these Polish prelates feared that a Catholic Poland would be inundated by secular notions of westernization brought about by membership in the European Union.

In 1995, Primate Josef Cardinal Glemp argued that E.U. accession "involves not only politics. The Polish Church also perceives it as a moral issue and warns against turning citizens into lay figures at the price of entering the rich proprietors' club."[31] Expressing the widespread trepidation shared by the Church's leadership, Glemp warned that "we could find ourselves in a situation where some people might say: 'Take us under your wing and we will make everything resemble you in every way.'"[32]

Following in-depth discussions with the European Commission in 1998, Glemp and his colleagues formally and officially declared their support for Polish E.U. accession, though in something less than ringing terms. Despite Bishop Pieronek's subsequent claim that this position was endorsed "calmly and unanimously" by his fellow bishops, Glemp admitted that some members of the episcopate remained "somewhat reserved" on the question.[33] Usually counted as a cosmopolitan voice among the Polish bishops, Pieronek nevertheless stated, "I most fear that which is habitually called the Western culture and which is quite often a distortion of that culture. The popular name for this," he said, "is McDonaldization."[34]

Undeniably, the Catholic Church is a hierarchical religious body. Arcane and archaic cannon law governs the complex relationship between national episcopal conferences and the Vatican curia as well as between local bishops and the bishop of Rome. However the working mores of ecclesiastical politics within Catholicism dictate that neither national episcopal conferences nor individual bishops can readily contradict a clearly defined, publicly articulated position of the supreme pontiff. To do so would call into question the bishops' teaching authority under Catholic law, which is validated by the legitimacy of those bishops' communion with their pope. Once Pope John Paul had expressed his support for the E.U. expansion to include Poland and the other former communist states of east central Europe, Glemp and Pieronek had few options. They could be ambivalent about it; they could have reservations; technically speaking, they could even offer their own views on a matter that was not subject to papal infallibility. But in terms of their understanding of their role in the Church as bishops, they simply could not publicly contradict the Polish pope.

Not everyone in the Polish Church felt the same level of institutional restraint. Though polls conducted among Polish priests found that 84 percent of them shared or at least accepted the position of the pope and the bishops on E.U. membership in 1998, a small number of Polish priests most definitely did not.[35] In a major public relations challenge for the bishops and the pope, some opponents mounted a vociferous campaign against membership in the European Union from the Catholic radio station, Radio Marija.

Operated by Father Tadeusz Rydzyk, Radio Marija became notorious in Poland and the Vatican by the mid-1990s for its vitriolic criticism of anti-Polish people and groups, as defined by their general worldview or their effect on postcommunist Polish society. Devoted to rescuing the authentic Catholic national identity from the ravages of the communist era, Rydzyk and his followers vigorously opposed what they saw as the Western infection brought about by E.U. membership.

This opposition movement was always in the minority, both within the formal structure of the Church and among the Polish population. Nevertheless, Radio Marija and its allies on the Catholic nationalist right are worthy of attention incommensurate with their numbers because within their rhetoric and worldview lie the central political questions and options now available to the Church in democratic postcommunist Poland. The question of European Union membership is important in its own right, and it is perhaps more important still as a symbolic representation of the deeper question of what kind of Poland will emerge from the revolution of 1989, and what role the Catholic Church can and should play in Polish society.

The debate is not really between liberal and conservative, or between accommodation and faith. Despite all the fusillades of vitriol between Radio Marija and the Polish episcopate, the two sides actually agree that at this historic moment the Polish Church must defend the Polish and Catholic national heritage; the Church must preserve those religious traditions and social practices that have always, even under communism, rendered Poland distinctively and recognizably Catholic. They do not want the Polish revolution to follow the path of the French Revolution, in which society devolved into secularism, thus forcing the institutional church to become marginalized.

The question is fundamentally a procedural one. The basic dispute within the millennial Polish Church is over its policies to achieve these goals, not whether they should be the goals in the first place. As Polish Catholicism undergoes profound procedural challenges, it is still led by a cadre of bishops who were trained in the communist era to view the government as an implacable enemy, and to view themselves as unelected representatives of the true national will. These notions made good sense when Poland was run by a government whose ideology was imposed from the outside and whose public policies were institutionally, socially, and morally anathema to the Catholic leadership.

However, Poland is now a stable and vibrant democracy whose government presumably advances policies that are an expression of the public's interest. Of course, the Polish bishops will object to some of those policies, and they will seek to advance the Church's teachings within the political process. The traditional top-down style of political leadership exercised by Wyszynski, Glemp, and Wojtyla is not an appropriate approach to democratic politics. No one should expect a Jeffersonian wall of separation between the Church and a Polish state whose population is more than 90 percent Roman Catholic. The bishops' political pronouncements—whether on Poland's entrance into the European Union; on Poland's development of a just and growing economy; or even on Poland's regulation of marriage, religious education, or abortion—will be dealt with in the open arena of democratic politics and not by elite negotiation or in the private spaces of political subversion.

Conclusion

The leaders of the Polish Church are enduring the wrenching process of learning to participate meaningfully in a political system where virtually everything is new. In short, the revolution has been won, but the effort at consolidation continues. Moreover, that effort at consolidation continues on two very closely related tracks. The first track, well understood by the Polish bishops, is the effort to retain the Church's public and influential role in Polish politics. The second track is to retain the religious faithfulness and the institutional loyalties of Polish Catholics that will form the very basis of any role that the bishops would like to play in democratic politics in the decades to come. That second track is not easy to tread in the context of the democratization of politics, the commercialization of society, and Poland's return to Europe through accession to the European Union. Can anyone really argue that these complex processes now under way in Poland will get any simpler or any more amenable to the influence of the Catholic Church in the post–Wojtyla era?

Notes

1. Bogdan Szajkowski, *Next to God. . . . Poland: Politics and Religion in Contemporary Poland* (New York: St. Martin's Press, 1983).

2. Scott Paltrow, "Poland and the Pope: The Vatican's Relations with Poland, 1978 to the Present," *Millennium: Journal of International Studies* 15 (1986): 3.

3. Adam Michnik, *The Church and the Left* (Chicago: University of Chicago Press, 1993).

4. Norman Davies, *God's Playground: A History of Poland* (New York: Columbia University Press, 1982), particularly vol. 2.

5. Maryjane Osa, "Creating Solidarity: The Religious Foundations of the Polish Social Movement," *East European Politics and Societies* 11 (Spring 1997): 339–65; Jan Kubik, *The Power of Symbols and the Symbols of Power: The Rise of Solidarity and the Fall of State Socialism in Poland* (University Park: Pennsylvania State University Press, 1994).

6. J. Bryan Hehir, "Papal Foreign Policy," *Foreign Policy* 78 (Spring 1990): 41.

7. Paltrow, "Poland and the Pope," 16.

8. "Church Official on State Rapport, Constitution," Foreign Broadcast Information Service, European Union, FBIS-EE.U.-94-148, August 2, 1994, 36.

9. The constitution is available at http://www.sejm.gov.pl. This quotation is from the preamble.

10. Ibid., articles 18 and 38.

11. Ibid., article 25, paragraph 4.

12. The author obtained an English-language copy of the treaty from Martin Pernal, an official in the Polish government department that negotiated the concordat with the Holy See. This particular quote is from article 22 of the text.

13. This statement was made by Primate Josef Cardinal Glemp. See FBIS-EE.U.-97-126, May 6, 1997.

14. This is similar to the argument made in Jose Casanova, *Public Religions in the Modern World* (Chicago: University of Chicago Press, 1994), 92–113.

15. Stephen Engelberg, "Pope Calls on Poland to Reject Western Europe's Secular Ways," *New York Times*, June 8, 1991.

16. Ibid.

17. The encyclical *Slavorum Apostoli* was reproduced in *Origins*, July 18, 1995.

18. For the pope's statements, see section 3 of "1000 Year Anniversary of the Death of St. Adalbert: Homily of John Paul II," Gniezno,Poland. 3 June 1997. Available at http://www.vatican.va/holy_father/john_paul_ii/travels/documents/hf_jp-ii_hom_03061997_en.html.

19. Ibid., section 4.

20. Ibid., section 5.

21. Ibid., section 2.

22. Section 3 of "Message of John Paul II to the Polish Bishops." Krakow, Poland, 10 June 1997. Available at http://www.vatican.va/holy_father/john_paul_ii/travels/documents/hf_jp-ii_mes_08061997_bishops_en.html.

23. For the pope's statements, see section 3 of "Homily of John Paul II at the Ecumenical Prayer Service." 31 May 1997. Available at http://www.vatican.va/holy_father/john_paul_ii/travels/documents/hf_jp-ii_spe_31051997_ecum-prayer_en.html.

24. The document appears in full in *Origins*, July 31, 2003, 153–76.

25. Ibid., 151.

26. Ibid., 171.

27. Ibid., 172.

28. Ibid., 173.

29. Ibid., 171.

30. Ibid.

31. "Cardinal Glemp Warns against Joining E.U.," FBIS-EE.U.-95-159, August 17, 1995.

32. Ibid.

33. "Polish Primate Backs NATO and E.U. Membership," *Global News Bank*, October 12, 1997.

34. "Catholic Bishop Views Risks Connected with E.U. Membership," FBIS-EE.U.-97-325, November 26, 1997.

35. Institute of Public Affairs, "Polish Catholic Priests and the European Integration: Main Research Results," March 1998.

Chapter 7

The Catholic Church in Ireland and Northern Ireland: Nationalism, Identity, and Opposition

WILLIAM CROTTY

THIS CHAPTER ANALYZES THE ROLE of the Roman Catholic Church in the Republic of Ireland as well as in Northern Ireland. It examines the Irish Church, its former prominence, and its changing contemporary role; the impact of economic development in Ireland in creating a new social, political, and moral culture in the nation; the scandals the Church has had to contend with; and the Church's present status in Irish society. It also analyzes the Northern Irish Church and its emphasis on moderation, peace, and cooperative efforts to establish a more stable governing arrangement. Its role as conciliator will be increasingly important following the Irish Republican Army's (IRA) July 2005 announced intention to end its thirty-six-year paramilitary struggle against the British, to "dump arms," and to become involved in the democratic peace process.

At one time, the Irish Church was the dominant social institution in pre-and postindependence Ireland. While it has adopted a role more familiar to competitive, pluralistic democracies in recent years, the Irish Church still commands overwhelming political power and influence, based largely on a membership that constitutes roughly 90 percent of the churchgoing population. Although ecclesiastically organized as one church, the Northern Irish Church is profoundly different from the rest of Ireland. It is the cultural symbol and community force representing a historically disadvantaged and discriminated religious minority. As an advocate of peace and reconciliation in a country torn by centuries of sectarian strife and religious bigotry, the Northern Irish Church finds itself in an extraordinarily difficult position.

Democracy, Interest Groups, and the Roman Catholic Church

The religious sphere revolves around the meaning of life and the existence of supernatural or transcendental reality. In many societies, one religion develops a monopoly within the religious sphere and, consequently, over the nation's spiritual and moral behavior; it becomes the dominant or established church. In contrast, the political sphere revolves around debates, analyses, and commentaries about how life can be best organized and developed. Different parties, organizations, and groups produce different discourse. Within democratic society, a church is obliged to become an interest group to vie for influence within civil society.[1]

Without question, the Roman Catholic Church is, and has been, the dominant church in Ireland. The following section focuses on how a dominant or established church has participated in and contributed to religious and political debate and discussion.[2] It also sheds light on the process whereby a dominant church is forced to adapt to a democratic society that is transforming itself into secular state.

The Irish Church

According to Finnegan, the Irish Church was "more revered and powerful than any such institution in any other European state" because "the conjunction of the Church's right for religious liberty with the Irish quest for political liberty meant that devotion to the Church was devotion to the country. Moreover, the Gaelic Ireland movement associated devotion to the Church with Irish cultural identity."[3] Similar to the role played by the Polish and the East Timorese Churches described in chapters 6 and 8, respectively, the Irish Church became intertwined with Irish nationalism, the society's cultural identity, and opposition to foreign colonization. The Church became the symbol of Ireland in the minds of the nation's people, the preserver of its value, and the one instrument of the society that was not subjugated by the British.

This made for a strong bond between the Irish people and "their" Church, one that has influenced state policy and social conduct to this day. Finnegan and McCarron write

> The Catholic Church was increasingly autonomous, creating its own education system and shaping public opinion, and although it accepted union with Britain at the institutional level it was associated with Irish nationalism at the functional level. The press was free and there was a free market economy. The conditions that foster democracy and stabilize it thus were present in Ireland. Ireland had developed institutions without a backward peasantry or a dominant landlord class, as well as family farms and autonomous institutions of Church, press, and political parties. The institutions of society were in effect modern and even somewhat pluralistic even though the values were traditional and organic.[4]

As a result, the Church emerged as dominant in its relationship with the state. The Church was directly associated with the fight for Irish nationalism, the

achievement of independence from Britain in 1922, and its post-1922 survival
as an independent state. Its values were the state's concerns and priorities. State
values thus reflected a "'social capital' or strong bond between people concerning trust, cooperation, equality, and community. . . . Thus the long-term social
capital or civil society built in Ireland . . . contributed to the establishment and
stability of democracy."[5]

The predominant role of the Church in the state's creation formed Ireland's
identity, its democratic experiment, and its social policies. "The Irish form of
democracy blended together Catholicism, constitutionalism, authoritarianism,
neo-corporatism, and Europeanization in the environment of a traditional culture with a developed civil society undergoing a process of transformation."[6]
From all of this, a traditionalist culture with the Church as its anchor evolved
an atypical state and church–state relationship.

The apogee of the Irish Church's influence during the postindependence era
was the 1937 constitution, championed by Eamon de Valera, who subsequently
became Ireland's prime minister and driving political force. The 1937 constitution acknowledged the Irish Church "as the guardian of the faith professed by
the great majority of the citizens." Conservative social doctrine was inserted into
the 1937 Constitution, including the primacy of the family, and the crucial role
of the woman as homemaker and mother, and prohibitions against divorce. Although not the "official" state church, the relationship was close enough to raise
uncomfortable questions for a liberal democratic political system.

The values of the Irish state and Church reflected the realities of the new
nation: rural, socially conservative, overwhelmingly Catholic, parochial, and
deeply traditional in family matters and cultural norms of behavior. Ireland had
suffered severely under the British occupation and the country's division in the
1922 treaty. Compounding this unfortunate colonial experience was the lack of
natural resources in Ireland, and its overreliance on a single crop in the nineteenth century. The resulting Great Famine prompted several waves of emigra-
tion of young and most able compatriots to America, Europe, and elsewhere
around the world. Those Irish children remaining were educated in parochial
schools that emphasized a traditional classical curriculum, as opposed to a scientific and technologically oriented one, and deemphasized a selfish, business-
oriented mentality. This, combined with Church teachings that emphasized
humanity, docility, and obedience to authority, made for a particularly passive
Irish personality: retiring, unassuming, obedient, self-deprecating, and self-criti-
cal. These qualities coexisted with a unique sense of humor; superb oral, musi-
cal, and written traditions; and personal warmth that continues to distinguish
Irish culture. These were not qualities that fostered a bold and aggressive state
presence in international and economic affairs.

When not applied to its legendary obsession with the bottle, the "Irish
Curse" described the Irish inability to compete economically and create wealth,

the nation's continuing economic problems, and its inability to compete successfully with other countries in the global economic arena. For those only familiar with Ireland's current reputation as the "Celtic Tiger," this may prove hard to accept. The fundamental economic policies and restructuring of the nation's economy that began in the late 1950s and early 1960s have rightly been referred to as an economic "miracle." It has transformed the once rural, slow-to-grow economy of Ireland into a globally competitive nation, considered by some business corporations as the "gateway to Europe." Ireland's primary asset has been its highly educated, hard-working, English-speaking labor force and its advantageous geographical position. With the assistance of European Union financing and planning, Ireland has transformed itself into a powerhouse of global economic trade and finance. Its gross national product and gross domestic product have soared, and its per capita income parallels or exceeds that of England, among others. This has enabled Ireland to bypass the manufacturing stage of development to engage the information age, and it is now highly competitive in the era of globalization.

The approach taken to date has been reactive to both social change and scandal. How the Church leadership confronts the forces of social change will determine its future role in Irish society. But the Church does have a role to play, especially in the areas of the state's social and international policy. The Irish state has already embraced many policies congruent with the ideals promoted by Roman Catholicism, such as its emphasis on peacekeeping, humanitarian aid to needy countries, and nonaggression in military affairs.

The depths of the societal changes driven by economics are hard to overestimate. Because these forces were outside of the Church's sphere of influence, the Church will have to adjust to a fundamental change in the thinking and the social, political, and economic situation in Ireland. Thus, after centuries as the society's most powerful institution, the Church is adapting to a new role. It may not be a totally welcome one, yet it is the challenge to both a meaningful survival and a source of relevance in a distinctly different society.

The Church, the State, and Social Policy

Both the Irish Church's humanitarian concerns and its resistance to change in its basic theological principles influence its approach to social policy. During the nation's formative years, the Church was the principal provider of social welfare and service agencies and the principal force of consequence in developing social policies. Substituting for the underfunded government, the Church made significant investments in education, schools, health care, hospitals, orphanages, homes for unwed mothers, and in providing for welfare recipients and the unemployed up through the late 1950s and early 1960s. The Irish Church also played a major role in the preservation and restoration of Irish culture, the Irish language, and the country's historical traditions.

Thus, the Irish Church enjoyed the goodwill and support of the people for centuries. Yet there was a price to pay. The hierarchy of the Irish Church was comprised of conservative leaders who believed that any social change challenged Church doctrine. Such changes included the role of women in Irish society, the sexual liberation that followed the mass availability of the pill and other anticonception methods; the acceptance of divorce as a legitimate option; and abortion, potentially the most continually divisive of all the issues.

These social changes coincided with the adoption by the Irish state of new economic development strategies in the 1960s and the reversal in the state's role and priorities, which affected society and the influence of the Church. The government encouraged foreign direct investment in the Irish industrial sector, which transformed the country's agriculturally based economy into a more industrial- and service-based economy. Cities and towns grew at the expense of the countryside. Government expenditure on health, education, and welfare increased to meet the needs of a developing society. The modernization of Irish society was given a new priority.[7]

The changing economic and social circumstances since 1960 suggest to some that the Irish state is becoming less Catholic, that life in Ireland is no longer directed by religious values, and that the Irish Church is losing its power over the people's hearts and minds.[8] It is an unfamiliar role for the Irish Church and for those who grew up with traditions of family, church, and community. The new age of internationalism, economic and national success, diminished spirituality, changing lifestyles, and sexual liberation evolved within a relatively brief period of decades. Still, much of the old Ireland and its social commitments and worldviews have remained in its social priorities.

The Periodization of Social Services

There is a rich and detailed literature on the Church's role in providing social services from the eighteenth century through various stages up to the 1950s. In broad terms, these stages proceeded from paternal colonialism, through the establishment of Church-operated social institutions, up to the current situation characterized as the state's assumption of control of social institutions. The principal stages are as follows.

Preindependence

In the nineteenth century, the Irish suffered under the Poor Laws and the confiscation of land and then the Great Famine. These crises led to the establishment of a statewide health care and educational system that was in large part managed by the Church. Interestingly, Catholics were prohibited from attending the nation's premier university, Trinity College, which was a Protestant institution.

The Period 1900–22

During the period from 1900 to 1922, the Irish government adopted a British-style old age pension and national insurance scheme. The era was dominated by the Easter Rebellion of 1916 and the Government of Ireland Act of 1920, which created the six-county Northern Ireland alliance with Great Britain. Finally, the Irish Free State was established in 1922.

The Period 1922–59

During the period from 1922 to 1959, "survival, not social policy, was the main preoccupation of the new Irish State." Europe and the world experienced a depression; World War II, during which time Ireland remained neutral; and the creation of the pre- and postwar welfare state on the European continent. But Ireland did not create a welfare state. Rather, the most powerful social institution in the country, the Catholic Church, took over many of the responsibilities of the state in these areas.

Forces to change social priorities emerged during the 1950s. Though the adoption of parliamentary acts or a restructuring of social services delivery systems did not occur, interest groups mobilized around social policy concerns in order to educate a broader public. In these terms, the period marked the beginning of a long-term, experimental approach to addressing social ills.

The 1960s

Beginning in the 1960s, the state increased its capabilities and resources. Economic benefits were included in contracts with various social groups, while the government cooperated with private and nongovernmental associations to meet the nation's social priorities. In many basic respects, this represented a state-initiated corporatist structural approach. Social programs were not integrated as they were in most European countries, but rather represented "opportunity costs," or ad hoc solutions. Despite the state's laudable success, many of the poor, the less educated, rural populations, and the elderly were left behind.[9]

The 1960s saw the beginnings of actual social reform. Two factors were important: The recently adopted economic strategy financed initiatives that envisioned a new and aggressive role for the state in areas of social concern. And as Himes describes in chapter 1 of this volume, the second involved the Church and the pronouncements of Vatican II, which proclaimed a new approach to societal needs, namely, that the "common good embraces the sum total of all those concerns of social life which enable individuals, families, and organizations to achieve complete and efficacious fulfillment."[10] This was a revolutionary turn of events, one with worldwide consequences, for a religion and hierarchy as conservative and doctrinaire as that of the Catholic Church. Vatican II established an environment in which the Church could approve major changes. Yet,

> despite a decade of economic expansion, of inward foreign investment and growth in manufacturing employment, the sixties were limited in their social achievements. Attitudes were gradually changing in the general population as to the need for widespread social and welfare interventions and reforms, but the results were in many instances too limited to have an impact on the general living and working conditions.[11]

The 1970s

During the 1970s, the embryonic social movements of the 1950s crystallized into organized groups and social movements with political promise. "A pluralism [was introduced] into social policy discussion," which was new in its extensiveness and in presenting alternative social approaches to problems.[12] This no doubt was the major hallmark of the 1970s.

Although the debate over priorities was livelier than in previous decades, the outcome was disappointing. Following its entrance into the European Community in 1973, structural funds were made available to Ireland. Eventually, these funds and the rapidly developing economy had the most long-run impact on improving social conditions. However, the two major oil crises of the 1970s limited the government's ability to improve social services.

The 1980s

The worldwide recession of the 1980s hit Ireland hard. As the government tightened outlays and restricted access to a number of social programs, the future role of the country in the global economic arena was placed in doubt. Though the government clearly recognized the severity of the social problems in housing, education, and welfare institutions, it still lacked the financial means to build new housing units and to hire teachers and health care workers. "The OECD [Organization for Economic Cooperation and Development] warned the government of Ireland against any moves towards increasing government expenditure, towards allowing real wage increases or increasing borrowing. Social developments, as a consequence, would have to be postponed or rely on an increase in taxation of those already at work."[13]

The most contentious social issues of the day—abortion, birth control, divorce, and, more generally, the role of women in society—continued to be vigorously debated. In these areas, the Church was very active in opposing change. Although stating that the laity should vote their conscience, the Irish bishops strongly opposed referendums on divorce and on abortion; from the pulpit, priests condemned the constitutional amendments as being destructive of the family. The referendums were defeated by roughly a 2 to 1 vote, with Dubliners voting for, and the rural areas against, the proposed changes. The decade did end on a high note.[14] The "Celtic Tiger" period (1987–97) had begun. It would transform the country and its global role thereafter.[15]

The 1990s

Normally, states develop a comprehensive set of social policies, of resources, rights, entitlements, and systems of redistribution. However, by the beginning of the 1990s, social policy in Ireland had skipped this phase.[16] Social benefits were integrated into collective bargaining agreements, brokered by the government among corporations, trade unions, and other related groups (farmers, collectives, contractors, suppliers, and the like). Furthermore, the government's Program for Economic and Social Progress (1991–93) called for "fundamental structural reforms, especially a continuation of the radical tax reform begun under the Program for National Recovery, a major assault on long-term unemployment and a restructuring of our social services, in particular social welfare, the health services, education and housing."[17] This approach, and the problems, continued through the 1990s and into the new century.

Ireland does not have a European-style welfare state. Rather, it has drifted toward "a mixed economy of welfare" by instituting a series of plans and agreements providing a faulty social umbrella for its citizens and by ignoring, or at least limiting, the equitable distribution of social resources to unorganized groups such as the less educated, nonunion, and nonprofessional sectors of the society.[18] An uneven tax policy also has contributed to the disproportionate share of costs and absence of equal benefits for the poor, the elderly, and the less well off in general.[19]

With the success of the government's outwardly oriented strategy of development, the country's standard of living improved remarkably.[20] However, social benefits were tied to the dynamic flows of the national and international economy, which is a continuing concern for any country adopting an outwardly oriented strategy, such as Ireland or even mainland China, as discussed by Reardon in chapter 13. During this period, the Church advocated an increase in humanitarian aid, as well as support for its social services, schools, and hospitals, and it vigorously fought for key social issues, such as abortion, divorce, and the role of women and the family, that it considered important for a moral society's conduct.

Ireland has embraced a corporatist mentality in relation to old age pensions, unemployment, health insurance, and, to a lesser extent, educational needs. The Church still provides services and social institutions of consequence—schools, hospitals, relief support—but the magnitude and impact are considerably less than during the nation's formative period. The Church has influenced the humanitarian thinking of those who frame the nation's social policy, and it continues to oppose social practices that it believes undermine its beliefs and its moral authority. It has resisted modernization and the changing lifestyles that mark a new, postmaterialist phase in Irish development.

Studies of Irish youth "suggest [a] growing pluralism in young people's outlook on life, and a greater focus on the individual and his or her experience as the locus for moral judgment."[21] Moral relativity could well be one of the most significant problems confronting the Church. It is a far cry from the absolutism, consensus, and power that existed in the past. The Church has experienced problems of its own that have served as much as anything else in recent years to change how it is perceived in Irish society and what its future influence may be.

The Current State of the Irish Church

The Church is undergoing a transformation forced not only by the restructuring of society but also by institutional problems it has long ignored. The number of seminarians is declining, and controversies abound over the issue of celibacy and the ordination of women. Fears related to the decline of Irish family life have generated an intense internal debate over the role of women in society, homosexuals, and civil unions. For various reasons, the Church has been forced to close parochial schools, hospitals, and relief agencies. As with the American Church described by Jelen in chapter 4, there have also been the sex scandals. A number of Church clergy have been involved in extramarital affairs, with some of these unions bearing children. Damning new evidence has revealed the use of corporal punishment and the abuse of children and women (the "Maggies," or unwed mothers) in the Church's care dating back to the 1950s.

Although such problems are not unique to Ireland, the result of these controversies and the restructuring of society is a weakened Irish Church. Consequently, the Church's influence over the state has diminished. Irish society has undergone a fundamental restructuring in the half century since World War II. A successful economic development strategy has significantly improved the living standards of the Irish people and propelled Ireland into the forefront of global competition. As the state has rejected its insular past, the Irish Church has been hesitant to confront this "new" Irish society. Similar to the experience of the countries of Latin Europe, discussed by Manuel and Mott in chapter 3, Ireland very much remains a "Catholic country," but the precise meaning of that statement remains highly unclear.

The Northern Irish Church

The Northern Irish Church is fundamentally different from the Catholic Church in the Republic of Ireland. By any standard, the religious acrimony and warfare in Northern Ireland have been a nasty business. The British government facilitated the settlement of Northern Ireland by Protestants during the colonial period, which exacerbated religious conflicts with the Catholic community. The Northern Irish government and its state police, along with the British military force and the Protestant paramilitary "defense" and "volunteer" organizations, have violently opposed the Catholic presence. The result has been a ghettoization of Catholics and systematic discrimination in housing, education, and the workplace.

The Irish community has responded in many ways. John Hume emphasized peaceful cooperation and the initiation of a civil rights movement, based on the example of the American South in the 1950s and 1960s. Others have chosen Sinn Féin and Gerry Adams as their political representatives. The extremists have joined the IRA and other such paramilitary organizations to conduct campaigns of violence and assassinations to oust the British, retaliate against the Protestants, and reunite Ireland as one country of thirty-two counties. Add to this the Orange Order, which is an exclusive Protestant organization that promotes Protestant society by commemorating its Protestant heritage. The "Marching Days" beginning on July 12 each year—intended to celebrate the 1688 victory at the Battle of the Boyne of the Protestant William of Orange over the Catholic King James II, thus ending permanently the Catholic claim to the English throne—are considered highlights of the Protestant calendar. Unfortunately, the "Marches" wind their way through Catholic enclaves, a provocative move that ensures resistance, trouble, and often violence.

The intent of the Orange Order and its junior affiliates and lodges is not only to conduct the Marching Days parades but also to provide "a demonstration of Protestant power and a proof that nothing has changed . . . since the Boyne."[22] It is an ugly situation with the divide structured along religious lines. Their objective is to socialize young Protestants into "the belief of their community," thus keeping alive from one generation to the next the religious hatreds of preceding generations.[23] The Orange Order and the Reverend Ian Paisley have exercised considerable influence over the Ulster Constabulary and the Northern political parties. Not surprisingly, Catholics are formally barred from membership in the Orange Order.

The Northern Irish Church and the nonfundamentalist Protestant churches have counseled moderation and nonviolence to achieve a permanent peace. The Catholic and Protestant churches exercise their moral powers of persuasion, issue statements of support for peace processes, and condemn sectarian violence. They also promote more conventional, pastoral activities, such as conducting weddings, presiding at funerals, and providing social activities such as dances, Boy Scouts, and bingo. For Catholics in particular, the Church can be the center of social life. "Churches are so widely influential that it is difficult to disentangle their role from that of other institutions of the society. . . . Church affiliation is important, not just for itself, but because it spills over into other activity."[24] "Some Church leaders have worked actively to assuage community divisions. . . . Church leaders have, on the whole, acted as bridge builders. . . . The leaders of the four main churches—Catholic, Presbyterian, Church of Ireland [Anglican], Methodist—meet regularly and probably more often than their counterparts in most parts of Christendom."[25] These meetings and the ecumenical spirit they engender are not shared by the fundamentalist Protestant leadership symbolized by Paisley and his followers. In fact, the Paisley-type provocateurs have the greatest visibility and hold the least compromising positions.

Religious divisions are kept alive, and it would appear quite successfully, by fundamentalist ministers and by the Orange Order and its sister organizations. These contribute to a climate of fear, repression, and retaliation that has marked the Irish political scene for generations. Both Catholic and Protestant extremists appear more able to set the political agenda, including derailing any serious peace efforts, than do the major churches.

The extremist Catholics were involved with the IRA's terrorist activities, the Derby "massacre" of 1972, and the "blanket" rebellion led by Bobby Sands, a turning point in gaining international attention for the Catholic civil rights crusade begun in the 1960s.[26] The continuing activities of Catholic and Protestant ultramilitarists, over which the establishment churches clearly exercised little control, reinforced the bitterness, anger, hatred, and frustrations that marked living in Ulster. Although not a promising setting for peaceful negotiations, both sides mobilized centrists and peace advocates throughout the North. The ultimate, and seemingly most promising, result was the Good Friday Peace Agreement of 1998, which among other things established a legislative assembly and executive for Northern Ireland. Though both institutions were suspended in October 2002, the peace process was given new life following the IRA's decision to "dump arms" in July 2005. Assuming that the IRA's decommissioning is a success, it will be up to Ian Paisley's Democratic Unionist Party to form a new government with Sinn Féin. Yet neither the established political parties nor the churches will be able to rely on the more radical militarists to abide by a ceasefire.

What Ruane and Todd refer to as "brutal class distinctions," reinforced in a globalized economy, continue. For some, this is the key to relieving the religious and economic issues that prevail in daily life.[27] As for religion in general, Ruane and Todd write: "Acceptance of church authority has decreased, as has the willingness to affirm a religious identity, although secularizing tendencies in Northern Ireland are slower than in other parts of the United Kingdom."[28]

These matters remain. There was great hope for the Good Friday Agreement, but it has proven difficult to put its complex institutional framework into operation to meet its ambitious timetable. Meanwhile, the old religious antagonisms persist, the Catholic and principal Protestant denominations do what they can, and the extremists exercise just enough leverage to keep the status quo and the fears and animosities these revive generally intact.

Conclusion

The Catholic Church in the Republic of Ireland was once politically dominant, and it is now attempting to fashion a new role for itself in response to the challenges of the contemporary era. The Catholic Church in Northern Ireland currently faces sectarian violence and civil rights deprivations directed against its population. The Northern Irish Church is seeking a model of interreligious cooperation born of pluralism and tolerance, which are characteristic of a fully matured liberal democratic state. The hope is that something along these lines will eventually prevail.

Notes

1. Tom Inglis, Mach Zdzistaw, and Rabat Mazanek, eds., *Religion and Politics: East–West Contrasts from Contemporary Europe* (Dublin: University College of Dublin Press, 2000), 6–7.

2. Inglis, Zdzistaw, and Mazanek, *Religion and Politics*, 4; see also Tom Inglis, *Moral Monopoly* (Dublin: Gill and Macmillan, 1998).

3. Richard B. Finnegan, *Ireland: The Challenge of Conflict and Change* (Boulder, Colo.: Westview Press, 1983), 73.

4. Richard B. Finnegan and Richard McCarron, *Ireland: Historical Echoes, Contemporary Politics* (Boulder, Colo.: Westview Press, 2000), 232.

5. Ibid.

6. Ibid., 233.

7. See Joseph J. Lee, *Ireland 1912–1985: Politics and Society* (Cambridge: Cambridge University Press, 1989); J. H. Goldthorpe and C. T Whelan, eds., *The Development of Industrial Society in England* (Oxford: Oxford University Press, 1994); and Kieran A. Kennedy, "The Irish Economy Transformed," *Studies: An Irish Quarterly Review* 87, no. 345 (1998): 333–42.

8. See William Crotty and David E. Schmidt, eds., *Ireland and the Politics of Change* (New York: Longman, 1998); Michele Dillon, *Debating Divorce: Moral Conflict in Ireland* (Lexington: University of Kentucky Press, 1993); Michele Dillon, "Catholicism, Politics, and Culture in the Republic of Ireland," in *Religion and Politics in Comparative Perspective*, eds. Ted G. Jelen and Clyde Wilcox (Cambridge: Cambridge University Press, 2002), 47–70; and M. MacGréil, *Religious Practice and Attitudes in Ireland* (Maynooth, Ireland: Survey and Research Units, Department of Social Studies, Saint Patrick's College, 1991).

9. Niamh Hardiman, "Taxing the Poor: The Politics of Income Taxation in Ireland," *Policy Studies Journal* 28, no. 4 (2000): 815–42; Richard Breen and Christopher T. Whelan, *Social Mobility and Social Class in Ireland* (Dublin: Hill and Macmillan, 1996).

10. See http://www.vatican.va/archive/hist_councils/ii_vatican_council/.

11. Pauline Conroy, "From the Fifties to the Nineties: Social Policy Comes Out of the Shadows," in *Irish Social Policy in Context*, eds. Gabriel Kiely, Anne O'Donnell, Patricia Kennedy, and Suzanne Quinn (Dublin: University College Dublin Press, 1999), 38.

12. Kiely et al., *Irish Social Policy*, 9; ibid., 39.

13. Conroy, "From the Fifties," 43.

14. Finnegan and McCarron, *Ireland*, 176–77.

15. William Crotty and David E. Schmitt, eds., *Ireland on the World Stage* (London: Longman/Pearson, 2002).

16. Conroy, "From the Fifties," 45.

17. *Program for Economic and Social Progress*, 1991, 8, quoted in Conroy, "From the Fifties," 46.

18. Conroy, "From the Fifties," 47.

19. Hardiman, "Taxing the Poor"; Breen and Whelan, *Social Mobility*. Also see Richard Breen, Damian Hannan, David Rottman, and Christopher Whelan, eds., *Understanding Contemporary Ireland: State, Class, and Development in the Republic of Ireland* (Dublin: Gill and Macmillan, 1990).

20. James L.Wiles and Richard B. Finnegan, *Aspirations and Realities* (Westport, Conn.: Greenwood Press, 1993); Jonathan Haughton, "The Dynamics of Economic Change," in *Ireland and the Politics of Change*, eds. William Crotty and D. Schmitt (London: Longman, 1998); Tony Fahey, "The Catholic Church and Social Policy," in *Social Policy in Ireland*, eds. Sean Healy and Brigid Reynolds (Dublin: Oak Tree Press, 1998); John Bradley, "The Irish Economy in an International Perspective," in *Ireland on the*

World Stage, eds. Crotty and Schmitt, 46–65; John Fitzgerald, "Ireland: A Multicultural Economy," in *Ireland on the World Stage*, eds. Crotty and Schmitt, 66–82. Niamh Hardiman, "The Political Economy of Growth," in *Ireland on the World Stage*, eds. Crotty and Schmitt, 168–88.

21. John Fulton et al., *Young Catholics at the New Millennium* (Dublin: University College Dublin Press, 2000), 9.

22. Larsen, as quoted in John Whyte, *Interpreting Northern Ireland* (Oxford: Clarendon Press, 1996), 31.

23. Whyte, *Interpreting Northern Ireland*, 30.

24. Ibid., 26.

25. Ibid., 27–28.

26. Finnegan and McCarron, *Ireland*, 331–32.

27. Joseph Ruane and Jennifer Todd, *After the Good Friday Agreement: Analysing Political Change in Northern Ireland* (Dublin: University College Dublin Press, 2002), 113.

28. Ibid.

Chapter 8

The East Timorese Church: From Oppression to Liberation

Alynna J. Lyon

AFTER CENTURIES OF SERVING THE interests of the colonial elite, the Roman Catholic Church in East Timor has emerged as a heroic advocate of human rights and national autonomy during the past three decades. Currently, the Church acts as a peacemaker and provides a venue for the building of a non-violent East Timor, or as it is officially known today, Timor-Leste. This chapter explores the chameleon nature of the Church as it reluctantly became the predominant international advocate of East Timor's independence, and, in the process, turned itself into an integral part of the modern political, cultural, and spiritual landscape of East Timor.[1]

Building on previous academic studies, this chapter focuses specifically on the Church's role in mobilizing the independence movement in East Timor.[2] The chapter traces the Church's interactions with the East Timorese, the Indonesian government, and the international community. Relying on the social movements' literature, the chapter uses a model of political mobilization to showcase how the East Timorese Church facilitated the consolidation of Catholic and Muslim identities and provided the independence movement with key resources. The chapter provides one explanation of a particular relationship between the people of East Timor, Indonesia, the international community, and the Catholic Church.

History of Foreign Rule

East Timor presents a tragic case of human suffering. Although an estimated 200,000 have died in recent political struggles, East Timor's Australian and Indonesian neighbors were painfully aware of the conflict for decades.[3] Yet, only fragmentary rumors of torture and unlawful imprisonment occasionally trickled out from this remote island 400 miles north of Australia into the international arena.

This international neglect ended abruptly in August 1999, when the people went to the polls to end years of colonial rule and Indonesia's military occupation. With this first triumph of democracy, the international community finally awoke to the struggles of this nation. A United Nations observer team registered voters and monitored polling stations as more than 75 percent of the people of East Timor cast their ballot for independence. Unfortunately, in a bizarre turn of events, a group of anti-independence militias attacked the East Timorese, setting fire to their homes, looting cities, and wiping out entire villages. Despite this violence, East Timor is viewed as a success story. In May 2002, East Timor gained its independence and changed its name to Timor-Leste. It joined the United Nations as the 191st member state in September of the same year.

For centuries, international politics—with its colonial history, world wars, the cold war, and growing emphasis on human rights—influenced life on the eastern part of the island. Over time, colonial powers, superpowers, and regional powers manipulated events, which created both a domestic and international crisis. In addition to the cost in human life, this internal war destroyed the economy and its infrastructure, stymied development, scarred social relations between Muslims and Catholics, and created a serious refugee problem as people scattered throughout the island.

Through these events, the Catholic Church played a significant part—as both oppressor and liberator. The Church initially was a tool of colonialism, then abandoned the territory during Japan's invasion during World War II, and subsequently returned to struggle with the people of East Timor against neocolonialism.

Geography and the East Timorese People

East Timor occupies the eastern portion of an island situated between Indonesia and Australia. The terrain of East Timor is dramatic, with high mountain ranges dropping down to large plains that reach to the sea. The Sea of Timor, located between the island and Australia, holds vast oil reserves, which makes control of the territory appealing to its neighbors. Timor has never been completely secluded; even before the Europeans arrived, maritime explorers from China and India often visited the island.

Today, diverse languages, ethnicities, and histories create a patchwork of people living in East Timor. Most observers identify two primary ethnic groups: the Belu, descendants of the Malays, who settled in the southern portion; and the Atoni, who primarily are concentrated in the central highlands. There are also several smaller ethnic groups, such as the descendants of African slaves brought by the Portuguese. East Timor is home to a kaleidoscope of cultures, with at least eleven different languages, including Tetum; Timorese, also known as Vaiqueno; Portuguese; and Indonesian. At the same time, Indians, Chinese,

Indonesians, the Dutch, and the Portuguese exposed the people to a rich variety of religious and cultural practices. The population has grown from 442,378 in 1950 to 800,000 people in about 2004. Although there is diversity in language and ethnicity, it is estimated that more than 90 percent of the East Timorese are Catholic, with 750,000 members, 31 parishes, and 101 priests.[4]

Portuguese Colonialism and the East Timorese Church

The saga of modern East Timor begins when traders from Portugal landed in about 1515 and declared it a Portuguese colony. The first missionary to East Timor, the Dominican father Antonio Taveira, arrived soon thereafter to begin baptizing some 5,000 Timorese. In 1702, a permanent mission was established in Lifao and was later transferred to Dili in 1769. By 1780, Portuguese Timor held approximately fifty churches, which served as an administrative arm of the Portuguese colonial power as missionaries played a "dual role . . . as both priests and military commanders."[5]

Under colonial rule, priests wore many hats. Initially, Portuguese colonial administrators were aided by Dominican and Jesuit missionaries, who served as both instruments of the state and the Church. In this capacity, they built schools and monasteries, which facilitated the socialization of islanders into Portuguese colonial norms. One communication between the Vatican and Portuguese authorities claims, "Portuguese Catholic missions are considered to be of imperial usefulness; they have an eminently civilizing influence."[6]

The Dutch also made colonial claims to portions of the island, resulting in a dispute between the colonial powers over control of the island and its lucrative sandalwood trade in the 1600s. In a compromise, the Dutch gained control over the western half of the island, while the Portuguese administered the eastern half; following negotiations with the International Court of Justice, this arrangement became legally binding in 1914. Two Timors thus were established—East Timor, with a Catholic Portuguese tradition; and West Timor, with a connection to the Protestant Netherlands.

Politics within Portugal forced the Church to leave East Timor from 1834 to 1874 and again from 1910 to 1920. In 1920, an uprising in East Timor gave one indication of indigenous aspirations to be free from external rule. The Portuguese military forces easily squashed the insurrection, killing more than 3,000 people and silencing dissent for several decades.[7] Under the Portuguese leader Antonio Salazar, Portugal established the Colonial Act of 1930, which centralized political control over the colonies and over Catholic operations on Portuguese territory; Salazar implemented similar policies in conjunction with the Vatican in Portugal's African colonies, as Linda Heywood describes in chapter 11 of this volume.

Kohen describes the Church as an important source of support against exploitation and physical attack. "It would be inaccurate and unfair to see the Church in the colonial period exclusively as an unquestioning arm of the metropolitan power, though some clergy were certainly in this category. . . . Many missionaries were regarded as community leaders and had a higher prestige than the civil authorities."[8] The Catholic missionary activity was deeply embedded in the educational and political institutions before World War II and the invasion of Japan. By the 1930s there were almost 19,000 Catholics and a minor seminary in Saibada, which remains in operation in present-day Dare.

World War II and Cold War Politics

East Timor also felt the dramatic international events of the 1940s, when the island became a battleground in the Pacific Theater of World War II. Because East Timor was a strategic point to block Japanese forces, Australia established a forward military post on the island. Nevertheless, the Japanese successfully invaded East Timor in February 1942; during the resulting three-year occupation, more than 60,000 East Timorese were killed by allied bombings and famine.[9] Having fled during the Japanese invasion, Catholic administrators returned with the Portuguese colonial rulers after 1945. Subsequently, the East Timorese Church focused on conversion and educating the East Timorese by teaching both the native Tetum language and Portuguese. An important element of the Church's success in conversion was its tolerance for local religious customs. However, the new converts' depth of conviction was relatively shallow, and many continued their indigenous religious practices.[10]

From the 1950s to mid-1970s, the East Timorese Church grew, as indicated in table 8.1, and the number of priests, nuns, and churches almost doubled.[11] Even into the 1960s, the East Timorese Church administered 60 percent of the schools; by 1974, 57,000 students attended these schools.[12] Carey argues that during this time the Church expanded its influence among the indigenous people and gained standing in local villages. The relationship may be conceptualized as triangular, in that the Church provided an important link among the indigenous population, the colonial power, and the local government.[13]

Following the 1974 Portuguese revolution, Angola and Mozambique were granted their independence, thus raising the question of East Timor's status. With high expectations for autonomy, several local political parties were formed, including the Revolutionary Front for an Independent East Timor, or Fretilin, which advocated a Marxist, independent East Timor. Promoting the redistribution of land and wealth, Fretilin eventually declared East Timor an independent country on November 28, 1975. The Australian consul, James Dunn, wrote that the new government "clearly enjoyed widespread support or cooperation from the people . . . leaders of the victorious party were welcomed."[14] Despite the declaration, most countries did not recognize the new government. It took two decades and thousands of deaths for an independent East Timor to be established.

TABLE 8.1.   MEMBERS OF THE EAST TIMORESE CHURCH,
1930–90

Year	No.	Population (%)
1930	19,000	4
1952	60,000	13
1973	196,670	29
1990	672,975	90

Sources: For 1930, John G. Taylor, *Indonesia's Forgotten War: The Hidden History of East Timor* (London: Zed Books, 1991), 17; and http://www.library.uu.nl/wesp/populstat/Asia/easttimc.htm. For 1952 and 1973, James Dunn, *East Timor: A People Betrayed* (Milton, Queensland: Jacaranda Press, 1983), 50. For 1990, José Ramos-Horta, *Funu: The Unfinished Saga of East Timor* (Trenton, N.J.: Red Sea Press, 1987), 201.

The Invasion

When the Republic of Indonesia became independent from the Dutch, it absorbed West Timor into its territory and hoped to absorb East Timor. Again, international politics changed the path of history in East Timor. When General Suharto defeated the formidable Indonesian Communist Party and consolidated his control over the state, the United States found a natural ally to help contain the spread of communism in Southeast Asia. Suharto knew that neither the United States nor other foreign powers would stop Indonesia's long-term plans to unite the island under one government.

On December 7, 1975, Indonesia invaded East Timor. Naval ships and warplanes brought 20,000 Indonesian troops to East Timor.[15] In describing the events, a Catholic bishop remarked, "The soldiers who landed started killing everyone they could find. There were many dead bodies on the streets—all we could see were the soldiers killing, killing, killing."[16] The assault was successful, for the new government collapsed and hundreds of thousands of people fled to the mountains to escape the killing, rape, and torture. Unlike the Japanese invasion during World War II, both foreign- and native-born priests stayed to protect their local communities or fled with them into the mountains of East Timor. This commitment to the people deepened the relationship between the Church and the indigenous population.[17] What had been a fairly superficial relationship became substantial and meaningful.

Less than two weeks after East Timor's declaration of independence, President Suharto proclaimed East Timor as Indonesia's twenty-seventh province.

Indonesia subsequently relocated many East Timorese from their mountainous homes to coastal villages. Years later, an Indonesian official would proclaim, "We have done more for East Timor in twenty years than the Portuguese did in four-and-a-half centuries."[18] However, the people of East Timor did not share this sentiment. During the five years following the invasion, the Timorese guerrilla organizations launched a series of attacks against Indonesian security forces. An estimated 100,000 people were killed during the invasion, and approximately 40 percent of the population died between 1975 and 1980 from war-related famine.[19]

The Transitional Role of the Church, 1974–1999

Rebuffing Indonesian government attempts to incorporate the local church under state control, the Vatican placed the East Timorese Church under direct Vatican control. As a result, subtle changes occurred in the relationship between the East Indonesian Church and the East Timorese; and not-so-subtle tensions arose between the Vatican and the Indonesian state. Under the policy of *integrasi*, Indonesia sought three objectives that sparked the Church's vocal opposition: language laws, population control, and religious conversion.

To promote integration and cement its control over the local population, Indonesia outlawed the Portuguese language and declared Bahasa Indonesian the national language. This triggered protest from the Church. Budiardjo and Liong explain the source of the tension:

> In 1981 the Indonesian administration tried to force the Church to accept linguistic *integrasi* by stipulating that Portuguese should no longer be used during Mass and should be replaced by Indonesian. The clergy rejected this request and asked the Vatican for permission for Portuguese to be replaced by Tetum. The Vatican gave its approval in October 1981. This change in language has helped integrate the Church even more closely with the community.[20]

In addition to resisting the invaders, the East Timorese Church empowered the local population by eliminating the use of the "new" colonial language and legitimating the use of indigenous languages.

Tensions also arose when the Church clashed with Indonesian authorities over a family-planning program to reduce the East Timorese population growth rates. The Indonesian government implemented compulsory fertility control in the form of birth control pills, hormonal injections, implants in women, and sterilization programs.[21] The East Timorese Church and its Vatican administrators directly opposed all Indonesian population control policies as violations of fundamental human rights. Finally, both the local church and the Vatican took offense at the Indonesian policies advocating the conversion of the East Timorese people to Islam.

In response to the Indonesian actions, the East Timorese Church moved to protect its interests, which coincided with indigenous interests. Both the Church and the local population had a vested interest in resisting the invaders and their attempts to control the language, religion, and even the physical bodies of the Timorese. Assuming an advocacy role after the invasion, priests quietly protested against the treatment of the East Timorese. Catholicism thus became a counter-response to Indonesian assimilation attempts, which had an added result of increasing Catholic conversions.[22] The role of the Church had changed dramatically from that of colonial times, when the Catholic Church held a position of power under the Portuguese government. As Lundry writes, "Before the invasion, priests were aloof and disdainful of rural Timorese. The Church was identified with the state and the clergy was charged with implementing government policies."[23] After the invasion, however, the Church was separated from the state as the Islamic-based Indonesian government no longer welcomed it.

Despite the tensions with the Church, Indonesia did grant several privileges. The Jesuits were allowed to publish a relatively uncensored weekly newspaper, *Seara*, which provided an early forum for debate on language rights and the education system.[24] Another Catholic newspaper, *A Provincia de Timor*, served as a venue for political dialogue about the Indonesian presence. Taylor argues that these publications and the Jesuit schools facilitated the establishment of early political parties, and in certain cases advocated independence.[25] At the same time, the Church remained fairly neutral.

The Resistance Movement and the Catholic Church

The occupation of East Timor became a pebble in Indonesia's shoe. Under the political leadership of the prosocialist Fretilin party, the Armed Forces of the National Liberation of East Timor emerged to confront the Indonesian military. Hundreds of young men went to the mountains to join the resistance. The Timorese were determined in their quest for independence, invoking the slogan *Pátria ou Morte!* (Fatherland or Death!) as they went into battle. One rebel, Jose Xanana Gusmão, organized the Revolutionary Council of National Resistance to bring together several groups that were fighting the Indonesians separately. Students organized another urban-based group to fight on the streets of the capital city. The result was a network of guerrilla fighters that offered a powerful force against the military presence. In response, the Indonesian government stationed between twenty and forty thousand troops to enforce its rule.[26]

With the emergence of the socialist resistance movement, the Church was placed in a challenging position. Fighting to establish a secular, communist government, Fretilin regarded the Church as a symbol of colonial oppression. Yet the resistance movement and the Catholic Church coexisted in the mountains; their mutual concern for the populous helped form a bond between the revolutionaries and the priests. Carey argues, "They provided an essential moral dimension to the nationalist struggle."[27] The East Timorese Church faced the moral issues of social justice, Indonesian pressure to comply with its edicts, and the mandates from the Holy See in Rome. The Vatican chose to walk a fine line between both factions because it did not want to isolate Indonesia. The official Vatican position called for recognizing the rights of the East Timorese people.

Tensions emerged between religious officials in East Timor and the Holy See as a result of the Vatican's relationship with Indonesia. Advocates for human rights felt betrayed by the Vatican's lack of attention to the plight of the East Timorese. After the separation with Portugal, many in the East Timorese Church felt abandoned because "they were forced to reconstruct their Church amidst the carnage and destruction of war."[28] In fact, some felt deserted by the silence of the Vatican in the face of devastation. This tension strengthened the bonds between the local community and the local church, further distancing the East Timorese Church from the Vatican. Once an extension of the colonial power, the East Timorese Church had gone native. It now associated with the people rather than the government, leading one author to refer to the transition as the "Timorization" of the Church.[29] The Church in East Timor became increasingly appealing to the people, resulting in a quadrupling of the Catholic conversions in the years after the Indonesian occupation to nearly 60 percent of the total East Timorese population.[30]

Monsignor Martinho da Costa Lopes personified the tension and internal struggle facing the local church. He was a vocal advocate of the independence movement and was the first Timorese leader of the East Timorese Catholic Church. Due to the "unsettled status" of East Timor following the events of 1975, he was not designated a bishop, although the Timorese often referred to him as their "bishop." Initially accepting the rules of the Indonesian Army, he was regarded has an "old-school conservative" leader who only reluctantly denounced Indonesian atrocities. Yet, after witnessing the growing atrocities against the East Timorese, such as the massacre of 500 women and children under Indonesian occupation, he proclaimed, "I feel an irrepressible need to tell the whole world about the genocide being practiced in Timor so that, when we die, at least the world will know we died standing."[31] After his protest letters were publicly issued to the international media, the U.S. Congress, and the Australian Parliament, the Indonesian authorities accused him of a "reputed support of Fretilin."[32] Undaunted, he called for the United Nations to intervene and limit support for Indonesia.[33] Under pressure from the government in Jakarta, the Vatican removed da Costa Lopes in 1983 for inciting nationalist sentiment.

As it expanded its role in Indonesia, the Vatican attempted to depoliticize the East Timorese Church by appointing a younger and more consolatory representative. These efforts backfired. A thirty-five-year-old native of East Timor, Carlos Filipe Ximenes Belo, served as the apostolic administrator from 1983 to

1988; in 1988, he was appointed bishop. After witnessing violence, murder, and the suffering of the East Timorese people, Belo attempted to communicate directly with the Indonesian militias. Not receiving a response, he wrote letters to the Vatican and UN secretary general Javier Pérez de Cuéllar stating, "We are dying as a people and a nation."[34] Belo used this remarkable correspondence with the international community to request a referendum on independence for East Timor. In addition to Belo, 5 cardinals, 32 archbishops, 77 bishops, and more than 1,300 Church leaders signed the letter. In response, Pope John Paul II stated that

> in most firmly condemning the violence, which has also been furiously unleashed against the personnel and property of the Catholic Church, I implore those responsible for so many acts of wickedness to abandon their murderous and destructive intentions. It is also my heartfelt wish that as soon as possible Indonesia and the International Community will put an end to the slaughter and find effective ways to meet the legitimate aspirations of the Timorese population.[35]

The Vatican could no longer ignore the events in East Timor. In October 1989, Pope John Paul II traveled to East Timor. Before the papal visit, Bishop Belo dropped a political bomb in an interview with CNN when he proclaimed that "we can verify that there is genocide, a cleansing" within East Timor.[36] In his sermon to the people of Dili, the pope expressed his hope that "those who have responsibility for life in East Timor will act with wisdom and goodwill towards all."[37] However, rather than creating peace, the pope's visit increased tensions. The papal mass incited widespread anti-Indonesian demonstrations, which resulted in clashes between Indonesian security forces and student protestors.

Through his fervent advocacy, Belo became the international spokesperson against the Indonesian occupation, thus catching the attention of the Vatican and Jakarta. Belo's official residence became a sanctuary for East Timorese in their flight from the violence. Placed under strict surveillance by the Indonesian militias, Belo survived several attempts on his life. The Vatican subsequently transferred Belo to a new, less visible diocese in Bacau. Yet, when Belo and José Ramos-Horta, vice president of the National Council of Timorese Resistance, shared the 1996 Nobel Peace Prize, Belo and the East Timorese problem were now placed fully in the international limelight.

The East Timorese Church also experienced divisions over the issue of Indonesian rule. There were those that actively participated in the resistance movement. Father Domingo Soares, who also was known as *padre maubere* (father of the resistance), was a highly visible campaigner in the National Council for East Timorese Resistance. Some East Timorese Church officials, such as Mario Vieira, opposed the politicization of the Church by arguing that "the Church should be neutral."[38] The Vatican, for the most part, followed a policy of neutrality and attempted to separate itself from events in East Timor. The Vatican was very careful not to isolate Indonesia because it was concerned that the minority Indonesian Catholic population would be "destroyed by unnamed enemies."[39] The Vatican also avoided a confrontation with Jakarta in order to realize a more long-term goal of expanding the Indonesian Church. Therefore, "the little ones are being sacrificed for big interests."[40] Moreover, the Vatican assumed that President Suharto unhesitatingly would use the military government to repress any threats to the Muslim community.

According to Edward W. Doherty, the late American diplomat turned adviser to the U.S. Catholic bishops, "Vatican diplomats are like any other diplomats, no different than the Americans or the French or the Russians: their main purpose is to improve the relations with the government of the country where they are accredited."[41] Kohen contends that the "Vatican diplomats would argue that they were being realistic . . . and East Timor would surely reconcile itself to Indonesian rule sooner or later."[42] Cardinal Roger Etchegaray, president of the Pontifical Council for Justice and Peace, argued the official position in February 1996, stating:

> I am aware that an international political problem exists concerning East Timor. It is not my competence to enter into that question. As a friend, however, I wish to say to all those involved: believe in the power of dialogue, of dialogue among yourselves and of dialogue outside the country. And I express complete encouragement, as the Pope himself has done on numerous occasions, for all the efforts of dialogue at present in course.[43]

East Timor Enters the World Stage: The Santa Cruz Massacre

Manuel and Mott discuss in chapter 3 the importance of the Church in extraordinary times of life. While the funeral of former French president François Mitterrand demonstrated the continued importance of the Church during critical times, funerals can also become forums to vent frustration. In October 1991, Catholics gathered at the Santa Cruz Cemetery in Dili for the funeral of a teenage boy who had died fighting the Indonesian forces. After placing flowers at the gravesite, the mourners initiated a series of anti-Indonesian protests, resulting in the deaths of 271 people, the wounding of 382, and the "disappearance" of 250 other protestors.[44]

The Santa Cruz Massacre had the greatest impact on focusing international attention on East Timor. The international media broadcast throughout the world bloody images of Indonesian forces killing women and children, thus challenging the veracity of Indonesian accounts of the massacre. Carey writes, "It was impossible, given this visual evidence, for the Indonesian authorities to deny that killings had taken place or that the Indonesian army had been involved."[45]

Yet the Indonesian government referred to the event as a "regrettable incident."[46] Several Western governments, including Canada and Denmark, halted aid shipments, while the U.S. Congress placed a temporary ban on the sales of arms and small weapons to Indonesia.

The 1990s in East Timor began and ended with violence. In 1995, violence broke out between Muslim settlers and Catholic East Timorese youth. In addition, two Protestant churches were burned to the ground. The incidents were blamed on the resistance movement. In 1997, the Asian financial crisis and economic turmoil shook the region and destabilized the government in Indonesia. Under intense political pressure, Indonesia's President Suharto resigned in May 1998. With a change in government, optimism for change in the twenty-seventh province increased. The new Indonesian president, B. J. Habibie, thus was faced with critical political and economic crises; he thus hinted that the best solution for East Timor might be independence.

The Referendum

In June 1998, the United Nations successfully negotiated an agreement with Indonesia to allow a "popular consultation" to determine whether the people of East Timor wanted independence. In the August 30, 1999, referendum, 98 percent of the voting population turned out, and a resounding 78.5 percent of voters declared their desire to be liberated from Indonesia's control.[47]

Within hours after the September 4 announcement on independence, pro-Indonesian militia forces went on a rampage; they committed acts of murder, arson, destruction of property, and forced deportation. Reports of attacks on refugees seeking asylum in churches also shocked the world, as did attacks on the churches themselves. Catholic priests and nuns were specifically targeted, resulting in the evacuation of Bishop Belo and many of his followers to Australia. Archbishop Jean-Louis Tauran, the foreign minister of the Vatican, reported that "we are facing another genocide, a genocide that does not spare the Catholic Church."[48] Reports found at least two Catholic priests and six nuns were killed. The Reverend Franscisco de Vasconcelos Ximenes, the head of the Protestant Church in East Timor, was killed in the violence as well. This new wave of bloodshed forced 600,000 people to flee their homes; 130,000 refugees fled to Indonesian-controlled West Timor.[49] Conservative reports indicate that at least 7,000 people died in the first few days after the announcement.[50] The pebble in Indonesia's shoe hit the world with the force of a grenade.[51]

In response to international calls to end the violence, the United Nations created a peacekeeping mission called the United Nations Assistance Mission in East Timor (Unamet), for the dual purposes of restoring peace and order in East Timor and assisting in promoting the successful transition to independence. Australia led the International Force for East Timor (Interfet), which was composed of 9,150 military personnel and 1,640 police officers who entered East Timor on September 20, 1999.[52] The operation was authorized to use "all necessary measures" to "restore peace and security" and provide disaster relief.[53] In October 1999, the Indonesian Assembly gave President Habibie a vote of no confidence, which resulted in Abdurrahman Wahid, a Muslim cleric, assuming the Indonesian presidency. With a change in political administration came another change in the policy toward East Timor. Twenty-five years after its invasion, Indonesia's assembly reversed the 1975 decree annexing East Timor and recognized the 1999 independence referendum, and it ordered its 25,000-strong military force to leave East Timor. As the military withdrew, thousands of East Timorese gathered in the streets of Dili to celebrate the end of foreign occupation.

On February 29, 2000, President Wahid traveled to East Timor's capital and apologized for twenty-five years of bloodshed and past abuses. Expressing Indonesia's new commitment to rebuilding peaceful relations, Wahid declared, "I would like to apologize for the things that have happened in the past . . . for the victims, to the families of Santa Cruz, and those friends who are buried here in the military cemetery."[54] The president of Portugal, Jorge Sampaio, facilitated the rebuilding of good relations with Indonesia and assisted East Timor in its quest for autonomy, peace, and stability. In addition to his formal apology, Wahid held several trials to determine whether members of the Indonesian military were responsible for the violence that occurred after the referendum. In shocking testimony, several Indonesian soldiers admitted to killing civilians in East Timor.[55]

The Church as a Conduit of Collective Action

Just like the Irish and Polish churches described in previous chapters, the East Timorese Church provided essential support to the resistance movement in mobilizing against Indonesian occupation. Tilly defines mobilization as "the process by which a group goes from being a passive collection of individuals to an active participant in public life."[56] Before people actually protest in the streets, establish paramilitary groups, or take up arms, there are several necessary preconditions. McAdam views the ethnic mobilization of the U.S. civil rights movement as the product of several forces.[57] He highlights the influence of southern African American churches on establishing solidarity, providing leadership for the movement, and gathering the necessary resources for collective action. For McAdam, mobilization is the product of three general forces: cognitive liberation, the presence of resources, and the opening of political opportunity structures.

This model offers a compelling framework for looking at the influence the Catholic Church had on the mobilization of the independence movement in East Timor and can be applied to the Church in other subjugated states, such as preindependence Ireland and Poland. By changing the cognitive liberation variable to focus on the politicization of identity, the model can highlight the role the East Timorese Church played in the independence movement. This allows for a more focused exploration of how the Church influenced group cohesion and the politicization of identity, as well as the group's access to material goods and services or resources.

The first tier of the model focuses on identity—a particular group must feel solidarity and communal ties before it can be an effective political actor. The politicization of identity began very early in East Timor's history. The Portuguese, particularly through their Catholic missionaries, created a foundation for identity-based strife. The colonial experience actually promoted group solidarity, for indigenous communities saw each other as allies against the colonial occupiers. The common colonial experience led the indigenous community to commit itself to a collective definition and to perceive their indigenous identity as unique and relevant for acquiring political power. The Indonesian invasion cemented these feelings of identity and solidarity, particularly once Indonesia attempted to integrate the East Timorese people by imposing their language and religion upon them. For twenty-three years, Jakarta employed several tactics to dilute the Timorese identity, including the sending of thousands of Javanese and Balinese migrants into East Timor to begin the process of assimilation.[58] In addition, it implemented an extensive educational system to assimilate the Indonesian language, history, religion, and national symbols. Despite these attempts, Indonesia's efforts only served to further solidify the Tetum language and the Catholic religious identity. Indeed, Anderson points out that the East Timorese were never resocialized by the Indonesians. Rather, assimilation policies bolstered group coherence and common identity. The East Timorese became even more aware of their communal ties as common victims of external oppression.[59] When blatant resistance to "Indonesianization" resulted in increased brutality, these communal ties only strengthened.

The Catholic clergy played a decisive role in maintaining the indigenous language of Tetum. As a product of Vatican II and the vernacularization of the Roman rite, Tetum replaced Portuguese as the liturgical medium in East Timor. As the depositor of cultural rights, the East Timorese Church became synonymous with resistance to Indonesia, and thus it came under attack, such as during the Santa Cruz Massacre of 1991.[60] In addition to promoting East Timorese identity by protecting Tetum, Catholicism itself was now part of the indigenous identity.

The East Timorese Church as a Resource for Collective Action

The most essential component of political action is power. A group's power, measured by its access to resources, is essential for its ability to organize people to act collectively. Groups cannot act effectively within the political arena without accumulating resources, such as money, weapons, technologies, information services, communication channels, and loyalties. Jenkins and Perrow argue that key to the "rise to insurgency is the amount of social resources available to unorganized but aggrieved groups, making it possible to launch an organized demand for change."[61]

The second variable focuses on the resources provided to insurgents. McAdam writes, "The generation of insurgency develops not from an aggregate rise in discontent but from a significant increase in the level of resources available to support collective protest."[62] Here, the presence of the Catholic Church contributed hope and optimism of an effective resistance. The Church's access to the international community was just as important to long-term success as Fretilin's acquisition of weapons.

In addition to money, weapons, leadership, communication systems, and sanctuary, leadership is important to internal cohesiveness, establishing tactics, and organizing protest activities. Political entrepreneurs are a powerful resource. They stir the cauldron, foster alliances, gather capital, and raise awareness. Political entrepreneurs precipitate conflict by politicizing collective identity, that is, by dramatizing grievances or threats to common interests or by pointing out opportunities to promote and further such interests by organized action.[63] According to Kingdon, "Entrepreneurs . . . lie in wait—for a window to open."[64] Bishop Belo is such a political entrepreneur. In fact Arnold Kohen argues that Bishop Belo became both the religious and de facto political leader of East Timor.[65]

The Catholic schools also provided an organizational component for the creation of the resistance organization. Most of the members of Fretilin were educated in parochial schools; many studied for the priesthood.[66] Carey highlights the important role of the colégios—Catholic communities that provide assistance to the widows and orphans of the Fretilin fighters.[67] One author echoes this observation: "The East Timorese Church represented the only form of indigenous, popular civil society tolerated by the state. As a result, the two were inseparable: civil society in East Timor was Catholic."[68]

Within East Timor, the Church provided a safe haven, an organizational framework, and an institutional alternative to Indonesian colonization. Kohen writes, "In a place where simply walking on the street could be deadly, it was the only public institution that provided a measure of protection to the people."[69] The Church served as witness to the violence in East Timor. It rebutted claims by the Indonesian government that downplayed casualties and denied connections, and it did so with a moral authority that left little room for the international community to doubt the Church's testimony. In addition, the Church was immune to Indonesia's attempts to restrict access to the area by foreigners: "The Church was the only local institution capable of communicating independently with the outside world and of articulating the deep trauma of the East Timorese people."[70] Applying this theoretical model to East Timor, it is clear that the

Catholic Church was both actively involved in the domestic political saga as well as in the international political mobilization against Indonesia.

The Future of the Church in East Timor

Even with its independence, East Timor remains in transition. Almost half the people who fled East Timor after the referendum remain in refugee camps in West Timor. Despite an international presence, peace and order have been difficult to establish. In October 1999, border clashes broke out among UN peacekeepers, Indonesian policemen, and anti-independence militias. The frequent fighting on the West Timorese border indicates that, although the Indonesian military forces are gone, the island's militias are prepared to fight. In addition, the economy of the country is in a shambles. Most of the country's infrastructure was destroyed in the fighting, leaving roads and communications systems unusable. Japan and Portugal are financially supporting East Timor's effort to reestablish its economy. However, after three hundred years of Portuguese domination, followed by three decades of Indonesian occupation and intimidation, the East Timorese are wary of outside assistance that may mask yet another threat to their independence and self-determination.

After serving twenty years in a jail in Jakarta as a political prisoner, the former rebel leader Jose Xanana Gusmão is now the elected president of East Timor. In a recent speech, he told his fellow East Timorese that both the country and people of East Timor were starting from zero. Traub explains, "East Timor lacks the most basic necessities: not just doctors, dentists, accountants, lawyers, and police, but also tables, chairs, pots, and pans. Even in Dili, the capital, stop signs, traffic signals, and streetlights are nowhere to be found."[71] With high unemployment, gang violence has erupted within Dili. Another issue facing the country is the role that Fretilin will play in the government. It remains to be seen how a rebel organization, trained in guerilla warfare, can adapt to the day-to-day governing of a country.

East Timor is beginning a long journey toward peace. The East Timorese Church is playing an important role in strengthening community structures, the search for justice, rebuilding, and recovery. Appeals for solidarity and religious tolerance dominate the current agenda of the Reverend Basilio do Nascimento, East Timor's new Catholic bishop of Baucau. At the same time, he has actively petitioned for international financial support to sustain the Church's educational and social programs. The East Timorese Church is focusing on refugee return from West Timor and the rebuilding of physical and political infrastructures. The Church is also active in the documentation and verification of human rights violations in East Timor and in searching for a balance between reconciliation and justice.

The Catholic Church in East Timor presents a fascinating case of the Church in transition. The Church experienced a profound conversion as it emerged from an instrument of oppression to one of liberation. It became an indigenous institution, taking a path separate from the Vatican. Here we find two strategic actors: the Vatican in its efforts to balance international strategic interest; and Bishop Belo and others of the indigenous Church, who became the cornerstone of the liberation movement. The Church "not only eased the suffering of the East Timorese population, but engendered a sense of nationalism that fueled the movement for independence."[72] The indigenous Church provided pride and honor to the movement and renewed optimism in the face of waves of almost three decades of violence and destruction.

Notes

1. For the "Catholic Church as strategic actor" approach, see Stathis Kalyvas, *The Rise of Christian Democracy in Europe* (Ithaca, N.Y.: Cornell University Press, 1996); Anthony Gill, *Rendering unto Caesar: The Catholic Church and the State in Latin America* (Chicago: University of Chicago Press, 1998); and Carolyn Warner, *Confessions of an Interest Group: The Catholic Church and Political Parties in Europe* (Princeton, N.J.: Princeton University Press, 2000).

2. Arnold Kohen, *From the Place of the Dead: The Epic Struggles of Bishop Belo of East Timor* (New York: St. Martin's Press, 1999); Richard Tanter, Mark Selden, and Stephen R. Shalom, eds., *Bitter Flowers, Sweet Flowers: East Timor, Indonesia, and the World Community* (Oxford: Rowman & Littlefield, 2001).

3. Seth Mydans, "A Timorese Era Closes Quietly as Army Goes," *New York Times,* October 31, 1999.

4. Donald E. Weatherbee, "Portuguese Timor: An Indonesian Dilemma," *Asian Survey* 6 (December 1966): 684.

5. *New Catholic Encyclopedia,* 2nd ed., s.v. 2002. Peter Carey, "The Catholic Church, Religious Revival, and the Nationalist Movement in East Timor, 1975–1989," *Indonesia and the Malay World* 27, no. 78 (1999): 78.

6. Cited in H. M. Hill, "Fretilin: The Origins, Ideologies and Strategies of a Nationalist Movement in East Timor" (M.A. thesis, Monash University, 1978), 22.

7. John G. Taylor, *Indonesia's Forgotten War: The Hidden History of East Timor* (London: Zed Books, 1991), 11.

8. Kohen, *From the Place of the Dead,* 44–45.

9. James Dunn, *East Timor: A People Betrayed* (Milton, Queensland: Jacaranda Press, 1983), 23–26.

10. Carey, "Catholic Church," 79.

11. Dunn, *East Timor,* 50.

12. John Taylor, *East Timor: The Price of Freedom* (London: Zed Books, 1999), 17.

13. Carey, "Catholic Church," 79.

14. Dunn, *East Timor,* 54.

15. Taylor, *East Timor,* 201.

16. "Interview with Former Bishop of East Timor," *Tapol Bulletin* 59 (September 1983). Cited in Taylor, *East Timor,* 68.

17. Carey, "Catholic Church," 80.

18. Peter Carey, *East Timor: Third World Colonialism and the Struggle for National Identity* (Coventry, U.K.: Research Institute for the Study of Conflict and Terrorism, 1996), 16.

19. Taylor, *East Timor*, 90; Peter Carey and G. Carter Bentley, *East Timor at the Crossroads: The Forging of a Nation* (Honolulu: University of Hawaii Press, 1995), 6.

20. Carmel Budiardjo and Liem Soei Liong, *The War against East Timor* (London: Zed Books, 1984), 121.

21. Roy Pateman, "East Timor, Twenty Years After: *Resistir e Vencer*," *Terrorism and Political Violence* 10, no. 1 (1998): 123. Also see http://www.etan.org/et2001c/november/01-3/0etwoman.htm.

22. Pateman, "East Timor," 124.

23. Chris Lundry, "From Passivity to Political Resource: The Catholic Church and Nationalism in East Timor," *East Timor Action Network* / *U.S.*, Spring 2000; http://www.etan.org/etreligious/2001a/polresrce.htm.

24. Carey, "Catholic Church," 80.

25. Taylor, *East Timor*, 26–27; Mathew Jardine, *East Timor's Unfinished Struggle* (Boston: South End Press, 1997), 11.

26. Elaine Brière, "East Timor: History and Society," in *East Timor: Occupation and Resistance*, ed. Torben Retboll (Copenhagen: Narayana Press, 1998), 30.

27. Carey, "Catholic Church," 70.

28. Ibid., 81.

29. Lundry, "From Passivity to Political Resource."

30. "The Agony of East Timor," *America* 181, no. 8 (1999): 3.

31. See http://www.ewtn.com/library/ISSUES/TIMOR.TXT.

32. Kohen, *From the Place of the Dead*, 109–14.

33. "Msrg. Da Costa Lopes," *New York Times*, March 5, 1991.

34. Bishop Carlos Filipe Ximenes Belo in a letter UN secretary general Pérez de Cuéllar, February 1989. In Kohen, *From the Place of the Dead*, 137.

35. Pope John Paul II, September 9, 1999.

36. "Agony of East Timor," 3.

37. Pope John Paul II, "Speech in Taci-Tolu," October 12, 1989.

38. Sian Powell, "Church on a Tightrope of Neutrality, " *Australian*, August 28, 1999.

39. Kohen, *From the Place of the Dead*, 112–13.

40. Ibid, 113.

41. Ibid.

42. Cited by Kohen, *From the Place of the Dead*, 113.

43. Roger Etchegaray, "Cardinal Etchegary Visits East Timor," in *Briefing: The Official Journal of the Catholic Bishops' Conference of England, Wales, and Scotland* (London: Catholic Communications Service, 1996).

44. Carey, "East Timor," 20.

45. Ibid., 20.

46. Matthew Jardine, *East Timor: Genocide in Paradise* (Tucson: Odonian Press, 1995), 17.

47. Neil King Jr. and Jay Solomon, "We Are No Fools: Diplomatic Gambles at the Highest Levels Failed in East Timor," *Wall Street Journal*, October 21, 1999.

48. Seth Mydans, "Priests and Nuns Become Targets of Terror," *New York Times*, September 12, 1999.

49. Peter Carey, "Secede and We Destroy You," *World Today*, October 1999, 4–5.

50. Ibid.

51. Ali Alatas, Indonesia's foreign minister, often used this descriptive phrase; cited in Michael E. Salla, "Creating the 'Ripe Moment' in the East Timor Conflict," *Journal of Peace Research* 34 (1997): 449–66.

52. Christopher Wren, "UN Creates an Authority To Start Governing East Timor," *New York Times*, October 26, 1999.

53. Jeffrey Bartholet and Ron Moreau, "The Hunters and the Hunted," *Newsweek*, September 27, 1999, 38.

54. "Wahid Apologizes to East Timorese Victims," February 29, 2000, FBIS-EAS-2000-0229.

55. *New York Times*, May 10, 2000.

56. Charles Tilly, *From Mobilization to Revolution* (New York: McGraw-Hill, 1978), 69. This concept should not be confused with Karl Deutsch's use of the term, which refers to transformative social processes. Karl Deutsch, "Social Mobilization and Political Development," *American Political Science Review* 55, no. 3 (1961): 493–515.

57. Doug McAdam, *Political Process and the Development of Black Insurgency* (Chicago: University of Chicago Press, 1982), 51.

58. Alberto Arenas, "Education and Nationalism in East Timor," *Social Justice* 25, no. 2 (1998): 131.

59. Benedict Anderson, *Imagined Communities* (London: Verso, 1983), 25.

60. Nancy Melissa Lutz, "Colonization, Decolonization and Integration: Language Policies in East Timor, Indonesia," paper presented at the annual meeting of the American Anthropological Association, Chicago, November 20, 1991.

61. Joseph Craig Jenkins and Charles Perrow, "Insurgency of the Powerless: Farm Worker Movements (1946–1972)," *American Sociological Review* 42, no. 2 (1977): 250.

62. McAdam, *Political Process*, 21.

63. Milton J. Esman and Shibley Telhami, *International Organizations and Ethnic Conflict* (Ithaca, N.Y.: Cornell University Press, 1995), 10.

64. John W. Kingdon, *Agendas, Alternatives, and Public Policy* (New York: Harper-Collins, 1984), 188.

65. Kohen, *From the Place of the Dead*, 17.

66. Taylor, *East Timor*, 47.

67. Carey, "Catholic Church," 83.

68. Lundry, "From Passivity to Political Resource." Also see http://www.etan.org/etreligious/2001a/polresrce.htm.

69. Kohen, *From the Place of the Dead*, 17.

70. Carey, "Catholic Church," 83.

71. James Traub, "Inventing East Timor," *Foreign Affairs* 79 (July/August 2000): 74–89; the quotation is on 74.

72. Lundry, "From Passivity to Political Resource," http://etan.org/ereligious/2001a/polresrce.htm.

Part Four

THE CHALLENGE OF JUSTICE

THIS PART OFFERS THREE OF the volume's most compelling case studies detailing the Catholic Church's paradoxical struggle for justice. These chapters on Brazil, Rwanda, and Angola each recall that the Roman Catholic Church itself can be understood in paradoxical terms—sometimes heroic and courageous, and other times cowardly and spineless—in the face of social injustice, poverty, and even genocide.

In chapter 9, Christine Kearney provides an important analysis of the development of liberation theology in Brazil as a unique Catholic response to poverty and oppression, and the subsequent Vatican reaction to that approach. Her account of the Catholic Church taking a preferential option for the poor in the face of military dictatorship, human rights abuses, and poverty speaks to the tension between the Church's traditional role as a member of the ruling elite to its new role as, in Himes's framework, "Church as people of God." Kearney first offers a brief history of church–state relations in Brazil and then discusses the shifts toward liberation theology in the 1960s and away from it in the 1980s and 1990s. She concludes with a discussion of how Catholicism has managed to remain robust in a democratic Brazil.

Chapter 10 examines the 1994 genocide in Rwanda. This contribution by the Rwandan Jesuit priest Elisée Rutagambwa speaks in a powerful way to the Church in tension and paradox, and it offers the volume's most theological analysis. A word of introduction is in order: Rutagambwa lost some forty family members in the Rwandan genocide, including his father, brother, four-year-old sister, grandparents, and two uncles, and he was forced to spend part of his childhood as a refugee. His chapter offers a detailed history of the role of Catholicism in Rwanda, shows how the church was complicit in the genocide, and offers some strategies for the Church to become an agent for national reconciliation and healing.

Linda Heywood's account in chapter 11 of the Catholic Church in Angola is a clear example of the church as a strategic moral actor. She details the historical development of the Catholic Church in Angola and then highlights the watershed pastoral letter of November 1989, in which the Angolan bishops called upon the warring factions in the postindependence civil war to end the hostilities, respect human rights, and hold free elections. As a strategic moral actor, the bishops positioned the Angolan Church to be an advocate for peace, and in so doing they gained the respect of all sides.

Chapter 9

The Brazilian Church: Reintegrating Ontology and Epistemology

Christine A. Kearney

THE EMINENT HISTORIAN Thomas Skidmore tells us that in March of 1500, King Manuel of Portugal celebrated a special mass to mark the launch of his greatest fleet of ships. The fleet was to sail around the tip of Africa to India, repeating Vasco da Gama's famous voyage of a few years earlier. To announce Portugal's dedication to the Christian mission, the ships' flags were emblazoned with crosses. But the fleet never made it to India. The lead ship, captained by Pedro Álvares Cabral, blew off course, and on April 23 of the same year landed in what today is the state of Bahia in Brazil. Cabral promptly claimed the "new" land for the king of Portugal and the Holy Church, and he called it Terra da Vera Cruz, Land of the True Cross.[1] Thus Brazil was born, and thus the Roman Catholic Church marked it from the very beginning.

Catholicism is without doubt an integral part of Brazil's historical, intellectual, social, political, and economic identity. Brazil is the largest Catholic country in the world, with more than 130 million Catholics, and for most of Brazil's five-hundred-year history, Catholicism has been the official state religion.[2] However, despite this apparently secure position, the Church's role in Brazilian society, and its relationship to secular authority in particular, have been complex, changing, and not always straightforwardly powerful.

During the colonial period (1500–1822), crown authorities and wealthy land-owners dominated Church officials both institutionally and morally. Given the great distance, the colonial Catholic Church in Brazil had a limited and periodic connection to Rome, a fact that compounded its dependence on secular authority. This pattern continued after independence during the imperial period (1822–89). The First Republic (1889–1930) saw the Brazilian Catholic Church lose its position as the official state religion but, ironically, also allowed it to reconnect with Rome and to develop an institutional identity and authority separate from the Brazilian state. During the dictatorship of Getúlio Vargas (1930–45), Church authorities lobbied for and secured the reinstatement of Catholicism as Brazil's official religion. This period also witnessed a close collaboration of Brazilian Church leadership with state authorities, especially on matters of social policy.[3] This pattern continued under the Second Republic (1945–64), but it changed again markedly during the military dictatorship years (1964–85), when the Catholic hierarchy abandoned its conservative support of the state and, under the banner of liberation theology, became a key advocate of social justice, human rights, and democratic reform.[4]

Most recently, since Brazil's return to democracy in the mid-1980s, scholars have noted an apparent decrease in the Brazilian Catholic Church's influence. They have highlighted the weakening of liberation theology–inspired social movements, such as the *comunidades eclesiais de base* (ecclesiastical base communities, or CEBs); the silencing of liberal clergy by Rome; and, finally, the remarkable increase in Pentecostal churches' influence.[5] Although this chapter does not dispute these trends, it does propose that the evidence also supports an optimistic outlook for Brazilian Catholicism.[6] Viewed in historical and cultural context, Catholicism is actually quite robust in Brazil, and it may well be on the verge of reclaiming some of the religious ground "lost" to the Pentecostals.

The chapter has four sections. The first offers a brief history of Brazilian Church–state relations, focusing on enduring patterns and structures. The second describes the period since the 1960s, and especially the two major shifts in the Brazilian Church's orientation during this time, first toward liberation theology and then back toward "traditional" concerns in the 1990s. The third section assesses the strength of the Catholic Church in Brazil today. Finally, the conclusion draws implications, both for the possible future(s) of Catholicism in Brazil, as well as for the study of religion by social and political scientists.

Church and State in Brazil: Background

Brazil was a Portuguese colony for more than three hundred years—much longer than any of the United States were British colonies and longer than Brazil has been an independent state. Not surprisingly, the colonial period left deep marks on Brazilian society, including the religious realm. "From the very beginning," the Brazilian economist Celso Furtado once said, "Brazil was a business." It was an asset to be exploited.[7] An opportunistic, mercantile attitude shaped Brazil's development. Economically, it led to an emphasis on agricultural and extractive enterprises, which tended to be both land and labor intensive. These, in turn, justified a reliance on African slavery, with Brazil becoming the second largest slave society in the Americas and one of the last to abolish slavery in 1888. Politically, the Portuguese colonial administration resembled that of Spanish America. A few favored subjects owned most of the land, and a hierarchical bureaucracy linked them and local administrators to the crown; but on the ground in Brazil, the landed elite and administrators had a great deal of freedom.[8] Socially, the main consequence of this system was an extraordinary level of inequality—between rich and poor, landowner and landless, white and black.[9]

The Catholic Church's place in this colonial milieu was paradoxical. On the one hand, in psychological and spiritual terms, the Church was quite potent. The Portuguese took very seriously their duty to Christianize the indigenous Brazilians and African slaves. Order priests, especially Jesuits, helped them in this mission and also assumed responsibility for education, health care, and record keeping. Christian values infused and shaped institutions, in both Portugal and the new world. There was very little separation between secular and sacred authority, state and church, cosmology and history.[10]

Nevertheless, as an institution in its own right, the colonial Church was quite weak. The Portuguese crown had authority from the papacy to establish dioceses, appoint bishops, collect tithes, and interpret papal directives. Indeed, for the entire colonial period and beyond, Rome had almost no direct contact with or effective authority over the Brazilian Church.[11]

As a result, the Catholic Church became enmeshed in the patriarchal family relationships and patron–client networks that ruled Brazil. At the same time, Catholicism itself became part of a melding of Iberian, indigenous, and African cultures that yielded distinctively "Brazilian" institutions and ideologies, including religious ones. Indeed, by the time of independence in 1822, Brazilian Catholicism was a syncretistic amalgam of beliefs and practices drawn from medieval Christian doctrine and African and Amerindian religions, as well as Portuguese folk superstition and magic.[12]

Independence did not alter much the contours of Brazilian society, nor did it change significantly the Catholic Church's position within it. No social revolution occurred. Instead, Brazil began independent life as a constitutional monarchy with a member of the Portuguese royal family as monarch.[13] This peaceful transition allowed for continuity. There now was an indirectly elected national assembly (to vote for electors, one had to be male, twenty-five years old, Catholic, born free, and own property), but it had little power compared with the emperor and his ministers.[14] The economy remained agricultural, slave based, and foreign trade driven, with Britain replacing Portugal as the key outside influence. Most significantly, however, the Catholic Church remained subordinate to the state, and if anything it grew weaker, as the Brazilian emperors took steps to centralize power and to rein in local potentates.[15]

However, the empire's fall in 1889 and the founding of the First Republic (1889–1930) led to important changes. In socioeconomic terms, Brazil altered markedly in some respects. Slavery ended in 1888, and a manufacturing economy began to emerge. The elite's composition and outlook also shifted. There was substantial immigration from Europe, as well as increased urbanization and improvements in education.[16] A "modern" elite, committed to further Brazilian "progress," became prominent, especially within the military.[17] Politically, the First Republic created a more decentralized and accountable government, with a wider (if still limited) franchise and greater opportunities for political party development.[18] But beneath this veneer lurked older trends. Brazil continued very unequal economically and divided racially, with its republican political institutions distorted by clientelism, paternalism, and periodic military interference.

For the Catholic Church, both the First Republic and the subsequent Vargas dictatorship (1930–45) were important formative years. The Constitution of the First Republic disestablished the Catholic Church, which caused some real losses (e.g., of property and control over education). However, it also freed the Brazilian Church for the first time in its history from direct state oversight. The episcopate was able to establish ties with Rome and to bring its doctrine and practices more into line with the orthodox European, and especially Iberian, Catholicism of the time. The number of dioceses and parishes increased, as indicated in table 9.1, as well as the number of priests, monks, nuns, and lay leaders.[19] These trends were strongest in urban areas, and affected mainly the middle and upper classes there, while in the countryside traditional folk Catholicism continued, and the Church remained integrated with and dependent on local systems of "patrimonial-paternalist domination."[20] Ideologically, Church leaders also took on many of the causes of European Catholicism, such as the economic plight of the working-class family and the fight against communism, even though these had little to do with Brazilian reality.[21]

TABLE 9.1.   BRAZIL'S ARCHDIOCESES AND DIOCESES, 1500–2000

Year	Archdioceses	Dioceses
1500–1600	..	1
1700	1	3
1800	1	6
1900	2	17
1920	12	39
1950	17	67
1960	28	96
1970	32	122
1980	35	162
1990	36	195
2000	39	207

Source: CERIS, http://www.ceris.org.br/estatistica/ quadros_estatisticos.asp.

The Church emerged in this period as a powerful societal actor in its own right, one with privileged access to Brazil's government leaders. Dom Sebastião Leme da Silveira Cintra (1882–1942), first the bishop coadjutor and later the cardinal archbishop of Rio de Janeiro, was a key figure in this transition. Leme was a savvy leader, whose perhaps wisest move was to forge an alliance with Vargas, Brazil's modernizing dictator and a very influential political figure for much of the twentieth century. Both men benefited from the relationship. With Leme's help, Vargas was able to take power peacefully. In addition, Leme periodically used Catholic organizations he had helped establish (e.g., the Catholic Electoral League) to support Vargas's policies. In return, Vargas helped Catholicism be reinstated as Brazil's official religion, and he ensured that key Catholic values—such as a ban on divorce—became public policy.[22]

The Catholic leadership's support for Vargas (and for subsequent political regimes) rested on much more than institutional self-interest; it included common values as well. A good example is Vargas's "corporatist" reforms. As Manuel and Mott discuss in chapter 3 of this volume, many Catholic countries adopted corporatist models during the 1920s and 1930s. These policies involved requiring economic actors to join functionally specific peak organizations (labor, agriculture, business, etc.), which the state, in turn, carefully managed. This mode of organizing interest groups was in line with Pope Leo XIII's *Rerum Novarum*, and it enjoyed the support of the Vatican.

Vargas's corporatism is just one example of a broader—though not complete—overlap of interests and values that existed between the Brazilian Catholic Church and the Brazilian state.[23] The Church's conservative, anticommunist, urban-middle-class outlook meshed well with the state's drive for orderly "progress." It meant that the Catholic hierarchy largely supported government initiatives during these years. This is not surprising. For even though the Church had gained institutional independence from the Brazilian state and had become a strong actor in its own right, it had also been shaped in important ways by the same historical and sociological factors that had fashioned Brazil's governing elite.

The Brazilian Church's support of the status quo lasted through the Vargas years (1930–45) and much of the Second Republic (1945–64). Meanwhile, more political, economic, and social changes continued to transform Brazilian society. Politically, Vargas's fall in 1945 ushered in another Republican regime with a wider franchise and stronger political parties than previously. Women now had the vote, and more Brazilians could pass the literacy test. The effective franchise grew to between 35 and 50 percent of the adult population, and political power was decentralized somewhat. Elections tended to be corrupt, and party identities still derived more from personalities, personal loyalties, and local patron–client networks than from abstract ideals or platforms. They also divided along pro- and anti-Vargas lines.[24]

By the early 1960s, the gulf between pro- and anti-Vargas elements was quite pronounced. Economic matters played an important part in this polarization. Particularly after 1950, Brazil continued the ambitious state-led industrialization program initiated under Vargas. These efforts yielded spectacular results. Manufactures became a large proportion of Brazilian exports, and the economy grew at unprecedented rates. In sheer economic size, Brazil's gross domestic product approached the world's twelve largest. In addition, under state tutelage, Brazil's infrastructure (roads, ports, telecommunications) improved dramatically. Not surprisingly, a significant shift of labor to these new economic sectors followed, and masses of poor Brazilians migrated from the Northeast to the industrial South in search of work. In a few short decades, the country evolved from a largely agricultural, rural society to one that was highly industrialized and urban.[25]

One problem with this rapid economic development was that it raised expectations amongst the lower classes—expectations that the Brazilian elite could not (or would not) satisfy. Brazil had always been terribly unequal. The difference in this period, however, was that a substantial number of Brazilian have-nots were now politically aware, concentrated geographically in urban areas, and enfranchised. As such, they constituted a source of potential instability, especially when mobilized by "irresponsible" populist leaders such as Vargas and his followers. At the same time, the ambitious industrialization programs of the Second Republic—which the Brazilian elite largely agreed were needed if Brazil was to become a country of first rank—did not come cheaply. And rather than tax the rich to fund them, successive administrations preferred instead to repress wages and/or print money. The cumulative effects of these policies included government deficits, high inflation, and restless workers. By April 1964, with a leftist follower of Vargas in the presidency threatening socialist measures and staging mass demonstrations, Brazilian military officers had had enough. They carried out a coup that ushered in more than twenty years of military rule.[26]

To Liberation Theology and Back Again: The Brazilian Church since 1964

Although the Church's stance prior to the military dictatorship was largely conservative and supportive of the status quo, as early as the 1950s a more "critical" orientation began to develop. This "Liberationist" Church became dominant in the 1960s and 1970s, and it captured the hopes and imaginations of observers both within and outside Brazil.[27] The Church's relationship to the state altered dramatically. It went from a close ally of the state on most issues to a vocal critic of the military government's social justice record. At the same time, the Church broadened its target constituency, from a focus almost exclusively on the urban middle and working classes to one that included the poor everywhere in Brazil.

A number of influences—national and international, intellectual and spiritual, strategic and institutional—shaped this transformation. Institutionally, the National Conference of Brazilian Bishops (Conferência Nacional dos Bispos do Brasil, CNBB), founded in 1952, was an important factor in that it provided more effective leadership than ever before. It was a central forum in which Brazil's geographically dispersed Church leaders could formulate common programs, coordinate activities, and share information. The CNBB also helped link the Brazilian Church to regional (the Latin American Conference of Bishops) and international (the Vatican) Catholic institutions. Finally, the CNBB successfully mobilized financial resources, both domestically and internationally. Ralph Della Cava speculates that from "the mid–nineteen seventies until the fall of the Berlin Wall in 1989, the Brazilian church was probably the single largest beneficiary of worldwide Roman Catholic philanthropy."[28]

The Liberationist movement in Brazil also drew strength from external Catholic developments. These included the Vatican II reforms of the 1960s, as well as the 1968 meeting of Latin American bishops in Medellín, Colombia, which outlined a regionwide "preferential option for the poor." The latter took inspiration from both Vatican II and liberation theology. Indeed, Brazilian Church leaders were a vanguard for the liberation theology wave that swept Latin America.[29] Locally, it had important consequences. First, the Church supported basic education and literacy campaigns in poor areas. Second, the CNBB sponsored issue-specific pastorals and commissions. These operated independently of parish and diocesan structures and included the Pastoral Land Commission, the Indian Missionary Council, and the Pastoral Workers' Commission. Finally, the CNBB encouraged the formation of CEBs, which were groups of about twenty individuals who met to discuss topics ranging from the Bible and the sacraments to social and political issues affecting the local community. By the late 1980s, it is estimated that there were perhaps one hundred thousand CEBs operating throughout Brazil.[30]

Finally, the military regime (1964–85) helped consolidate and focus the Brazilian Church's already growing Liberationist tendencies. The generals pursued economic development and social peace with a tenacity unprecedented even in Brazil, a country where "order and progress" were well-established goals.[31] Their industrialization projects hurt significantly the Church's new constituency, poor Brazilians. And to silence its opponents, the military also used torture, imprisonment, deprivation of political rights, exile, and occasionally execution.[32]

As a result, the Catholic Church, led by the CNBB, became the military's most powerful critic. It publicized military atrocities both domestically and internationally. It mobilized the CEBs, pastorals, and commissions to pressure for democratic reform. It supported opposition labor unions, political parties such as the Partido dos Trabalhadores (PT, or Workers' Party), and (later) social movements like the Movimento Sem Terra (MST, or Landless Movement).

Moreover, in the process, it educated and empowered a generation of leaders, many of them from traditionally disadvantaged sectors of Brazilian society: the rural poor, *favela* (urban slum) dwellers, Afro- and indigenous Brazilians, and women. Indeed, the Liberationist Catholic Church may have been the most significant contributor to Brazil's key democratic events of the 1980s: the return to civilian rule in 1985, the adoption of a new constitution in 1988, and the election by universal suffrage of a president in 1989.[33]

The years of Brazil's military dictatorship, then, saw the Brazilian Catholic Church adopt new goals, institutional forms, and modes of influence vis-à-vis the state. The preferential option for the poor meant a concern for Brazilians' material conditions and a commitment to their well-being in this world as well as the next. It also saw the formation of new organizations that were grassroots in nature, in contrast to the urban-middle-class Catholic organizations that already existed. Finally, these changes meant that the Church became more than an organization oriented toward the elite that influenced the state from "the top" by pursuing goals mostly having to do with traditional morality. It now also exerted influence "from below," on behalf of all Brazilians, and for much broader "this-worldly" goals.[34]

Nevertheless, during the 1980s and 1990s, the Brazilian Church retreated from its Liberationist stance and returned to more "traditional" concerns and modes of influence.[35] The Vatican under John Paul II played an important role in this process. The pope saw liberation theology as too close to Marxism, and he worked to decrease its influence throughout Latin America. In Brazil, Rome began reviewing seminary instruction and warned São Paulo archdiocesan leaders, for example, that they should not use the figure of "Christ as Revolutionary," which was a central image in liberation theology, to justify antipoverty initiatives.[36] In 1985, the Vatican censured two leading Brazilian liberation theologians, Leonardo and Clodovis Boff. The pope also started replacing "Liberationist" Brazilian bishops with more conservative ones, and he instructed the Brazilian episcopate not to participate directly in politics.[37] The pope's message was clear, and even though the Brazilian Church did not abandon its Liberationist activities altogether, it certainly began to tone them down. Church leaders publicly shifted away from grassroots social justice activities and toward more traditionally religious concerns, such as promotion of the sacraments.[38]

At the same time, the Liberationist Church's very success in helping return democracy to Brazil probably had a dampening effect on further activism. Once the military leaders departed, and "democrats" replaced them, there seemed less need for overt Church involvement in politics. There were now political parties and other secular organizations that could protect Brazilians' rights and interests. Thus, Church leaders naturally reverted to their former ways of interacting with the state. That is, they once again became movers behind the scenes, communicating directly and personally with state officials on matters of religious importance. For example, during José Sarney's term as president, from 1985 to 1990, Dom Luciano Mendes de Almeida, the secretary general and later president of the CNBB, was a "constant fixture in the halls of power" and a close adviser to Sarney.[39] He and other Church leaders consulted with Sarney on a number of matters, including the safety of missionaries in the Brazilian interior, the Brazilian government's economic development plans for the Amazon, violence by landowners against rural workers, and censorship of a controversial film about the Virgin Mary. Still other Brazilian clergy lobbied government leaders— not entirely successfully—against family-planning programs and anti-AIDS initiatives that promoted condom use.[40]

Finally, the behavior of poor Brazilians themselves also provided some justification for the Brazilian Church's retreat from Liberationist doctrine and activity. During the 1980s and 1990s, large numbers of the poor left Catholic grassroots organizations, such as the CEBs, and joined other social movements. More alarming, from a religious standpoint, they also began to join Protestant— and particularly evangelical—churches in great numbers. As table 9.2 illustrates, between 1980 and 2000, the number of Brazilians declaring themselves Catholic declined by about 15 percent. In the same period, those claiming to be evangelicals increased by about 8 percent. The implication is that a good portion of the Catholic losses went to the evangelicals.

Brazilian Catholic leaders, as well as the Vatican, watched these numbers with dismay, and some explained them as the consequence of the Liberationist era's neglect of the spiritual lives of Brazilians. In addition, survey data indicated that many Brazilians—including poor Brazilians—had been turned off by the political aggressiveness and militancy of many Liberationist Church organizations.[41]

TABLE 9.2.   RELIGIOUS COMPOSITION OF BRAZIL

Aspect	1940	1950	1960	1970	1980	1990	2000
Population (millions)	41.2	61.9	70.2	94.1	119.0	146.8	169.8
Catholics (%)	95.0	93.4	93.0	91.7	89.0	83.3	73.6
Evangelicals (%)	2.6	93.4	4.0	5.2	6.6	9.0	15.4
Spiritists (%)	1.1	93.4	1.4	1.3	1.2	1.6	1.7
Others (%)	0.8	93.4	1.0	1.0	1.2	1.0	1.8
No religion (%)	0.5	93.4	0.5	0.8	1.8	5.1	7.3

Sources: IBGE 2000 Census, www.sidra.ibge.gov.br/bda/tabela/protabl.asp?z=t&o=1, "As Influências da Lógica Mercadológica Sobre As Recentes Transformações Na Igreja Católica." [The Influence of Marketing Logic on the Recent Transformations in the Catholic Church], Revista de Estudos da Religião (no. 2 / 2003): 1–23.

Consequently, this was another factor in persuading the Brazilian Catholic Church to revise its agenda and tone down its Liberationist rhetoric. It also motivated the Church to study ways of competing with the Pentecostals.

Scholars trace the success of the Pentecostal movement in Brazil to several factors.[42] First, the Pentecostals are physically present in poor areas of Brazil, particularly in the big cities. There are few Catholic churches in the poor neighborhoods but many Pentecostal churches. Second, the Pentecostals have a direct way of dealing with poor people's problems of unemployment, alcoholism, domestic abuse, gang violence, and drug addiction. They say that demons cause them, and exorcism cures them. "They bring the Bible and prayer to combat revolvers and machine guns: the fire of the Holy Spirit against the fire of weapons."[43]

By contrast, the Catholic Church generally prefers to address the structural causes of these problems and to work for legal and social reforms. Third, Pentecostal preachers promise the poor that they will reap immediate material rewards for their faith in Christ Jesus. They say that living a "clean" life (abstinence, sobriety, hard work), and giving lots of money to their evangelical church will earn them worldly riches. Catholics do not preach this way. Fourth, they insist that their members practice no other religion. They forbid and vilify adherence to Catholicism, as well as to the so-called possession cults, including *umbanda*, *candomblé*, and Kardecism. For its part, Catholicism has traditionally tolerated religious syncretism in Brazil. Finally, Brazilian Pentecostals use aggressive proselytizing, modern media, and electoral politics to advance their agenda, while Catholics have been slow to adopt these practices.[44]

The Pentecostals saw a spiritual and material deficit among Brazil's marginalized, and they capitalized on it. But their example has given Catholics a wake-up call, as well as hints about what methods to use in making a comeback. Brazilian Catholics, at all levels, have certainly responded. First, a strong Catholic Charismatic movement has emerged that appeals to the same spiritual yearnings that Pentecostalism satisfies. It has active lay participation and leadership, and it enjoys the support of both the Brazilian episcopate and Rome. Second, the Church is giving renewed support to traditional Catholic groups that venerate Jesus, the Holy Spirit, the Virgin Mary, and the saints. Finally, Church leaders are making special efforts to appeal to young people. They sponsor retreats, special youth masses, and other gatherings that are designed to be uplifting and joyful. Many of these efforts take advantage of popular music. There are even "pop-star priests" who fill stadiums, attract thousands to their regular masses, and have top-selling compact disks.[45]

Are these initiatives too little and too late? The jury is still out, but some see them as a potential revival and credit them with luring back middle-class Catholics who had been disenchanted with liberation theology's excesses, attracting the young and reconverting Pentecostal defectors to Catholicism, and helping to reverse the decline in religious vocations.[46]

Assessing the Brazilian Church Today

As leading scholars on the Brazilian Church aptly remind us, the Catholic Church is not an organization like any other. In the first place, "the Church" is actually *many* churches, encompassing a range of actors and organizations, with noticeably different material interests and, sometimes, even theological bents. Second, the Brazilian Church, in addition to being a national institution, is also part both of an international Catholic "state" centered in Rome and a transnational network of Catholic organizations. Finally, the Brazilian Church has goals that transcend mere material or political ones; they include a *spiritual* mission.[47]

For these reasons, we must assess the Brazilian Church's current role in Brazilian society in a nuanced fashion. It is tempting to romanticize the Church's political role during the Liberationist era and to mourn its passing.[48] However, the Church's traditionalist turn in the 1980s and 1990s does not represent a complete change in policy; nor does it spell disaster for Catholic influence in Brazilian society. Catholic leaders continue to work for social justice and they have not altogether abandoned their grassroots organizations. Their focus on devotional issues rather than sociopolitical ones is a necessary part of their mission, and their use of elite-level influence is neither new nor sinister. Most important, there is evidence that the Church's current policies and methods are effective, even from the perspective of competing with the Pentecostals.

Although the Catholic Church has lost much of its zeal for social mobilization, it continues to work for democracy and social reform. For example, the Church has supported a number of progressive initiatives, including Brazil's first Bill of Rights, anti-police brutality legislation, prison reform legislation, policies to protect street children, land reforms and policies to protect landless workers, public housing reforms, health care reform, and the like. In addition, the Brazilian Bishops' Council continues its activities, albeit on a smaller, less public scale, with the CEBs, the Pastoral Land Commission, the Indian Missionary Council, and the Pastoral Workers' Council. Finally, the Catholic Church supports and works with other progressive organizations in Brazil, including the MST and the PT, whose leader, Luís Inácio "Lula" da Silva, was elected president of Brazil in 2002.[49]

Moreover, liberal members of the clergy still have some influence in the CNBB, whose directives and public statements continue to express social justice concerns. For example, in April 1996, the CNBB published a four-year plan called Rumo ao Novo Milenio (Way to the New Millennium). It outlined the council's intentions to work on the human rights initiatives outlined above.[50] In addition, by opening an office in Brasília, the CNBB set up a direct line with national policymakers. Its staff is available to consult with the members of the executive and legislative branches, as well as to aid them in their social programs. The goal is to support social justice and democratic "nation building" without becoming directly involved in formal politics.[51] In other words, the CNBB aims to be a sort of "moral watchdog" for Brazilian society.[52]

The Brazilian Catholic Church's conservative turn, then, has not been complete. But has its current model of state/societal influence been effective, and has it cost Catholicism influence in Brazil? These are difficult questions, mainly because the empirical evidence is ambiguous. On the one hand, the census data discussed in the last section seem to indicate losses to the Catholic Church, as evidenced by the decline in the number of Brazilians declaring themselves to be Catholic and the increase in the number of Brazilians claiming to be evangelicals or to have no religion at all. But some Brazilian scholars have questioned the conclusions that should be drawn from these figures.

In a recent article, Alberto Antoniazzi writes that the census figures are misleading for a few reasons. First, and most important, there is ample evidence that many Brazilians practice more than one religion. For example, a 2002 study sponsored by the Center for Religious Statistics and Social Investigations (Centro de Estatística Religiosa e Investigações Sociais, or CERIS) conducted interviews in the six major metropolitan areas of Brazil and found that 25 percent of those interviewed attended the services of more than one religious denomination. In most cases, individuals were practicing Catholicism, as well as one or more of the possession cults, including *umbanda*, *candomblé*, and Kardecism.[53] The census questionnaire, however, allows the respondent to list only one religion. This means, second, that the actual numbers of Catholics and possession cult members were probably miscounted in the 2000 and previous censuses. In fact, Antoniazzi thinks that in previous censuses the numbers of Catholics were probably inflated somewhat, and therefore that the declines shown for Catholicism in 2000 were probably not as sharp as the numbers suggest. At the same time, he observes that Brazilians in general have been becoming more educated, worldly, and self-reliant. Thus the increases in the numbers of "no religion," as well as the declines in the reported numbers of Catholics, may reflect not so much actual changes as the increased willingness of respondents to list non-Catholic options first.[54]

Despite these caveats, however, the census data do show a significant increase in the numbers of Pentecostal Brazilians. And because the Pentecostals expressly forbid their adherents to patronize the possession cults, or any other religion, their reported numbers are probably fairly accurate—that is, the "multiple-religious-affiliation" factor can be assumed to have less of an effect on them. Or can it? Historically, Brazilians have combined elements of different religions in their spiritual practices. The Catholic Church has tended to tolerate and at times even to encourage this syncretism. This tolerance can be interpreted as a weakness of Catholicism vis-à-vis Pentecostalism. But Pentecostalism itself is not free of influences from other Brazilian religions. Birman and Leite argue that the evangelicals' exorcism rites in particular depend to a substantial degree on the values and spiritual sensibilities of Catholicism and the possession cults, even while they condemn them. As a result, one can speak of a "syncretic Pentecostalism" in Brazil.[55] Only more sensitive polling and survey methods will be able to confirm or deny the existence of this trend, as well as what it may mean for the relative strength of each denomination within the syncretistic potpourri that is religion in Brazil.

Nonetheless, it is safe to say that Catholicism is unlikely to lose its preeminent place in the mix. Certainly, the Church needs to do more to attract and retain members, and it especially needs to do a better job of being actively present in poor Brazilian neighborhoods. These are areas where the Brazilian Catholic Church can learn from the successes of the evangelical churches. But the Catholic Church's broader influence in Brazilian society should not be underestimated either. This brings us again to the issue of whether the influence strategy that the Church has adopted in the post–1985 period is really effective. Here, a few observations are in order.

First, the Brazilian Church's current influence strategy may be somewhat elitist but also has some distinct advantages. In general, the strategy fits well with Brazil's political structures—its strong executive, weak political parties and legislature, pervasive patron–client relations, and corporatist interest organizations. Moreover, movements that are too radical have a tendency to alienate influential sectors of the Brazilian population, as well as to invite repression—and this is especially true at the local level. Witness the frequent massacres of rural workers, indigenous groups, and the like that get in the way of landowners, mining companies, and other wealthy Brazilians. The government no longer formally represses civilians, but it has not been all that effective at stopping this kind of violence.[56] So working for gradual change from above, while lending support and protection for grassroots initiatives, shows political acumen on the part of the Brazilian Catholic leadership.

Second, many Brazilians view politics with cynicism. They have good reason. There have been several scandals involving government officials who use their offices to funnel public resources, contracts, and other favors to their friends, family members, and supporters. The most egregious example is President Fernando Collor, who was impeached in 1992 for taking bribes and brokering favors.[57] Another is the illegal fundraising and bribery scandal that currently is threatening the credibility of the Worker's Party and Lula da Silva's government, as well as Lula's reelection prospects.[58] After Brazil's return to democracy, the Catholic Church could have created or formally allied itself with a political party—as it has done with Christian Democratic parties in many other Latin American and European countries. Instead, the Brazilian Church has chosen, as it has done many times in the past (e.g., under Cardinal Leme), to remain outside the political fray. This choice has had the advantage of shielding the Church from the dirt that often flies in Brazilian politics and has also allowed it to speak more convincingly for *all* sectors of Brazilian society, rather than be labeled partisan.

This strategy may be paying off. Throughout the 1990s, the Church has consistently topped the list of institutions that Brazilians say they most trust. For example, in a telephone survey conducted by Latinobarometer in 2001, respondents were asked how much confidence they had in various national institutions, including the Church. The results, shown in table 9.3, reveal that in Brazil 58 percent of those polled said they had "a lot" of confidence in the Church. By comparison, the army received an "a lot" of confidence rating of 30 percent; the judiciary of 18 percent; the president of 15 percent; the police of 14 percent; the National Congress of 9 percent; and political parties of only 6 percent. These results are startling—not only for the low esteem in which Brazilians hold most of their democratic institutions but also for the high regard that they have for the Catholic Church. The results of the survey are similar for the rest of Central and South America; but nowhere else, except in Venezuela, does the Catholic Church receive the high approval rating that it does in Brazil.[59] Surely, the Church leadership's choice to exert influence from outside formal politics, as well as to use its historic place as a privileged corporate actor to effect reform from the top, has contributed to the unparalleled credibility that the Catholic Church enjoys in Brazil today.

Conclusion

The Brazilian Catholic Church's five-hundred-year history shows it to be a highly adaptable and influential institution in Brazilian society. As political, economic, and social changes have occurred, the Church has tailored its policies and influence strategies to suit new realities. A short-term focus may reveal a decline in the last decades of the Church's overtly activist and grassroots orientations, as well as an increase in challenges to the Church's hegemony from other religious and secular movements. But a longer-term view suggests that the Church's role as a privileged corporate actor in Brazilian politics has endured, and that its place in Brazilian culture, at both the elite and popular levels, remains pivotal.

Nevertheless, recent events do have implications for the Brazilian Church's policies going forward. The successes of the Pentecostals highlight areas where Catholicism can do better. In particular, Church leaders need to continue to pay closer attention to Brazilians' spiritual needs than perhaps they did during the Liberationist era. The CNBB and the clergy are aware of this imperative, and their efforts to attract young people and to make the sacraments more accessible are steps in the right direction. But more could probably be done to help Brazilians—and especially poor Brazilians—cope with day-to-day problems and the toll these take on spiritual well-being. Ideally, more churches would be built in poor

TABLE 9.3. CONFIDENCE OF LATIN AMERICANS IN VARIOUS NATIONAL INSTITUTIONS
(% OF RESPONDENTS)

Institutions	A lot	Some	A Little	None	No Reply	Don't Know
Brazil						
Armed forces	30	23	28	16	1	2
The Church	58	16	16	8	1	1
National Congress	9	14	40	31		24
The judiciary	18	21	38	20	2	2
Police	14	17	40	27	1	1
Political parties	6	14	38	39	1	2
The president	15	17	34	31	1	2
South America						
Armed forces	16	28	34	21	1	1
The Church	45	26	18	11		
National Congress	5	19	36	36	1	2
The judiciary	8	21	39	29	1	1
Police	8	23	37	31	1	1
Political parties	4	16	34	44	1	1
The president	9	23	34	33	1	1
Central America						
Armed forces	11	15	33	36	5	
The Church	56	23	18	10	1	
National Congress	8	15	36	38	3	
The judiciary	8	17	39	33	3	
Police	10	17	39	32	1	
Political parties	5	13	34	45	3	
The president	10	16	36	36	2	
Latin America						
Armed forces	14	24	33	26	2	1
The Church	49	23	18	10	1	
National Congress	6	18	36	37		21
The judiciary	8	19	39	31	2	1
Police	9	21	37	31	1	
Political parties	4	15	34	44	2	1
The president	9	21	35	34	1	1

Note: The survey also asked about trust in television; survey performed by telephone in each country; country sample size varied from 993 to 1,207; South America was 1,207; Central America was 5,961; and Latin America was 18,038.

Source: Latinobarometer Telephone Survey, 2001, available from *Polling the Nations*, http://poll.orspub.com/poll/lpext.dll?f=templates&fn=main-h.htm.

neighborhoods, and more clergy would be stationed there. But in practice, this solution is probably not feasible. Part of the problem, of course, is that vocations have not been keeping up with increases in population, as illustrated in table 9.4, so the Brazilian Church—similar to the Catholic Church in many other countries—finds itself understaffed.

Years of high inflation, a crushing national debt, decreases in government funding for social programs, and increases in unemployment have strained both Brazil's and the Church's resources to the hilt. But perhaps these gaps can continue to be filled by Brazil's traditionally active laity and the CEBs, along with funding from international sources.

Finally, our analysis has some important implications for social science theory. The Brazilian Catholic Church is a uniquely multilayered and multidimensional institution. It acts within a national context, but, as Ferrari argues in chapter 2, it is also part of an international Catholic "state" headquartered in Rome, as well as a transnational network of Catholic organizations. The Church is typical of political actors in general in that it has institutional interests that it strategically pursues. But it is unlike other actors in the sense that it is bound not only by mundane self-interest but by moral and spiritual imperatives as well. As arguably the oldest institution in Brazil, the Catholic Church has resources that are different from those of just about any other Brazilian institution, religious or secular. These derive not just from the number of adherents it has at any given point, or the money in its coffers, or the number of buildings it owns—although these things also count. Rather, the Catholic Church in Brazil can invoke cultural and psychological resources that come from five hundred years of infusing Brazilian institutions. In other words, it exercises power in the Gramscian sense.[60] The public outrage in reaction to the 1995 *chute na santa* (goal kicking the saint) incident—when a Pentecostal bishop from the Universal Church of the Kingdom of God disrespectfully touched a statue of Our Lady of Aparecida with his foot on live television—is a poignant example of this fact.[61]

The Brazilian Church's special status thus demonstrates that power combines both material and ideological elements—a prominent truth in this era of combating religious "extremism." It also challenges our usual categorizations of institutions—by function, geographic scope, and/or material circumstances—and stretches definitions of actor self-interest. Religious institutions do not act solely according to economic incentives; nor can their behavior reliably be predicted on this basis. Gauging their power and influence requires both a contextual sensibility and a willingness to view human beings as more than material creatures. It also requires a longer-term perspective than political scientists are normally able to take, as well as a commitment to explaining *continuity* as well as short-term change. Without these adjustments, the Liberationist episode in Brazilian Church history takes on too large a significance and masks Catholicism's historic and enduring structural strengths.

TABLE 9.4. BRAZIL'S PARISHES AND CLERGY, 1970–2000

Aspect	1970	1975	1980	1985	1990	1995	2000
Parishes	5,577	5,947	6,341	6,788	7,357	7,901	8,787
Inhabitants per parish	16,701	17,645	18,698	19,443	19,672	19,722	19,324
Total clergy	13,092	12,589	12,688	13,207	14,198	15,310	16,772
Diocesan clergy							
Total	5,040	4,952	5,159	5,551	6,560	7,724	9,207
Brazilian-born	3,866	3,777	4,010	4,623	5,607	6,810	8,295
Foreign-born	1,093	1,172	1,102	928	952	911	911
No response	81	3	47	..	1	3	1
Order Clergy							
Total	8,052	7,637	7,529	7,656	7,638	7,586	7,565
Brazilian-born	3,788	3,620	3,643	4,293	4,720	4,967	5,319
Foreign-born	4,262	4,017	3,884	3,363	2,913	2,618	2,237
No response	2	..	2	..	5	1	9
Inhabitants per clergyman	7,114	8,335	9,344	9,993	10,193	10,178	10,124

Source: CERIS, www.ceris.org.br/estatistica/quadros_estatisticos.asp.

For these reasons, this study invites social scientists to shift their perspective from the standard view. It asks us to look not only at the agents of change (parties, interest groups, social movements, institutions, classes) but also at the context within which they act. It encourages us to take the long view, rather than to focus too narrowly on short-term events and shifts. Finally, and most important, however, this study of the Brazilian Church sheds special light on the concrete effects that abstract factors—such as beliefs, ideas, and culture—can have on political actors' goals and the policy decisions they make. In short, to paraphrase Manuel and Mott's argument in chapter 3, this study is an invitation to reintegrate ontology and epistemology.

Notes

1. Thomas E. Skidmore, *Brazil: Five Centuries of Change* (Oxford: Oxford University Press, 1999), 5–8.

2. Estimates vary as to the exact number. According to figures compiled by the National Conference of Brazilian Bishops (CNBB, http://www.cnbb.org.br) in March 2004, 73.9 percent of Brazil's 177.8 million people were Catholics. These are close to figures provided both by the Brazilian Institute for Geography and Statistics (IBGE, http://www.ibge.gov.br), as well as by Brazil's Center for Religious Statistics and Social Investigations (CERIS, http://www.ceris.org.br).

3. Throughout this chapter, I use "the Church," "the Brazilian Church," and "the Brazilian Catholic Church" interchangeably.

4. Thomas C. Bruneau, *The Political Transformation of the Brazilian Catholic Church* (Cambridge: Cambridge University Press, 1974), chap. 1 passim.

5. See, e.g., Patrícia Birman and Márcia Pereira Leite, "Whatever Happened to What Used to be the Largest Catholic Country in the World?" *Daedalus* 129, no. 2 (2000): 271–90.

6. Similar views are expressed by, among others, Madeleine Cousineau, "Not Blaming the Pope: The Roots of the Crisis in Brazilian Base Communities," *Journal of Church and State* 44 (2003): 349–65; and Edward L. Cleary, "The Brazilian Catholic Church and Church–State Relations: Nation-Building," *Journal of Church and State* 39, no. 2 (1997): 253–72.

7. Interview with author, Rio de Janeiro, October 1995.

8. Skidmore, *Brazil*, 10–14, 25–26.

9. On enduring colonial social patterns, see Sérgio Buarque de Holanda, *Raízes do Brasil*, 26th ed. (São Paulo: Companhia das Letras, 1995), 39–40, 57–62; and Gilberto Freyre, *Casa-Grande & Senzala: Formação da Família Brasileira sob o Regime da Economia Patriarcal*, 18th ed. (Rio de Janeiro: J. Olympio, 1977), li. On race in Brazil, see Carl Degler, *Neither Black Nor White: Slavery and Race Relations in Brazil and the United States* (Madison: University of Wisconsin Press, 1971); and Thomas E. Skidmore, *Black into White: Race and Nationality in Brazilian Thought* (New York: Oxford University Press, 1974).

10. Cleary, "Brazilian Catholic Church," 255. Francisco M. P. Teixeira, *História Concisa do Brasil* (São Paulo: Global, 1993), 69; cited in Cleary, ibid.

11. Bruneau, *Political Transformation of the Brazilian Catholic Church*, 16.
12. See Yvonne Maggie, *Medo do Feitiço: Relações entre Magia e Poder no Brasil* (Rio de Janeiro: Arquivo Nacional, 1992); Donald Ramos, "Gossip, Scandal and Popular Culture in Golden Age Brazil," *Journal of Social History*, Summer 2000, 887–912; and Carole A. Myscofski, "The Magic of Brazil: Practice and Prohibition in the Early Colonial Period, 1590–1620," *History of Religions* 40, no. 2 (2001): 153–76. On indigenous Brazilians, see John Hemming, *Red Gold: The Conquest of the Brazilian Indians* (Cambridge: Harvard University Press, 1978). Because of the Brazilian Church's isolation, and the absence of links with Rome, Brazilian Catholicism remained virtually untouched by events in Europe (e.g., the Reformation and Counter-Reformation), as well as by changes in Roman Catholic doctrine brought about by the various councils (e.g., the Council of Trent).
13. Skidmore, *Brazil*, 35–42.
14. Leslie Bethell, "Politics in Brazil: From Elections without Democracy to Democracy without Citizenship," *Daedalus* 129, no. 2 (2000): 5-7.
15. Skidmore, *Brazil*, 43–55.
16. Ibid., 84–92.
17. See Christine A. Kearney, "The Comparative Influence of Neoliberal Ideas: Economic Culture and Stabilization in Brazil," Ph.D. diss., Brown University, 2001, chap. 5.
18. Bethell, "Politics in Brazil," 7.
19. Bruneau, *Political Transformation of the Brazilian Catholic Church*, 35–37, chap. 2 passim.
20. Procópio Camargo, *O Movimento de Natal* (Brussels: Centre de Documentation sur L'Action des Églises dans le Monde, 1966), 214; quoted in Bruneau, *Political Transformation of the Brazilian Catholic Church*, 49.
21. Bruneau, *Political Transformation of the Brazilian Catholic Church*, 43–47.
22. Ibid., 41–47. See also Scott Mainwaring, *The Catholic Church and Politics in Brazil, 1916–1985* (Stanford, Calif.: Stanford University Press, 1986).
23. W. E. Hewitt, "Catholicism, Social Justice, and the Brazilian Corporatist State since 1930," *Journal of Church & State* 32, no. 4 (1990): 831–50, for a detailed discussion of Brazilian corporatism.
24. Skidmore, *Brazil*, 127–30.
25. Ibid., 138–49.
26. Thomas E. Skidmore, *Politics of Brazil, 1930–1964: An Experiment in Democracy* (New York: Oxford University Press, 1967), 294–302.
27. The liberation theology literature is vast. Some good introductory texts include Gustavo Gutierrez, *A Theology of Liberation: History, Politics and Solution*, trans. and ed. Sister Caridad Inda and John Eagleson (Maryknoll, N.Y.: Orbis Books, 1973); Leonardo Boff and Clodovis Boff, *Introducing Liberation Theology*, trans. Paul Burns (Maryknoll, N.Y.: Orbis Books, 1987); and Phillip Berryman, *Liberation Theology* (Philadelphia: Temple University Press, 1987).
28. Ralph Della Cava, "Transnational Religions: The Roman Catholic Church in Brazil & the Orthodox Church in Russia," *Sociology of Religion* 62, no. 4 (2001): 542.
29. Scott Mainwaring, "Grass-Roots Catholic Groups and Politics in Brazil," in *The Progressive Church in Latin America*, ed. Scott Mainwaring and Alexander Wilde (Notre Dame, Ind.: University of Notre Dame Press, 1989), 151–52.

30. Ibid., 151. See also John Burdick, *Looking for God in Brazil: The Progressive Church in Urban Brazil's Religious Arena* (Berkeley: University of California Press, 1993); and Madeleine Cousineau Adriance, *Promised Land: Base Christian Communities and the Struggle for the Amazon* (Albany: State University of New York Press, 1995).

31. Kearney, "Comparative Influence of Neoliberal Ideas," chap. 5.

32. Skidmore, *Brazil*, 163–66.

33. Ralph Della Cava, "The 'People's Church,' the Vatican and *Abertura*," in *Democratizing Brazil: Problems of Transition and Consolidation*, ed. Alfred Stepan (New York: Oxford University Press), 143–47; Mainwaring, "Grass-Roots Catholic Groups and Politics in Brazil," 166–71. See also José Ivo Follman, "Progressive Catholicism and Left-Wing Party Politics in Brazil," in *The Church at the Grassroots in Latin America: Perspectives on Thirty Years of Activism*, ed. John Burdick and W. E. Hewitt (Westport, Conn.: Praeger, 2000), 53–67; Margaret Keck, *The Workers' Party and Democratization in Brazil* (New Haven, Conn.: Yale University Press, 1992); and Emir Sader and Ken Silverstein, *Without Fear of Being Happy: Lula, the Workers' Party, and Brazil* (New York: Verso, 1991).

34. W. E. Hewitt, "Origins and Prospects of the Option for the Poor in Brazilian Catholicism," *Journal for the Scientific Study of Religion* 28, no. 2 (1989): 127–30.

35. Understandably, much recent scholarship has attempted to understand this shift's causes and significance. See, e.g., the works collected in *The Church at the Grassroots in Latin America*, ed. Burdick and Hewitt.

36. *Folha de São Paulo*, May 30, 1984, 6, cited in Hewitt, "Origins and Prospects," 131.

37. Thomas C. Bruneau and W. E. Hewitt, "Catholicism and Political Action in Brazil: Limitations and Prospects," in *Conflict and Competition: The Latin American Church in a Changing Environment*, ed. Edward L. Cleary and Hannah Stewart-Gambino (Boulder, Colo.: Lynne Rienner, 1992), 53–54.

38. Hewitt, "Origins and Prospects," 127–30.

39. Ibid., 129.

40. Ibid.

41. See Thomas C. Bruneau and W. E. Hewitt, "Patterns of Church Influence in Brazil's Political Transition," *Comparative Politics* 22, no. 1 (October 1989): 39–61; and W. E. Hewitt, *Base Christian Communities and Social Change in Brazil* (Lincoln: University of Nebraska Press, 1991).

42. See Rowan Ireland, *Kingdoms Come: Religion and Politics in Brazil* (Pittsburgh: University of Pittsburgh Press, 1991); David Lehmann, *Struggle for the Spirit: Religious Transformation and Popular Culture in Brazil and Latin America* (Cambridge: Polity, 1996); and David Martin, *Tongues of Fire: The Explosion of Protestantism in Latin America* (Oxford: Basil Blackwell, 1990).

43. Birman and Leite, "Whatever Happened," 281.

44. Ibid., 278–80.

45. Ibid., 284–85; and Peter B. Clarke, "'Pop-Star' Priests and the Catholic Response to the 'Explosion' of Evangelical Protestantism in Brazil: The Beginning of the End of the 'Walkout'?" *Journal of Contemporary Religion* 14, no. 2 (1999): 203–16.

46. Della Cava, "Transnational Religions," 544; Clarke, "'Pop-Star' Priests," 208–10.

47. Bruneau and Hewitt, "Catholicism and Political Action in Brazil," 47–49;

Mainwaring, "Grass-Roots Catholic Groups and Politics in Brazil," 152–58; and Cleary, "Brazilian Catholic Church," 269–72.

48. See Edward L. Cleary, *Crisis and Change: The Church in Latin America Today* (Maryknoll, N.Y.: Orbis Books, 1985); and W. E. Hewitt, "The Changing of the Guard: Transformations in the Politico-Religious Attitudes and Behaviors of CEB Members in São Paulo, 1984–1993," *Journal of Church and State* 38 (1996): 115–36.

49. Cleary, "Brazilian Catholic Church," 265–69.

50. Conferência Nacional dos Bispos do Brasil, *Rumo ao Nôvo Milénio: Projeto de Evangelização da Igreja no Brasil em Preparação ao Grande Jubileu do Ano 2000* [Approaching a New Millennium: Evangelization Project for the Church in Brazil in Preparation of the Jubilee 2000] (São Paulo: Editorial Salesiana Don Bosco, 1996), cited in Cleary, "Brazilian Catholic Church," 262–63.

51. Clovodis Boff, "Uma análise de Conjuntura da Igreja Católica no Final do Milénio," *Revista Ecclesiástica Brasileira* 56 (March 1996), cited in Cleary, "Brazilian Catholic Church," 266.

52. Della Cava, "Transnational Religions," 545.

53. CERIS, *Desafios do catolicismo na cidade* (São Paulo: Paulus, 2002), cited in Alberto Antoniazzi, "As Religiões no Brasil Segundo o Censo de 2000," *Revista de Estudos da Religião* 2 (2003): 76.

54. Antoniazzi, "As Religiões no Brasil Segundo o Censo de 2000," 76–77.

55. Birman and Leite, "Whatever Happened," 285.

56. Paul E. Amar, "Reform in Rio: Reconsidering the Myths of Crime and Violence," *NACLA Report on the Americas* 37, no. 2 (2003): 37–42.

57. Timothy J. Power, "Political Institutions in Democratic Brazil: Politics as a Permanent Constitutional Convention," in *Democratic Brazil: Actors, Institutions, and Processes*, ed. Peter B. Kingstone and Timothy J. Power (Pittsburgh: University of Pittsburgh Press, 2000), 31.

58. Raymond Colitt, "Lula Rejects Proposal to Step Down at End of Term in Brazilian Crisis," *Financial Times* (London), August 5, 2005, 6.

59. One could argue that the survey's sample size and the method used (telephone) may reduce the results' representativeness. But even if the results only reflect the opinions of the middle and upper classes, they are still remarkable. For country-by-country results, see *Polling the Nations*, http://poll.orspub.com/poll/lpext.dll?f=templates&fn=main-h.htm.

60. The Church combines material *and* ideological power. David Forgacs, ed. *The Antonion Gramsci Reader* (New York: New York University Press, 2000), chap. 6.

61. For the full story and an interesting interpretation, see Patricia Birman and David Lehmann, "Religion and the Media Battle for Ideological Hegemony: The Universal Church of the Kingdom of God and TV Globo in Brazil," *Bulletin of Latin American Research* 18, no. 2 (1999): 145–64.

Bibliography

Brazilian Institute for Geography and Statistics [Instituto Brasileiro de Geografia e Estatística, IBGE], Sistema de Recuperação Automática (SIDRA). *Banco de Dados Agregados*. Download from http://www.ibge.gov.br.

Bruneau, Thomas C. *The Church in Brazil: The Politics of Religion*. Austin: University of Texas Press, 1982.

Burdick, John. "What Is the Color of the Holy Spirit? Pentecostalism and Black Identity in Brazil." *Latin American Research Review* 34, no. 2 (1999): 109–31.

Center for Religious Statistics and Social Investigations (Centro de Estatística Religiosa e Investigações Sociais). *Quadros Estatísticos*. Download from http://www.ceris.org.br.

Doimo, Ana Maria. "Social Movements and the Catholic Church in Vitória, Brazil." In *The Progressive Church in Latin America*, ed. Scott Mainwaring and Alexander Wilde. Notre Dame, Ind.: University of Notre Dame Press, 1989.

Drogus, Carol Ann. "Popular Movements and the Limits of Political Mobilization at the Grassroots in Brazil." In *Conflict and Competition: The Latin American Church in a Changing Environment*, ed. Edward L. Cleary and Hannah Stewart-Gambino. Boulder, Colo.: Lynne Rienner, 1992.

Furtado, Celso. Interview with the author, October 1995, Rio de Janeiro.

Guerra, Lemuel. "As Influências da Lógica Mercadológica Sobre As Recentes Transformações Na Igreja Católica" [The Influence of Marketing Logic on the Recent Transformations in the Catholic Church]. *Revista de Estudos da Religião*, no. 2 (2003): 1–23.

Lehmann, David. "Charisma and Possession in Africa and Brazil." *Theory, Culture & Society* 18, no. 5 (2001): 45–74.

Mainwaring, Scott. "The Catholic Church, Popular Education and Political Change in Brazil." *Journal of Interamerican Studies and World Affairs* 26, no. 1 (1984): 97–124.

Martins, Andrea Damacena, and Lucia Pedrosa de Pádua. "The Option for the Poor and Pentecostalism in Brazil." *Exchange* 31, no. 2 (2002): 136–56.

Nagle, Robin. "'Pelo Direito de Ser Igreja' ['For the Right to be Church']: The Struggle of the Morro da Conceição." In *The Church at the Grassroots in Latin America: Perspectives on Thirty Years of Activism*, ed. John Burdick and W. E. Hewitt. Westport, Conn.: Praeger, 2000.

National Conference of Brazilian Bishops (Conferência Nacional dos Bispos do Brasil). *Estatísticas Sobre a Igreja no Brasil* [Statistics on the Church in Brazil]. Download from http://www.cnbb.org.br.

Scalon, Maria Celi, and Andrew M. Greeley. "Catholics and Protestants in Brazil." *America*, August 18–25, 2003, 13–15.

Serbin, Kenneth P. "Church–State Reciprocity in Contemporary Brazil: The Convening of the International Eucharistic Congress of 1955 in Rio de Janeiro." *Hispanic American Historical Review* 76, no. 4 (1996): 721–51.

United Nations Development Program. *Human Development Reports*. http://hdr.undp.org/statistics/data/.

World Bank. *World Development Indicators Online*. http://devdata.worldbank.org/dataonline.

Chapter 10

The Rwandan Church:
The Challenge of Reconciliation

ELISÉE RUTAGAMBWA, S.J.

IN THE YEARS IMMEDIATELY FOLLOWING World War II, when the truth of the Holocaust proved much worse than anyone believed possible, global reaction was unanimous: Crimes of this magnitude must never be allowed to happen again. But the firm imperative "never again" heard in the late 1940s has become something closer to "again and again." One such example is the 1994 genocide in Rwanda, in which nearly a million Tutsis and moderate Hutus were murdered.[1] The Rwandan genocide has clearly challenged the international community's commitment to the "never again" principle, and it has brought shame upon the world's most prominent moral force, the Roman Catholic Church.[2] Indeed, in the face of clear and indisputable evidence, the Rwandan Church leadership has been reluctant to acknowledge that Church members— including clergy—were directly involved in the killings, and took too long to use the term genocide. Similar to the Protestant and Roman Catholic churches in Germany during Word War II at the time of the Holocaust, the Rwandan Church has remained largely silent or ambiguous in the face of these modern-day atrocities.[3]

Today, however, the Church is starting to help Rwandan society recover and move toward reconciliation. Deep skepticism toward the Church remains, particularly among those who witnessed the 1994 genocide and recall the Church leadership's complicity with the killing. There is only one clear way for the Church to foster peace and unity in Rwanda: A decade after the genocide, the Church must confess its mistakes and willingly engage in the process of its own internal healing. Such healing is important for any religious institutions that have endured the divisions and atrocities visited by internal strive and civil war.

Historical Background

At least three important historical factors contribute to the Rwandan Catholic Church's present difficulty in serving as an instrument of reconciliation: first, the Church's failure in evangelization; then the devastating impact of its ongoing collusion with political power; and finally, its failure to address the genocide in 1994. Let us examine each of these issues.

The Failed Policy of Evangelization

Rwanda has a population of nearly 8 million and a geographic area of 16,365 square miles. The nation is located in the African Great Lakes region, and it shares borders with the Democratic Republic of the Congo to the west, Tanzania to the east, Burundi to the south, and Uganda to the north. Rwanda was colonized by Germany until the end of World War I, and it was subsequently controlled by Belgium until it achieved independence in 1962. Its population is composed of three social groups—the Hutus, Twa, and Tutsis—all of which share the same language, religion, and culture.

The country is one of the most Christianized nations in Africa. According to the 1991 Rwandan census, 89.8 percent of the population claimed membership in a Christian church—62.6 percent Catholic, 18.8 percent Protestant, and 8.4 percent Seventh-Day Adventist.[4] The evangelization of Rwanda began in the early 1900s while the country was already under German colonial rule. Following Germany's defeat in World War I, the League of Nations presented Belgium with a mandate to administer what was then known as Rwanda-Urundi. The White Fathers (Pères Blancs) missionaries settled in the country and recruited adherents. However, they faced resistance from King Musinga, who saw Christianity as a threat to traditional beliefs and national unity. At the urging of Bishop Léon Class, the Belgian colonial administration deposed Musinga and enthroned his son Mutara III, who soon converted to Catholicism.[5] After the king's baptism, Rwanda was consecrated to Christ the King and became a virtual Christian kingdom.

Influenced by racist nineteenth-century anthropological and racial studies, the Catholic missionaries undertaking the evangelization were deeply prejudiced against the African peoples.[6] Accordingly, they dismissed everything related to Rwandan religious and cultural traditions as paganism. Drawing from the reports of their travels, Cardinal Charles Lavigerie, the founder of the White Fathers, surmised that Africans generally lacked a sense of religion: "It is doubtful whether Negroes have any sense of another life and the immortality of the soul. In any case, they do not seem to have any religion apart from gross superstitions without any form of culture and which resemble to witchcraft."[7] These views echoed those of the German philosopher Hegel:

All our observations of African man show him as living in a state of savagery and barbarism, and he remained in this state to the present day. The Negro is an example of animal man in all his savagery and lawlessness, and if we wish to understand him at all, we must put aside all our European attitudes. We must not think of a spiritual God or of moral laws; to comprehend him correctly, we must abstract from all reverence and morality, and from everything which we call feeling. All this is foreign to man in his immediate existence, and nothing consonant with humanity is to be found in his character.[8]

On the basis of new reports from knowledgeable African missionaries who lived closely with the Africans, however, Cardinal Lavigerie modified his views. Although eventually acknowledging the humanity of the Africans and their sense of religion, the cardinal could never accept the idea that the Rwandans were equal to the Europeans.

Catholic missionaries fractured Rwandan civil society by prohibiting native religious and cultural traditions and by forcing people to renounce their secular beliefs. Specifically, by introducing a dualistic Manichean worldview in which people were either "saved" or "damned," the missionaries created significant cleavages in Rwandan civil society. New converts were separated from their unconverted family members, thereby abolishing the role of their ancestors, who traditionally served as intergenerational "glue," that is, as mediators between the living and the dead. Thus the Judeo-Christian bipolar vision, divided between the Bakristu (Christians) and Bapagani-Bashenzi (pagans), replaced the traditional tripolar view.[9] The newly baptized congregants (Bakristu) became a distinctive social group having little in common with the nonconverts (Bashenzi). The social typology distinguishing Bakristu from Bapagani-Bashenzi was realized by relocating new converts away from the nonbaptized, and introducing new symbols and rites such as the wearing of rosaries or religious medallions.

This new identity schema served as the foundation of the new collective memory of Rwandans, to the detriment of their identity. After the majority of Rwandans were baptized and the traditional religion was prohibited, the dual identity schema Bakristu-Bashenzi became irrelevant. But when the powerful new ethnic ideology emerged following the colonial divide, it was transformed into a new dual identity schema of the Hutus and Tutsis.

Missionaries engaged in evangelization also mistakenly supported the colonial political tactics of "divide and rule." They endorsed ethnic divisions among Hutus, Tutsis, and Twa. Yet this ethnic division was a falsely conceived ethnic ideology, which presented them as exclusive and hostile groups. According to this colonial ethnic ideology, all Tutsis were rulers and all Hutus were servants. Hence, just as the colonizers relied on the Tutsi chiefs to cement their political power, the missionaries chose the Tutsi hierarchy as their tool for evangelization.[10] With the Rwandan Church's support, the colonial administration appointed the Tutsi hierarchy to the new colonial administration. In turn, the Tutsi elite received many privileges, including private schools that were built for their children, who were destined to work for the colonial administration.

The Hutus and Tutsis do not belong to exclusive or hostile ethnic groupings. Traditional Rwanda was markedly different. In Rwandan culture, cattle breeding was associated with wealth and prestige. Therefore, as the Tutsis were generally pastoralists and the Hutus agriculturalists, the Tutsis had more influence and dominated the leadership. However, while the Tutsi pastoralists were settling the land, the categories of Hutus and Tutsis became so dynamic that they could not be conceived simply as fixed groups. As many historians who wrote about Rwanda have observed, a rich Hutu could become a Tutsi and a poor Tutsi could become a Hutu.[11] In addition, there was much intermarriage. The socio-economic division among them, therefore, was exacerbated largely by the ethnic interpretation applied by the Rwandan Church missionaries.

At the end of the 1950s, as decolonization swept through the African continent, King Mutara III and a group of his national council members vowed to initiate important reforms. In response to their demands for independence from colonial rule, the Belgian administration and the missionary church leadership adopted a new tact: They shifted their support from the Tutsi hierarchy to the Hutu elite and, in turn, blamed their divisive policies on the former.[12] The Tutsi chiefs who had once been praised for their superiority and their natural-born leadership qualities were now condemned as enemies of the Church and white people, and they were accused of being strangers who had invaded the Hutu people's lands in order to exploit them. This colonial strategy sought to undercut the authority of the Tutsi, and, in so doing, position the Belgians as the true protectors of the Hutu people. Essentially, the colonial authorities, with the support of the Church, played one group off of the other so that the real exploiters and invaders—the Belgian colonizers and the white missionaries—could maintain their dominant position in Rwandan society.

The Rwandan Genocide of 1959

Swiss Bishop André Perraudin was the most prominent Church figure in this policy shift. When he was appointed to Kabgayi Diocese, he did not question the Church's divisive methods of evangelization.[13] Although he claimed to promote charity among his followers, he continued to pursue the same divisive tactics. In the late 1950s, Perraudin and the Belgian colonial administration decided to support the Hutu republican movement, which was an extremist political party led by Catholic-trained Hutu intellectuals. With colonial and Church support, this Hutu-republican party called the Party of the Hutu Emancipation Movement (PARMEHUTU) won the 1959 elections and assumed power. But instead of restoring unity and social justice, the PARMEHUTU indiscriminately blamed the colony's ills on the Tutsis, and with the aid of the Belgian colonial administration, it initiated the first Rwandan genocide by massacring more than 20,000 Tutsis, while another 200,000 escaped abroad to neighboring states or were exiled. Those who remained in the country were denied most of their basic rights.[14]

The "demonization" of the Tutsis preceded the 1994 genocide. Even though this was a clear and grave human rights violation, Bishop Perraudin and his senior aides dismissed these events as a social revolution intended to redress social injustices. For thirty years, these views were not questioned.[15] Thus, the world ignored the 500,000 Tutsi refugees, as history textbooks for schoolchildren and the World Bank alike praised Rwanda's development as a model of democracy.[16]

Official Ethnic Discrimination

When the president of the Second Rwandan Republic came to power in 1973 and instituted the new political party called the Mouvement Révolutionnaire National pour le Développement, or National Revolutionary Movement for Development, official ethnic discrimination was sanctioned under the so-called policy of ethnic and regional balance. Under this policy, each Rwandan was ethnically identified from birth, resulting in the Tutsis' systematic exclusion from all important areas of national life. Thus, it became easy to determine membership in each ethnic group. Although this policy was clearly unjust, Church leaders justified it as a corrective measure for the former colonial exclusion of the Hutus.[17] To the Catholic bishops, Tutsis were still the oppressors of Hutus, even after thirty years of exclusive Hutu power.

The actual Church practice of evangelization in Rwanda, which in theory is intended to promote unity and the love of God, instead divided Rwandans and played a role in unleashing sectarian violence. During this time, the Rwandan Church was certainly more preoccupied with power and political influence than with authentic Christian values. For missionaries and local church leaders, the strategy adopted for the policy of evangelization encouraged the conquest of numerous converts at the expense of nurturing their moral quality. Pastoral work stressed visible aspects of Church life, such as the sacraments, liturgy, and service (diakonia), while other important aspects, such as personal conversion, Communion (koinonia), and issues concerning peace and justice, enculturation, and dialogue, were neglected.[18] Concerned primarily with its power, the Church remained silent toward ethnic discrimination and related social injustices.

Collusion with Power

The Church's collusion with political power proved to be another evil in its mission of evangelization in Rwanda. Since its establishment, Rwandan Church leaders could not resist involvement with morally questionable political leaders.[19] This continued until the end of the Second Republic in 1994.

During the colonial period, as Rutayisire and Muzungu argue, "The Catholic Church was a component of the State, its right hand. In this system of 'co-management accomplice,' [the Church] mixed with political power and could not disown it, since it drew its subsistence from it."[20] Longman also noted a co-operative network relationship between different churches and the state. On the one hand, the colonial administration relied on the churches—Catholic and Protestant—to provide costly public services such as education, health care, and social work. In return for this support, the colonial administration gave missionaries free access to the population and exempted them from taxes, thus strengthening church–state ties.

Under the First and Second republics (1962–94), the collusion of the Rwandan Church with political power intensified. As Ugirashebuja writes, "[The Church] had considerable privileges such as the quasi-monopoly of education, a powerful audience among the political elite, possession of much unused land, and important exemptions in the tax system."[21] The cooperative working relationship between the missionaries and the colonial administrators was passed on to the new political elite and Church leaders. Individual churches and the state cooperated in extending control over the population, regulating its behavior, and integrating it into the new economic and political system. In some cases, church leaders echoed political speeches in preaching or pastoral letters, and they even carried out political functions.[22] For instance, the former archbishop of Kigali, Vincent Sengiyumva, once served as a member of the central committee of the ruling party.[23]

Timothy Longman observes that a private cooperative relationship was reinforced by the close relationship shared by the new leaders of both the Rwandan Church and state; some had family ties, some were close friends and neighbors, and others were former classmates in the missionary schools.[24] These cooperative relationships became problematic when religious colleagues tolerated political leaders, who were engaged in corruption or adopted dictatorial attitudes. This created an alliance of powerful ethnic and regional self-interest in which both groups cooperated in fiercely defending the status quo.

The Genocide and the Church's Failure to React

Following the conclusion of the Arusha Accords between the Tutsi Rwandan Patriotic Front (RPF) and the Rwandan government in 1992, which provided for a cease-fire, and after the deaths on April 6, 1994, of the presidents of Rwanda and Burundi, the Armed Forces of Rwanda and various militia groups—namely, the Hutu-dominated Interahamwe—took control of the Rwandan government.[25] These Hutu extremists assassinated Agathe Uwilingiyimana, a Hutu moderate and Rwanda's first female prime minister, and they then broadcast anti-Tutsi propaganda on local radio and in the newspapers, which incited Rwanda's second large-scale massacre of Tutsis and moderate Hutus, which lasted until July 1994. As the Rwandan military and the Interahamwe were turning the country into killing fields not seen since the Cambodian holocaust of the mid-1970s, the United Nations peacekeeping forces in Rwanda (known as UNAMIR) were inexplicably ordered to adopt a position of "impartiality." The genocide started on April 6 and lasted a hundred days.

One of the most publicized acts of brutality occurred in the city of Kivumu, at Nyange Church, where the Interahamwe bulldozed a local Catholic Church in which some three thousand Tutsis had sought refuge. As the walls collapsed, those escaping were slashed to death by machete-wielding Hutus. Following a hundred days of genocide and nearly a million deaths, the Rwandan Hutu regime was replaced by Tutsi RPF forces who put an end to the genocide. Some 2 million Hutus fled for their lives to neighboring countries, accompanied by some of the core perpetrators of the genocide.

Faced with these flagrant government-sponsored violations of basic human rights—and with countless murders taking place in churches and Catholic school buildings—the Rwandan Church, unbelievably, did not protest. The biship's first statement deploring the killings was issued on April 10, 1994, but it let the government off the hook, instead offering a vague condemnation of "those who act under the influence of anger, grief, and revenge."[26] Although the bishops knew that the Tutsi-dominated RPF troops were not involved in the genocide, they nonetheless cowardly implicated the RPF troops in a statement, calling upon the Rwandan authorities and the RPF officials

> to hold consultation meetings without complications in order to institute the broad-based transitional government in respect to the UN Security Council's recent resolution. The Rwandan authorities and RPF officials should avoid the temptation of sinking the country into another perilous, fratricidal, and divisive war.[27]

A second statement issued by Church leaders on April 16, 1994, distorted the events as an ethnic war, in which Hutus and Tutsis were killing each other equally, thereby masking its genocidal nature.[28] Later statements continued to conceal the true nature of the killing. Though the bishops knew that the Hutu-controlled Rwandan Armed Forces were behind the killings, they called upon the government "to keep their concern for everyone's security without discrimination." In what was arguably the Rwandan bishop's lowest moment, they published a letter in the April 1994 edition of the *Osservatore Romano*, which paid "tribute to the Rwandan Armed Forces for taking security concerns to heart."[29] Further, they expressed "their satisfaction at the institution of a new government"—the government that was urging Hutus to kill Tutsi—"to which they promised their support."[30] Finally, "they called upon all the Rwandans to ease the task of the new government by responding to their call favorably and helping them to achieve their mission."[31]

Some priests and nuns were directly involved in the killings, while other members of the clergy acted as accomplices by gathering Tutsis into church buildings, where they were slaughtered. The Rwandan Church's statements made no mention of responsibility for these acts.[32] To the contrary, the Church assisted those priests and nuns in finding safe havens in other countries to avoid facing trials in later years.[33]

For years following the events of 1994, the Church was reluctant to recognize its historical role in the division of Rwandan civil society as well as its role in the genocide. In fact, Church authorities avoided the word "genocide" altogether. True to their historical pattern of following former governments, the Rwandan Church continued to depict the genocide as a civil war in which Tutsis and Hutus were equally to blame. Further, Church leaders resumed celebrating the Eucharist as if nothing had happened: There were no ceremonies of purification or proper burials for those Christians whose corpses were still lying in church buildings; nor was there any attempt to call the perpetrators to account for their pernicious crimes. Even when the Rwandan Association of the Survivors of the Genocide (known as IBUKA), with the support of the postgenocide government, suggested that some of the churches where people had been slaughtered be turned into memorials for quiet prayer and societal healing, Church authorities rejected the idea out-of-hand, offering a series of lame excuses, such as the idea that memorials would generate division among Christians, or that only bishops were allowed to be buried in the churches.[34]

The sentiment of Rwandan Church leaders toward the victims of the genocide can be described as one of indifference—at best. Although the Church leaders expressed legitimate concern for the refugees of the genocide, they never distinguished clearly between the persecuted (genuine refugees) and the persecutors (those seeking escape from trials for their crimes). The reference to both groups as "refugees" was an insult to the persecuted, and it lessened the seriousness of the crimes committed by the persecutors. Perhaps the most scandalous statement by a Church official about the genocide was uttered by Bishop Phocas Nikwigize of the Ruhengeri Diocese. In his interview with De Volkskrant on June 26, 1995, he dismissed the genocide as something simply human and, therefore, understandable:

> What happened in 1994 in Rwanda was something very human. When someone attacks you, you have to defend yourself. Within such a situation, you forget that you are a Christian; you are then first and foremost a human. . . . These Batutsi were collaborators, friends of the enemy. They were in contact with the rebels. They had to be eliminated so that they could not betray any more.[35]

The Church's continuing unconditional support for criminal regimes, its appalling reluctance to speak out when crimes negating its very raison d'être are perpetrated, and its unrepentant attitude after the genocide—all have profoundly discredited its own mission, leading many people to become deeply skeptical about its ability to promote reconciliation.

Conditions for the Rwandan Church to Promote a Genuine Reconciliation

How can the Church possibly play the role of a reconciler when it has always been part of the problem by colluding with oppressive political regimes? Should not the Church begin by acknowledging its own errors and reconciling itself before any social engagement in the larger work of reconciliation in civic society? These are critical questions that Church leaders need to face with honesty and humility, for in so doing is the only sign of hope for a genuine renewal within the Church.

Although the Church hierarchy has miserably failed to address the genocide, it is important to note that small numbers of individuals have shown admirable devotion to Christian morals and virtues.[36] There were Christians—Catholic and Protestant, priests, nuns, and laity—who risked their lives for the sake of their fellow human beings. Some members betrayed the Church's mission, but others acted with true faith and commitment to the Gospel.[37] It is in this small measure of true faith and commitment to Christian values and morals that we see evidence of hope for reconciliation. The faith and commitment of the heroes and heroines provides a foundation upon which to build and work toward the Church's renewal.

For the Rwandan Church to credibly work for reconciliation, it must, at a minimum, fulfill the following three conditions. First, it must directly and clearly confess all its sins associated with the genocide. Second, it needs to honestly, and in full view of the world, reveal the root causes and mechanisms that led to the genocide. Third, it must recommit itself to its distinctive character as the "Body of Christ"—that is, for the national reconciliation to be truly Christian oriented, this spiritual dimension should not be ignored. Though it may be difficult and humiliating for an institution that has had its hand in sowing division, it is nonetheless the only way to bring about true reconciliation and unity. Let us now examine each of these conditions.

A "Cheap Reconciliation" Should Be Avoided

As Robert Schreiter writes, in situations subsequent to mass violence, "a cheap reconciliation is a form of false reconciliation which consists of dealing with a history of violence by suppressing its memory."[38] One way to suppress memory, to which perpetrators and their accomplices often resort, is to put the violent history in the past and push people to begin anew. This reduces reconciliation to a hasty process that seeks to normalize the situation without seriously addressing the causes of violence.

For example, the new Rwandan government attempted in 2001 to promote an annual commemoration of the genocide and the "Gacaca jurisdictions," which is a grassroots judicial system aimed at restoring the truth and trying the perpetrators of the 1994 genocide.[39] Yet the perpetrators of the genocide and their supporters opposed such initiatives for fear that they would promote hatred and incite vengeful acts. However, as Schreiter rightly observes, "Suppressing memory does not take the violence away; it only postpones its expurgation. Such an attempt grows out of a fundamental misunderstanding of the process of reconciliation, not realizing that there is more to reconciliation than a cessation of violence."[40] In some cases, this "cheap" reconciliation is advocated by Church leaders or well-meaning but naive outsiders who believe they are fulfilling the Christian virtue of forgiveness, with no serious consideration of responsibility. Unfortunately, such a hasty, "cheap" reconciliation simply ignores what true forgiveness dictates in this situation—namely, an honest, public, and complete confession of sins—and leaves the impression that the violence is condoned.

The undermining of genuine reconciliation is a major problem. Calling those who have suffered to forget what they have endured is a form of indifference to their suffering, and it only serves to perpetuate and aggravate the oppression. In this regard, Wiesel argues:

> Indifference is not a beginning, it is an end. And, therefore, indifference is always the friend of the enemy, for it benefits the aggressor—never his victim, whose pain is magnified when he or she feels forgotten. The political prisoner in his cell, the hungry children, the homeless refugees—not to respond to their plight, not to relieve their solitude by offering them a spark of hope is to exile them from human memory. And in denying their humanity we betray our own.[41]

For his part, Schreiter puts it powerfully: "To trivialize and ignore memory is to trivialize and ignore human identity, and to trivialize and ignore human identity is to trivialize and ignore human dignity. That is why reconciliation as a hasty of peace is actually the opposite of reconciliation. By forgetting the suffering, the victim is forgotten and the causes of suffering are never uncovered and confronted."[42] In fact, to deny memory is to side with death and the enemy. And to forget about the dead is to kill them a second time.

To achieve a profound reconciliation, the most appropriate first step is to comfort the victims. The Church should make sufficient time for grieving and remembering their loved ones, while recognizing that reconciliation is a long, unpredictable journey. Under no conditions should the victims be forced or rushed into reconciliation.

It is critical that the Church take steps to promote honesty in its own actions and in society at large. Without this approach, the Church risks a possible resumption of violence. Therefore, to bring about a genuine reconciliation, the Church must liberate itself from the real causes of violence and eradicate them.

As Schreiter states, "Liberation is not just liberation from the violent situation, but also liberation from the structures and processes that permit and promote violence."[43] That is, liberation is a precondition to reconciliation. For him, "conflict is not peripheral to the process of reconciliation but is met at its very heart. If the sources of conflict are not named, examined, and taken away, reconciliation will not come about. What we will have is a truce, not a peace."[44]

Unfortunately, the Rwandan Church has remained defensive about its role in the country's civil strife.[45] Church leaders have answered criticism for their mistakes by claiming that the Church itself is being persecuted. As Rutayisire says in his criticism of the Rwandan Church's attitude during the first ethnic cleansing of 1959, "In clerical circles, there has never been any attempt to analyze the causes of the violence of November in order to set a common strategy and initiate concerted and appropriate actions. The refusal or the fear of the analysis is perceived in the abstract tone employed, which is not appropriate to promote their historical knowledge."[46] Rutayisire gives another example, in recounting the words of the bishop of Nyundo Diocese: "The violence which has strongly struck Rwanda and, particularly the Diocese of Nyundo, has been allowed by God with the purpose of salvation. All that has crushed and made us suffer only in order to lead us to a total redemption."[47] This type of explanation does no good, and it actually tends to worsen the situation.

Christian Reconciliation versus Secular Mediation Techniques

Conflict resolution studies and secular mediation techniques have become fashionable in the contemporary age. The underlying principle of these approaches is that both parties have legitimate interests that cannot be totally satisfied as they wish. Therefore, the process consists of balancing the interests and asking the parties to give up some of their interests for the sake of reconciliation. From a Christian point of view, this model sounds realistic. It acknowledges that conflict can arise while people try to maintain their legitimate interests and values. Like Christian-oriented reconciliation, this approach recognizes a minimum sense of human dignity because it takes seriously the claims of all parties. In addition, it is not a speedy process, for it requires some conditions to be fulfilled to end the conflict.

The key distinguishing element between "reconciliation as a managed process" and "Christian reconciliation" is the fact that the former is reduced to a technical rationality. Christian reconciliation does not count solely on human resources and skills. Genuine Christian reconciliation relies on spirituality and God's grace.

Of course, this neither minimizes the value of reconciliation as a human responsibility nor abdicates responsibility in the face of the violence provoked by political oppression. Instead, this approach acknowledges the tremendous complexity of the task of reconciliation in particular situations where social relations have so profoundly deteriorated. As Schreiter explains, "Whereas reconciliation as a managed process is something to be mastered, Christian reconciliation is something to be discovered as God's grace is given to those concerned."[48] In this sense, he insists, "Reconciliation becomes more of an attitude than an acquired skill; it becomes a stance assumed before a broken world rather than a tool to repair that world. . . . Reconciliation is more spirituality than strategy."[49]

In the Rwandan situation, the "reconciliation as a managed process" approach is familiar. Such calls were heard both before and after the genocide. Most surprising was the call by some countries that hoped to rescue their former allies—now suspects of genocide—by bringing the victims to the negotiation table with their former executioners, without any prior trial for their crimes. In this case, reconciliation cannot be perceived only in terms of the interests of the negotiating parties because there are also subjective dimensions: Both sides do not have legitimate interests in Rwanda.

As we can learn from the Holocaust of World War II, in a situation of genocide, the persecuted and the persecutors do not each have legitimate interests. For there to be justice and societal healing, all the subjective elements and their social impact simply cannot be translated into identifiable interests to be put on the bargaining table. Thus, if the Church is to work for true reconciliation and lasting peace in this context, it must make its own voice heard through a spiritual approach to supplement the reconciliatory efforts of the government and the other nonreligious social actors.[50]

Catholic Liturgy, Ritual, and Genuine Reconciliation

Perpetrators of genocide and other crimes against humanity often avoid any attempt at reconciliation largely due to a guilty conscience and a refusal to assume responsibility. These are profound obstacles to the process of reconciliation and impediments to the individuals' inner peace. Thus, victims and perpetrators need a space where they can express their concerns and find some kind of therapy before the genuine steps to reconciliation can be undertaken. In the Church, this is addressed through liturgy and pastoral ministry.

One of the most important components of the Church's liturgy is its ritual. Indeed, as Schreiter has noted, "Rituals play a prominent role in touching parts of our lives and expressing deeply-felt but repressed feelings, such those experienced by the victims of mass violence and persecution. . . . The drama of ritual can speak of that for which we have no words."[51] To illustrate this, he describes the purification of the National Stadium in Santiago. Following the 1973 military coup d'état engineered by General Augusto Pinochet against the elected Marxist administration of Salvador Allende, military authorities transformed the National Stadium into a death camp, where some nine hundred people were executed, and many others simply disappeared, never to be seen again. In the aftermath of the return of civilian rule in Chile in 1990, discussed by Lies and Malone in chapter 5 of this volume, the Church used the Catholic purification ritual as a way of remembering those who had perished in the stadium. These kinds of rituals give the families an opportunity to mourn their loved ones and ensure that they rest in peace. In addition, they engender a sense of solidarity among fellow Christians, which strengthens the victims and empowers them to confront the challenge of reconciliation.[52]

Another important ritual is the celebration of the sacrament of reconciliation, commonly known as confession. This both helps the perpetrators take responsibility for their acts and extends the sinful consciousness to the whole Christian community and society at large. As Schreiter notes, "This may prove especially useful when the Church itself finds that it has sinned and needs to repent. Ways need to be devised to capture once again the wealth of that sacrament for these kinds of situations."[53] In other words, the sacrament should be a public, energizing practice that helps people understand the implication of their social sin and find new ways for common healing.

The Eucharistic ritual is vitally important, as Schreiter notes, because of its theological meaning and practical effect. Eucharistic theologies and practices vary among churches, but they all stress the need for deliverance from the suffering of violence. Schreiter writes:

> Gathering around the Eucharistic table, the broken, damaged, abused bodies of individual victims and the broken body of the Church are taken up into the body of Christ. Christ's body has known torture; it has known shame. In his complete solidarity with the victims, he has gone to the limits of violent death. And so his body becomes a holy medicine to heal those broken bodies of today.[54]

In other words, the Eucharist acquires a significant role in reconciliation inasmuch as it identifies the victim with Christ. It actualizes the story of the innocent one who suffers and dies but who cannot vanish that way. Like Christ, through death, the victim comes to the fullness of life. What is attractive about this approach is that the remembrance is active and aims at redemption. Rather than retaining anger while awaiting the opportunity to take revenge, suffering becomes a transforming force that helps individuals and their societies work for peace and reconciliation and heal from the ill effects of violence.

Of course, even these liturgical practices cannot easily achieve this role without sound and concerted pastoral action. This is particularly relevant to the Rwandan Catholic Church, which faces a demanding task of reconciliation and has yet to adjust to the new social realities subsequent to the genocide. Given the reduction in numbers of clerics caused by the genocide and the enormous need for personal care that the process of reconciliation requires, the Rwandan Catholic Church must review its pastoral structures and reconsider its methods of communicating the Good News.[55]

In this respect, the Catholic Church already has the advantage of serving as a place where Christians of all conditions converge to satisfy their spiritual need. Thus, what Christians need is more organized and accessible structures that address their concerns for reconciliation, both as individuals and community. One such structure could be the small Christian communities, where both laypeople and clergy could meet and discuss constructive issues concerning the Church's mission in their particular situation. Such communities could also serve as prophetic places where the recovery of a unified church community could liberate itself from the demons of the past. Given the urgency of the mission of reconciliation, a special ministerial board should also be convened to coordinate and monitor all pastoral activities related to the mission of reconciliation, similar to those established by the Archdiocese of Santiago to address the human rights abuses perpetuated on the people of Chile by Pinochet's government.[56]

Conclusion

It is often taken for granted by Church leaders that since the Church is intimately related to Christ Jesus and is a mediator of God's grace, it will surely achieve the ministry of reconciliation. However, as the history of the Rwandan Church has painfully shown, the Church is also subject to human weaknesses and sin. Over the years, Rwandan Catholic leaders have chosen to collaborate with oppressive regimes, with total disregard and indifference to the abuses and the tragic suffering imposed upon their victims. In this respect, reconciliation is as much needed within the institutional Church itself as it is in Rwandan society. The Church is a graced and spiritual body that possesses the seed of its own regeneration, but it would be naive and perhaps irresponsible to idealize the role of the Church as a reconciler without first challenging its own mistakes. For that reason, an "unconditional reconciliation" by the Church is not possible. If the Rwandan Church is to contribute to any level of reconciliation and bring about what Himes calls in chapter 1 a "church as communion," it must first consider its own failings, avoid the temptations of a "cheap" reconciliation, and be genuinely open to the complex challenges of societal healing through a resolute belief in God's plan of uniting humanity.

Notes

1. See http://news.bbc.co.uk/1/hi/world/africa/1288230.stm.

2. United Nations, Convention on the Prevention and Punishment of the Crime of Genocide, adopted by Resolution 260 (III) A of the United Nations General Assembly on December 9, 1948; http://www.hrweb.org/legal/genocide.html.

3. Harry James Cargas, *When God and Man Failed: Non-Jewish Views of the Holocaust* (New York: Macmillan, 1981), ix; Theo Tschuy, *Ethnic Conflict and Religion: Challenge to the Churches* (Geneva: World Council of Churches Publications, 1997), 24.

4. Government of Rwanda, *General Population Survey of 15 August 1991: Analysis of the Final Results* (Kigali: Government of Rwanda, 1994).

5. Josias Semujanga, *Origins of Rwandan Genocide* (New York: Humanity Books, 2003), 79.

6. Ian Linden, *Christianisme et pouvoir au Rwanda 1900–1990* [Christianity and power in Rwanda 1900–1990] (Paris: Éditions Karthala, 1999), 17.

7. Cardinal Lavigerie, "Premieres and deuxièmes instructions aux missionnaires de l'Afrique Equatoriale" [The first and second set of instructions to the missionaries of Equitorial Africa] (1878 and 1879), and other letters found in "Instructions aux Missionnaires," quoted by Van der Meersch, *Le Catéchuménat au Rwanda, de 1900 à Nos Jours* [The Rwandan Catechumens from 1900 to Today] (Kigali: Pallotti Press, 1993), and requoted by Gatwa Tharcisse, *Rwanda Eglises: Victimes ou Coupables?* [Rwandan Churches: Victims or Culprits?] (Yaounde: Éditions Haho Lome, 2001), 66.

8. Friedrich Hegel, *Lectures on the Philosophy of World History: Introduction— Reason in History*, trans. A. H. B. Nisbet (New York: Cambridge University Press, 1975), 177.

9. Semujanga, *Origins*, 82.

10. André Linard, *"Les Deux Erreurs du Monde Catholique"* [Two Mistakes in the Catholic World], *La Cité*, January 5, 1995.

11. For more information, see Linden, *Christianisme et pouvoir*, 22.

12. Paul Rutayisire, "Silences et compromissions de la hiérarchie de l'Eglise Catholique au Rwanda" [Silence and compromise among the Catholic Church hierarchy in Rwanda], *Au Coeur de l'Afrique* 2–3 (1995): 428.

13. Andre Perraudin, *Un Evêque au Rwanda* [A Priest to Rwanda] (Paris: Editions Saint-Augustin, 2003), 60.

14. See http://www.gov.rw/government/historyf.html.

15. Rwanda was granted official independence from Belgium on July 1, 1962.

16. Peter Uvin, *Aiding Violence: The Development Enterprise in Rwanda* (Bloomfield, Conn.: Kumarian Press, 1998), 40–42, 44.

17. Paul Rutayisire and Bernardin Muzungu, "L'ethnisme au coeur de la guerre" [Ethnism at the heart of the war], *Cahiers Centre Saint-Dominique* 1 (August 1995): 70.

18. Rutayisire, "Silences et compromissions," 426.

19. Gerard Prunier, *Rwanda: Le genocide* [Rwanda: The genocide] (Paris: Éditions Dagorno, 1999), 49. Also see Antoine Mugesera, "A l'origine de la desintegration de la nation rwandaise" [At the origin of the disintegration of the Rwandan nation], *Les Cahiers Evangile et Societé*, June 1996, 46–58; and Mugesera, *Rwanda : L'Eglise Catholique à l'epreuve du genocide* [The Catholic Church's proof against genocide] (Greenfield Park, Calif.: Les Éditions Africana, 2000).

20. Rutayisire and Muzungu, "L'ethnisme," 70.

21. Ugirashebuja Octave, Ugirashebuja, "L'Eglise du Rwanda après le génocide" [The Rwandan Church after the genocide], *Etudes*, February 1995, 221.

22. Conférence des Evêques Catholiques du Rwanda, *Recueil des lettres et messages de la Conférence des Evêques Catholiques du Rwanda publiées pendant la période de la guerre (1990–1994)* [Collection of letters and messages from the Catholic Bishops' Conference of Rwanda published during the war (1990–1994)] (Kigali: Pallotti Presse, 1995).

23. Faustin Rutembesa, Jean Pierre Karegeye, and Paul Rutayisire, *L'Eglise Catholique*

à *l'epreuve du génocide* [The Catholic Church's proof against genocide] (Montreal: Les Éditions Africana, 2000), 34.

24. Timothy Longman, "Empowering the Weak and Protecting the Powerful: The Contradictory Nature of Christian Churches in Central Africa," *African Studies Review* 41, no. 1 (April 1998): 42–72.

25. "Interahamwe" may be translated as "Those Who Stand Together" or "Those Who Fight Together."

26. *Bulletin de la Conférence des Evêques du Rwanda* [Bulletin of the Rwandan Bishops' Council] 3–4 (1994–95): 4.

27. Ibid.

28. Ibid., 5.

29. Ibid., 4.

30. Ibid.

31. Thadee Nsengiyumva, "Communicato dei Verscovi cattolici del Rwanda" [Communications of the Catholic Bishops of Rwanda], *Osservatore Romano*, April 11, 1994.

32. Among other examples, see the case of the Sovu nuns. African Rights, ed., *Rwanda Not So Innocent: When Women Become Killers* (London: African Rights, 1995), 155–94.

33. African Rights, ed., *L'Abbé Hormisdas Ngengiyumva accusé de genocide, protégé par l'Eglise* [Father Hormisdas Ngengiyumva accused of genocide, protected by the Church], *Report*, November 27, 2001.

34. A compromise was finally reached under pressure from the government and survivors.

35. Phocas Nikwigize, "Interview with Catholic Bishop Phocas Nikwigize," *Els de Temmermen: De Volkskrant*, June 26, 1995.

36. African Rights, ed., "Rwanda: Tribute to Courage," *Report*, December 2002.

37. See http://www.winne.com/rwanda/bf05.html.

38. Robert J. Schreiter, *Reconciliation: Mission & Ministry in a Changing Social Order* (Maryknoll, N.Y.: Orbis Books, 1992), 19.

39. See http://www.penalreform.org/english/theme_gacaca.htm.

40. Schreiter, *Reconciliation*, 21.

41. Elie Wiesel, "The Perils of Indifference," paper delivered April 12, 1999, Washington; http://www.americanrhetoric.com/speeches/ewieselperilsofindifference.html.

42. Schreiter, *Reconciliation*, 19.

43. Ibid., 22.

44. Ibid., 23.

45. Rutembesa, Karegeye, and Rutayisire, *L'Eglise Catholique*, 41.

46. Paul Rutayisire, "L'Eglise Catholique et la decoloniasation ou les illusions d'une victoire" [The Catholic Church and decolonization or the illusions of victory], in *L'Eglise Catholique*, ed. Rutembesa, Karegeye, and Rutayisire, 42.

47. Ibid.

48. Schreiter, *Reconciliation*, 23.

49. Ibid.

50. R. Scott Appleby, *The Ambivalence of the Sacred: Religion, Violence, and Reconciliation* (Lanham, Md.: Rowman & Littlefield, 2000). Also see Raymond G. Helmick

and Rodney L. Petersen, *Forgiveness and Reconciliation: Religion, Public Policy, and Conflict Transformation* (Philadelphia: Templeton Foundation Press, 2001).

51. Schreiter, *Reconciliation*, 74.

52. Ibid., 66.

53. Ibid., 75.

54. Ibid., 76.

55. During the genocide, the Rwandan Church lost 3 bishops, 103 diocesan priests, 53 religious men in orders, and 66 religious women from different congregations. See Jean Damascène Bizimana, *L'Eglise et le genocide au Rwanda* [The Church and genocide in Rwanda] (Paris: L'Harmattan, 2001), 9.

56. Schreiter, *Reconciliation*, 66.

Chapter 11

The Angolan Church: The Prophetic Tradition, Politics, and the State

LINDA HEYWOOD

THE CALL TO BE BOTH prophetic and political has presented a major problem for the Roman Catholic Church in Angola. During the time of Portugal's authoritarian "New State," or Estado Novo, which was in power from 1926 to 1974, Portuguese colonial authorities used the Angolan Church as a convenient ally to subvert the liberty of Portuguese and Africans alike. The postcolonial Marxist state also attempted to manipulate the Angolan Church following independence, from 1975 to 1992. This chapter examines the ideological challenges from the colonial, postcolonial, and revolutionary states, which eventually forced the Roman Catholic Church to adopt a prophetic role in Angolan political and social life.

The Church's prophetic and political role is especially important in Angola, where according to Pepetela, religion "is in everything. The Movement cadres are steeped in religiosity, whether Catholic or Protestant. And not only those of the movement. Take any party. . . . A party is a Church."[1] Scholars have analyzed the enduring significance of the Catholic and Protestant churches in contemporary Angolan politics.[2] Indeed, the most recent study of the connections between church and state in Angola has criticized the churches for failing to carry out their duty of being the prophetic voice for the people in the wilderness of despair and suffering.[3]

The New State and the 1940 Concordat

Although supportive of Portuguese exploration in central Africa, the Vatican did not undertake a comprehensive missionary effort in Angola as it had in East Timor, a process well described by Lyon in chapter 8 of this volume. To consolidate its colonial control and to finance missionary efforts, the Portuguese colonial administration turned to non-Portuguese Catholic, Baptist, Methodist, and Church of Christ missionaries to work among the major African ethnic groups in the colony—the Congos to the north, the Kimbundu in the Luanda region, and the Ovimbundu in the central part of the colony. Beginning in the late nineteenth century, the Holy Ghost Fathers headquartered in France, along with members of other secular orders and a sprinkling of Portuguese Catholic laity, increased their operations in Angola.

However, by the early twentieth century, the situation was bleak. After inspecting the Angolan missions, the Jesuit provincial for Portugal decried the poor state of Catholic work in the Angolan colony, whose missionaries were slowly dying out. Most of the priests in the field had served for more than forty years and were about seventy-five years old. More alarmingly, there were not enough new priests to replace them. Indeed, at the time, the Jesuits had only thirty-two missions, seventy-seven priests, and fifty-five auxiliary brothers in the field.[4]

Although the Angolan Catholic Church had numerically more converts, the Protestants (British Baptists, American Methodists, and the Canadian and American Church of Christ) enjoyed greater financial and organizational strengths. The Protestant churches thus offered African Angolans more opportunities for education and health services that allowed them to become assimilated (assimilados) into the colonial state. The North American Protestant Church of Christ missionaries established a series of health, educational, and social institutions among 3 million of the Ovimbundu, the largest Angolan ethnic group.[5] The Methodists attracted significant numbers of Kimbundus in Luanda and its hinterland; they offered a range of educational and health training for the thousands of Kimbundus making their homes in the slums of the capital, Luanda.[6] The Baptists provided similar services for the Kongo-speaking areas. Because Protestant institutions were so extensive, Angolan colonial officials worried about the establishment of an informal Protestant "parallel state" among the African population.

To undermine the work of the Protestant missionaries who were "denationalizing" the Angolan Africans, the state co-opted the Angolan Church to act on the state's behalf; similar forms of corporatism had been established in Latin Europe and Latin American in accordance with the 1891 papal encyclical Rerum Novarum and its later incarnation, the 1931 Quadragesimo Anno. The Portuguese leader, Antonio Salazar, was a staunch Catholic and "closet priest" according to his Protestant critics (he is also discussed by Manuel and Mott in chapter 3.[7] In 1926, Salazar and the Vatican signed the João Belo Statute, which provided state funding to the Portuguese Church to undertake African evangelization.[8] To control the Church, Salazar signed the famous 1940 Concordat and Missionary Accord; one year later, he signed the Missionary Statute with the Vatican. The Portuguese Church now was responsible for the "native educational system," which was limited to primary education and to overseeing the "Portugalization" of the Africans. If Portuguese missionaries were not available, the Holy See was obligated to send foreign missionaries, as long as they agreed to be "subject to the laws and courts of Portugal."[9]

The Angolan Church now was confronted with a contradiction between its prophetic and political roles in modern society. By accepting the state's financial and political support, Church officials guaranteed the survival of the Church's prophetic role. Yet dependence on the state ultimately drew the Angolan Church deeper into the oppressive colonial system and weakened its political voice, which was so essential at this crucial juncture in Angolan history. Responding in 1933 to missionary complaints concerning the treatment of Angolans in the central highlands, Angolan bishop Moisés Alves de Pinho reminded the missionaries that "it is not for their work of evangelization that the state appreciates our mission . . . [their] interest is in civilization and nationalism."[10] In fact, this was the attitude of the Church for the next several decades, as missionaries were warned "not to mix in politics," which the state accused the Protestants of perpetrating.[11] This emphasis on "civilization and nationalism" versus evangelization and justice dominated the life of the Angolan Church for decades.

Up to the 1940 Concordat, the Angolan Church relied on the Holy Ghost Fathers, Jesuits, and clergy of the local dioceses (a total of 169), along with Sisters of Saint Joseph of Cluny (whose presence in Angola dated from the latter part of the nineteenth century).[12] With the Concordat, the Angolan Church saw its government subsidy rise from $99,236 (4,961,825 escudos) in 1940 to $564,514 (28,225,675 escudos) in 1960. The Angolan Church now assumed complete responsibility for the education and socialization of Angolan Africans. To advance the civilizing goals of the Portuguese colonial state, the Catholic seminary located in the central highland city of Caala noted in a 1944 report that "the native priest who graduates from this seminary . . . would not be a catechist but a precious help in civilization which the Portuguese wish to give to her colonial children."[13]

By 1960, the number of Africans claimed by the Church in its parishes and missions had substantially increased, accounting for 500,000 in Luanda and Malange, 309,000 in the Kongo, and more that 1 million in the Ovimbundu highlands.[14] Indeed, in 1960 the Angolan Church claimed 51 percent of the Angolan African population, the Protestants claimed 17 percent, and the remaining 32 percent were non-Christian. The number of African priests increased from 8 in 1933 to 330 (and 300 seminarians) in 1960.[15] The number of schools for Africans also increased significantly.

Some members of the Angolan Church disagreed with the emphasis on the prophetic over the political and the growing dependency of the Church on the state. One such early critic was Padre A. Saraiva—editor of the *Missões de Angola e Kongo*, published by the Order of the Holy Spirit—who opposed the forced colonial labor policies in Angola. The newly nominated Angolan bishop of Nova Lisboa (renamed Huambo after independence) publicly criticized the indiscriminate selection of African men for long-term labor indenture, which was "wrecking Christian family life." Responding to such criticism, the colonial authorities blocked the entry of "liberal" Catholic missionaries.[16] During the 1950s, Catholic priests such as Alfredo Mendes faced harsh judicial questionings for positions that they took in defense of the Angolan population.[17]

The Response of the Protestant Missionaries

Some Protestants, envious of the close alliance between the Angolan Church and the New State, accused the Angolan Catholics of deliberately destroying Protestant institutions. According to the Protestant missionary D. V. Waln, Catholics had established one mission station in the central highlands region of Chilesso in 1933, which already enjoyed a thriving African Protestant community. By 1940, the Catholics had built 110 outstations, all of which where within a stone's throw of the Protestant missions. These Catholic missionaries taught that Martin Luther was a "polygamist and drunkard," and that Jesus Christ was the founder of Roman Catholicism.[18] Merlin Ennis lamented that "after all our outstations had been established [in Elende] and the work of consolidation already underway, the Roman Catholics established six stations. . . . These are all supported with government funds, and not by the Catholic Church."[19]

Ennis criticized the Angolan Church's hostility toward the Protestant missionary work, and he lambasted the Vatican agreements as being "in spirit and content . . . contradictory to international treaties."[20] The Protestants accused the Angolan Church of colluding with the state to refuse Protestant missionary permits, while simultaneously allowing German, Alsatian, and other non-Portuguese Catholics easy access to the Angolan missionary field.[21] Indeed, the head of the Portuguese secret police—commonly known as PIDE, for Polícia Internacional e de Defesa do Estado, or the International Police for the Defense of the State—reportedly stated, "The bishop says, 'they are only spies.'"[22]

At the time, Protestants had a formidable educational and social presence among the three major Angolan ethnic groups. In the central highlands and neighboring regions, Protestants missionaries numbered 60 individuals, and included pastors, agronomists, teachers, doctors, and nurses. Angolan Africans also held important administrative and spiritual positions in the missionary structure, including 150 Ovimbundu pastors and several hundred unlicensed and licensed Ovimbundu teachers, as well as nurses, deacons, and catechists. These foreign and indigenous Protestant missionaries served a population of more than 60,000 communicants and several hundred thousand "adherents," who were associated with the Church of Christ in central Angola. Foreign missionaries and African leaders led a well-managed community at their 7,817-acre training complex at

Dondi, which supplied personnel to eight hospitals, two hundred or more bush clinics, a large hostel that housed Ovimbundu in Nova Lisboa, and the hundreds of churches and elementary and preparatory schools that operated throughout the central highlands and the coastal areas. The Protestants' impact thus went far beyond the Ovimbundu highlands, from Lobito on the coast to the central highlands and beyond.[23]

Unlike the Catholic missionaries, the Protestants successfully straddled both the prophetic and political arenas. Protestant missionary teachers disregarded the law by allowing their Ovimbundu students to communicate using both their native Umbundu and Portuguese languages.[24] Publicly criticizing the brutality of Portuguese labor policies, Protestant missionaries acted as a buffer between the Angolan Africans and the colonial state.[25] Whereas Catholics condoned the state's forced labor policies, its routine beatings with a wooden stick known as "*palmatória*," and the limited primary school education system, the Protestants offered a wide range of opportunities to their converts.

Nevertheless, the Protestants recognized that they had to comply with state demands in order to continue their work in Angola. Protestant missionaries were warned to be cautious in exposing Portuguese injustice, because in Angola "we enjoy much freedom and many privileges which are curtailed in other parts of Africa. It therefore behooves us to count our blessings rather than bemoan our difficulties."[26] This attitude allowed the Protestant churches to straddle the prophetic and political divide. Thus it is not surprising that the Angolan leaders who rebelled against the colonial state in 1961 were trained in Protestant schools.

The Nationalist Struggle of 1961–1974

In the wake of the outbreak of the liberation war in 1961, church–state relations in Angola underwent another dramatic shift. Colonial state officials identified the Protestant missionaries as enemies of the Portuguese colonial state for fostering the growth of anti-Portuguese sentiments among Africans and for deliberately creating institutions outside the state. The colonial regime also criticized the Protestants for supporting the Movement for the Liberation of Angola (Movimento Popular de Libertação de Angola, or MPLA) and the coalition of the Union of the People of Angola (União dos Povos de Angola, or UPA) and the Front for the Liberation of Angola (Frente Nacional de Libertação de Angola, FNLA).[27]

Thus between 1961 and 1963, the colonial government reduced the number of Protestant missionaries from 256 to 141, and by the late 1960s the number had fallen precipitously to 11.[28] Although more muted, the state also expelled 16 Catholic priests and imprisoned 9 others suspected of being revolutionary sympathizers.[29] Until 1974, Catholic and Protestant leaders were held hostage to a colonial state intent on holding on to power. Whereas Protestant missionaries had used subterfuge to avoid the unjust demands of state officials, they were more cooperative after 1961. As the Methodist missionary Raymond Noah admitted, "We always worked on the principle that we should do all we could to cooperate with government authorities."[30]

This close linkage of religion and politics exposed the contradictions between the Church's prophetic and political roles. During his 1965 speech to the United Nations and his 1969 speech in Kampala, Uganda, Pope Paul VI recognized the principle of self-determination for colonial states.[31] The Vatican's new position affected the younger missionaries arriving in Angola during the late 1960s and early 1970s. With post–Vatican II's popularization of liberation theology and the vernacularization of the Catholic Church, a new progressive wing arose within the Angolan Church, whose hierarchy was increasingly Africanized.[32] Some Angolan Catholics joined their fellow Protestants to form the leadership of the MPLA and Holden Roberto's government-in-exile that formed in Leopoldville in 1962.

However, the Angolan Church continued its support for the colonial state. In 1969 Jonas Savimbi, the leader of the Union for the Total Independence of Angola, or A União Nacional para a Independência Total de Angola (UNITA), stated that "few missionaries who are still in Angola are preaching an adulterated Gospel as they cannot attack Portuguese atrocities without fear of reprisals. When they have to keep quiet, they condone colonialism and PIDE activities."[33] Angolan Catholic leaders thus remained silent to demands that the Vatican should disassociate itself from the Portuguese Church to protest Portuguese atrocities in the nationalist war. Conversely, Protestants publicly promoted their political role on behalf of the Angolan Africans, pointing out that colonial officials regarded them as dangerous because they had "strong foreign ties. They practice a subversive radical democracy . . . [and] also destroy the unity and harmony of the Portuguese community which is being promoted by the Catholic Church."[34]

During the 1960s, Protestant leaders in Canada, the United States, and the United Kingdom openly aligned themselves with the liberation movements; by 1965 these Protestants supported four hundred Angolan students in various postsecondary institutions throughout the world.[35] However, the Catholic Church continued to serve the state by opening more Angolan schools. By 1975, the Angolan Church had established 3,396 Catholic primary schools employing 3,894 teachers or monitors and educating 157,821 students. In addition to establishing rudimentary schools in African villages to prepare Africans for entry into primary school, the Angolan Church ran several high schools and many postprimary institutions for training students for business, health care, woodworking, and the like.[36] However, this extensive educational system catered mainly to the white and mulatto populations, and it never reached the majority black Angolan Africans. Postsecondary education was outside their reach, although the Church did offer a limited number of scholarships to Africans.[37]

Because of its cooptation by the colonial state, the Angolan Church was never an independent agent. Forced to comply with state regulations, it remained segregated from the African masses, and it played a minimal role in the training of the emerging African political leadership, who "came out of [the Protestant] tradition." Protestants who were banned from working in Angola continued to exercise a moral voice by reminding the revolutionary leaders of "the tradition which is the foundation of a free Angola."[38] Yet, despite the 1970 meeting between Pope Paul VI and the leaders of three liberation movements in the Portuguese African colonies (Amilcar Cabral of Guinea-Bissau, Marcelino dos Santos of Mozambique, and Agostinho Neto of Angola), Catholic missionaries who supported the liberation movement had to do so surreptitiously.[39]

The MPLA, Marxism, and the Angolan Church

Angolan critics viewed the Church in 1974 as inseparable from the colonial state, which they derisively described as a "Catholic Fascist regime." When the liberation movements were transformed into political parties, the Protestant church played the "more important political role."[40] Following the April 25, 1974, Portuguese coup, hundreds of thousands of Portuguese settlers and many Catholic priests and nuns scrambled to leave Angola. As a result, the advocacy of the Angolan Church's hierarchy and local clergy was absent as the contest of power among the MPLA, FNLA, and UNITA degenerated into civil war and chaos.[41] Under these circumstances, the MPLA leadership planned its attack against the Angolan Church with the ultimate goal of establishing an antireligious, Soviet-style state.

After the MPLA gained control of the state, party officials adopted policies that deprived the Angolan Church of the status and privileges it had enjoyed under the colonial regime. Indeed, the Marxist leadership hoped that within several decades all religious life would disappear from Angola. To that end, President Antônio Agostinho Neto and the MPLA leadership abrogated the Angolan Constitution, which had guaranteed that "all religions shall be respected and the state shall afford churches and places and objects of worship protection as long as they comply with state law."[42] Neto publicly attacked the Angolan churches, accusing them of being "anti-patriotic and anti-national."[43]

Parish and village churches were the first targets of the antichurch campaigns. Any Catholic or Protestant missionary who appeared sympathetic to UNITA faced harassment. Father Tarsisio, who was pastor of 25,000 Ovimbundu living in the central highlands area of Alto Hama, recalled that the "MPLA would not openly stop the Masses, but on Sundays they would organize alternate activities to take place at the same time as the church service. The MPLA did not want people going to church because it was against its Marxist ideology."[44]

The state continued its antireligious rhetoric during the period 1977–78, when President Neto argued that "Catholics and Protestants could not join the party" and speculated that within fifty years "there will be no church in Angola."[45] At its annual meeting in 1978, the MPLA Political Bureau decided that priests and missionaries must register as foreign residents and could only operate as foreign residents and not as institutions. Moreover, the Political Bureau ordered the registration of "legitimate" churches and institutions, prohibited new construction for religious purposes, banned church and religious organizations that "promoted disobedience and disregard for the law," and outlawed "women's, youth, and labor organizations of a religious nature." A newly established party committee supervised all religious publications.[46]

Responding to these antichurch initiatives, the Angolan Catholic bishops issued a pastoral letter criticizing the government takeover of religious educational institutions, the education of Angolan children in socialist countries without parental consent, and the state's reliance on "atheistic propaganda." The bishops also publicly criticized the government for failing to uphold the constitutional guarantees of religious freedom; Radio Vatican reported that the Angolan people "suffered discrimination for their beliefs and often lost the custody of their children."[47]

Publicly condemning the pastoral letter as "an insult to our people, our government, and the MPLA Workers' Party."[48] President Neto approved the closure and nationalization of the Catholic Radio Ecclesia.[49] The government-controlled newspaper *Jornal de Angola* printed a series of attacks accusing the bishops of being counterrevolutionaries. The government defended its actions against the Angolan Church by arguing that "the Church enjoyed a very privileged position" during the colonial period and that "any government that wants to take control of its educational system and carry out any equitable land reform policy was bound to clash with the [Angolan] Church."[50]

Despite its rhetoric of socialist atheism and its antichurch legislation, the government had no intention of alienating all religious groups. Indeed, even as the party moved against the nationwide Catholic institutions, the Baptist missionaries in northern Angola, and Protestant missionaries in central Angola, the MPLA sought to ally itself with the Methodist Church as its new political partner. The Methodists and their strong Kimbundu membership, who made up the base of the MPLA, had been friendly with the MPLA since the early days of the liberation struggle. When the Baptist-trained Congos (FNLA) allied with their Church of God-trained Ovimbundu (UNITA) to fight against a Marxist-led MPLA, Angolans had no doubt that the MPLA was allied with the Methodists. The Methodist bishop Emelio Carvalho, who formalized the relationship between the revolutionary state and the Methodist Church, was described as "a great political man of MPLA."[51] Roberto de Almeida, the MPLA Central Committee secretary for ideology, described the Methodist Church in Angola as a "religious institution with an important history of remarkable deeds during the great epic of our people's liberation."[52] Thus the MPLA considered the Methodist Church a religious entity inseparable from the revolutionary state.

Eventually, the MPLA was confronted with an intractable and expensive war against UNITA. The war cost 60 percent of the government's annual budget, which ruined the economy and led to the death of hundreds of thousands of Angolans. Facing a large refugee population and imminent starvation, the MPLA leadership was forced to pull back from its antichurch policies of the early 1970s and court the very churches that it had persecuted.

MPLA officials subsequently opened a new propaganda front by dispatching teams of ambassadors to reassure American and European church officials of their vital role in Angolan reconstruction. The MPLA now called on the churches to reform their institutions to meet the needs of the oppressed Angolan population. However, the government still emphasized ideological considerations in its rapprochement strategy. De Almeida reminded officials of the World Council of Churches in 1984 that Angola was a secular state.[53]

Rediscovery of the Angolan Church's Prophetic and Political Voice

Faced with a growing crisis in the 1980s, the Angolan Church hierarchy adopted an ambitious moral agenda to confront the state in order to straddle both the prophetic and political spheres. Though cautious of renewing its alliance with the state, the Angolan Church of the 1980s worked with its Protestant counterparts to pursue issues of ecclesiastical needs and social justice among the expanding Angolan population of more than 6 million people. By 1983, the Angolan Church had relied upon 13 bishops, 312 priests, 51 brothers, and 714 nuns to expand its food, education, counseling, health, and other service operations.[54] Citing Pope John Paul II's call for all African Catholics to assume political and social service positions aimed at "energizing African society with the spirit of evangelism," the Angolan bishops advised Catholics working with the state to always keep "the integrity of their faith and the right to practice it."[55] The 1980 pastoral letter also explained the Angolan bishops' refusal of the government's invitation for two priests and a bishop to join the National Assembly, because they would be unable to fulfill both their ecclesiastical and their National Assembly duties.[56]

However, the Angolan bishops had become more politically aggressive by 1984, when they called upon the MPLA-led government and UNITA to work toward reconciliation. The bishops' call for reconciliation publicly challenged the official state position, which regarded UNITA as an illegitimate organization created by South Africa and led by illegitimate leaders. The bishops noted that "the fratricidal war" had led to unnecessary suffering by the Angolan people, with "dislocations of the population, destruction of families, hunger, sickness, death, and other evils of a moral nature." For the first time, the bishops called for an end to the war so that the Angolan family could be "truly reconciled." The bishops proposed to work with the other Angolan churches and people to bring about conciliation; they asked all the Angolan dioceses to promote a permanent prayer for reconciliation.[57]

The Angolan Church also implemented a reconciliation strategy with their fellow Protestant churches to pursue a joint moral agenda. Among these new Protestant allies, the Church found the ecumenical spirit that had been sorely lacking during the colonial period. Maria Chela Chikueka described a religious community in UNITA's capital where Protestant "ministers and [Catholic] priests took turns in delivering the sermon."[58] Eva Chipenda, whose husband, José Belo Chipenda, was named secretary of the All Africa Conference of Churches in 1987, described how Protestants joined Catholics in the meetings and activities at the Center of Studies of Theology and Culture in Lobito.[59] Having grown up in colonial Angola, where Protestant and Catholic Africans did not mix, Chipenda commented that "the usual practice was for the Catholics to take care of their converts in their missions and schools and for the Protestants to do so in theirs."[60] Catholic priests and nuns remained in Jamba, where they continued to work with their Protestant counterparts to maintain the educational, religious, health. and other institutions for the large refugee population. Two Protestant missionaries who visited Jamba in 1985 observed that many of the civilian and military personnel there had been former members of the Protestant community in the highlands. Yet among the Protestants was a Catholic congregation, including "seven priests and five nuns."[61]

Although the new ecumenical strategy empowered the Angolan Church to engage the state, the Church still faced an uphill battle to achieve its moral agenda. Reflecting on the tenth anniversary of Angolan independence, fourteen archbishops and bishops decried the social calamities that had resulted from a decade of war. They called on the MPLA and UNITA partisans, in the name of "all the victims of this conflict," to put down their arms and take up peace.[62] In their 1989 "Message to the Leaders of UNITA and MPLA-PT," the bishops stressed that "Angolans want to be one people, a real nation," and they called on Christians to "continue their prayers so the leaders of the MPLA-PT and UNITA, through the intercession of the Immaculate Heart of Mary, Patron Saint of Angola, find the road to true peace."[63] For the first time since independence, the Angolan Church directly confronted the state.

As expected, MPLA officials challenged the bishops' authority to interfere in political affairs and reminded them of the subordination of the Angolan Church to the state.[64] Accusing the bishops of colluding with the United States and "the armed bandits of UNITA," MPLA officials said that the bishops were possibly committing treason by engaging in "political actions that objectively serve the interests of the enemies of the People's Republic of Angola." The state thus warned the bishops not to "give counsel to those who don't need it or take the place of the state under which they are integrated." Finally, the bishops were reminded to "render to Caesar what is Caesar's and to God what is God's."[65]

Carrying out the Angolan Church's prophetic and political roles on behalf of the underrepresented paid off by the late 1980s. Although the government did not give up plans to subordinate the Church, the MPLA officials were forced to adjust their policies toward the Angolan Church for several reasons. The MPLA's war with UNITA was stalemated, thus forcing the MPLA to reconcile with the Angolan Church. Officials slowly realized that the Angolan Church was not an enemy of the MPLA or the state but an advocate for peace. Perhaps most important, the MPLA had lost its propaganda monopoly, as the pulpit could now outmaneuver the state press. The November 1989 bishops' letter, read throughout Angola, called on both the MPLA and UNITA to end the hostilities and hold free elections. As a result, the Angolan Civic Association joined with the Angolan Church to pressure the MPLA and UNITA to respect human rights. The Angolan Church had rediscovered its political voice.

The Bicesse Accords, 1991

The 1991 Bicesse Accords, which formalized procedures for reconciliation and free elections, was a major political breakthrough for the Angolan Church.[66] MPLA officials had realized that an alliance with the Angolan Church was essential to ensure its political survival in a democratic Angola. With the help of sympathetic Angolan Church officials such as Cardinal Dom Alexandre de Nascimento, the state began to repair its relationship with the Church by inviting Pope John Paul II to visit Angola in 1992 and by establishing formal diplomatic ties with the Vatican.

MPLA officials deftly handled the pope's 1992 visit to Angola, which included an official welcome at the airport, an outdoor mass in war-ravaged Huambo in the Ovimbundu highlands, and a mass amid the ruins of Angola's five-hundred-year-old Catholic Cathedral in Mbanza Kongo, the capital of Zaire province, and formerly known as São Salvador, the ancient capital of the Kingdom of Kongo. Angolans for the first time witnessed Marxist officials consorting with the pope and the Angolan clergy on MPLA-controlled radio and television. Not long after the pope's visit, the Angolan president, José Eduardo, who had been a dedicated Marxist, married for the first time in the Angolan Church.

One scholar of contemporary Angolan politics suggests that the new relationship was nothing more than "political dating" (namoro politico), for it highlighted the MPLA's search for legitimacy in the face of UNITA's threat. Others have accused the MPLA of using the papal visit "as a vote-catcher among the Catholics" for the November 1992 elections.[67] Perhaps the most accurate interpretation came from the Angolan people themselves, who argued that "it is better to be ruled by a robber than a murderer" (*Vale mais un gatuno no poder do que un assino*).[68] Thus, the Angolan Church remained vigilant, especially following the 1992 elections, which did not bring the expected end to the internal conflict.

As the Angolan civil war continued throughout the 1990s, the suffering of the Angolan people increased exponentially. Unfortunately, their suffering was compounded by the diversion of humanitarian aid by corrupt MPLA officials.[69] The Angolan Church continued to work with the Protestant churches to vigorously promote democracy and justice in Angola. Working with Catholic Relief Services and other organizations, the Church delivered needed services to displaced Angolans. The Church strengthened its educational and social services initiatives to a growing number of Angolans who had become dissatisfied with the state-controlled system. The capstone of the Church's educational initiatives was set in February 1999 when the Catholic University of Angola opened its doors to 320 Angolan students. During a ceremony thanking the president of the American "Citizens Energy" for the donation of books and computers, Cardinal de Nascimento stated that "the goal of the Catholic University is to educate young people who . . . will form new generations of students and help the country re-discover the values of education that a terrible prolonged war has obscured."[70]

Although Pope Paul VI had been reluctant to speak on political issues dividing countries and nations, Pope John Paul II strongly supported the Angolan Church's new prophetic and social justice roles and regarded Angolan reconciliation as a top priority.[71] In 1997 the Vatican reestablished diplomatic ties with Angola, a gesture that the pope had refused to adopt during his official 1992 visit to Angola. With the support of the local Protestant churches and now the Vatican, the Angolan Church became an even more potent political actor advocating reconciliation and peace. When UNITA and the MPLA returned to war in 1999, the bishops adopted a dramatic and unorthodox position that the war did not represent the "people's voice or the people's interest." In an effort to achieve "a new mentality" that valued peace,[72] the Angolan bishops launched the "Movement towards Peace" (Movimento pro Pace). Reaching out to all believers as well as secular forces including Angolan politicians, the movement urged the MPLA and UNITA to sue for peace.

The resolve of the Angolan Church to be the prophetic and political voice for all Angolans strengthened in the face of kidnappings, murders, and intimidation that its staff and members faced.[73] With the direct support of Pope John Paul, the Angolan Church joined other religious leaders in 2000 to convene a Congress for Peace. The congress publicly condemned the war for continuing "to destroy the country, to decimate its people and to widen the gulf of hatred between Angolans."[74] Empowered by the Church's new moral imperative, Father Simões of São Francisco Parish in the Viana municipality directly condemned the MPLA's wanton execution of Ovimbundu people suspected of supporting

UNITA. Insisting that he was not a UNITA supporter, Father Simões argued that "as a representative of God and the Church," his duty was "to state the truth, to denounce errors, and to defend the oppressed."[75]

Conclusion

Beginning in the 1980s, the Angolan Church transformed itself to play a remarkable moral and political role in war-torn Angola. Analyzing church–state relations in Angola, the *Washington Post* published articles in 2001 titled "In Angola Church Is a Surrogate State" and "Missionaries Fill Void in Vital Services." The *Post* discovered that the independent news outlets in Angola were not "as popular or as outspoken as the Archdiocese's Radio Ecclesia."[76] The article proceeded to profile Sister Maria José, who was the seventy-year-old head of the local Catholic charitable organization, Caritas. Having worked as an Angolan missionary for decades, Sister Maria José represented the new type of socially and politically committed Catholic missionary.

Following the death of UNITA's leader Jonas Savimbi in early 2002 and the end of the civil war, the state accepted the Angolan Church's prophetic and political roles to achieve a strong and stabile Angolan society. In 2004, the Angolan Ministry of Education approved the Angolan Church's petition to establish new schools and other educational facilities as well as to train educational staff.[77] The state also allowed the representative of the Angolan archbishop, Brother João Domingos, to accept 5,000 copies of the Portuguese Roman Catholic Bible from the Lusophone Bible Society. Despite having broadcast critical comments about the state in 2003, Radio Ecclesia was allowed to continue to serve as a voice for the Angolan people.[78]

The relationship between the state and the Angolan Church had come a long way since the colonial and revolutionary periods. By 2000, the Angolan Church had weathered a devastating civil war and substantial ideological attacks to emerge as a potent prophetic and political leader in an independent Angola.

Notes

1. Pepetela, *Mayombe: A Novel of the Angolan Struggle* (Portsmouth, N.H.: Heinemann, 1983), 77.

2. John Marcum, *The Angolan Revolution* (Cambridge, Mass.: MIT Press, 1969); Lawrence Henderson, *Angola: Five Centuries of Conflict* (Ithaca, N.Y.: Cornell University Press, 1979); Lawrence Henderson, *The Church in Angola: A River of Many Currents* (Cleveland: Pilgrim Press, 1992); Didier Péclard, "Religion and Politics in Angola: The Church, the Colonial State, and the Emergence of Angolan Nationalism (1940–1961)," *Journal of Religion in Africa* 27, no. 2 (1998): 160–86; Maria Guadalupe Rodrigues, "The Catholic Church in Contexts of Crisis: The Case of Angolan Independence," *Current Research on Peace and Violence* 13, no. 4 (1990): 235–43.

3. Benedict Schubert, *A Guerra e as Igregas, Angola 1961–1991* (Geneva: P. Schettwein, 2000).

4. Manuel Nunes Gabriel, *Angola: Cinco Seculos de Cristianismo* [Angola: Five Decades of Christianity] (Lisbon: Literaly, 1978), 365.

5. Linda Heywood, *Contested Power in Angola, 1840s to the Present* (Rochester: University of Rochester Press, 2000), 92–122.

6. For the work of the Methodists, see Lawrence Henderson, *A Igreja em Angola* [The Church in Angola] (Lisbon: Editorial Alem Mar, 1990), 225–28.

7. American Board Conference for Foreign Missions, Merlin Ennis, "Portuguese Colonial Adminstration in Angola," 2.

8. Guadeloupe Rodrigues, "Catholic Church in Contexts," 237.

9. Péclard, "Religion and Politics," 167.

10. "B. Moisés Pinho, Bishop of Angola and Congo to Monseigneur," Archives General de R. Peres du St. Esprit, boite 485, November 10, 1939.

11. Catherine Ward Tucker, *A Tucker Treasury: John T. Tucker—Reminiscences and Stories of Angola, 1883–1958* (Winfield, U.K.: Wood Lakes Books, 1984), 118.

12. Henderson, *A Igreja*, 130.

13. Heywood, *Contested Power in Angola*, 102.

14. Réné Pélissier, *Colonie du Minotaure* (Paris: Montamets, 1978), 445–52; Heywood, *Contested Power in Angola*, 101.

15. Henderson, *A Igreja*, 130.

16. American Board Conference for Foreign Missions, John T. Tucker, "Labour Conditions in Africa . . . Angola," 1944, 3.

17. Os Bispos Católicos de Angola, "Nota Pastoral, Luanda," May 14, 1980, 2.

18. American Board Conference for Foreign Missions, D. V. Waln, "Why Recruits?" October 28, 1940, 1.

19. American Board Conference for Foreign Missions, Merlin W. Ennis, "Report," 3.

20. American Board Conference for Foreign Missions, Merlin W. Ennis, "The Missionary Enterprise Still Has Frontiers," 2.

21. American Board Conference for Foreign Missions, Merlin W. Ennis, "Africa Calls," December 1, 1944.

22. Ibid.

23. E.g., see Heywood, *Contested Power in Angola*, chap. 5.

24. Statement made by Mr. Malcolm McVeigh before the Angola Committee, United Nations Archives, DAG 4/4.2, box 10, McVeigh, 15.

25. Edward A. Ross, *Report on Employment of Native Labor in Portuguese Africa* (New York: Abbott Press, 1925). Ross included in his critique of Portuguese labor several instances of abuses of African labor as described to him by Protestant missionaries.

26. United Methodist Church, General Board of Global Missions, File 602-A, Correspondence, Minutes of 24 Conference of the Evangelical Alliance, 13, 1956.

27. United Methodist Church, General Board of Global Missions, New York, File 669; Raymond Noah, "An Account of Experiences in Angola, Africa during the Years 1960–61,"14. For the outbreak of the liberation wars, see John Marcum, *The Angolan Revolution: Vol. 1: Exile Politics and Guerrilla Warfare, 1962–1976* (Cambridge, Mass.: MIT Press, 1969).

28. Heywood, *Contested Power in Angola*, 79.

29. United Church of Christ, Angola, 1964, File 486, Conference Baptist Missionary Society, "The Baptist Missionary Society and Angola, A Statement—January 1964," 2; see also Guadeloupe Rodrigues, "Catholic Church in Contexts," 238.

30. United Methodist Church, General Board of Global Missions, New York, File 669, 6.

31. Guadeloupe Rodrigues, "Catholic Church in Contexts," 238.

32. Péclard, "Religion and Politics," 170.

33. American Committee on Africa, New York, 1969, "Open Letter to Protestant Missionaries Who Served in Angola," J. M. Savimbi, October 1969, 3.

34. United Methodist Church, General Board of Global Missions, New York, File 842, Conferences, Accra Conference and Argentina Conference, Lawrence Henderson, "Report on Angola, April 1968," 2.

35. United Church of Christ, File 511, "Proposals Regarding Protestant Mission Work in Angola," L. W. Henderson, June 17, 1965, Confidential Report to Angola Committee, 7.

36. Os Bispos Católicos de Angola [Catholic Bishops of Angola], November 28, 1980, 2.

37. United Nations Archives, DAG 4/4.2, box 10, "Statement Made by Mr. Malcolm McVeigh before the Angola Committee," 1961.

38. United Methodist Church, General Board of Global Missions, New York, File 946, Program Conferences, Joel Norby to Samuel Abrigada, December 12, 1973.

39. For the reaction of Jonas Savimbi to this incident, see American Committee on Africa, Angola, Doc. 1, Dr. Jonas Savimbi, Interview, 1970, 9.

40. American Committee on Africa, New York, "African Scenario, 1974–79," 1.

41. United Methodist Church, General Board of Global Missions, New York, File 985, "All Angolan Conference," Eugene Cardoso, Camono, Angola, August 13, 1975.

42. American Committee on Africa, New York, Angolan Press Release, Luanda, July 21, 1984, 5.

43. The antichurch campaigns resembled the anti-Protestant campaigns of the earlier Portuguese colonial regime, as officials targeted the Catholic and Protestant educational institutions and missions. Like their New State counterparts, the MPLA viewed the churches as their main competitors to leading civil society.

44. Karl Maier, *Angola: Promises and Lies* (London: Sherif, 1996), 50.

45. Henderson, *A Igreja*, 402.

46. American Committee on Africa, New York, Angolan Press Release, Southern Africa, E. 1 VIII, March 1978.

47. As quoted in Michael Wolfers and Jane Bergerol, *Angola in the Front Line* (London: Zed Books, 1983), 182.

48. Ibid., 183.

49. *Washington Post*, January 27, 1978.

50. *National Catholic Register*, April 1, 1979.

51. United Methodist Church, General Board of Global Missions, "All Angolan Conference," 2.

52. American Committee on Africa, New York, Angolan Press Release (Angop), Luanda, July 21, 1984, 5.

53. See http://www.mongabay.com/reference/country_studies/angola/all.html.

54. American Committee on Africa, New York, APS News and Features Bulletin, 7.

55. Os Bispos Católicos de Angola, May 14, 1980, 2.

56. Ibid., 3.

57. Os Bispos Católicos de Angola, February 17, 1984.

58. Maria Chela Chikueka, *Angola Torchbearers* (Toronto: Chela Book Group, 1999).

59. Eva de Carvalho Chipenda, *The Visitor: An African Woman's Story of Travel and Discovery* (Geneva: Risk Books, 1996), 75–76.

60. Ibid.

61. American Committee on Africa, New York, "Church Delegation Visits Christians in the UNITA-Controlled Area of Angola," November 1985, 4. The delegation comprised Lawrence Henderson and Betty Bridgman.

62. Carta Pastoral Dos Bispos de Angola e São Tomé, "Firmes Na Esperança: Reflexão pastoral apôs dez anos de independencia" [Pastoral Letter from the Catholic Bishops of Angola and São Tomé: "Firm in Hope: A Pastoral reflection after ten years of independence"], Conferência Episcopal de Angola e São Tomé, 1986, 11–12.

63. "A Message from the Angolan Bishops" Luanda, November 11, 1989.

64. "A Deus o que e de Deus, Resposta do MPLA" [The God who is God: Response to the MPLA], November 3, 1989, 1.

65. Ibid.; "Message from the Angolan Bishops."

66. "Bicesse Accords," http://www.incore.ulst.ac.uk/services/cds/agreements/pdf/ang1/pdf.

67. *New York Times*, June 5, 1992.

68. As quoted by Tali, "About Pope John Paul II Visit to Angola in 1992," 3.

69. George Wright, *The Destruction of a Nation: United States Policy towards Angola since 1945* (London: Pluto Press, 1997), 142.

70. "Cardonal do Nascimento and Joe Kennedy Send Books, Computers, to Catholic University of Angola," Boston, June 7, 1999, http://www.angola.org/reference/pressrel/prce060799.html.

71. *New York Times*, June 5, 1992.

72. Human Rights Watch, "Angolan Civil Society and Human Rights," http://hrw.org/reports/1999/angola/Angl1998-11.htm.

73. For the attacks on Catholic missionaries in Angola see, "16 Catholic Children Kidnapped in Angola, 18 October 2001," http://www.christiansoldiers.org/Pers011018.html; and "Angolan Missionaries Abducted as Pope Appeals for Peace," http://cwnews.com/news/viewstory,cfm?recnum=13505.

74. "Churches Call for Cease-Fire," http://www.actsa.org/Angola/apm/apm0801.htm.

75. Maier, *Angola*, 127.

76. *Washington Post*, March 22, 2001.

77. "Ministry of Education Approves Catholic Church Schools," Luanda, January 31, 2002; available at http://www.angola.org.

78. Angolan Press Agency, "Catholic Church Apologizes to Head of State," February 21, 2003.

Part Five

THE CHALLENGE OF
ACCOMMODATION

IN CHAPTER 1 OF THIS VOLUME, Kenneth Himes argues that the early Church was lacking both political and military influence, and, as such, patiently endured the larger political dynamic all around. That description speaks very clearly to the contemporary situation for the Catholic Church in India and China, and to a lesser extent, in the Congo. In all three cases, the respective national churches have faced the challenge of accommodation to civil authorities. In this, they have sought to create some protective space in civil society for their flock.

In chapter 12, Mathew Schmalz highlights the often tenuous position of Catholicism within Hindu India. Representing less than 2 percent of the total population, the Catholic community has tried to make itself indispensable to the larger culture by its significant contributions in education, health care, and orphanages. Even so, many influential members of the Indian political elite consider the Catholic Church to be an antisecular, antinational force, and they have strongly criticized it for its policy of conversions. And yet, Christianity is very much a part of the fabric of Indian society; Saint Thomas the Apostle is said to have first brought Christianity to India in A.D. 52, and there are Syrian rite Christians in the southern state of Kerala who have practiced their faith for almost 2,000 years. For its part, the Roman Catholic Church arrived in India with the Portuguese in 1498, and it was established under Saint Francis Xavier. Under Portuguese rule, there were both forced conversions in the areas they controlled—Portuguese India mainly consisted of Goa, Daman, and Diu, along with some smaller holdings, located south of Mumbai (Bombay)—and their colonial pattern of intermarriage with Hindu families created a new breed of Luso-Indian Catholics in the subcontinent. When the Portuguese were finally expelled from India in 1961, they left behind an indigenous Goan Catholic minority culture. So although Catholics only constitute a small community within India's vast and diverse population, the Indian Church has a reliable population base and presence, which, according to its critics, generates a power that far exceeds the number of its adherents. Chapter 12 fully explores the theme of how the church deals with state authorities in an effort to secure a safe place for its religious activities in civil society.

Lawrence Reardon argues in chapter 13 that the Chinese Communist authorities view the Catholic Church to be an antinational, antirevolutionary, and foreign presence, and have sought to eliminate it. Reardon details the history of Christianity in China, with special emphasis on the half-century struggle between the Communist state and the Vatican to control the hearts and minds of Chinese Catholics. The result of this struggle has actually been the division of China's 12 million Catholics into three groups: those who belong to the open, state-controlled patriotic Church; those who belong to the illegal, underground Church, which regards the pope as the vicar of Christ; and those whose loyalties are divided between the state and the pope. The theme of how Rome and the local church seek to negotiate space under Communist control and atheistic secularism dominates this chapter.

In the volume's concluding chapter, the African Jesuit Priest Yvon Elenga argues that the Catholic Church has been a successful agent of civil society under democratization in his native Congo. The situation is less dire in the Congo for Catholics than in India or China, in that they represent some 42 percent of the total population, but they still face some difficulties from civil authorities. The author suggests that whenever the Catholic Church raises questions about issues such as abortion and corruption, it does so to reflect Catholic social teaching and to participate in the dynamics of democratization. That is, in confronting many difficult and dangerous situations, the Congolese Church has acerbated its relationship with the state all the while attempting to create space for itself and its flock in civil society.

Chapter 12

The Indian Church:
Catholicism and Indian Nationhood

MATHEW N. SCHMALZ

AFTER THE INDIAN GOVERNMENT RECOGNIZED Vatican City as a state
and exchanged ambassadors, Pope John Paul II announced that he would make
a state visit and a "pilgrimage" to India in 1986. The Catholic Bishops Council
of India (CBCI) promulgated several documents that invoked the spirit of the
Second Vatican Council to renew the Indian Church.[1] Many Indian Catholics
hoped that the papal visit would bring international attention to the Indian
Catholic movement as well as add credibility to Catholic contributions to Indian civil society. These hopes were concealed in language that sought to contain or negate the political resonance of the papal visit; according to the Catholic
periodical *The Examiner*,

> the very presence of the Pope should be for us a sign and hope of the unity which
> is necessary to solve the manifold problems which beset the Church and country.
> The Pope will not be expected to offer concrete solutions to the political and so-
> cial problems that often lead to divisions and disunity. The Church was not given
> a mission in the political, social and economic order. Christ set it as a religious
> one.[2]

To affirm its religious nature, the papal visit was presented under the theme,
"A Call to Unity." The pope would first visit Delhi and Shillong, then travel
south to Goa and Bombay.[3] Great care was taken not to raise any issues that
might be considered controversial. The pope generally refrained from talking
about conversion, caste, abortion, and other incendiary issues. Instead, he invoked Mahatma Gandhi and his legacy to speak in general terms about the quest
for justice. The only controversial event occurred when the pope criticized the
Goan hierarchy for allowing only priests inside the Basilica of Dom Bosco for
his mass, while nuns and Catholic laity were forced to remain outside. Such

rhetorical restraint was essential, given the often tenuous position of Catholicism within independent India.

Controversy was indeed waiting for the pope. Upon his arrival in New Delhi, demonstrators met him with placards opposing conversions and denouncing the foreignness of Catholicism. Wider protests had been planned, but 300 demonstrators were arrested as a "precautionary measure" before they began their march.[4] Recognizing the controversy that the papal visit could incite, Urdu-language periodicals with a largely Muslim readership welcomed the pope. Also attempting to quiet the controversy, the *Hindustan Times* published an editorial describing the pope's visit as "sentimental" and of "little political significance."[5]

Nevertheless, such views were in the minority as many Indian journalists portrayed the Catholic Church as an antinational force.[6] The issue of conversion was the centerpiece of an article in the Hindi news magazine *Awakash* alleging that foreign missionaries received tens of millions of rupees from abroad.[7] In the widely circulated Hindi periodical *Dinman*, Ramsevak Srivastav initially praised the significant contributions of Catholic colleges, schools, and hospitals to Indian society, but he then proceeded to argue that the Church violated Indian traditions of secularism.[8] For Srivastav, conversions to Christianity represented a failure of Hinduism; Catholicism was a "time bomb" waiting to explode within Indian society.

Such fears were echoed by Hindu nationalist leaders. Balraj Madhok, the head of the Hindu nationalist organization Rashtriya Swayamsevak Sangh (RSS), spoke of plans to "convert 200,000 Indians to Christianity" as a "present" for the pope.[9] Madhok attributed the government's reception of the pope to the influence of Sonia Gandhi, the Italian-born wife of then–prime minister Rajiv Gandhi. The invective surrounding Catholicism only worsened with John Paul II's return visit in 1998. Hindu groups took out full-page advertisements asking the pope to renounce conversion. When he affirmed conversion by promulgating his postsynodical apostolic exhortation *Ecclesia in Asia*, Hindu communities throughout the world protested.[10]

The controversy surrounding the papal visits to India crystallized deep and long-held suspicions about the Catholic presence in Indian society. As early as three years after Indian independence, the state government of Madhya Pradesh accused foreign missionaries of using financial incentives to convert members of tribal groups.[11] In a recent series of widely publicized books, the journalist Arun Shourie branded Christian exclusivism as antinational. In many ways, the animus directed against Catholicism is surprising. Catholics constitute a relatively small community within India's vast and diverse population. However, the Indian Church has a presence and, some would say, a power that far exceeds the number of its adherents. This institutional visibility has attracted much protest and praise.

To explore the tensions between Catholicism and Indian nationhood, this chapter argues that Catholicism is firmly rooted in Indian culture but is also associated with colonial and foreign domination. The indigenous yet foreign character of Indian Catholicism is the fundamental problem confronting the institutional church, just as it is with the Chinese Church and the early American Church, respectively described in chapters 13 and 4 of this volume. Central to Catholicism's understanding of itself in Indian society is its essential contributions to building Indian nationhood through its extensive work in education and health. However, the crucial point of contention between Catholicism and the Indian government is conversion, which often puts Catholicism in a rather precarious position. Thus, Indian Catholicism must negotiate its relationship with a civil society oscillating between Hindu nationalism and secular democracy.

A Brief History of Catholicism in India

As in the Chinese case, South Asians considered Roman Catholicism to be a foreign religion controlled by a foreign power. Catholic schools have often catered to the elite of Indian society and quite conspicuously use English as the medium of instruction. Catholic communities are often identifiable by their distinct customs. But Indian Catholics generally do not perceive Catholicism as being irreducibly foreign, even though they paradoxically value its association with "otherness." Such ironies are the result of Catholicism's history as both a tradition rooted in Indian culture and a religion undeniably associated with colonialism.

Precolonial Catholic Presence

Catholic tradition holds that the Apostle Thomas brought Christianity to India in A.D. 52.[12] Settling at Cragamore on the Malabar Coast, Saint Thomas began to spread the Gospel among the Hindu community. Approximately ten years after his arrival, seven churches had been established and the small Christian community was consolidated.[13] Thomas' missionary efforts led him to Mylapore, where he was martyred.[14] Though it would be difficult indeed to confirm the accuracy of stories concerning Saint Thomas in India, many Indian Catholics consider these stories historically true and a symbolically important marker of Catholicism's roots in South Asia.

The first record of foreign contact with Christian communities in India was in A.D. 345, when Thomas Canav and a group of Syrian Christians settled in Travancore in southern India;[15] presumably the use of the Syro-Malabar liturgy began soon thereafter. Within the indigenous Varna system—the traditional hierarchical division of Hindu society into four classes: Brahmin (priest),

Kshatriya (warrior), Vaishya (merchant), and the Shudra (servant)—Christians were placed somewhere between the warrior and the merchant classes. Five centuries later, another wave of Syrian Christians immigrated to southern India. Because the Syriac Church had separated from Rome during the Nestorian controversy, Christianity in India developed independent of Rome until the Portuguese settled in Goa in 1498.

Colonial and Postcolonial Catholicism

In 1514, Pope Leo X ceded "rights of patronage" to Portugal over the churches and trading stations established from Bombay to Tuticorin.[16] The reestablishment of papal influence first brought the Franciscans and then the Jesuits to India, with Goa elevated to an episcopal see in 1536. The sixteenth and seventeenth centuries saw an aggressive expansion of missionary activities. The Jesuit Francis Xavier settled among low-caste pearl fishermen in Travancore and translated both the Nicene and Apostles' creeds into Tamil.

During this stage of Christianity's development, Catholicism became inextricably identified with foreign customs and political domination. All foreigners were called *parangi*, a term that soon became pejorative and synonymous with the Portuguese and Christians.[17] *Parangis* wore leather shoes, ate meat, and drank wine, which were practices forbidden to high-caste Hindus. By slaughtering cows to eat beef, the Portuguese identified themselves with Untouchable outcastes. For a high-caste Hindu to convert to *parangi* Catholicism meant degradation and pollution. In response to such perceptions, Roberto De Nobili, an Italian Jesuit, founded a mission in Madurai and adopted the lifestyle of a Hindu renunciant as a means of adapting Catholicism to indigenous cultural standards.[18] Jesuits also sent emissaries to the court of the Mughal emperor Akbar in the Muslim-dominated north. At the end of the seventeenth century, Catholicism could claim 300,000 adherents in India and Ceylon (Sri Lanka).[19]

The three centuries leading up to Indian independence was largely devoted to institutional consolidation. Catholic missionaries successfully established various ecclesiastical jurisdictions in the north, but they did not gain substantial numbers of converts. In the south, Catholicism was torn by dissention. Some Syrian rite Catholics, resenting the Vatican's influence, established the Mar Thoma Church with full Syriac rites. During British rule, Christian missionaries were given preferential treatment, but these were Protestant missionaries; Catholicism was largely sidelined from participation in political discourse, except in Goa, where the Portuguese held colonial power. Some Catholics were quite active in opposing British rule. Brahmabhadhav Upadhyaya of Bengal, who advocated an Indian style of Catholicism, published a series of scathing newspaper editorials criticizing British rule; as a result, he was imprisoned for sedition and died in prison in 1904.[20] Upadhyaya's life is emblematic of the continuing struggle of Indian Catholicism to negotiate its relationship with the Indian civil society and nation-state. Clergy in southern India were largely Indian, while those in northern India were foreign. The religious life of Catholicism was perceived as "the other." Nonetheless, in preindependence India, the Indian Church established schools and hospitals, which later became the foundation of its influence.

The advent of Indian independence in 1947, along with Portugal's 1961 expulsion from Goa, removed the formal ties between the Indian Church and the colonial power. The importance of the Indian Church was affirmed by the Vatican when Valerian Gracias of Bombay was made a cardinal in 1950. Presently, Catholicism in India is divided into three rites: the Roman or Latin rite, which predominates in the north and among poorer classes on the south Indian coast; the Syro-Malabar rite, which predominates in Kerala state and in parts of northern India; and the Syro-Malankara rite, which continues an often bitter feud with its Syriac counterpart. Overall, the Indian Church has the fourth largest number of Catholic bishops of any country, even though many of the dioceses in the northern India have fewer than a thousand Catholics. Presently, India also has five cardinals. Catholics in India, combining the three rites, number about 20 million or about 2 percent of India's population of 1 billion, 80 to 85 percent of whom are Hindu, with 10 to 15 percent being Muslim.

Catholicism and Indian Nationhood

India is a federal republic and parliamentary democracy. The president serves a largely ceremonial role as chief of state while the prime minister remains head of government. The legislative assembly is divided into the Rajya Sabha (the council of states) and the Lok Shabha (assembly of the people) and reflects India's political diversity and range of national and regional political parties. By virtue of its Constitution, promulgated on January 26, 1950, India is a secular state. Indeed, K. M. Panikkar observed soon after independence that the "new democratic, egalitarian and secular state is not built upon the foundations of ancient India, or of Hindu thought."[21] According to Gerald Larson, conceptions of the Indian nation-state owe much to Western democratic ideals that became influential in India during the period of British rule.[22] But this secular understanding of nationhood has not been without its own tensions, which have forcefully emerged during the last decade.

Until the 1990s, the Indian political system was dominated by the Congress Party, led initially by Jawaharlal Nehru, one of the architects of Indian independence. After Nehru's death, and that of his successor Lal Bahadur Shastri, Nehru's daughter, Indira Gandhi, emerged triumphant as leader of the Indian National Congress Party, also known as the Congress Party or the Congress (I) Party. After Indira Gandhi was assassinated by her bodyguards, she was succeeded by her son

Rajiv. After Rajiv Gandhi's murder by a suicide bomber during a campaign that was expected to return him to power, the fortunes of Congress (I) faded as the Indian government was dominated by the nationalist Bharata Janata Party (BJP) between 1996 and 2004.

The rise of this avowedly Hindu party has had broad implications for Indian nationhood and Catholicism's relationship with the Indian state. The BJP and its ideological forbearer, the RSS, have relentlessly critiqued the official secularism of the Indian state. Though a civil code applies to Hindus, Sikhs, Buddhists, and Christians, Muslims are subject to their own personal law, the Sharia, which has distinctively Islamic requirements for divorce and inheritance. Quotas for lower castes, officially known as "Scheduled and Backward Classes," are maintained not only for admission to education and government employment but also for some elected positions. For many Hindu nationalists, such accommodations to religious and social minorities not only expose Indian secularism as a sham, but also threaten the national integrity of India itself. The continuing evolution of Indian secular democracy and resurgent Hindu nationalism constitute the overarching framework for Catholic involvement in Indian civil society. Such involvement affirms the commitment of Catholicism to the Indian state through the promotion of development programs and religious inculturation, while simultaneously challenging what are perceived to be threats to religious liberty and to the advancement of low-caste groups that have long been ostracized in Indian society.

Religion and Development

Even though India has experienced remarkable economic growth during the past decade, its gross national product per capita stands at a very low $480. Though India has always struggled with poverty, the continuing expansion of the HIV/AIDS epidemic and the demographic shift resulting from female foeticide have also brought significant challenges to Indian civil society. As part of an independent India, the Indian Church has affirmed its work for social justice as central to its role within Indian society. However, the CBCI, from its inception in 1944 until 1970, did not approve any comprehensive statements on the question of social justice. CBCI documents emphasized internal Church affairs and the proper maintenance of charitable organizations. In fact, the CBCI standing committee argued in 1952 that the best contribution the Church could make to "the country's welfare" would be through "her educational and social welfare activities."[23]

The CBCI's first programmatic statement on social justice, "Poverty and Development," was released on International Workers Day in 1971. The CBCI directly focused Indian Catholicism on social justice issues:

Because we are firmly convinced of the fundamental Christian truth that every man is my brother, we also hope that we can respond to the times reveal themselves so eloquently in the cries for justice and liberation from the fetters of an exploitative society that by its social structures perpetuates the enslavement of millions. The Church is very much with the prevailing movement in India to do away with the root causes of poverty through its concern and active participation in programs geared to its causes.[24]

While "personal and relief services will always have their important place," the focus of the Church's work was to transform social structures.[25] In later communications to the Bishop's Synod in Rome, the CBCI outlined its approach to social change: first, the clergy itself should adopt a simpler lifestyle; second, Catholic educational institutions, which traditionally catered to the most affluent sections of Indian society, should educate students as agents of social reform and also earnestly seek to recruit poorer students for admission; third, the Indian Church should assume a more active role in Indian civic discourse.

Looking at the CBCI's pronouncements within the context of global Catholicism, what is initially apparent is the influence of the Second Vatican Council. Seminal documents such as *Evangelii Nuntiandi* and *Gaudium et Spes*, whose significance is discussed by Himes in chapter 1 of this volume, constitute the foundation of Indian Catholicism's move from a state-centered to society-centered Church. But there is also a very specific Indian agendum. The 1970s were heady days in Indian politics. Indira Gandhi was flush with victory over Pakistan and the creation of Bangladesh. One of her campaign slogans was "*Gharibi hatao*" (Banish poverty). Quite clearly, the CBCI was aligning itself with Indira Gandhi's populism, which drew upon various Indian visions of socialism as well as Gandhism. When Indira Gandhi proclaimed the 1975 emergency and effectively suspended Indian democracy, the Indian Church was largely mute, even when faced with forced sterilization campaigns.

The sterilization campaigns of 1975 represented a radical method of dealing with the perennial issue of India's rapid population growth. The Indian government has increasingly favored such aggressive population control measures since the failure to implement the "rhythm method" as a means of family planning during the country's first five-year development plan. In 1996, the CBCI explicitly condemned "coercive methods being practiced in the country such as forced sterilization, abortion and pressure put on health and other personnel in government and other hospitals to propagate and enforce means that go against their conscience."[26] The CBCI's attitude toward population control emphasizes the social context of child rearing.

Generally, the Indian Church identifies population growth as symptomatic of deeper underlying issues that Indian society must address, particularly the distribution of wealth and economic development. The CBCI advocates natural family planning as the most conducive method to developing family harmony, because the population question must be understood within the context of the totality of married life. In India, one occasionally discovers earnest nuns going from village to village attempting to teach the practice of natural family planning. However, within the context of daily parish life, contraception or sterilization is not standard fare in Indian Catholic homiletics. Such an aggressive stance would be controversial, given the extensive but largely unsuccessful efforts of various Indian governments to control population growth.

Abortion is relatively inexpensive and widely available in India. In a CBCI symposium on bioethics in 1986, speakers lamented that the Indian Church had not responded aggressively to the legalization of abortion in 1971.[27] Though the Indian Church denounces abortion, there is nothing remotely resembling the American right-to-life movement. But abortion in India is primarily used to choose the sex of children, resulting in a demographic widening of the ratio between men and women. The prevalence of ultrasound machines and mobile sex selection clinics has made it quite easy for families to selectively abort female fetuses. The Indian Church was one of the nongovernmental bodies that took a strong stance in favor of prohibiting female infanticide. In 1994 the Pre-Natal Regulation and Prevention Misuse Act was passed, making female infanticide illegal, although it is still widely practiced.

The Indian Church has most aggressively focused on the spread of HIV/AIDS. Approximately 1 percent of the Indian population is infected with HIV, and the virus is spreading rapidly, largely through heterosexual sexual activity and drug use. The Indian Church has worked closely with governmental and nongovernmental organizations in developing educational programs designed to provide education regarding the transmission of HIV.[28] The Church's response to the AIDS epidemic was in some ways prompted by the widely publicized refusal of a Catholic priest to allow one of his parishioners to be buried in the Catholic cemetery after he had died of AIDS.[29] The Indian Church has most prominently been engaged in preventing discrimination against those infected with HIV/AIDS and has publicly opened all its hospitals to those infected with the virus. Within Indian civil society, issues surrounding sexuality are not discussed as openly as they are in Western societies. Within this context, the Indian Church's approach to the HIV/AIDS epidemic is quite distinctive in its openness.

Inculturation

Catholicism's efforts to contribute to Indian nationhood extend to conceptions of the religious life of Catholicism itself. Given the widespread association between Catholicism and various understandings of "foreignness," Roman or Latin rite Catholicism in India began an earnest attempt to adapt its religious life to Indian cultural standards. The so-called Indian "inculturation" movement conventionally is placed within the framework of the reforms of the Second Vatican Council and its openness to religious pluralism.

In the West, Catholic adaptation to Indian culture is most closely identified with the work of two foreigners, Henri Le Saux and Bede Griffiths, who came to India to adopt a life of radical renunciation. But within the context of Indian Catholicism, the Indian theologian D. S. Amalorpavadass had the most decisive influence on the inculturation movement. Born in Pondicherry, a former French colony in India, and educated in France, Amalorpavadass took charge of the National Liturgical Center in Bangalore.[30] Empowered by the reforms of the Second Vatican Council and a variety of indults *ad experimentum*, Amalorpavadass envisioned an experimental Indian rite mass that would supplant the imported Roman or Latin rite.[31] Though not approving Amalorpavadass's most radical reforms, the Vatican issued "12 Points of Adaptation," which allowed a variety of accommodations to Indian culture in the Latin rite mass: Priests dressed in ochre robes characteristic of renunciants, and the Bible and the Eucharist were honored through offerings of flowers and incense. Characteristically, Hindu images such as the lotus were also utilized. Amalorpavadass envisioned these adaptations as bridging the gap between Catholic and Indian identities. Moreover, such adaptations were designed to embrace Indian culture and nationhood. Amalorpavadass and many Indian bishops hoped that Catholicism would no longer be seen as foreign but as very much a part of the Indian nation.

Such advocates of inculturation were continuing a long tradition of Catholic fascination with India. Indologist missionaries, such as Roberto De Nobili and Abbe Dubois, produced some of the finest ethnographic accounts of Hindu religiosity.[32] In one sense, India has always been seen as prime mission territory. Yet in another sense, Hinduism has often been understood as a kind of mirror image of Catholicism—both embrace a clerical hierarchy, the use of images, and a tremendous diversity of practice.

Amalorpavadass had entered into a political debate about Indian identity that is at the center of Indian political life and institutions. In writing about the enculturation movement, the Indian sociologist K. N. Sahay predicted that it would lead to Catholicism's full acceptance within Indian society.[33] Hindu nationalists, however, had a much different view. The social critic Sita Ram Goel branded enculturation as a cynical attempt to win converts by dressing up Catholic religiosity in Indian garb.[34] Just as colonial powers once exploited India, Catholicism was now exploiting and consuming Indian religiosity without regard to appropriate boundaries of difference.

Ironically, many Indian Catholics also resisted inculturation. South Indian Catholics took Amalorpavadass to court to stop the experimentation; they believed that these adaptations threatened their own distinctive identity. Many north Indian Catholics are converts from the Untouchable castes; they resist the reforms as a concession to Brahmin religiosity. Hinduism is a very diverse religion, and of course India is a religiously diverse nation. Given all the facets of Hinduism and Indian religiosity that could presumably be accommodated, engaged, or integrated into Catholic religious life, it is interesting that Catholicism has chosen high-caste forms of religiosity. Far from being an irenic attempt to open Catholicism to Indian culture, inculturation represents an accommodation to an incipient ideology of Indian nationhood—and one that is generally not amenable to Catholicism itself.

The Conversion Controversy

At the center of the discourse surrounding enculturation remains the issue of conversion. Whether an accurate characterization or a stereotype, it is widely said that Hinduism is a majority religion with the insecurity of a minority religion. Hinduism was pilloried and attacked under British rule. The British government also patronized Protestant missionaries who attempted, generally quite unsuccessfully, to convert the "natives." Mahatma Gandhi often commented that he admired Christ but did not admire most Christians or Christian churches.[35] What Gandhi found most offensive was Christian claims to absolute truth and its strategies of conversion. Given the attitude many Christian missionaries have expressed toward Hinduism and Indian religiosity, debate over conversion has been a consistent and contentious feature of Indian political life.

At the heart of the conversion controversy are different readings of the Indian Constitution. Freedom of religion is guaranteed according to article 25 (1) approved by the Constituent Assembly as part of the Indian Constitution during the early days of Indian independence. The article provides that "subject to public order, morality and health and to the other provisions of this part, all persons are equally entitled to freedom of conscience and the right to practice and propagate religion." Indian Catholics have long argued that the Constitution explicitly allows conversion if conversion is understood to proceed from a free conscience. For example, Valluvan Clarence Motha, a prominent legal expert at Loyola College in Madras, argues that

> to propagate religion means to spread and publicize one's religions convictions for the edification of others. The word propagate indicates persuasion and exposition without any element of coercion. It is immaterial whether the propagation is made by a person in his individual capacity or on behalf of some Church or institution. The right to propagate one's religion does not give the right to any one to forcibly convert any person to one's religion.[36]

With regard to evangelization, the Indian Church's efforts have been very circumspect. While Protestant catechists and missionaries are known to conduct campaigns ridiculing Hindu gods, Indian bishops would never condone such aggressive efforts. It is only in the northeast India states of Assam, Mizoram, and Arunchal Pradesh that the Indian Church has gained substantial numbers of converts in recent decades.

Underlying the issue of conversion is the question of "forced conversion," whose definition often leads to more circumscribed interpretations of constitutional guarantees of religious freedom. In his continuing polemics against Christianity, the Indian journalist Arun Shourie observes that the Constitution makes explicit that "nothing in this Article shall affect the operation of any existing law or prevent the State from making any law a) regulating or restricting economic, financial, political, secular or other secular activity which may be associated with religious practice; b) providing for social welfare and reform."[37] These constitutional articles render illegal the receiving of money from abroad, conversion, and any overt involvement in political discussion.

Shourie's arguments articulate deeply held suspicions of Christian activity within Indian society. Missionaries have long been the subject of distrust in Indian society, and various state governments have passed legislation banning forced conversions, which are defined as those based upon financial inducements. Since Indian independence, many state governments have established commissions that have investigated missionary activities and have claimed that missionaries did in fact use financial incentives to entice converts. In his 1956 report to the Madhya Pradesh government, Justice M. B. Rege drew attention to loans, food aid, and hospital access preferentially given to Christian converts. This led him to conclude, "We cannot call conversions for pure material gain fraudulent in the strict sense of the word; but in our view the preaching of any religion must be based on very strong and pure ethical foundations and conversion without strong faith, must be depreciated as being unspiritual and unethical."[38]

The Indian Church has often labeled such charges as baseless given the wide-ranging nature of its social work. Nonetheless, the states of Madhya Pradesh and Orissa have drastically curtailed activities of the Indian Church and other Christian denominations. It is very difficult to verify the allegations of forced conversion, especially because Catholic and Protestant denominations are lumped together in an undifferentiated whole. In his polemical writings, Shourie conflates English Protestant missionaries, the CBCI, the Bible, and various Vatican documents, which he simply regards as "the Christian Church." He thus does not appreciate the dramatic differences between the various Christian denominations.[39]

What does seem clear, however, is that the distribution of foreign aid to Catholic converts constitutes a strong financial incentive to convert, even though it perhaps was not intended to be some sort of quid pro quo. Because of the dynamic created by its distribution of clothes, food, and scholarships, the Indian Church has curtailed or stopped its most aggressive aid programs.[40]

Catholicism and Caste

The Indian Church has continually protested any restrictions on religious activity and denied the use of financial incentives to encourage conversion. Generally, the protest against restrictions placed upon Catholic missionary activities, or the granting of visas to foreign priests, has been framed in terms of broader Catholic discussions of human rights and religious freedom. However, the Indian Church has specifically focused on the conversion among the Untouchable castes, which are now described as the Dalits (the oppressed or crushed).

Within the four classes of traditional Hindu society, a person still belongs to the class one is born into regardless of occupation. Jawaharlal Nehru was a Brahmin even though he was prime minister. These classes subdivide into particular castes. Thus, there are multiple endogamous classes within specific castes. This hierarchical system is based upon distinctions between purity and pollution. If one is involved in a particularly polluting occupation, such as tanning or street sweeping, one has correspondingly low rank within the hierarchy. Outside the system entirely are the Untouchables, who are considered to be so polluted that even their touch is considered defilement. Though Untouchability has officially been abolished, Untouchables in the rural areas are still subject to a variety of restrictions— from being denied access to communal sources of drinking water to being segregated into colonies outside villages. During the past hundred years, the vast majority of converts to Catholicism have come from Untouchable castes.

The issue of caste within Indian society is a matter of considerable debate. Western scholars have been criticized for overemphasizing or "fetishing" hierarchy within Indian civilization.[41] However, the caste is undeniably one of the primary issues within Indian civic discourse. Since Indian Independence, the government has pursued a wide-ranging program of compensatory discrimination designed to benefit the Untouchables.[42] Not only are political or administrative positions set aside for members of Scheduled and "Backward Classes," there are also quotas, officially called "reservations," for Scheduled Caste employment and university admission. Christians of Scheduled Caste origin, however, are not legally entitled to these benefits. According to the President's Constitution (Scheduled Castes) Order 19 of 1950, only Hindus are in the "Scheduled Caste" category. This position was affirmed in the cases of *Michael v. Venatsuaram* and *Guntur Medical College v. Mahau Rao*, wherein it was determined that a convert to Christianity ceases to belong to the caste system.[43] Although preference benefits were eventually extended to Buddhists and Sikhs of Scheduled Caste origin, Christians have been consistently excluded.[44]

The Indian Church's reaction to the issue of quotas was initially quite muted. The CBCI in 1982 peripherally mentioned that quotas should "perhaps" be set aside for "the weaker sections" of society.[45] However, by 1988 the CBCI had passed a resolution committing itself to changing legislation that allowed Christians of Scheduled Caste origin to benefit from the expansive preference system.[46] In the 1990s, the Indian Church organized a series of demonstrations to demand the inclusion of Christians in Scheduled Caste quotas.[47]

Although none of these actions had any impact upon legislation, the Indian Church inserted itself more forcefully into the national debate on caste. Many Indian journalists argued that such demonstrations are incomprehensible because there is no conception of caste in Christianity. And such demands for preference benefits only further divide Indian society along caste lines. The Christian response to such arguments is that Dalit Christians live in a caste society and are subject to the same discrimination as other "Hindu" members of Scheduled Castes. Moreover, if there is no caste in Christianity, quotas for Dalit Sikhs and Buddhists are illogical, because neither religion embraces the caste system. The quota system is quite controversial—to demonstrate against this aggressive program of affirmative action, young Brahmins have immolated themselves in protest. According to the mainstream Indian media, the preference system encourages the rigid filling of quotas and nepotism, which has led to a decline in educational standards and qualifications for government service. Interestingly, the Church's agitation for quotas for Christian Untouchables marked a turning away from its key national constituency. Many of the most influential Indian political and civic leaders were trained in Catholic English medium schools; these leaders were most threatened by an expansion of the quota system. While the Indian Church has pulled back from the most aggressive forms of aid for Catholic Untouchables, it nonetheless represents one of the most ardent advocates for the rights of Untouchables regardless of their religious identity.

Catholicism and Hindu Nationalism

The rise of the Bharata Janata Party (BJP) in the 1990s threatened India's constitutional commitment to secularism. The BJP's ideological forebear, the RSS, is vehemently anti-Muslim. The BJP and the RSS are committed to building a temple to the Hindu god Ram over the ruins of a mosque in the northern Indian city of Ayodhya, which is an issue that has periodically sparked deadly riots among Hindus and Muslims. The BJP and RSS also oppose the concessions made to Muslims in Indian law. Though Christianity is certainly not as much a target as Islam, Catholicism in particular is often branded as antinational.

The position of the BJP and the RSS vis-à-vis the Indian Church became an international issue in 1999. Anti-Christian violence occurred in areas of India where the Catholic Church had aligned itself with low-caste converts. For example, in the central Indian state of Madhya Pradesh, nuns were raped; in the eastern coastal state of Orissa, several priests were murdered.[48] In Gujarat, the birthplace of Mahatma Gandhi, several Untouchable communities of Catholic converts were put to the torch. The Indian government made a variety of public statements decrying the violence but sought to disassociate itself and its RSS cadres from any association with it—either as actual instigators of the violence or for creating what would be called in India a "communalistic" atmosphere that encouraged religious violence. The Indian Church implicated the government's role and reaffirmed its support of the lower castes that were the primary victims of the violence. Yet the violence against Catholic Christians undeniably brought into sharp focus the issue of conversion, long the most incendiary point of contention among the Indian Church, the Indian government, and Indian civil society.

Conclusion

Walter Fernandes argues that the Indian Church has unevenly combined two approaches to the issue of Indian national integration. First, it has tried to promote its own interests while finding a "mode of living" among other religious groups.[49] Second, Catholicism has tried to develop an "understanding" among elite groups that implicitly recognize Hindu dominance.[50] Catholicism's efforts to promote social justice and religious freedom would fall under the first approach, while enculturation would represent the second. Though Fernandes argues that an aggressive "prophetic" voice would constitute a third approach to national integration on the basis of "justice," the Indian Church seems reluctant to set itself in opposition to Indian elites, as Fernandes recommends.

The issue of Catholicism's presence within Indian society once again came into sharp relief with the unexpected success of Congress (I) in the 2004 Indian national elections. Sonia Gandhi, the widow of Indira Gandhi's son Rajiv, was widely expected to assume the post of prime minister. But her Italian birth, her halting Hindi, and her Catholic identity made the possibility of her holding the reins of government politically untenable. Though Catholics have held positions of authority in government and the military, the perception of Catholicism as a foreign religion that is ultimately controlled by foreigners remains a dominant theme in Indian political and civic discourse.

Notes

1. "Pastoral Letter of the CBCI Standing Committee on the Occasion of Pope John Paul II's Visit to India," *The Examiner*, August 3, 1985, 697–98, 719.

2. Eddie Fernandes, "What's the Significance of the Pope's Visit to India?" "Our Vineyard" column, *The Examiner*, January 1986.

3. The terms "New Delhi" and "Delhi" are used interchangeably in this chapter.

4. "Tin Sau Hindu Mahasabha Gireftar" [300 Hindu Mahasabha Arrested], *Quami Morcha*, February 2, 1986.

5. For a representative editorial, see "Pop Jaun Paul ki Acchi Batein" [The Good Words of Pope John Paul], *Qaumi Morcha*, February 3, 1986; S. Venkat Narayan, "On the Path of Peace," *Hindustan Times*, February 2, 1986.

6. "Pop ki Yatra" [The Pope's Trip], *Dharmyug*, February 2–8, 1986; Kanchan Gupta, "A Tour Too Many?" *Telegraph*, February 2, 1986; "The Papal Visit to India," *Times of India*, February 3, 1986; Paravin Dakshan, "The Oldest Church in India," *Sunday*, February 2–9, 1986; Thomas Abraham, "Papacy: Pulls and Pressures," *Frontline*, January–February 1986, 9–11.

7. Rajnish, "Kya Kar Rahi Hain Isai Mishanariyan?" [What Are Christian Missionaries Doing?] *Awakash*, February 28, 1986.

8. Ramsevak Srivastav, "Kya Katholik Carc Sacmuc ek Taim Bam Hai?"[Is the Catholic Church Really a Time Bomb?], *Dinman*, February 2–8, 1986.

9. Balraj Madhok, "Pop ki Bharat Yatra" [The Pope's Indian Journey], *Dinman*, February 2–8, 1986.

10. For the complete English text of *Ecclesia in Asia*, see http://www.vatican.va/holy_father/john_paul_ii/apost_exhortations/documents/hf_jpii. For the reaction among the diaspora Hindu communities, see "Pope: 'Convert all Hindus,'" *Hinduism Today*, February 2000, 24.

11. Government of Madhya Bharat, *The Christian Missions Enquiry Committee's Report* (Indore: Government of Madhya Bharat, 1956).

12. See P. Thomas, *Christians and Christianity in India and Pakistan* (London: George Allen & Unwin, 1954), 11–27; Stephen Neill, *A History of Christian Missions* (London: Penguin Books, 1986), 44–45; and M. R. James, *The Apocryphal New Testament* (Oxford: Oxford University Press, 1926), 364.

13. A. Mathias Mundadan, *History of Christianity in India: From the Beginning up to the Middle of the Sixteenth Century* (Bangalore: Church History Association of India, 1989), 21–36.

14. Ibid., 44–46.

15. F. E. Keay, *A History of the Syrian Church in India* (New Delhi: ISPCK, 1960), 19.

16. Jose Luiz, *Evangelization in Uttar Pradesh* (Bombay: Coordination Center, Saint Xavier's College, 1974), 24.

17. Stephen Neill, *A History of Christianity in India: The Beginnings to 1707 A.D.* (Cambridge: Cambridge University Press, 1984), 280.

18. On Roberto De Nobili, see De Nobili, *Preaching Wisdom to the Wise: Three Treatises by Roberto De Nobili, S.J., Missionary and Scholar in 17th Century India*, trans. Anand Amaladass, S.J., and Francis X. Clooney, S.J. (Saint Louis: Institute of Jesuit Sources, 2000); see also Vincent Cronin, *A Pearl to India* (New York: E. P. Dutton, 1959).

19. Luiz, *Evangelization*, 26.

20. For more on Brahmabhab Upadhyaya, see Julius Lipner, *Brahmabandhab Upadhyay: The Life and Thought of a Revolutionary* (New Delhi: Oxford University Press, 1999).

21. K. M. Panikkar, *The State and the Citizen* (Bombay: Asia Publishing House, 1956), 28.

22. Gerald Larson, *India's Agony over Religion* (Albany: State University of New York Press, 1995), 4.

23. CBCI, "Report on the Meetings of the Standing Committee," in *The Social Teaching of the Church*, ed. John Desrochers (Bangalore, 1982), 199–200.

24. CBCI, "Report on the 1971 CBCI Meeting in Bombay," in *The Social Teaching of the Church*, ed. John Desrochers (Bangalore: Centre for Social Action, 1982), 121.

25. Ibid.

26. CBCI, *Population and Development* (New Delhi: CBCI Centre, 1996), 12.

27. C. J. Vas, "Medical Overview and Laity Concerns," in *Colloquium on Bio-Medical Issues*, ed. CBCI (Bombay: Bharat Printers, 1986), 20.

28. An overview of the CBCI's work for HIV/AIDS education may be found at http://www.cbcihealth.com/.

29. See http://www.cdcnpin.org/PrevNews/2004/jan04/update011404.txt.

30. My discussion here draws upon my previously published analysis of Amalorpavadass's work; see Mathew N. Schmalz, *"Ad Experimentum*: Theology, Anthropology and the Paradoxes of Indian Catholic Enculturation," in *Theology and the Social Sciences*, ed. Michael Barnes (Maryknoll, N.Y.: Orbis Books, 2001), 161–80.

31. See D. S. Amalorpavadass, *New Orders of the Mass for India* (Bangalore: National Biblical, Catechetical, and Liturgical Centre, 1974). Indults *ad experimentum* are quoted by the pope to deviate from common church law or practice.

32. Abbé J. A. Dubois, *Hindu Customs, Manners and Ceremonies*, trans. Henry K. Beauchamp (Oxford: Clarendon Press, 1906).

33. K. N. Sahay, *Christianity and Culture Change in India* (New Delhi: Inter-India Publications, 1986).

34. Sita Ram Goel, *Catholic Ashrams* (New Delhi: Voice of India, 1988).

35. Mahatma Gandhi, *The Collected Works of Mahatma Gandhi*, vol. 65 (New Delhi: Government of India, 1964), 47–48.

36. Valluvan Clarence Motha, "Conversion: A Fundamental Right," in *Christianity in India: Its True Face*, ed. CBCI Commission for Evangelization (Thanjavur: Don Bosco Press, 1981), 61.

37. Most recently, see Arun Shourie, *Harvesting Our Souls: Missionaries, Their Designs, Their Claims* (New Delhi: ASA Publications, 2000), 49–50.

38. M. B. Rege, *Christian Missions Enquiry Committee* (Indore: Government of Madhya Bharat, 1956), 10.

39. See Arun Shourie, *Missionaries in India: Continuities, Changes, Dilemmas* (New Delhi: ASA Publications, 1994).

40. See Mathew N. Schmalz, "Images of the Body in the Life and Death of a North Indian Catholic Catechist," *History of Religions* 39 (November 1999): 177–201; see also Schmalz, "Dalit Catholic Tactics of Marginality at a North Indian Mission," *History of Religions* 44 (February 2005): 216–51.

41. On this point, see Arjun Appadurai, "Is Homo Hierarchicus," *American Ethnologist*, 13 (1986): 745–61.

42. For a general discussion of compensatory discrimination, see Mark Galanter, *Competing Equalities: Law and the Backward Classes in India* (New Delhi: Oxford University Press, 1984).

43. See Julian Saldanha, S.J., "Legal Barriers to Conversion," *Indian Missiological Review* 5 (January 1983): 16–22; and Lawrence Sundaram, S.J., "Problems of Coverts Before and After Conversion," in *Christianity in India: Its True Face*, ed. CBCI Commission for Evangelization (Thanjavur: Don Bosco Press, 1981).

44. Dalit Sikhs were included in the reservation system in 1956, and Dalit Buddhists were added in 1990.

45. CBCI, *Report of the General Meeting 1982* (New Delhi: CBCI Centre, 1982), 46.

46. CBCI, *Report of the General Meeting 1988* (New Delhi: CBCI Centre, 1988).

47. See "Caste Conscious," *Sunday*, December 16, 1995.

48. Celia W. Dugger, "Attacks on Christians Unsettle Rural India," *New York Times*, January 23, 1999; "47 Suspected Militants in India Charged with Missionary's Death," *New York Times*, January 25, 1999; "India's Christians: A Double Standard," *New York Times*, February 19, 1999. Also see U.S. State Department, *Annual Report on Religious Freedom for India, 1999*; http://www.state.gov/www/global/human_rights/irf_rpt/199/irf_india99.html.

49. Walter Fernandes, *The Role of Christians in National Integration* (New Delhi: Indian Social Institute, 1988), 35.

50. Ibid.

Chapter 12

The Chinese Catholic Church: Obstacles to Reconciliation

LAWRENCE C. REARDON

FOLLOWING THREE DECADES OF PERSECUTION and suppression, Christianity in China is enjoying a renewed sense of vibrancy and growth. Churches that were once used as pigsties, grain silos, and automotive repair centers have reopened to serve China's 21 to 80 million Christians.[1] The Protestant and Catholic churches are enjoying an upsurge in popularity as China's masses increasingly search for religious alternatives to the atheistic credo of Marxism–Leninism–Mao Zedong Thought.

Similar to the Indian and the early American churches analyzed in this volume, the Chinese Church is a minority church that has had a contentious relationship with the state. Unfortunately, the Catholic Church in China is divided internally. Though the three rites within the Indian Church are the result of centuries of migration, well described by Schmalz in chapter 12 of this volume, the division of Mainland China's 12 million Catholics is the direct result of a decades-long political struggle between the state and the Vatican. This struggle has resulted in three different churches: the open, state-controlled patriotic Church (hereafter called the open Church); the illegal, underground Roman Catholic Church, which regards the pope as the vicar of Christ with singular authority (hereafter called the underground Church); and Chinese Catholics whose loyalties are divided between the Communist state and the Vatican. Sources in Hong Kong estimate that more than one-third of Chinese bishops (38 percent), priests (36 percent), nuns (33 percent), and seminarians (37 percent) belong to the underground Church.[2] Although somewhat abated, the resulting conflicts within the Mainland Catholic movement have slowed reconciliation attempts and inhibited the growth of Catholicism, especially compared with Protestant counterparts.[3]

The Vatican has enjoyed limited success in influencing the state's religious policies during periods of moderate control. However, since the early 1980s, the

Vatican's pastoral strategy has inhibited reconciliation within the Chinese Catholic movement and has antagonized communist elite leaders, who have prevented formal diplomatic recognition of the Vatican. As with the Rwandan case discussed in chapter 10, reconciliation among all China's Catholic Churches—including the Hong Kong and Taiwanese Catholic churches not analyzed in this chapter—remains an elusive but necessary precondition to achieve the "Church as communion" as described by Himes in chapter 1.

Chinese Policy Cycles

China's religious policies have been affected by a cycling between moderate and conservative/ideological policy positions. Elite decision makers coalesce around like-minded elites among the twenty-five to thirty-five top policy elites, thus forming "opinion groups."[4] Such groups vie for the support of the preeminent leader to gain control of the policy process. Once successful, the opinion group or groups undergo a process of readjusting previous policies and introducing innovative policies. The implementation process is the most complex, as problems often arise, requiring midcourse policy corrections. If such corrections fail, a competing opinion group will intervene, claiming that the state faces a crisis. The ruling opinion group thus can lose its legitimacy, resulting in the transfer of power to its elite competition.

Key to this approach is the Weltanschauung of the individual decision maker, formed by particular beliefs and life experiences.[5] Communist elites share certain basic opinions of the Catholic Church, which are strongly rooted in China's historical legacy and communist ideology.[6] During the Imperial period, religious beliefs were incorporated in the official state orthodoxy of Confucianism: "Imperial rule and Confucian view of the subjects' loyalty to the state went hand in hand with mutual enforcement."[7] The state accepted Buddhism, Daoism, and later Christianity as long as they "recognized the state's political authority, accepted its leadership in all social spheres and carried out its policies." Contemporary Chinese elites continue to share this historical view that the state must dominate religion.[8]

Second, Communist elites view the Catholic Church as a foreign church with foreign leaders (yang jiao). As with the Indian Church described in chapter 12, Western missionary churches, schools, and hospitals were considered foreign enclaves, where foreign priests under the protection of foreign colonial military powers acquired political power.[9] Because this "usurpation" of China's sovereignty continued during the Republican period (1911–49), the Chinese Communist Party (CCP) attacked the Church as early as 1928.[10] By diplomatically recognizing the Japanese puppet state of Manchukuo in 1934, establishing the Legion of Mary to fight communism, and recognizing Taiwan as China's legitimate government after 1949, the Vatican further alienated the CCP, whose elites viewed the Vatican as nothing less than a foreign enemy interfering in China's internal affairs.

Finally, communist elites—whether they be those from China, Poland, or Angola discussed in this volume—share a similar atheistic opinion about religion. Adhering to Marx's view that "religion is the opiate of the people," Chinese Communist elites believe that religion is superstitious belief used to subjugate the working classes.[11] Only Marxism–Leninism–Mao Zedong Thought and science can liberate the masses.

Although sharing these basic views on religion, communist elites held differing opinions on the implementation of China's socialist transformation. Having participated in the Work-Study Movement (Qingong jianxue yundong) in Europe in the 1920s, key elites such as Premier Zhou Enlai and Vice Premier Deng Xiaoping enjoyed a deeper understanding of Western culture and society, including its religion.[12] During their sojourn in Europe, these future CCP leaders received financial aid from Father Lebbe (aka Lei Mingyuan), a Belgian priest who worked in Europe with the overseas Chinese students. A former overseas Chinese student, the renowned military commander Zhu De, reportedly asked the same Father Lebbe to celebrate a requiem mass for soldiers killed in Shaanxi Province in 1936.[13] Although other elites such as Mao Zedong were fascinated by the outside world, they seldom if ever ventured abroad and thus held a more pessimistic view of the international environment, foreign cultures, and religions. These elites adopted a more xenophobic view of the revolution and its economic and social policies.[14]

As a result of these different experiences and beliefs, elites developed different Weltanschauung, resulting in differing attitudes on how to achieve the revolution. Such differences have generated a cycling of policies toward the Catholic Church since the 1950s.

Elites' Tools of Control

China is ruled by the CCP, which is a hierarchically organized Leninist party that enjoys a high degree of policy autonomy and capacity. Since 1949, the preeminent leader (i.e., Mao Zedong, Deng Xiaoping, or Jiang Zemin) formally or informally controlled the three key power bases: the CCP, the government (i.e., the State Council), and the military. The preeminent leader cooperated with the members of the Standing Committee of the CCP's Political Bureau to determine all general policies, including those concerning religion and the Chinese Church. In turn, they depended on the United Front Work Department (Tongzhan Bu) to coordinate religious strategy.[15]

The State Council formulates and implements the actual religious policy dictated by the preeminent leader and the Political Bureau. The primary government organ is the State Administration for Religious Affairs (SARA), which until 2000 was known as the Religious Affairs Bureau (RAB); its Department B oversees China's Christian religions.[16] SARA is responsible for the registration of churches; the approval of church personnel; researching religious policy; and coordinating its efforts with other governmental organizations, such as the trade unions, women's associations, and youth groups.[17] With organizations at the national, provincial, municipal, and prefecture levels, the patriotic organizations are effectively the key agents overseeing RAB/SARA policy implementation. There are eight officially recognized organizations, including the Chinese Catholic Patriotic Association (CCPA), which was established in 1957.[18]

The most important organization within the open Church is the Chinese Catholic Representatives Assembly (CCRA). Meeting every five years, the CCRA "elects the leaders of the [CCPA and the Bishops' Conference], deliberates the work report and stipulates and amends the constitution."[19] The purpose of the Bishops' Conference is "to govern Church affairs according to the principle of independence and in a democratic spirit, conform to the concrete realities of our country, to study and explain the doctrines and morals 'to be believed and to be practiced,' and to represent the Chinese Church at international events."[20]

In addition to these tools of control, the Ministry of National Security exposes foreign agents operating within domestic religious structures and the Ministry of Public Security enforces State Council laws and regulations. Finally, grassroots-level neighborhood committees approve all religious places of worship.[21]

Religious Policy Cycling under Mao Zedong, 1949–78

During the Maoist period, Chinese elites shared the basic goals of eliminating all heterodox beliefs and establishing Marxism–Leninism–Mao Zedong Thought as the sole theological basis of society. Until 1957, these elites agreed to follow a relatively moderate, long-range strategy toward religion and the Roman Catholic Church. Premier Zhou Enlai, who also held the Foreign Ministry portfolio, argued that "as long as there was no opposition to the political power of the Chinese people and no support within the Church for American imperialism, relations with the Vatican could be maintained."[22] Zhou supported the ouster of foreign clergy, but he felt that the Chinese Church, whose adherents numbered about 3.5 million believers, should be tolerated as long as the state maintained ultimate control of their belief systems.[23]

Moderate Policy Implementation, 1949–57

READJUSTMENT. Following the outbreak of the Korean War in mid-1950, the CCP eradicated all perceived hostile foreign influences within China. By 1951,

China expelled the papal nuncio, Archbishop Antonio Riberi, and within two years, more than 5,500 Catholic missionaries were expelled.[24] The most prominent American case involved the arrests of Bishops James F. Walsh and Francis Ford in 1950. Accused of being spies for the United States during the Korean War, Bishop Ford died in a Chinese prison on February 21, 1952, and Bishop Walsh eventually was released from jail in July 1970.[25]

The CCP also persecuted pro-Vatican elements within the Chinese Catholic community, such as Bishop Gong Pinmei, the first Chinese bishop of Shanghai, who remained in prison until the mid-1980s. During September 1955, the arrests of other pro-Vatican bishops ensued, including the mass arrests of pro-Vatican Catholics in Shanghai and elsewhere. Just like all foreign-invested firms established during the "semicolonial" and Guomindang periods, the CCP nationalized religious schools, hospitals, and educational institutions.

INNOVATION. In the early 1950s, the CCP initiated the Three Self Movement (Sanzi yundong), which called upon all churches "to thoroughly, permanently, and completely sever all relations with American missionaries and all other missions, thus realizing the self-government, self-support, and self-propagation in the Chinese Church."[26] By 1957, the Vatican was replaced with a home-grown religious authority: the Chinese Catholic Patriotic Association (CCPA), which maintained only "purely religious relations with the Vatican" and "resolutely oppose[d] its use of religious pretexts and other underhanded activities to disrupt our just cause of opposing imperialism and promoting patriotism."[27]

IMPLEMENTATION. Following the expulsion of Archbishop Riberi in 1951, China severed all diplomatic relations with Vatican City. Despite the "Three Self" strategy, the CCP continued to acknowledge the religious authority of the Holy See, which appointed eighteen Chinese bishops between 1949 and 1955.[28]

VATICAN INFLUENCE OVER MODERATE POLICIES. Because the CCP's policies of the 1949–57 period were relatively moderate, the Vatican was able to influence Chinese elite policies toward the Church through nondiplomatic channels. Though Pope Pius XII issued two apostolic letters that were critical of the autonomous Church and the Three Self Movement, he retained limited authority to appoint new Chinese bishops. Unofficially, the Holy See also "granted local ordinaries in China special powers to empower priests to see to the proper leadership in their respective dioceses during the absence of the bishop or when he is prevented from exercising his proper authority."[29] This right was extended in 1957, which eventually led to the establishment of the underground Church. Some analysts argue that CCP policies of this period actually strengthened the Chinese Church by transforming a foreign religion into a local religion, something foreign missionaries had been unable to accomplish for more than a century.[30]

At the same time, the Chinese Revolution and the ensuing cold war divided the Mainland Chinese Church from Chinese Catholics who escaped to Hong

Kong and to the island of Taiwan, where the Republic of China (ROC) government had been reestablished. The Vatican retained its diplomatic relations with the ROC and strengthened its pastoral activities in Taiwan and the British colony, which became important outposts to observe and at times communicate with the Mainland Church. Though there has been a political reconciliation between the Mainland and Hong Kong since 1997, political and religious reconciliation with the ROC has yet to occur.

Ideological Policy Implementation, 1957–78

READJUSTMENT. Beginning in 1957, Mao Zedong asserted greater ideological influence over the policy elites. His first initiative, the Anti-Rightist Campaign of 1957, imprisoned those who represented the last vestiges of opposition to Mao's policies among the lower ranks of the party and the people, including those Chinese Catholics and prelates that supported the Vatican.[31] Second, Mao called for a Great Leap Forward in 1958, which affected all policy sectors, including the CCPA bishops and priests. Of the 145 dioceses at this time, only 25 were led by bishops.[32] Beginning in December 1957, the dioceses in Sichuan, Hebei, and Hubei provinces consecrated bishops without the consent of the Holy See. From April 1958 until April 1963, the CCPA continued this "self-reliance" strategy by consecrating fifty-one bishops, all of whom were required to reject the Holy See, including all "reactionary" commands and encyclicals.[33]

The failure of the Great Leap Forward temporarily delayed Mao and his ideologically driven colleagues. After 1964, Mao reasserted his control to implement the Cultural Revolution. The ideologues sought to eliminate all feudal and Western cultural influences, including religion and the Catholic Church. Members of the party's United Front Work Department and the State Council's RAB who had pursued the more moderate policies were purged and the CCPA was disbanded.[34] All churches, temples, and mosques were closed, and many were converted for use by local enterprises. Priests, ministers, and imams were sent to prisons, forced labor camps, or to exile in the countryside. To demonstrate their love of Chairman Mao, many priests and nuns were forced to give up their vows of celibacy and to marry.

INNOVATION. By May 1964, the People's Liberation Army issued the *Quotations of Chairman Mao* [*Mao zhuxi yulu*]. The Little Red Book contained snippets of wisdom from Mao's Collected Works that the entire nation would memorize. His works replaced the teachings of Confucius, the Daoists, the Buddhists, and Mohammed. Mao's writings became China's new Bible.

IMPLEMENTATION. Adorned with their sacred Mao buttons, the Chinese people constantly held study meetings to understand and live (*tihui*) Mao's philosophy. Songs and dances in praise of the chairman were composed based on Mao's quotations. Millions of Chinese made pilgrimages to Mao's birthplace and the sites of his most glorious victories. A lucky few million even glimpsed his glorious image in Tiananmen Square. Though foreigners could attend mass at Beijing's Nantang Cathedral beginning in Christmas 1970, the Chinese masses subsumed all religious beliefs to revere Mao, who had become China's "temporal god."[35]

VATICAN RESPONSE. Just before his death in 1958, Pope Pius XII issued his last apostolic letter to the Chinese Church, condemning the CCPA and the illegal appointment of bishops.[36] By 1959, the Congregation for the Propagation of the Faith ruled that the consecration of the CCPA bishops was "illicit but valid," because the appointment of the consecrating bishops had originally been approved by the Holy See. Similarly, all newly ordained priests were valid but had been illicitly ordained.[37] Connections with the Chinese Church were nonexistent in the 1960s. The majority of the fifty-eight "Chinese bishops" who attended the opening of the Second Vatican Council were not from Mainland China but from the Republic of China on Taiwan.

Religious Policy Cycling under Deng Xiaoping, 1978–92

After the Third Plenum of the Eleventh Communist Party Congress of 1978, a moderate elite leadership assumed control. Their shared, long-term goal was to accelerate domestic economic growth, which required a greater involvement with the global capitalist economy. Though continuing to oppose feudal and foreign corrupt influences, these moderate leaders appeared "indifferent to the question of religion and did not see Christianity as a threat."[38]

Moderate Policy Implementation, 1979–87

READJUSTMENT. After thirteen years of regarding Mao as their "temporal god," the Chinese dug up their kitchen gods, reconstructed their ancestral halls, and participated in religious services and festivals.[39] Beijing released many bishops, priests, and nuns jailed since the 1950s, and it began the process of returning Church property by either "giving back the land, buying it, or parceling out another piece in a different area."[40] Major cathedrals and smaller churches once again welcomed Catholic worshipers. By 1982, the Sheshan Seminary in Shanghai was reopened, followed the next year by the National Catholic Seminary in Beijing.[41]

To control China's resurgent religious community, the leadership revived the United Front; the RAB; and the Patriotic Associations, such as the CCPA. The CCP also approved the establishment of the Chinese Bishops' Conference, which gained greater administrative control of the open Chinese Church during the 1980s and early 1990s. Though the bishops continued to acknowledge the pope's spiritual authority, they ignored the Vatican's temporal authority by permitting CCP authorities to appoint Catholic bishops, beginning with Fu Tieshan of

Beijing in 1979.[42] Thus, few analysts were surprised when Chinese authorities refused to allow Deng Yiming to return to China after Pope John Paul II appointed him archbishop of Guangzhou in 1981.[43]

INNOVATION. Two key documents were issued in 1982 to guide the party and the government's religious policies. Article 36 of the new Chinese Constitution reaffirmed the freedom of religious belief, which protected all "normal" religious activities. More important, the Central Committee issued Document 82.19, which was a nuanced strategy designed to encourage both atheists and religious believers to concentrate on the country's foremost goal: economic modernization.[44]

IMPLEMENTATION. As the theoretical foundation of the People's Republic of China (PRC) began to crumble, some Chinese found a new source of psychological comfort in Christianity. The Ministry of Education knowingly hired Protestant missionaries as foreign teachers of English, who quietly conducted Bible study and promoted Christian fellowship activities. In coastal China, Christianity became synonymous with modernization, contributing to a "Christianity craze."[45] Because the government lacked funds to rebuild the churches and finance operations, Christian and non-Christian denominations established small for-profit enterprises and sought foreign financing.[46]

Within the Catholic community, this new openness translated to a greater exchange with the Universal Church. Starting in 1980, China invited Cardinals Roger Etchegaray and Franz Koenig to visit the Mainland, while CCPA delegations visited the Philippines, Belgium, and the United States. Beginning in 1982, prayers for the pope were included in Catholic missals and during mass. In April 1989, the Bishops' Conference upheld "the primacy and authority of Pope John Paul II" as the spiritual leader of the Catholic Church.[47]

VATICAN INFLUENCE OVER MODERATE POLICIES. Reacting to the new Chinese policies during his 1981 visit to Manila, John Paul II called for a renewed dialogue with the Mainland Chinese Church.[48] By 1987, the Holy See reached an accommodation with the CCPA resulting in the resignation of the surviving foreign "Chinese bishops." Cardinal Jaime Sin of the Philippines and the archbishop of Tokyo continued to engage the CCPA in dialogue, and even said mass in the CCPA church.

Simultaneously, the Vatican's Congregation for the Evangelization of Peoples actively supported the Mainland's underground Church.[49] Staffed by formerly imprisoned priests and bishops, the underground Church took advantage of the less restrictive climate to engage in surreptitious communications with the Holy See, to train priests loyal to the Vatican, and to consecrate bishops with the pope's blessing. While priests and the laity were still subject to arrest, the CCP generally tolerated the underground Church and its Protestant equivalent, the "home" churches.[50] However, this toleration had its limits.

Conservative Policy Implementation, 1987–92

READJUSTMENT. As communism was disintegrating in Eastern Europe, Chinese students, intellectuals, and workers were massacred during the Tiananmen Square Incident of June 4, 1989. Deng Xiaoping sided with his conservative colleagues within the party who promoted a more conservative political, economic, and social policy emphasizing nationalism.[51] These conservatives argued that their enemy's goal was to achieve the "peaceful evolution" of China, that is, China's transformation into a democratic state. Christianity, the Vatican, and Pope John Paul II were seen as the major protagonists who contributed to the downfall of European communism, as discussed by Byrnes in chapter 6.[52]

A senior Chinese leader, Chen Yun, argued in 1990 that "using religion to win over the masses—especially young people—has always been a favorite trick of both our domestic and foreign class-enemies. This is the bitter lesson of several of the communist-led countries that recently lost power."[53] To ensure the CCP's survival, the conservatives argued for a curtailment of foreign religious influences and the reimplementation of strict controls over religion.[54] Seeking to consolidate his support among the Political Bureau members, the newly appointed party leader Jiang Zemin supported these conservative initiatives.

Thus in February 1989, the Central Committee adopted the "Circular on Stepping up Control over the Catholic Church to Meet the New Situation."[55] To counteract the Vatican's support of the underground Church, the Central Committee strengthened the CCPA and the Bishops' Conference. As the underground Church was "running wild . . . deceiv[ing] people and incit[ing] them to resist the government," the government arrested underground bishops, attacked Catholic enclaves, and issued local regulations that restricted nonauthorized religious activities.[56] Underground Catholics were forced to repent and to promise to participate in the open Church.[57]

POLICY INNOVATION. In 1991, the Central Committee issued Document 91.6, "Some Problems Concerning Further Improving Work on Religion."[58] While reaffirming the moderate policies put forth in Central Committee Document 82.19 and the problem of "peaceful evolution," the CCP advocated the open codification of religious behavior to promote local government enforcement of unlawful religious activities.

POLICY IMPLEMENTATION. The CCP identified nine avenues of foreign religious penetration, including student and teacher academic exchanges, foreign teachers, Church-owned industries, and tourism.[59] Subsequently laws and regulations were issued to prevent religious activities in Chinese educational institutions and to prevent Chinese students from studying at foreign religious institutions.[60] "Abnormal" religious practices not protected by the constitution were defined as consisting of "any meeting, preaching or evangelism outside [officially designated] places."[61]

Religious Policy Cycling under Jiang Zemin and Hu Jintao, 1992–2005

Because of the threat to the overall "opening" development strategy, Deng Xiaoping broke with the conservatives following his trip to southern China (*nanxun*) in February 1992. Jiang Zemin, who had been appointed as the CCP leader in 1989, gained control of the party and the state; after Deng's death in 1997, Jiang also gained control of the military. This effectively made him the preeminent leader, although he was not as powerful as Mao and Deng.

Jiang and his moderate elite coalition members retained Deng's long-term goals of accelerated economic development. They further integrated China into the global economy by joining the World Trade Organization in 2001, and by allowing capitalists to join the party under the "Three Represents" concept.[62] By embracing these initiatives, Jiang fundamentally transformed the CCP. As for religious policy, Jiang maintained the controls imposed beginning in 1989, but the party and the government became less fearful of "peaceful evolution" and more interested in making money.[63]

Moderate Policy Implementation, 1992–2000

READJUSTMENT. While continuing to adhere to Central Committee Document 91.6, party elites returned to the relaxed attitude of the 1980s. This was apparent at the Fifth National Catholic Representatives Congress of September 1992, which adopted a constitution, imbuing the organization with greater legitimacy and decision-making authority over personnel appointments and policy implementation at the lower levels. Also, greater emphasis was placed on vocations for priests and nuns. Catholic seminaries and convents were allowed to hire foreign teachers and send seminarians and sisters abroad for training in Europe, the United States, and Hong Kong.[64]

POLICY INNOVATION. According to the head of the RAB, the "Three Phrase Directive" issued by Jiang Zemin at a November 1993 United Front conference "point[ed] to a new understanding that religious work will take."[65] Jiang extolled all cadre to "(1) completely and correctly implement the party's policy of religious freedom; (2) strengthen supervision over religious affairs in accordance with the law; and (3) positively guide religion to adapt to socialist society."[66] Six years later, Jiang clarified his position by stating that the party did not require the churches "to adapt to socialist society; religious believers only need to be law-abiding."[67]

Thus, the party's long-term goal had shifted. It was not to eliminate religion, as originally set forth in 1949, but to continue a coexistence with religious believers, who could publish their Bibles and hold prayer meetings as long as such activities were considered within the "norm." This complies fully with the spirit of Jiang's "Three Represents" approach formally announced in 2001, which was the same strategy that allowed capitalists to join the "communist" party. It also allowed the gradual assimilation of Hong Kong into Chinese society after 1997.

POLICY IMPLEMENTATION. In light of Jiang's "Three Represents" philosophy, the party and the open Church adopted two strategies in the 1990s to coexist with and co-opt the underground Church. Instead of arresting underground bishops, the CCPA and the Bishops' Conference actively courted underground bishops and priests—such as two underground bishops from Gansu and Henan—to join the open Church.[68]

Second, with the January 1996 visit of Archbishop Claudio Celli to Beijing, the PRC reopened diplomatic talks with Vatican City that had broken down following the 1989 Tiananmen Incident. Nearly two months following the return of Hong Kong to Mainland authority in 1997, Chinese foreign minister Qian Qichen laid out Beijing's position: Once political relations were resolved, religious issues could be discussed.[69] Thus the CCP had significantly changed its previous negotiating position by allowing a discussion of the Vatican relationship with the open Church, but this would come about only *after* Vatican City had severed diplomatic relations with Taiwan.[70]

VATICAN INFLUENCE OVER MODERATE POLICIES. By February 1999, the Vatican's secretary of state, Cardinal Angelo Sodano, stated that the Vatican was prepared to drop its diplomatic relations with Taiwan and that Chinese bishops would be appointed from a Vatican-approved list of candidates. This was the so-called Vietnam solution.[71] Jiang Zemin agreed to the normalization conditions following his 1999 visit to Europe, where leaders urged the reconciliation.[72] Therefore, on August 17, 1999, the Central Committee issued Document 99.26, "Regarding the Strengthening of Catholic Work in the New Circumstances." To deal with the prospect of greater Vatican inference, the state decided to reduce the bishops' authority by transferring greater administrative control to the CCPA; the state continued its policy of co-opting the underground Church bishops and priests, and arresting those "who stir up trouble." Most important, Document 99.26 stated that "the normalization of China–Vatican relations offers a beneficial opportunity to solve the problem of the underground Catholic forces. If we can use this opportunity . . . to win the majority of the underground Catholic forces over to our side, to convert them, then a key link in the Party Central's strategic plan will be realized."[73]

Throughout the 1980s and 1990s, Pope John Paul II sought to rebuild the bridge between the Chinese Church and the Universal Church.[74] By reaching an accommodation with Beijing, the Vatican also hoped to strengthen managerial control over the Chinese Church, improve direct communications, and help inoculate the Church from corruptive influences.[75] By January 1, 2000, the pope's desire to visit the Mainland during the Jubilee Year was all but realized.

Conservative Policy Implementation, 2000–2005

POLICY READJUSTMENT. On April 25, 1999, fifteen thousand members of the Falungong movement held a peaceful demonstration for sixteen hours in front of the Zhongnanhai leadership compound near Beijing's Forbidden Palace. Inside the compound, members of the Central Committee were both astonished and concerned.[76] Established in the early 1990s by Li Hongzhi, Falungong's mixture of Daoism, Buddhism, and *qigong* harkened back to the mid-nineteenth-century's Taiping, whose leader Hong Xiuquan believed himself to be Jesus' younger brother. Occurring during a similar period of spiritual unrest following the Western opening of China, the rebellion lasted nearly twenty years, and it cost the lives of more than 20 million Chinese.[77] Similarly, Jiang Zemin and the CCP leadership regarded the Falungong as a dangerous cult whose members had infiltrated the party and the state. Subsequently, after "discovering" within China other dangerous religious movements and cults such as the Unification Church, the state banned the movements, arrested tens of thousands of practitioners, and initiated a series of campaigns to root out the "infestation."[78]

Cults and unregistered religious groups were now considered a national security threat.[79] The National Peoples' Congress outlawed all "heretic cults" on October 30, 1999, followed in early 2000 by joint Central Committee / State Council Document 2000.5, "Opinion on Relevant Issues Concerning Dealing with Some Socially Harmful Qigong Organizations." The Ministry of Public Security was charged with the mission of specifying which organizations constituted cults and reeducating the "misled."[80]

Jiang Zemin's previous inclusive policies toward religion were closely reevaluated, especially after the seventeenth Karmapa Lama, one of the most senior Tibetan spiritual leaders, escaped to India in December 1999.[81] Between August 1999 and January 2000, the leadership changed its position on establishing diplomatic relations with Vatican City. On January 6, 2000, the open Church ordained five bishops without the pope's approval. Instead of a low-key diplomatic response, the Vatican employed a historically charged, "tit-for-tat" response by announcing the canonization of 120 Chinese martyrs killed during the 1900 Boxer Rebellion. To compound the situation, the Vatican chose October 1— the PRC's National Day—to perform the canonization ceremonies in Saint Peter's Square in front of ten thousand people. As Beijing's Bishop Fu Tieshan stated, "To choose today's date to canonize those so-called saints is a clear insult and humiliation. Today is a great holiday that celebrates the liberation of the Chinese nation from the invader and from the violent robbery of the imperialists and colonialists."[82] Not surprisingly, this concluded the efforts of Pope John Paul to bring about a reconciliation with the Mainland Chinese Church.

POLICY INNOVATION. During an expanded meeting of the CCP Central Committee and the State Council in December 2001, Jiang Zemin stated that under "the present domestic and international circumstances the party and government can only strengthen their leadership over religious work and their supervision over religious affairs. They cannot allow their control of religion to weaken. . . . [They must] protect the legal; wipe out the illegal; resist infiltration; and attack crime."[83] In essence, the leadership agreed to return to the spirit of Central Committee Document 91.6, but to use the new legal codes and undercover operations to control all illegal religious activities, including the underground Church.

POLICY IMPLEMENTATION. Since 2000, the Chinese state has tightened its managerial control of the open Church, increased arrests of underground bishops and priests, and destroyed illegal underground churches.[84] Most important, three documents were issued in March 2003 that effectively emasculated the Bishops' Conference. The state, through the CCPA, once again fully controlled the open Church.[85]

Conclusion: Policy Cycling, Pastoral Strategies, and Reconciliation

The differing opinions among Chinese policy elites have caused a cycling of moderate and ideological/conservative policies directly affecting the policy toward the Chinese Church and the Vatican. The three preeminent leaders, Mao Zedong, Deng Xiaoping, and Jiang Zemin, initially implemented relatively moderate policies toward society and religion. As their tenure progressed, however, these leaders were confronted by crisis, forcing a change toward more ideological/conservative policy positions. Further research should be undertaken to determine whether differences among communist leaders in other countries, including the Polish and Angolan cases covered in this volume, had a similar influence on religious policy. In chapter 11, for instance, Heywood argues that Angolan Movimento Popular de Libertação de Angola (MPLA) leaders had strong connections with the Methodist Church that affected the communist MPLA's policy toward religious institutions.

Jiang Zemin's adoption of a more conservative position toward religion and the Chinese Church after 1999 was different. The Falungong threat elevated the importance of religious policy to a central position in state affairs, along with economic development and national defense strategies. Clearly, this does not bode well for the future of "illicit" religious movements, such as the underground Church. As of May 2006, the actions of Jiang's Communist Party successor, Hu Jintao, demonstrate that the leadership continues to view uncontrolled religious movements as key threats to national stability. Yet with the realization of the key role of religion in maintaining national stability, China's top leaders might be more open to new initiatives from the Vatican to bring about reconciliation.[86]

The Vatican enjoyed limited influence with the Chinese Communist authorities during moderate policy cycles; the Vatican also overcame problems with other communist states to realize reconciliation, most recently with the Vietnamese Church. Thus it remains unclear why the Vatican has not taken advantage of the Chinese elites' moderate policies to bring about greater reconciliation since the 1980s. Instead, the Vatican has adopted a divisive pastoral strategy of engaging the open Church and aggressively promoting the underground Church. Possibly Church leaders were influenced by the pope's desire to overcome world communism, or by the strong influence within the Vatican of conservative anti-communists and the Taiwanese Catholic Church. Whatever the case, the Vatican's dual strategy has exacerbated political relations with Beijing, provided an excuse for Communist conservatives to arrest underground Church leaders, and divided the laity. This pastoral strategy failed to achieve overall reconciliation during John Paul's papacy.

Reflecting on 400 years of the Vatican's relationship with China, Pope John Paul II stated before his death, "I feel deep sadness for these errors and limits of the past. . . . For all this I ask the forgiveness and understanding of those who may have felt hurt in some way by such actions on the part of Christians."[87] This was a profound apology from the pope. It will be up to Pope Benedict XVI and his successors to learn from past errors and choose the appropriate pastoral strategy to deal with the Chinese state and heal divisions among Chinese Catholics.

The Vatican might find guidance from Rutagambwa's chapter 10 on the Rwandan Church, which provides a detailed blueprint for reconciliation between implacable foes to realize, following Himes, a "Church as communion." Such a comprehensive and lasting reconciliation could only be achieved if the Vatican manages to successfully negotiate a treaty with the local authorities that would unite the open and underground mainland churches with the Hong Kong and Taiwanese Catholic churches, creating a Greater Chinese Church. Such a profound religious reconciliation would no doubt contribute to an overall political reconciliation between the PRC and the ROC on Taiwan.

Notes

The author is especially grateful to Henrietta Harrison, Ted Jelen, Beatrice Leung, Thomas Massaro, S.J., and Robert Whitaker for commenting on drafts of this chapter, and for the support provided by the Universities Service Centre, Chinese University, Hong Kong.

    1. David Aikman, *Jesus in Beijing* (Washington, D.C.: Regnery, 2003), 7–8.
    2. Betty Ann Maheu, "China Church and News Digest, 2003," *Tripod* 23, no. 132 (Spring 2004): 63.
    3. Richard Madsen, *China's Catholics* (Berkeley: University of California Press, 1998): 7–10; John Cioppa, "The Catholic Church in China: Between Death and Resurrection," *Tripod* 12, no. 76 (July–August 1993): 15; Richard Madsen, "Catholic Revival during the Reform Era," *China Quarterly* 174 (June 2003): 469–74. In a critique of

an earlier draft, Henrietta Harrison argues that in Shanxi, growth was also impeded by a general lack of evangelization as well as the "ethnic" nature of Shanxi Catholicism.

4. Kenneth Lieberthal and Michel Oksenberg, *Policy Making in China* (Princeton, N.J.: Princeton University Press, 1988), 35–62.

5. For a more complete discussion, see Lawrence C. Reardon, *Reluctant Dragon: Crisis Cycles in Chinese Foreign Economic Policy* (Seattle: University of Washington Press, 2002), chap. 1.

6. Eric O. Hanson, *Catholic Politics in China and Korea* (Maryknoll, N.Y.: Orbis Books, 1980).

7. Xiqiu Fu, "Guest Editor's Introduction," *China Law and Government* 36, no. 2 (March–April 2003): 4.

8. Liu Peng, "Church and State Relations in China: Characteristics and Trends," *Tripod* 15, no. 88 (July–August 1995): 6.

9. Madsen, *China's Catholics*, 31.

10. John F. Donovan, *The Pagoda and the Cross* (New York: Charles Scribners' Sons, 1967), 111–13.

11. Fu, "Guest Editor's Introduction" (no. 2), 7.

12. Marilyn A. Levine, *The Found Generation* (Seattle: University of Washington Press, 1993); Marilyn A. Levine and Chen San-Ching, *The Guomindang in Europe* (Berkeley: Institute of East Asian Studies, University of California, 2000).

13. Beatrice Leung, *Sino-Vatican Relations* (New York: Cambridge University Press, 1992), 73–76; Levine and Chen, *Guomindang*, 16, 178–85.

14. Reardon, *Reluctant Dragon*, 32–37.

15. Liu Peng, "Church and State Relations," 9.

16. Anthony S. K. Lam, *Decades of Vacillation*, trans. Norman Walling, S.J. (Hong Kong: Holy Spirit Study Centre, 2003), 29.

17. Fu, "Guest Editor's Introduction" (no. 2), 6; Lam, *Decades*, 28.

18. Central Committee Document 82.19, issued March 31, 1982, in *The Catholic Church in Present-Day China*, by Anthony S. K. Lam, trans. Peter Barry, M.M., and Norman Walling, S.J. (Hong Kong: Ferdinand Verbiest Foundation / Holy Spirit Study Centre, 1994), 277; Central Committee Document 99.26, issued August 17, 1999, trans. by *Tripod* Staff, *Tripod* 20, no. 116 (March–April 2000): 34.

19. Central Committee Document 99.26, 35.

20. Ibid.

21. Lam, *Decades*, 41.

22. Michael C. Mi, "Five Obstacles to Sino-Vatican Reconciliation," *Tripod* 16, no. 95 (September–October 1996):7.

23. B. B. Chang, "An 'Independent, Autonomous and Self-Administered' Church," trans. Norman Walling, S.J., *Tripod* 19, no. 112 (July–August 1999): 6; Anthony S. K. Lam, *The Catholic Church in Present-Day China*, trans. Peter Barry, M.M., and Norman Walling, S.J. (Hong Kong: Ferdinand Verbiest Foundation / Holy Spirit Study Centre, 1994), 33; Angelo S. Lazzarotto, "The Chinese Church at the Second Vatican Council," trans. Betty Ann Maheu, M.M., *Tripod* 17, no. 100 (July–August 1997): 49.

24. Lazzarotto, "Chinese Church," 49.

25. Holy Spirit Study Centre Staff, "A Chronology of the Catholic Church in China

in the Context of Selected Dates in World and Chinese History," *Tripod* 13, no. 76 (July–August 1993): 35–37; Donovan, *Pagoda*, 181–203.

26. G. Thompson Brown, *Christianity in the People's Republic of China* (Atlanta: John Knox Press, 1986), 84, as cited in Aikman, *Jesus*, 153.

27. Lam, *Catholic Church in Present-Day China*, 35.

28. Chang, "Independent, Autonomous," 6; Lam, *Catholic Church in Present-Day China*, chap. 2.

29. "Letter to the Shanghai Diocese from Cardinal Fumasoni-Biondi," March 7, 1957, in *Catholic Church in Present-Day China*, ed. Lam, 22–23.

30. William T. Liu and Beatrice Leung, "Organizational Revivalism: Explaining Metamorphosis of China's Catholic Church," *Journal for the Scientific Study of Religion* 41, no. 1 (2002): 121–38.

31. Leung, *Sino-Vatican*, 96.

32. Liu and Leung, "Organizational Revivalism," 128.

33. Paul, "An Appeal from China's Underground Church," trans. Norman Walling, S.J., *Tripod* 19, no. 112 (July–August 1999): 27. For a listing of appointments, see Lam, *Catholic Church in Present-Day China*, 226–29.

34. Leung, *Sino-Vatican*, 99–102.

35. Luo Yu, *Henansheng tianzhujiao shi* [The history of the Catholic Church of Henan Province] (Taipei: Furen Daxue Chubanshe, 2003), 222–25; Holy Spirit Study Centre Staff, "Chronology," 37; Lam, *Catholic Church in Present-Day China*, 51.

36. Lazzarotto, "Chinese Church," 49–50.

37. Lam, *Catholic Church in Present-Day China*, 40.

38. Francis Mi and Betty Ann Maheu, "China's Religious Policy: 1981–1999," *Tripod* 19, no. 113 (September–October 1999): 25.

39. Sergio Ticozzi, "Popular Religion in China Today," trans. Betty Ann Maheu, M.M., *Tripod* 15, no. 85 (January–February 1995): 26.

40. Anthony Lam, "The Catholic Church in China: Conflicting Attitudes," *Tripod* 20, no. 115 (January–February 2000): 29–30.

41. Holy Spirit Study Centre Staff, "Chronology," 43–48.

42. Lam, *Catholic Church in Present-Day China*, chap. 7; Chang, "Independent, Autonomous," 12.

43. Lam, *Catholic Church in Present-Day China*, 61–66; Chang, "Independent, Autonomous," 12–13.

44. For the English translation, see Lam, *Catholic Church in Present-Day China*, 262–86.

45. Author's fieldwork, 1984–88; Liu Peng, "Church and State Relations," 12; Mi and Maheu, "China's Religious Policy," 27.

46. Jean Charbonnier, "The Use of Religion for Economic Purposes," *Tripod* 14, no. 80 (March–April 1994): 5–28.

47. Lam, *Catholic Church in Present-Day China*, 66, 76.

48. Pope John Paul II, "John Paul II Speaks to China," *Tripod* 17, no. 100 (July–August 1997): 35; Holy Spirit Study Centre Staff, "Chronology," 46.

49. Madsen, *China's Catholics*, 41–42. Also see the Eight Directives issued by Cardinal Josef Toko, prefect of the Congregation for the Evangelization of Peoples, issued in May 1988, in Lam, *Catholic Church in Present-Day China*, 176.

50. Liu Peng, "Church and State Relations," 12.

51. Zheng Yongnian, *Discovering Chinese Nationalism in China* (Cambridge: Cambridge University Press, 1999).

52. Fu, "Guest Editor's Introduction" (no. 2), 7.

53. "Chen Yun Letter to Jiang Zemin," 4 April 1990, in *Asia Development Brief* (November–December 1994), as cited in Tony Lambert, "The Present Religious Policy of the Chinese Communist Party." *Religion, State & Society* 29, no. 2 (2001): 124. Also see Beatrice Leung, "The Sino-Vatican Negotiations: Old Problems in a New Context," *China Quarterly* 153 (March 1998): 135.

54. Liu Peng, "Church and State Relations," 5.

55. Central Committee / State Council Document 89.2, issued February 17, 1989, in Lam, *Catholic Church in Present-Day China*, 287–97.

56. Central Committee/State Council Document 89.2, 295–96; Holy Spirit Study Centre Staff, "Chronology," 62–65; Mi and Maheu, "China's Religious Policy," 12; Lam, *Catholic Church in Present-Day China*, 165.

57. Mi and Maheu, "China's Religious Policy," 19.

58. Central Committee/State Council Document 91.6, issued February 5, 1991, in Lam, *Catholic Church in Present-Day China*, 298–308.

59. Mi and Maheu, "China's Religious Policy," 14.

60. E.g., see State Council Document 94.144, issued January 31, 1994, in Lam, *Catholic Church in Present-Day China*, 255–57; Religious Affairs Bureau, "Rules for the Implementation of the Provisions on the Administration of Religious Activities of Aliens within the Territory of the PRC," issued September 26, 2000, in *China Law and Government* 36, no. 3 (May–June 2003): 81.

61. Liu Peng, "Church and State Relations," 9.

62. Bruce J. Dickson, *Red Capitalist in China* (New York: Cambridge University Press, 2003), 161–62.

63. Cioppa, "Catholic Church," 10.

64. Beatrice Leung and Patricia Wittberg, "Catholic Religious Orders of Women in China: Adaptation and Power," *Journal for the Scientific Study of Religion* 43, no. 1 (2004): 77–79; Cioppa, "Catholic Church," 11–13.

65. Ye Xiaowen, "A Review and Reflection on Religious Work at the Turn of the Century: Seriously Study and Solve Major Problems That Affect the Overall Situation," trans. Norman Walling, S.J., *Tripod* 20, no. 120 (November–December 2000): 28.

66. Xiqiu Fu, "Guest Editor's Introduction," in *China Law and Government* 36, no. 3 (May–June 2003): 4.

67. Peter Barry, "Their Voice Should Be Heard," *Tripod* 19, no. 110 (March–April 1999): 24–25; Jiang Zemin, "President Jiang Addresses Religious Representatives," *Tripod* 19, no. 110 (March–April 1999): 26.

68. Anhui Province, Department of Public Security, "The Bulletin of the Department of Anhui Public Security," issued March 6, 2001, in *China Law and Government* 36, no. 2 (March–April 2003): 53; Holy Spirit Study Centre Staff, "China Church and News Update: A Review January 1999–January, 2000," *Tripod* 20, no. 115 (January–February 2000): 64.

69. Mi and Maheu, "China's Religious Policy," 21.

70. Chang, "Independent, Autonomous," 20; *Tripod* Staff, "China Church and News Update," *Tripod* 16, no. 92 (March–April 1996): 51.

71. Holy Spirit Study Centre Staff, "China Church," 64; Madsen, "Catholic Revival," 475.

72. Jeroom Heyndrickx, "An Olive Branch for China," *Tripod* 21, no. 123 (Fall–Winter 2001): 67.

73. Central Committee Document 99.26, 33.

74. For the texts of the pope's appeals to China between 1981 and 1996, see Pope John Paul II, "John Paul," 35–38.

75. Madsen, "Catholic Revival," 484.

76. Beatrice Leung, "China and Falungong: Party and Society Relations in the Modern Era," *Journal of Contemporary China* 11, no. 33 (2002): 772–74.

77. Jonathan D. Spence, *God's Chinese Son* (New York: W. W. Norton, 1996).

78. Chang, "Independent, Autonomous," 3–5.

79. Fu, "Guest Editor's Introduction" (no. 2), 10.

80. Ministry of Public Security, People's Republic of China, "Notice on Various Issues Regarding Identifying and Banning of Cultic Organizations," *Gongtongzi* 2000.39, issued July 12, 2001, in *China Law and Government* 36, no. 2 (March–April 2003): 22–38.

81. *South China Morning Post*, May 31, 2004.

82. *Tripod* Staff, "China Church and News Update 2000," *Tripod* 20, no. 120 (November–December 2000): 65; for a chronology of the entire period, see 63–65. Also see "The Bulletin of the Department of Anhui Public Security," 43.

83. *People's Daily*, December 13, 2001, as cited in Fu, "Guest Editor's Introduction" (no. 3), 3.

84. *Washington Post*, June 23, 2004; *New York Times*, August 19, 2004.

85. "A Management System for Catholic Dioceses in China," trans. Peter M. Barry et al., *Tripod* 23, no. 130 (Autumn 2003): 5–36.

86. For a fairly optimistic interpretation of the State Council's 2005 "Regulations on Religious Affairs," see Anthony Lam, "A Commentary on the Regulations on Religious Affairs," *Tripod* 25, no. 136 (Spring 2005), at http://www.hsstudyc.org.hk/Webpage/Tripod/T136/T136_E03.htm.

87. Pope John Paul II, "Message of Pope John Paul II to China," *Tripod* 21, no. 123 (Fall–Winter 2001): 60.

Chapter 14

The Congolese Church: Ecclesial Community within the Political Community

Yvon C. Elenga, S.J.

THE RECENT WAVE OF DEMOCRATIZATION in Africa has enabled the Roman Catholic Church to participate in the political life of several African countries, including the Republic of the Congo.[1] Under the leadership of the Congolese bishops, the Church has sought to contribute to the country's political, economic, and social life—a rather complex task given the county's history of political instability and the fact that the Church has never enjoyed the same moral and legal authority as the secular state. This chapter examines how the Roman Catholic Church has tried to enliven the ecclesial community within the Congolese political community in order to promote the creation of a more just society.

The Church–State Relationship in Historical Perspective

The Republic of the Congo, also known as Congo (Brazzaville) and hereafter referred to as the Congo, was once part of the precolonial Bantu kingdom of Kongo, which occupied the contemporary states of Angola, the Congo, and the Democratic Republic of Congo. Following the struggle between France and Belgium to control the Congo River basin, the French occupied the river's right bank in 1885. By 1908, France established French Equatorial Africa, which encompassed the current states of the Congo, Gabon, Chad, and the Democratic Republic of Congo. Granted its independence in 1960, the Congo was subsequently governed by a series of leaders, including priests, Marxist-Leninists, democratically elected leaders, and the military.

During this tumultuous period, the Congolese Church has played an important role in Congolese politics. The Portuguese Franciscans first evangelized the Kongo kingdom in the sixteenth century, followed by the Holy Ghost Fathers in 1883. With the establishment of French colonial control, the Holy See created the Vicariate Apostolic of French Congo and Loango in 1886. By 1900, more than a thousand new Christians lived in Loango, which was a key mission station at the starting point of the caravan routes (*route des caravans*) heading to Brazzaville. Following decades of missionary work, today half the Congo's 3 million people belong to the Roman Catholic Church. Thanks to mutual understanding, self-commitment, and even tentative collaboration, the Church has enjoyed a relatively cooperative relationship with successive regimes ruling the Congo.

The Colonial Congo

Various problems beset the work of evangelization during the colonial period. This region has a long-standing tradition of political action through religious expression.[2] Following the collapse of the Kongo kingdom in the second half of the sixteenth century, a young woman called Kimpa Vita (aka Dona Beatrix) established the Anthonian movement, which attempted to reunify the kingdom in 1700. Like Joan of Arc, Kimpa Vita professed to have a prophetic vision of restoring the ancient kingdom to its former glory. Also like Joan of Arc, she was condemned for heresy and burned alive.[3]

During the period of French colonization, there were several messianic movements, including Matswanism. In 1926, André-Grenard Matswa founded the Fraternity of French Equatorial African Natives (l'Amicale des Originaires de l'Afrique Equatoriale Française). Matswa died in a French colonial prison in January 1942 while his partisans were still waiting for him. As a show of opposition, the Matswanists always refused to vote in any election. They saw the emergence of Fulbert Youlou as the rise of hope. He was ordained a Catholic priest in 1946. While engaged in his pastoral ministry in Brazzaville, Youlou learned of the plight of the local laborers, who were ill treated by the colonial administration. This led to his interest in politics, which was not shared by his bishop, Monsignor Michel Bernard, who subsequently assigned Youlou to work in a remote city.

Undeterred by missives not to engage in political activities, Youlou ran for political office in 1947 and again in 1951, resulting in a suspension *a divinis*—that is, he was not allowed to celebrate the sacraments. This did not stop Youlou, who founded his own party in May 1956, the Democratic Union for the Defense of African Interests. After gaining popularity as the mayor of Brazzaville—the country's largest city and the capital city of French Equatorial Africa—Youlou was narrowly elected president and prime minister of the newly independent Congo in 1960.

The Congolese Postcolonial Transition

Reacting to the catastrophic consequences of Western domination—namely slavery and colonization—the newly established African countries adopted two different approaches to discovering and defining their unique identities. The first one claimed that "Africanness" could be found in traditional narratives, which were based on an illusionary reconstruction of an "authentic" Africa. The second approach relied on ideologies such as Marxist-Leninism and Pan-Africanism.

To understand the development of postcolonial African states, let us first examine the three stages of colonial development. The first period, which started with the conquest of the African territories and ended in the 1930s, was characterized by administrative authoritarianism and decentralized despotism. The second phase, of so-called modernizing bureaucrats, spanned the 1940s and lasted until the time of the exciting promises of decolonization, as these bureaucrats tried to construct an African future in terms of modern institutionalization. Power remained centralized and interventionist during this second phase. The third period started on the eve of independence in the late 1950s. The new African leaders foresaw a promising new dawn for their newly independent nation-state, which enjoyed strong and effective political institutions, and they expected their newly decolonized continent to enter a new era of modernity.[4]

Yet this new dawn of the African "nation-state" model proved illusory, in part because it was based on the Western European experience, which proved to be irrelevant to the realities of postcolonial Africa. One example is the Republic of the Congo, which in January 2002 adopted its fourteenth constitution in its nearly forty years of political history.[5] This institutional instability shows quite clearly that for almost four decades the country has been unable to conform to the Western model of nation-states.

The Congolese Church under Various State Regimes

In the Congo, there is a separation between Church and state. Yet this separation does not prevent the Church from existing within the political order.[6] There have been four major phases of church–state relations in the Congo during the past fifty years. The first period began with the election of the priest-politician Fulbert Youlou to the presidency. During this period, there was a collaborative relationship between Church and state, especially in areas of education, health care, and youth activities. This first period ended in 1963, when trade union activists and opposition political parties deposed President Youlou.

The second period lasted from 1963 to 1968, when Alphonse Massamba-Débat presided over the country. The leftist National Movement for the Revolution was the sole political party permitted to function at that time. This regime also differed with the previous Youlou presidency in that it was far more aggressive toward clergy, some of whom were imprisoned and tortured. This new adversarial relationship resulted in the nationalization of all schools and the imposition of an official Marxist-Leninist credo on the state and society—a process very similar to the Chinese transition to socialism in the 1950s discussed by Reardon in chapter 13. During this period, the Congolese Church reacted quite strongly to the mistreatment of all Christians and the marginalization of the Catholic laity.[7]

The third period of church–state relations began with the assumption to power of Marien Ngouabi in 1968. Instead of an antagonistic relationship, the Congolese socialist state attempted to normalize church–state relations.[8] Ngouabi knew quite well that as an institution, the Congolese Church had played an important role in building schools and providing many other social services. He also thought that a fruitful collaboration with a preeminent actor such as the Church would be a good example of a so-called national unity. This "unity" was also geographical, for Ngouabi was a northerner, while the then–archbishop of Brazzaville, Cardinal Émile Biayenda, was from the south. When Ngouabi was assassinated in a coup d'état in March 1977, Cardinal Biayenda was kidnapped and murdered in an act of retaliation by Ngouabi's partisans. However, President Joachim Yhomby-Opango, who served from April 1977 to February 1979, and his successor, President Denis Sassou-Nguesso, who served from February 1979 to August 1992, continued Ngouabi's cooperative approach with the Congolese Church. The struggle for democracy in the 1990s marked the fourth period.[9]

The Congolese Church under Democracy

To understand the Congolese Church's role in promoting democracy, one first must understand the process whereby the Church accepted its new role as political agent. Following the Congolese economic crisis of the mid-1980s, the International Monetary Fund (IMF) provided emergency loans contingent upon the Congo's adoption of a stringent structural adjustment program. The IMF program put undue hardship on the Congolese people, forcing the Catholic bishops to issue a pastoral letter in April 1986, "The Christian, a Messenger of Peace," pleading for immediate relief for the suffering.[10] With the worsening of the socioeconomic situation in the late 1980s, the state adopted drastic measures, including the reduction of state salaries. The Catholic Church reacted by forming the National Council for the Apostleship of the Laity in the Congo. Its purpose was to call for the greater commitment of the laity as outlined by the Second Vatican Council's *Apostolicam Actuositatem* and to provide bishops with more accurate information on the situation around the country.

However, the Congolese Church did not work alone. For two decades before 1990, the Congolese state officially recognized the Roman Catholic Church, the Evangelical Church, the Salvation Army, the Kibanguist Church, the Congo Islamic Conference, the Terinkyo Church, and the Lassist Church.[11] To provide a "united front" for all Christians when confronting the atheistic ideology of the Marxist-Leninist regimes, the Congolese Ecumenical Council of Christian Churches (CECCC) was established in 1972. As had often occurred in the past, the Congolese Catholic Church joined other Christian denominations in addressing social issues and confronting the civil authorities.

Ecclesial Community in the Political Community

The fall of the Berlin Wall in 1989 and the collapse of the Soviet Union in 1991 reverberated around the world, including the Congo, where it inspired the Congolese democratic transformation between 1990 and 1992. Trade unions, students, and groups of politicians took advantage of this new democratic wave to argue for more freedom of expression and association. The Catholic Church played a major role in this democratic process. At the closing of their eighteenth plenary session on April 30, 1990, the Catholic Episcopal Conference issued a letter titled "All Are Called, Each by His Name." In this letter, the Congolese bishops called upon all men and women to participate "with all the spiritual, moral, and intellectual richness and all the energy that they draw from their lives in the country, in the modern form of democracy, the rule of law, economic initiatives, communication, and science."[12] With the convocation of the National Conference of Political Parties on November 1990, the bishops issued a second message, "Political Commitment, Nonviolence, Brotherhood," writing:

> We are taking the initiative to inform you of our reflections, of our preoccupations and of our wishes that we make in the light of the gospel and the tradition of the Church with a view to contributing to a peaceful evolution of our institutions towards a renewal of democracy, and to realistic development of our economy, of our culture and of our society.[13]

Realizing the winds of change, President Sassou-Nguesso called upon the Congolese Church in July 1990 to become more politically engaged. Church leaders responded by appealing for a new political era, for the establishment of a democratic system, and for the realization of a society in which all would be guaranteed justice, peace, and equality. The bishops were not solely advocating the end of one-party rule and the rejection of Marxism-Leninism; they also envisioned a radically new political order.[14]

Christian Community, Civil Society, and the 1990 National Conference

During the transition to democracy, the term "civil society" was popularly invoked but seldom understood. Some saw the emergence of the civil society as promoting older forms of mass organizations.[15] Others envisioned a new civil society in which the Congolese Church would be a major catalyst for democratic transformation. The National Conference of 1990 thus spent much time discussing the structure of the state and the role of private organizations in civil society, such as the Church.[16]

The opening of the National Conference on February 25, 1990, was a long-awaited opportunity to gather together representatives of nongovernmental organizations (NGOs), emergent political parties, charitable associations, independent personalities, and representatives of the various churches. Bishop Ernest Kombo of Owando was chosen to lead the National Conference. Ordained a Jesuit in 1973, Kombo was a pastor in two parishes in Brazzaville and concurrently served as a civil servant for nearly two decades. Bishop Kombo was eventually appointed president of the High Council of the Republic.

Kombo's election as chairperson of the Executive Committee of the National Conference can be understood in two ways. First, it followed the example of Benin, where Bishop Isidore de Souza, who was considered by all as an impartial observer, chaired the 1990 national conference. Second, his acceptance of the position coincides with the January 1991 publication of John Paul II's encyclical *Redemptoris Missio*, which emphasized the Church's duty to defend against political oppression.[17] The election of Bishop Kombo confirmed the Church as an impartial yet important political player. Kombo thus considered himself the representative of not only Catholics but all churches.[18]

From February to June 1991, two thousand national conference delegates engaged in tense debate and a full exchange of ideas. They shared a common goal of developing new institutions for a democratic Congo. They also shared a cathartic experience, for it was an opportunity to identify those responsible of the catastrophic collapse of the Congo. At the bequest of the churches, the conference did eventually adopt a code of fundamental moral values for political life, embodied in the Charter of the Rights and Freedoms of the Congolese Citizen. Yet the churches failed to convince those involved in murder and embezzlement to confess and apologize.

During this period of democratic transition (June 1991–August 1992), the Congolese Church was viewed as an important counterbalancing force to political society. Bishop Kombo was strongly urged to run for president. Yet Kombo argued that his "avocation" was politics but his vocation was the Church, which he loved above all else.

The Principle of Autonomy

A paradox has plagued Congolese church–state relations. Congolese Church leaders often took the initiative to speak out about any social issue, and they often were called upon by the state to intervene in several situations. Yet politicians were often put on the defensive, and they used outrageous criticisms of the Church to defend their positions. During the Marxist-Leninist regime, this confrontational relationship led to civil authorities threatening clergymen.

A similar paradox occurred during the period of the democratization. By 1992, the Congo had successfully made the transition to a multiparty democracy. When Congolese President Pascal Lissouba dissolved the National Assembly in November 1992 and called for new elections, opposition parties accused the government of not respecting the Constitution. To help resolve the crisis, the CECCC issued a message to all Congolese men and women recommending unity over the evil of division. When the National Assembly elections were held in May and June 1993, the Catholic bishops issued a letter, "The Christian and National Unity." They acknowledged the resistance to democracy and that the country was not yet free from social agitation.

In July 1993, tensions over the legislative election results erupted into widespread civil disorder. During an extraordinary meeting on August 6, 1993, the Congolese bishops issued its "Message for Peace and Reconciliation" in an effort to help restore order and stability. President Lissouba subsequently called upon the CECCC to declare the August 15 Independence Day as a day of prayer and reconciliation. On that day, a "Message to the Faithful and to All Men and Women of Good Will" was read during a service on the Boulevard des Armées. While tensions over the 1993 elections subsided, the long-awaited 1997 elections posed an even greater test for Congolese democracy.

The Promise of Reconciliation

Returning from France in 1997, the former Congolese leader Sassou-Nguesso carried out his campaign in the countryside to encourage popular support. Tensions grew during one of his tours to Owando when a soldier was killed. Sassou-Nguesso's private residence subsequently was surrounded on the pretext that he was harboring the killer(s). Thus began a traumatic war that spanned four months, only to end in October 1997, when the Angolan military intervened on behalf of Sassou-Nguesso. As in the past, Sassou-Nguesso appointed a new government, and he argued for a transition period before democracy could be reestablished.[19]

Although Congolese state leaders often attempted to exclude key Church leaders from the political sphere, they never hesitated to call upon them to intervene when needed. During the four months of fighting, Congolese Church leaders remained relatively silent. After Sassou-Nguesso gained power, his government convened the National Forum for Reconciliation in January 1998 to plan the transition back to democracy. Not only did the Congolese Church participate, but it also agreed under the auspices of the CECCC to accede to Sassou-Nguesso's request for intervention. By late 1998, the CECCC had organized an ad hoc committee chaired by Father Diafouka of the Orthodox Church. Unfortunately, gunmen interrupted the commission's meeting and murdered several clergymen. Subsequently, Catholic leaders were invited to facilitate negotiations with the rebels of Frédéric Bitsangou, also known as Pasteur Ntumi. In 2001, Catholic leaders did accept a peace mission, but they first required that fighting should stop unconditionally; that Catholic leaders would be fully empowered to achieve consensus; and finally, that their security would be guaranteed. Unfortunately, this mediation failed, as political ambitions trumped the search for equity.

Democratization Process and Religious Discourse

In the eyes of the Congolese people, the Catholic Church does not possess the same legitimacy as civil authorities to speak on public matters. Whenever it addresses or raises questions about issues such as abortion and corruption, the Church does so to reflect Catholic social teachings and to participate in the dynamics of democratization.[20] In confronting many difficult and dangerous situations, the Congolese Church has assumed the role of social critic.

The ambiguity of silence could not continue when facing a people who yearn for hope, truth, and peace. The Catholic Church, by far the predominant Christian denomination in the Congo—some 42 percent of the total population is Roman Catholic, and the Christian faith has undeniably has played an important role in the Congo—is often at odds with the political regime because it sponsors or supports various associations and commissions.[21] The Congolese Church has always tried to be a sign of the reign of God by promoting a culture of reconciliation and justice even under adverse conditions. Speaking on behalf of the CEECC during the burial of the archbishop emeritus of Brazzaville, Barthelemy Batantou, on May 4, 2004, Bishop Kombo delivered a eulogy that obliquely criticized the government. He first paid tribute to the late pastor and graciously asked him to intercede for the country still confronting grave political problems. The bishop also openly prayed for peace and reconciliation for the Congo. Among the attendees were President Sassou-Nguesso, members of governments, and many other guests from neighboring countries. Though some of the attendees were delighted with Kombo's veiled criticisms of the government, others found his remarks unfitting and even disrespectful for a funeral eulogy. The immediate reaction came then from Monsignor Mario Roberto Cassari, the papal nuncio in the Congo and Gabon. In a declaration made available in major newspapers, Cassari strongly criticized Kombo's eulogy.[22]

Finding Common Ground: Peace and Justice

The Church's advocacy of justice and peace has greatly acerbated its relationship with the state.[23] A primary issue of contention has been the country's petroleum resources, whose export provides the Congo with its main supply of foreign exchange. At the end of the 1997 civil war, the Church issued a letter titled "The Congo Hungers and Thirsts for Peace" (Le Congo a faim et soif de paix), which criticized three decades of oil revenue mismanagement. Although the Congo is the third largest oil producer on the African continent, it owed foreign creditors $5.4 billion at the end of 1999. For the bishops, this transparent mismanagement of petroleum revenue was more than a political error, but it brought up larger issues of social justice and long-term peace. Some 70 percent of the Congolese population was living under the poverty line, and 60 percent of the eligible population was jobless. Confronting such dramatic economic problems, the Congo faced a bleak future. Besides advocating better revenue management, the bishops also appealed in 2002 for the government to secure financial aid from the World Bank and the IMF.

In another message issued in 2001, titled "Dialogue, Truth, Justice and the Road to Peace" (Dialogue, vérité, justice, chemin de paix), the bishops argued, "There is no sustainable peace without good governance of national revenues, or without employment for the youth. Development and peace are never possible with the growth of scandalous inequalities between those who have and accumulate, and the rest of the population that have nothing."[24] The Congolese Church issued a third declaration in July 2002, which reviewed the mismanagement of oil revenue by previous political regimes. In collaboration with the Congolese Observatory of Human Rights, Secours Catholique (France), and Caritas (USA), the Congolese bishops have participated in a public campaign to call attention to oil revenue issues. Because the French petroleum company Total-Fina-Elf dominates the Congolese petroleum sector, the group sponsored an "Oil Plea" campaign in France that called for better and open management of the Congolese oil resources. In response to these appeals by the Catholic bishops, President Sassou-Nguesso promised to improve government management and to cooperate with the IMF and World Bank in implementing domestic economic reforms.

The political realm remains the ongoing challenge for the Congolese Church. As in many modern African countries, the Congo is still in the process of institutionalizing its new democratic society. Yet there is a long way to go. Church commissions have sought the drafting of a new national constitution that guarantees freedom of speech and association. The new democratic state must develop a more harmonious relationship with the churches. There is a need for new political personnel to replace those who have held thirty-year sinecures, political candidates should not be pursuing private interests, and the political environment needs to be peaceful.

Conclusion

Catholic social teaching has been and continues to be an inspiring instrument for those involved in the construction of political organizations, including democracy. Over the decades, Congolese Church leaders have had to respond to the changing political and social environment, which has shaped their views and inspired their ministry. They have not separated themselves from the state, and they are not competing for the same political or social status. Instead, the Roman Catholic ecclesial community has been working within the political community to achieve a just and equitable society in the Congo.

Notes

1. Ibrahima Mane, ed., *Etat, démocratie, sociétés et culture africaine* [State, democracy, and societies of Africa] (Dakar: Éditions Démocraties Africaines, 1996); P. Yengo, ed., "Identités et démocratie," in *Identités et démocratie en Afrique et ailleurs* [Identities and democracy in Africa and elsewhere] (Paris: Pointe-Noire, L'Harmattan, and Association Rupture, 1997); C. Toulabor, "Transitions et consolidations en Afrique" [Transition and consolidation in Africa], *Afrique 2000* 4 (February 1991): 55–70; Richard Joseph, ed., *State, Conflict, and Democracy in Africa* (Boulder, Colo.: Lynne Rienner Publishers, 1999).

2. G. Balandier, *Sociologie des Brazzavilles noires* [Sociology of black Brazzaville] (Paris: Armand Colin, 1955); M. Sinda, *Le Messianisme Congolais* [Congolese Messianism] (Paris: Payot, 1972); G. Nzongala-Ntalaja, *The Congo: From Leopold to Kabila: A People's History* (London: Zed Books, 2003), 48–49.

3. Another prophet in what is now Democratic Republic of Congo is Simon Kimbangu, who began his ministry in the Baptist community in the village of Nkamba. He influenced the fight for independence, which was proclaimed in 1960.

4. See the suggestions by Harris Memel-Fote, "Des ancêtres fondateurs aux pères de la nation: Introduction à l'anthropologie de la démocratie" [Founding ancestors of the fathers of the country: Introduction to anthropology of democracy], *Cahiers d'Études Africaines* 123 (1991): 263–85; P. T. Robinson, "Democratization: Understanding the Relationship between Regime Change and the Culture of Politics," *African Studies Review* 37, no. 1 (April 1994): 39–67; Mwayila Tshiyembe, "La science politique africaniste et le statut théorique de l'etat africain: Un bilan négatif" [African political science and the theoretical status of the African state: A negative balance], *Politique Africaine* 71 (December 1998): 109–32.

5. The first constitution was adopted in 1961. Since then, there have been seven constitutions and seven "Fundamental Acts." See A. Gabou, *Les constitutions congolaises* [The Conglese constitutions] (Paris: LGDJ, 1984); Félix Bankounda, "Congo-Brazzaville: Une Septième Constitution pour quoi faire?" [Congo-Brazzaville: What's the purpose behind the Seventh Constitution?], *Politique Africaine* 61 (March 2001): 163–69.

6. See J. Kerleveo, *L'Eglise Catholique en régime de séparation* [The Catholic Church in the divided regime], 3 vols. (Paris: Desclée, 1957–64); J. B. Trotabas, La Notion de laïcité dans le droit de l'Eglise Catholique et de l'état républicain [The idea of the laity in Catholic Church law and the republican state] (Paris: LGDJ, 1961); J. Moody, *Church and Society: Catholic Social and Political Thought and Movements, 1789–1950* (New York: Arts, Inc., 1953).

7. Bishop Michel Bernard, "Human Life Is Sacred," in *Pais mes agneau: Recueil des lettres pastorales des archevêques de Brazzaville 1964–1975* [Feed my sheep: Collection of pastoral letters from the archbishops of Brazzaville 1964–1975] (Brazzaville: N.p., 1977).

8. Ibid. The pastoral letters published during this period are "La place du Chrétien dans la communauté nationale" [The Christian's place in the national community] and "Le développement" [Development].

9. A. Okoko-Esseau, "The Christian Churches and Democratization in the Congo," in *The Christian Churches and the Democratization of Africa*, ed. Paul Clifford (New York: E. J. Brill, 1995), 148–67; A. Okoko-Esseau has identified three periods before the so-called democratization process, to which the author has added a fourth category.

10. Okoko-Esseau, "Christian Churches," 152.

11. The Terinkyo Church is an Asian movement, and the Lassit Church is a national prophetic sect.

12. *Paroles d'evêque* 5 [Words from the bishop] (Brazzaville: Episcopal Conference, 1990).

13. Ibid., 6.

14. Ecumenical Council, *Réflexion sur les conclusions de la IIe session ordinaire du Comité Central du Parti Congolais du Travail* [Reflections on the conclusion of the eleventh ordinary of the eleventh session of the Congolese Workers Party Central Committee] (1990).

15. As an allegedly Marxist country, the People's Republic of Congo has developed many political associations under the Congolese Socialist Youth Union, Revolutionary Union for Congolese Women, and Union Confederation of Congo.

16. See M. Mamdani and E. Wamba-dia-Wamba, eds., *African Studies in Social Movements and Democracy* (Dakar: Codesria, 1995); and C. Aké, *The Feasibility of Democracy in Africa* (Dakar: Codesria, 2000).

17. K. Jenkins, "Christian Churches in Africa: Agents of Change or Supporters of the Status Quo," *Geonomics* 3, no. 5 (1991): 6.

18. Ernest Kombo, "Nécessité et urgence d'un engagement communautaire" [The need and urgency of community engagement], *Telema* 3, no. 4 (1992): 52.

19. See L. Huron, ed., *Les transitions démocratiques: Actes du colloque international de Port-au-Prince* [Democratic transitions: Procedures of the Port-au-Prince international conference] (Port-au-Prince: Syros, n.d.); and R. Joseph, "The Reconfiguration of Power in Late Twentieth-Century Africa," in *State, Conflict, and Democracy in Africa*, ed. R. Joseph, 73–74.

20. M. Cheza, H. Derroitte, and R. Luneau, eds., *Les evêques d'Afrique parlent* [The african bishops speak] (Paris: Centurion, 1992).

21. "Mouvement pour la vie" [Movement for life] is an association whose main activity is the promotion of the value of life and campaign against abortion. "Commission Justice et Paix" [Commision for Justice and Peace] is more involved in social activism.

22. Bishop Kombo's address and the reaction of the nuncio are in *La Semaine Africaine*, May 20, 2004, 3.

23. There are the famous cases of priests or seminarians who have been tortured or killed: Louis Badila and Father Robir in 1965; the murder of Cardinal Biayenda in 1977; the death of Monsignor B. Gassongo in 1982; the imprisonment and torture of Father

Joseph Ndinga in 1988; the murder of Father Jan Czuba in 1998; and the assassination of the Christian mediators in Mindouli in 1998.

24. See http://www.cenco.cd/declarationcomiteperm.htm.

Bibliography

Allen, C. "Who Needs Civil Society?" *Review of African Political Economy* 73 (1997): 329–37.

Bayart, Jean-François. "Les Eglises Chrétiennes et la Politique du Ventre." *Politique Africaine* 35 (1989): 3–26.

Conus, Georges. "L'Église d'Afrique au Concile Vatican II." *Neue Zeitschrift für Missionswissenschaft* 30 (1974): 241–55, and 31 (1975): 1–18, 124–42.

Dorier-Apprill, Elizabeth. "Les enjeux socio-politiques du foisonnement religieux à Brazzaville." *Politique africaine* 64 (1996): 129–35.

Duteil, Armel. "Relations entre le socialisme et l'Etat dans la république populaire du Congo." *Spiritus* 88 (Septembre 1982): 5–31.

Haynes, Jeff. *Religion and Politics in Africa.* London: Zed Books, 1996.

Joseph, Richard. "The Christian Churches and Democracy in Contemporary Africa." In *Christianity and Democracy in Global Context*, ed. J. Witte Jr. (Boulder, Colo.: Westview, 1993).

Kasfir, N. "The Conventional Notion of Civil Society: A Critique." *Commonwealth and Comparative Politics* 36, no. 2 (July 1998):1–20.

Linz, J. J., and A. Stepan. *Problems of Democracy, Transitions and Consolidation: Southern Europe, South America and Post-Communist Europe.* Baltimore: Johns Hopkins University Press, 1996.

Mayeur, Jean-Marie. *La separation des eglises et de l'etat* [The church–state separation]. Paris: Éditions Ouvrières, 1991.

Mbembe, Achille. *Afriques indociles: Christianisme, pouvoir et état en société postcoloniale* [Disobedient Africa: Christianity, power and state in postcolonial society]. Paris: Karthala, 1988.

Muyembe, Bernard Munono. *Eglise, Evangelization et promotion humaine: Le discours social des evêques africains* [The church, evangelization, and promotion of humanity: The social discourse of African bishops]. Paris: Éditions du Cerf / Éditions Universitaires, 1995.

Oyatambwe, Wamu. *Eglise Catholique et pouvoir politique au Congo-Zaire: la quête démocratique* [The Catholic Church and political power in Congo-Zaire: The democratic quest]. Paris: L'Harmattan, 1997.

Père Christian. "Lettre ouverte au Nonce Apostolique" [Open letter to the Apostolic Nuncio]. *La Semaine Africaine*, May 20, 2004.

Tonda, Joseph. "De l'exorcisme comme mode de démocratisation: Eglises et mouvements au Congo de 1990 à 1994"[Exorcism as a means of democratization: Churches and movements in Congo, 1990–1994]. In *Religion et transition démocratique en Afrique* [Religion and democratic transition in Africa], ed. François Constantin et Christian Coulon. Paris, Karthala, 1997.

————. "Identités religieuses, identités ethniques et 'situations d'aliénation' au Congo" [Religious identities, ethnic identities, and "situations of alienation" in the Congo]. In *Identités et démocratie en Afrique et ailleurs* [Identities and democracy in Africa and elsewhere], ed. P. Yengo. Paris: Pointe-Noire, L'Harmattan, and Association Rupture, 1987.

Appendix A

Vatican Documents with Relevance to Church–State Issues

Documents of the Second Vatican Council

Constitutions

Gaudium et Spes (*Pastoral Constitution on the Church in the Modern World*), 1965
Lumen Gentium (*Dogmatic Constitution on the Church*), 1965

Declarations

Dignitatis Humanae (*Decree on Religious Freedom*), 1965
Nostra Aetate (*Declaration on the Relation of the Church to Non-Christian Religions*), 1965

Decrees

Apostolicam Actuositatem (*Decree on the Apostolate of Lay People*), 1965
Christus Dominus (*Decree on the Pastoral Office of Bishops*), 1965
Inter Mirifica (*Decree on the Media of Social Communications*), 1963
Unitatis Redintegratio (*Decree on Ecumenism*), 1964

Nonconciliar Documents

Apostolic Constitution

Ex Corde Ecclesiae (*On Catholic Universities*), 1990

Apostolic Exhortations

Ecclesia in Asia (*Post Synodal Apostolic Exhortation to the Church in Asia*), 1999

Ecclesia in Europa (*Post Synodal Apostolic Exhortation to the Church in Europe*), 2003

Familiaris Consortio (*On the Role of the Christian Family in the Modern World*), 1981

Apostolic Letter

Mulieris Dignitatem (*On the Dignity and Vocation of Women*), 1987

Encyclicals

Centesimus Annus (*On the Hundredth Anniversary of Rerum Novarum*), 1991

Evangelium Vitae (*The Gospel of Life*), 1991

Humanae Vitae (*On the Regulation of Birth*), 1968

Lamentabili Sane (*Syllabus Condemning the Errors of Modernists*), 1907

Mater et Magistra (*Christianity and Social Progress*), 1961

Pacem in Terris (*Peace on Earth*), 1963

Populorum Progressio (*On the Progress of Peoples*), 1967

Quadragesimo Anno (*On the Reconstruction of the Social Order*), 1931

Quantra Cura (*Syllabus of Errors of Pius IX*), 1864

Redemptoris Missio (*On the Permanent Validity of the Church's Missionary Mission*), 1991

Rerum Novarum (*On the Condition of the Working Classes*), 1891

Sollicitudo Rei Socialis (*On Social Concern*), 1987

Veritatis Splendor (*The Splendor of Truth*), 1993

Appendix B. Religious Concentration of the Countries Considered in this Volume

Country	Population	Catholic	Protestant	Jewish	Muslim	Hindu	Animist/Tribal	Other	Atheist/Agnostic/No Religion
						%			
Angola	11,190,786	38.00	15.00				47.00		0
Brazil	186,112,794	73.60	15.40				1.70	1.80	7.4
Chile	15,980,912	89.00	11.00	Negligible					
China	1,306,313,812		3–4 (Christian)[a]		1.00			92–98	
Congo, Republic of	3,030,126	42.65	7.35		2.00		48.00		
East Timor	1,040,880	90.00	3.00		4.00	0.50		2.50	
France	60,656,178	83–88	2.00		5–10				4 (unaffiliated)
India	1,080,264,388	1.58	0.72	1	13.4	80.5		1.8	
Ireland	4,015,676	88.4	3 (Church of Ireland); other Christian: 1.6					1.5	
Ireland, Northern	1,700,000	40.26	45.57						13.88 (not stated)
Italy	58,103,033	97.00						3.00	
Poland	38,635,144	89.8	1.6 (Protestant and Eastern Orthodox)						
Portugal	10,566,212	94.00						0.3	
Rwanda	8,440,820	56.50	26		4.60		0.10		1.70
Spain	40,341,462	94.00			1.00			6.00 (Muslims and Jews)	
United States	295,734,134	24.00	52.00	1.00	1.00			10.00	10.00

[a] Where the data do not indicate a distinction between Catholics and other Christians, that fact is noted by placing the percentage of Christians in the Protestant column with a notation that the percentage refers to all Christians.

Source: U.S. Central Intelligence Agency, *World Fact Book*, 2005.

Appendix C

Timeline of Significant Events in the Life of the Roman Catholic Church, 1800 to the Present

1800–23: Pius VII serves as 251st pope

1801: Concordat between France and Rome reestablishing the Church after the French Revolution

1823–29: Leo XII serves as 252nd pope

1829–30: Pius XIII serves as 253rd pope

1831–46: Gregory XVI serves as 254th pope

1846–78: Pius IX serves as 255th pope for 31 years, second longest in history

1857: The antiforeigner and anti-Catholic "Know-Nothings" gain influence in the United States

1869–70: First Vatican Council, or Vatican I

1878–1903: Leo XIII serves as 256th pope

1891: *Rerum Novarum* issued (on the need to improve labor conditions for workers)

1903–14: Pius X serves as 257th pope

1914–22: Benedict XV serves as 258th pope

1922–39: Pius XI serves as 259th pope

1929: Lateran Pact between the Vatican and Italy, establishing Vatican City as a city-state

1931: *Quadresimo Anno* (on the need for the reconstruction of a more just and equitable social order)

1939–58: Pius XII serves as 260th pope

1959–63: John XXIII serves as 261st pope

1960: John F. Kennedy becomes the first and only Roman Catholic elected U.S. president

1962–65: Second Vatican Council, or Vatican II

1963–78: Paul VI serves as 262nd pope

1967: *Populorum Progressio* (development of peoples)

1968: *Humanae Vitae* (on human life, denouncing birth control)

1970: *Novus Ordo* (establishing new order of the mass)

1978: John Paul I elected as 263rd pope

1978: John Paul II elected as 264th pope, from Poland; first non-Italian since the 16th century

1979: Mother Teresa wins Nobel Peace Prize for her work with orphans in India

1981: Assassination attempt wounds John Paul II; he eventually forgives his attacker; issues *Laborem Exercens* (commemorating *Rerum Novarum*)

1984: Lateran Pact revised so that the Catholic Church would no longer be the established church of Italy; United States establishes diplomatic relations with the Vatican

1994: *Ordinatio Sacerdotalis* (issue of ordination of women declared a subject "closed for all time"); John Paul II becomes first pope to condemn the Italian Mafia

1996: Bishop Carlos Filipe Ximenes Belo and José Ramos-Horta, vice president of the National Council of Timorese Resistance, share the Nobel Peace Prize

2000–5: Charges of molestation by some Catholic priests lead to the resignation or termination of some 250 priests in the United States; similar scandals rock other countries, including Ireland; over $100 million is awarded to victims in civil suits in the United States

2002: United States Conference of Catholic Bishops adopts policy to remove priests for one sexual transgression

2005: Pope John Paul II dies after an almost 27-year papacy, third longest in history

2005: Benedict XVI elected 265th pope, warns of a "dictatorship of relativism" in the world

2006: Pope Benedict XVI travels to Auschwitz, the former Nazi concentration camp in Poland. He called this visit "particularly difficult and troubling for a pope from Germany." News reports quoted Benedict asking aloud "Why, Lord, did you remain silent?" and "How could you tolerate this?"

Appendix D

World Values Survey: How Important Is Religion in Your Life?

TABLE 9.   How Important Is Religion in Your Life?

Country	Very	Rather	Not Very	Not at All
		%		
United States	54.4	26.2	14.4	4.9
Canada	30.7	30.8	25.4	13.2
Venezuela	61.2	24.0	9.2	5.6
Brazil	60.8	26.8	7.8	4.6
Peru	55.0	29.4	13.3	2.3
Dominican Republic	51.4	33.3	11.9	3.5
Colombia	49.2	38.8	10.6	1.5
Chile	47.1	29.6	17.4	5.9
Mexico	40.2	35.5	19.4	5.0
Argentina	37.6	27.7	21.9	12.8
Uruguay	23.1	26.5	30.8	19.6
Iceland	23.8	32.4	28.4	15.4
Ireland	47.8	35.7	12.6	3.8
Italy	30.7	37.0	20.7	11.6
Austria	24.9	37.0	27.4	14.0
Spain	24.1	37.0	27.3	17.3
Switzerland	19.2	37.0	31.4	20.5
Netherlands	18.9	37.0	30.9	27.1
Portugal	17.1	37.0	26.7	17.2
Britain	16.2	37.0	36.0	19.3
Belgium	15.3	37.0	27.4	27.3
West Germany	14.2	37.0	36.5	25.6
France	13.9	37.0	27.9	29.4
Norway	13.6	37.0	39.7	21.1
Sweden	9.8	37.0	41.0	30.6

(continued)

TABLE 9.   CONTINUED

Country	Very	Rather	Not Very	Not at All
			%	
Denmark	8.5	37.0	38.6	30.1
Poland	49.1	36.5	11.4	3.0
Romania	41.8	32.7	18.8	6.6
Bosnia and Herzegovina	35.1	39.4	17.6	8.0
Croatia	32.8	30.2	24.4	12.6
Serbia	26.0	29.7	29.9	14.4
Hungary	23.2	26.7	29.2	20.9
Slovakia	19.0	21.4	31.2	28.4
Slovenia	16.9	26.6	33.9	22.6
Bulgaria	13.6	21.8	33.6	31.1
East Germany	10.9	12.2	28.1	48.8
Czech Republic	7.5	14.3	25.8	52.4
Georgia	44.6	34.8	14.1	6.5
Azerbaijan	29.9	53.3	13.4	3.4
Armenia	26.6	39.1	24.0	10.3
Ukraine	20.9	32.5	26.8	19.8
Belarus	17.0	25.8	36.0	21.1
Lithuania	14.9	33.6	34.5	16.9
Finland	14.3	27.9	38.1	19.6
Russia	13.4	24.3	33.6	28.7
Bangladesh	82.4	16.2	1.0	0.0
Pakistan	80.5	14.1	5.3	0.0
Turkey	68.9	18.6	8.1	4.4
India	52.7	31.4	11.4	4.5
Philippines	78.5	19.5	1.8	0.0
Australia	23.3	24.8	32.5	19.3
South Korea	22.8	29.6	33.8	13.8
Taiwan	13.0	34.1	44.4	8.5
Japan	6.3	14.8	44.1	34.8
China	3.3	7.4	25.8	63.6
Nigeria	91.0	5.8	2.3	1.0
Ghana	88.3	5.3	5.3	1.1
South Africa	67.3	22.5	7.1	3.1

Note: Combined results of three waves of World Values Survey: 1981–82, 1990–91, 1995–97. France with a sample size of 2,202; Great Britain, 3,808; West Germany, 4,423; Italy, 3,366; Netherlands, 2,238; Denmark, 2,212; Belgium, 3,937; Spain, 7,661; Ireland, 2,217; United States, 5,706; Canada, 2,984; Japan, 3,269; Mexico, 4,878; South Africa, 7,267; Hungary, 2,463; Australia, 3,276; Norway, 3,612; Sweden, 3,010; Iceland, 1,629; Argentina, 3,086; Finland, 2,578; South Korea, 3,470; Poland, 2,091; Switzerland, 2,612; Brazil, 2,931; Nigeria, 3,770; Chile, 2,500; Belarus, 3,107; India, 4,540; Czech Republic, 930; East Germany, 2,345; Slovenia, 2,042; Bulgaria, 2,106; Romania, 1,103; Pakistan, 733; China, 2,500; Taiwan, 1,452; Portugal, 1,185; Austria, 1,460; Turkey, 2,937; Lithuania, 2,009;

Ukraine, 2,811; Russia, 4,001; Peru, 1,211; Venezuela, 1,200; Uruguay, 1,000; Ghana, 96; Philippines, 1,200; Georgia, 2,593; Armenia, 2,000; Azerbaijan, 2,002; Dominican Republic, 417; Bangladesh, 1,525; Colombia, 6,025; Serbia, 1,280; Croatia, 1,196; Slovakia, 466; Bosnia and Herzegovina, 1,200.

Source: Polling the Nations, http://poll.orspub.com/poll/lpext.dll?f=templates&fn= main-h.htm.

RELIGION IS VERY IMPORTANT

	Country	%
1	Nigeria	91.0
2	Ghana	88.3
3	Bangladesh	82.4
4	Pakistan	80.5
5	Philippines	78.5
6	Turkey	68.9
7	S. Africa	67.3
8	Venezuela	61.2
9	Brazil	60.8

Note: N = 58.

Contributors

Timothy A. Byrnes, Colgate University

William Crotty, Northeastern University

Yvon C. Elenga, S.J., Weston Jesuit School of Theology

Lisa L. Ferrari, University of Puget Sound

Linda Heywood, Boston University

Kenneth R. Himes, O.F.M., Boston College

Ted G. Jelen, University of Nevada, Las Vegas

Christine A. Kearney, Saint Anselm College

William M. Lies, C.S.C., University of Notre Dame

Alynna J. Lyon, University of New Hampshire

Mary Fran T. Malone, University of New Hampshire

Paul Christopher Manuel, Saint Anselm College

Margaret MacLeish Mott, Marlboro College

Lawrence C. Reardon, University of New Hampshire

Elisée Rutagambwa, S.J., Boston College

Mathew N. Schmalz, College of the Holy Cross

Clyde Wilcox, Georgetown University

Index